# INVESTIGATING CHILD EXPLOITATION AND PORNOGRAPHY

# INVESTIGATING CHILD EXPLOITATION AND PORNOGRAPHY: THE INTERNET, THE LAW AND FORENSIC SCIENCE

Monique Mattei Ferraro, JD, CISSP
Eoghan Casey, MS
Michael McGrath, MD, Contributor

ELSEVIER
ACADEMIC
PRESS

Amsterdam • Boston • Heidelberg • London • New York • Oxford • Paris •
San Diego • San Francisco • Singapore • Sydney • Tokyo

| | |
|---|---|
| Acquisitions Editor | Mark Listewnik |
| Project Manager | Sarah Hajduk |
| Associate Acquisitions Editor | Jennifer Soucy |
| Developmental Editor | Pamela Chester |
| Marketing Manager | Christian Nolin |
| Cover Design | Greg Smith |
| Interior Design | Kenneth Burnley |
| Composition | Best Set |
| Printer | Maple-Vail |

Elsevier Academic Press

200 Wheeler Road, Burlington, MA 01803, USA
525 B Street, Suite 1900, San Diego, California 92101-4495, USA
84 Theobald's Road, London WC1X 8RR, UK

This book is printed on acid-free paper. ∞

**Library of Congress Cataloging-in-Publication Data**
APPLICATION SUBMITTED


**British Library Cataloguing in Publication Data**
A catalogue record for this book is available from the British Library

ISBN: 0-12-163105-2

For information on all Academic Press publications visit our Web site at
www.books.elsevier.com/forensics

Printed in the United States of America
05   06   07   08   8   7   6   5   4   3   2   1

*When will our consciences grow so tender that we will act to prevent human misery rather than avenge it?*

Eleanor Roosevelt


*If we don't stand up for children, then we don't stand for much.*

Marian Wright Edelman

# CONTENTS

About the Authors     xi
Preface     xiii
Acknowledgments     xv

**SECTION I    THE INFLUENCE OF TECHNOLOGY**

1.   Overview     3
    1.1   Background     5
    1.2   History of Child Sexual Exploitation     6
    1.3   Child Pornography     8
    1.4   Technology and Child Exploitation     9
    1.5   Technology and Preferential Sex Offenders     15
    1.6   Development of Child Pornography Law     16
    1.7   International: The United Nations Convention on the Rights of the Child     18
    1.8   Conclusion     18
        References     19

2.   Internet Applications     21
    2.1   IP Addresses and Domain Name System     22
    2.2   E-Mail     23
    2.3   E-Groups and Mailing Lists     24
    2.4   List Serves     31
    2.5   Newsgroups, Discussion Boards, and Bulletin Boards     31
    2.6   Web Sites     33
    2.7   Chat Rooms and Internet Relay Chat     35
    2.8   Instant Messaging     36
    2.9   Web Cameras and Videophones     37
    2.10   File Transfer Protocol (FTP)     37
    2.11   Peer-to-Peer (P2P)     38
    2.12   Conclusion     39
        Resources     39

3.   Cyber Victims     41
    3.1   Victimology     45
    3.2   How to Protect Children Online     45
    3.3   Conclusion     47
        References     47
        Internet Resources     49

4.  Cyber Offenders                                                        51
    4.1   The Online Sexual Predator                                       53
    4.2   The Child Molester                                               57
    4.3   Modus Operandi: How Online Child Molester Operates               63
    4.4   Signature and the Online Child Molester                          69
    4.5   Profiling the Child Molester                                     71
    4.6   The Subculture of Child Pornography                              73
    4.7   Conclusion                                                       73
          References                                                       74

5.  Sources of Digital Evidence                                           79
    5.1   Open Computer Systems                                            81
    5.2   Embedded Computer Systems                                        88
    5.3   Communication Systems                                            91
    5.4   Peripheral Devices                                              97
          References                                                      97


SECTION II  INVESTIGATING INTERNET CHILD EXPLOITATION
6.  Undercover Operations                                                 101
    6.1   Self-Protection                                                  101
    6.2   Using Personal Equipment                                        103
    6.3   Setting Up Internet and Telephone Connections                   104
    6.4   Using Online Undercover Identities                              105
    6.5   Conducting an Online Investigation                              105
    6.6   Documenting Predisposition of the Suspect to Commit a Crime     107
    6.7   Preparing for a Meeting or Search                               107
    6.8   Agencies and Resources                                          112
    6.9   Conclusion                                                      113
          References                                                      114
          Internet Resources                                             114

7.  Collecting and Preserving Evidence on the Internet                    115
    7.1   Preserving Evidence on the Internet                             115
    7.2   Finding Evidence on the Internet                                116
    7.3   Collecting Remote Evidence                                      119
          References                                                      127

8.  Tracking on the Internet                                              129
    8.1   Attribution and Continuity of Offense                           130
    8.2   Tracking Internet Activities                                    135
    8.3   Overcoming Challenges to Attribution                            145
          References                                                      150

9.  Search and Seizure in Cyberspace I: Drafting Warrants and Warrantless Searches   151
    9.1   Search Warrant Drafting                                         151
    9.2   Search Warrants in General                                      154
    9.3   Child Pornography Sent via the Internet—Search Warrant for Internet
          Account                                                         156
    9.4   Enticement of a Minor                                           158

|        |                                                    |     |
|--------|----------------------------------------------------|-----|
| 9.5    | Grooming Evidence                                  | 158 |
| 9.6    | The Affidavit—Probable Cause                       | 159 |
| 9.7    | Arrest Warrants                                    | 165 |
| 9.8    | Warrantless Searches                               | 166 |
| 9.9    | Conclusion                                         | 170 |
|        | References                                         | 170 |

10. Search and Seizure in Cyberspace II: Executing the Search   171
|        |                                                    |     |
|--------|----------------------------------------------------|-----|
| 10.1   | Search Warrants                                    | 171 |
| 10.2   | Evidence Handling                                  | 178 |
| 10.3   | Obtaining a Second Warrant                         | 179 |
| 10.4   | Executing Internet Service Provider Search Warrants| 179 |
| 10.5   | Conducting Preliminary Interviews                  | 187 |
| 10.6   | No Knock Warrants                                  | 188 |
| 10.7   | Privileged Documents and Communications            | 188 |
| 10.8   | The Privacy Protection Act                         | 189 |
| 10.9   | Returning Seized Items                             | 189 |
|        | References                                         | 190 |

**SECTION III  FORENSIC EXAMINATION OF DIGITAL EVIDENCE**

11. Overview of the Examination Process                          193
|        |                                                    |     |
|--------|----------------------------------------------------|-----|
| 11.1   | Examination                                        | 195 |
| 11.2   | Analysis and Reconstruction                        | 209 |
| 11.3   | Challenges to Admissibility                        | 213 |
|        | References                                         | 215 |

12. Servers and Networks                                        217
|        |                                                    |     |
|--------|----------------------------------------------------|-----|
| 12.1   | Identification and Seizure                         | 218 |
| 12.2   | Preservation                                       | 219 |
| 12.3   | Examination and Analysis                           | 220 |
|        | References                                         | 224 |

**SECTION IV  THE LAW OF INTERNET CHILD SEXUAL EXPLOITATION**

13. Child Pornography                                           227
|        |                                                                |     |
|--------|----------------------------------------------------------------|-----|
| 13.1   | Evolution of Child Pornography Law Post-*Ferber*               | 235 |
| 13.2   | Possessing Child Pornography Can Be Prohibited                 | 236 |
| 13.3   | The Child Pornography Protection Act and the Free Speech       |     |
|        | Coalition Challenge                                            | 236 |
| 13.4   | Morphed Images                                                 | 237 |
| 13.5   | Virtual Child Pornography                                      | 238 |
| 13.6   | Conclusion                                                     | 241 |
|        | References                                                     | 241 |

14. Pre-Trial                                                   243
|        |                                                                |     |
|--------|----------------------------------------------------------------|-----|
| 14.1   | Introduction                                                   | 243 |
| 14.2   | Charging in Computer-Assisted Child Exploitation Cases         | 243 |
| 14.3   | Case Law Concerning Charging Decisions                         | 244 |
| 14.4   | What Constitutes Possession?                                   | 246 |

14.5    Multiple Computer Users                                              247
14.6    Plea Bargaining Considerations                                       249
14.7    Selection of Evidence                                                252
14.8    How Much Is Enough?                                                  253
14.9    Enticing a Minor to Engage in Sexual Activity                        253
14.10   Presenting Evidence                                                  255
14.11   Conclusion                                                           255
        Reference                                                            256

15.  Trial                                                                   257
15.1    Selecting the Jury                                                   257
15.2    Young Victims/Witnesses                                              259
15.3    Expert Witnesses                                                     261
15.4    Dissecting the Digital Forensics Expert's Report                     267
15.5    Defending the Charge                                                 278
15.6    Conclusion                                                           285
        References                                                           285

16.  Final Thoughts                                                          287
16.1    Setting Up an Online Child Exploitation Unit                         287
16.2    Locating Resources for Investigators and Prosecutors                 291
16.3    Looking Forward                                                      292
        Reference                                                            293

Index                                                                        295

# ABOUT THE AUTHORS

## MONIQUE MATTEI FERRARO, JD, CISSP

Monique Mattei Ferraro is an attorney and certified information systems security professional who works in the Connecticut Department of Public Safety Computer Crimes and Electronic Evidence Unit. She advises Connecticut's Internet Crimes Against Children Task Force and administers its legal and training components. She has worked in law enforcement since 1987. She is co-author of Connecticut's *Law Enforcement Guidelines for Computer and Electronic Evidence Search and Seizure*, with The Honorable Judge John Blawie, JD and Sergeant Andrew Russell, JD. She holds a Master's Degree from Northeastern University and a Law Degree from the University of Connecticut School of Law.

## EOGHAN CASEY, MS

Eoghan Casey is currently a senior consultant and forensic examiner with Stroz Friedberg LLC in Washington, DC. He was previously System Security Administrator for Yale University, and has received his BA in Mechanical Engineering from the University of California, Berkeley, and a Master's in Educational Communication and Technology from New York University. He is a frequent lecturer on computer security and computer crime and contributed to the *Encyclopedia of Forensic Science* (Academic Press, December 2000), *Criminal Profiling, 2nd Edition* by Brent Turvey (Academic Press, May 2002), and written *Digital Evidence*, now in its second edition (Academic Press, March 2004) and served as editor for the *Handbook of Computer Crime Investigation* (Academic Press, October 2001).

## MICHAEL McGRATH, MD

Michael McGrath, MD, is a Clinical Associate Professor, Department of Psychiatry, at the University of Rochester Medical Center in Rochester, NY. He is also Associate Chair for Ambulatory Services, Department of Psychiatry and Behavioral Health, at Unity Health System, in Rochester, NY.

Dr. McGrath divides his time between clinical, administrative, teaching, and research activities. His areas of special expertise include forensic psychiatry and criminal profiling. He has lectured on three continents and is a founding member of the Academy of Behavioral Profiling.

This work is the culmination of many years of study and work. During my under-graduate and graduate work, my primary research interests revolved around domestic violence, sexual assault, child abuse, and child exploitation. Femi-nism, the Constitution, freedom of expression and privacy, politics, and the dynamics of power are topics that seem to me to be intertwined with crime against women and children. As time marches on, I notice that more than twenty years have passed since I first began to study these issues. The issues have changed a bit, but they are just as interesting, just as in need of study, and just as intertwined as ever.

When the Internet was invented, a revolution began in the way we live our lives. A thousand years from now, the early days of the "Internet Age" will no doubt be considered of more historic magnitude than the Industrial Revolu-tion or the Iron Age. In a matter of fifteen years or so, the Internet has irre-versibly impacted every major human endeavor. The Internet has changed the way we communicate, the way we are educated, our economy, our sexuality, our politics and the way crime is committed. This book addresses the narrow area of investigating the online exploitation of children.

Those whose proclivities lead them to prey on children have unprecedented access to potential victims via the Internet. This book explores how the Inter-net has created an unlimited and barely regulated trade in child pornography and has opened the floodgates to the free exchange among child molesters. Sex offenders who prefer to have sex with children have nearly unlimited access to children when they use the Internet. Not only do sex offenders have free access to children and to child pornography through the Internet, but they also have the comfort and support of countless like-minded others just a mouse-click away.

When criminal activity was constrained by limits on transportation and tech-nology, law enforcement could confine itself to patrolling neighborhoods and playgrounds to protect children from those who would exploit or harm them. The Internet presents new and difficult challenges. This book aims to arm law enforcement officers, prosecutors, forensic scientists, students, and academics with awareness of emerging issues and tools.

If crime is on the streets, law enforcement personnel need to know the language of the streets. Crime on the information superhighway is no different. Police, prosecutors, the defense bar, and judiciary need to familiarize themselves with the vernacular of the Internet and high technology.

# ACKNOWLEDGMENTS

**Monique Mattei Ferraro**

I would like to thank my co-author, Eoghan Casey, who has been an excellent friend, colleague and co-author. I thank him for his guidance and support. One rarely finds friends who bring so much to the table. Whatever I do with him I find is better than anything I've done on my own.

Thanks to Andrew Russell for believing in me. His patience and friendship have seen me through years of exploration and growth. Joe Sudol has been very supportive of me and of my work on this book and other far-flung projects. My colleagues at the Computer Crimes and Electronic Evidence Unit have supported me and provided assistance in so many areas, it would be impossible to list. In particular, I want to thank Bruce Patterson for his forensic reports, research on experts, and for his support. Jim Smith is always there for me. Thanks, Jim, for lending expertise, search warrant language, and dedication to the cause. Ruth Torres has read many drafts and given her thoughtful commentary, suggestions, and abiding friendship. Dan Tramontozzi, Jeff McGurk, Steve DiPietro, John Farnham, Nick Juliano, Henry Doddenhoff, Brian Beshara, Nick Juliano, Ivan Torres, Christina Ferrante, and Brian Blakeman have all been unwavering in their support and making work a great place to be. Thanks especially to Jane Schneider for all of her assistance and support throughout.

My interns toiled endlessly for no pay and little else. Thanks to Rochelle Fleischman, Keely Stockman, Amie Danielson, Samir Termanini, A.J. Walmbolt, Steve Arcuri, Sarah Esidore, Alix Rosenberg, Ashlee Kelly, and Paul Battiste.

Thanks to my teachers and mentors. Special thanks to my professor, then boss and friend, John Bardelli, who taught me everything I know.

Thank you to the many excellent colleagues and friends who read drafts and offered salient commentary. Thanks especially to Jackie Sanford, Judith Rossi, and John Blawie.

Special thanks to our editor, Mark Listewnik, developmental editor, Pam Chester, associate acquisitions editor, Jennifer Soucy, and Project Manager, Sarah Hajduk, who have been helpful, supportive, and most of all, patient.

Finally, I could not do anything without the love and support of my family and many dear friends. My friends and family helped me with the important stuff—picking up my daughter from school, filling in for me when I couldn't be there, letting me sleep late when I had to. Thanks especially to my friend, Karen, my loving husband Albert, whom I adore and my daughter, Sara, and son, Nicholas.

## Eoghan Casey

I would like to express my deepest gratitude to Monique Mattei Ferraro for her guidance as we navigated this complex topic and for being the model of balance between life and work. I have always been impressed by her intelligence, quality of character, and sense of humor but never more so than during this joint endeavor. Her enthusiasm and vision challenged me to consider many aspects of our work in a new light, leading to a greater clarity in my understanding that I feel is reflected in this book.

I am also delighted to have this opportunity to formally recognize Mike McGrath's contributions to this work and to my development over the years. Thank you for your sage instruction and for your extraordinary friendship and wit.

Thanks to my friends and colleagues who have continually supported me personally and professionally. Thanks also to Mark Listewnik and the others at Academic Press for your patience and encouragement. Without all of your help, this book would not have been possible.

# SECTION I

## THE INFLUENCE OF TECHNOLOGY

# CHAPTER 1

# OVERVIEW

*I was born into an insane family where my grandfather physically and sexually abused me from a young age until I was fifteen. Part of what he did was send me to strangers' homes for child prostitution where I was also used for child pornography. My grandfather would take pictures of me, as well as show me haunting pictures of other kids who looked drugged and dazed.*

*Growing up and trying to fit into a normal life after so much abuse is hard. I have nightmares, flashbacks and struggle with everyday tasks that most people take for granted. . . . There is a haunting that surrounds me constantly, reminding me that I don't have control over keeping my past a secret. The pictures that were taken when I was so young are still out there. Who knows where they are and how many people have seen them. I wonder if they will show up when I least expect it. I am away from abuse now, but know that someone could be pleasuring himself while looking at my pictures or showing them to kids. (childlustrecovery.org 2003)*

Child sexual assault and exploitation were once limited to physical locations such as school playgrounds, church vestibules, trusted neighbors' homes, camping trips, and seedy, darkly lit back rooms of adult bookstores. Rapid increases in Internet usage have created a virtual hunting ground for those who prey on children and have fueled a brisk, multi-billion dollar trade in the associated illicit material. Online child exploitation includes all forms of sex abuse of children with an online nexus, particularly enticement of minors to engage in sexual activity; manufacture, distribution, and importation of child pornography; and child sex tourism.

> Sexual predators who travel to meet victims that they have acquired online are sometimes called **travelers**.

In addition to providing a new venue for child exploitation, the Internet reduces disincentives by providing anonymity and facilitating fantasy development. The Internet gives offenders easier access to support groups of like-minded individuals, reducing their sense of being marginalized (Taylor and Quayle 2003). The Internet is also very easy to use, making it readily accessible to even the least technologically literate among the population.

> The impact of these peer support groups can be profound, "normalizing" abnormal desires, enabling offenders to view their behavior as socially acceptable and possibly lowering their inhibitions to act on impulses that would otherwise remain fantasy. Additionally, these types of support groups can give offenders access to child pornography, children and technical knowledge that would otherwise be beyond their reach. (Casey, Ferraro, and McGrath 2004)

While the Internet has made the world smaller by bringing distant people and places within easy reach, computer storage media have grown larger to hold almost unfathomable amounts of information. Computer storage capacity has increased to the point at which a small personal computer hard drive can hold as much information as the United States Library of Congress. Child pornographers use this space to store personal libraries of tens of thousands of digital images. Additionally, people increasingly conduct their communications and store more records electronically—financial, personal, and otherwise.

Many people view their communications, online activities, and the information stored on their computers as private. Few people anticipate that law enforcement will ever discover their computer's contents—actually, few people realize the volume of information retained by their computer about their activities. To take advantage of the large amounts of data stored and transmitted using computers, investigators and lawyers must be cognizant of the way information is processed and stored by computers. We talk about "digital forensics" throughout the book. The term refers to the study of the technology, the way criminals use it, and the way to extract and examine digital evidence. Criminals are becoming aware of the risks and are taking steps to conceal their online activities. In response, digital investigators are developing methods and tools to see through such concealment behavior. This ongoing battle of wits, combined with rapid developments in technology, makes this a challenging and dynamic area requiring intelligent and dedicated investigators and attorneys.

Approximately half of the caseload in computer crime units involves the computer-assisted sexual exploitation of children. Despite the scale of this problem, or perhaps because of it, no published resources bring together the complex mingling of disciplines and expertise required to put together a computer-assisted child exploitation case. This work fills this void, providing police, prosecutors, and forensic examiners with the historical, legal, technical, and social background for the laws prohibiting child exploitation—in particular, child pornography—and enticing minors to engage in sexual activity using the Internet. In addition to providing guidance on the technical and legal aspects of child exploitation investigations, cases and associated data are presented to provide a deeper understanding of the crimes, victims, as well as offenders and the level of danger they pose to themselves, their victims, and investigating officers.

## 1.1) BACKGROUND

Children, by definition, are not capable of making the decision to have a consensual sexual relationship. Because of their tender years, lack of education and transportation, children are completely dependent on the adults responsible for their care. When a child is enticed into sexual activity, s/he is manipulated into the act—not a full participant. It simply is not possible for a child who is not granted full adult rights—to vote, to self-determination and self-support—to consent to sex with an adult. The law has sometimes referred to sexual activity between an adult and a person not yet of adult age as "statutory rape" because the sex was "consensual" but illegal by statute based on the difference in age between the partners. When the child is younger, the act has often been classified as "molestation," a watered-down, euphemistic term for the child's victimization. The authors consider sex between a minor (as defined by the jurisdiction) and an adult to be sexual assault. Sexual assault of a child can include kissing, fondling, oral contact to genitals, and penetration whether with an object or a part of the body.

Child pornography is a permanent record of a child's sexual assault that exploits the victim each time it is viewed for pleasure. It is impossible to gauge the damage that such an assault can have on a victim, family, and community.

**CASE EXAMPLE**

The case of Marc Dutroux shook Europe in the late 1980s. He was married and the father of three children. He owned several houses. A large source of his income was from the sale of young girls he kidnapped and sexually assaulted into prostitution and creating child pornography.

Dutroux was convicted of the rape and abuse of five girls and was sentenced to thirteen years in prison. He served only three years. Not long after his release, young girls began to disappear near his several houses. Police searched his houses, only to find nothing. Unfortunately, the police failed to search the basement of one of the houses where two teenaged girls were still alive—hidden and hoping to be saved.

> In 1996, police again searched one of Dutroux's houses where they found a soundproof concrete dungeon in the basement. Two girls, a fourteen-year-old and a twelve-year-old, were found in the dungeon. They were alive, but Dutroux sexually assaulted them and filmed the assaults. Police also found at least 300 child pornography images. Investigation revealed that Dutroux killed at least four girls and sexually assaulted many more. His final capture and conviction inspired public outrage that he had served only three of thirteen years for his initial crimes. The public demanded reform of the laws, the way the laws were enforced, and the punishments given to those preying on their children. (Bell 2003)

Offenders who intentionally seek out children and take advantage of their weaknesses for sexual purposes are a form of sexual predator. The weakness can be emotional, psychological, or physical—or any combination of these. There may seem to be some lack of clarity inherent in such a definition, as it would seem that a sex offender by definition is taking advantage of or exploiting the victim. Inherent in the description, though, is the expectation that the predator has, on some level, planned the offense.

> A **sexual predator** is defined by the authors as a sex offender who takes advantage of a weakness (or weaknesses) of a victim to further sexual exploitation of the victim, with at least some element of planning involved.

This chapter presents an overview of online child exploitation, examining the scope of the problem and providing a foundation for the rest of the book. The history of child exploitation and the way technology is used to facilitate it are explored. A section on how child protection laws developed in the United States and abroad is followed by a brief summary of the book's structure and contents.

The online child exploitation discussed in this book has two faces: child pornography, together with all of the activities necessary to perpetuate it (manufacture, distribution, importation, and possession), and the enticement of a minor to engage in sexual activity using an online facility. Sometimes the two crimes will be treated separately and sometimes together. Since the historical roots of the crimes are found in the sexual assault of children, we begin discussing the crimes together.

## 1.2) HISTORY OF CHILD SEXUAL EXPLOITATION

The history of childhood has been a nightmare from which we have only recently begun to awaken. The further back in history one goes—and the further away from

the West one gets—the more massive the neglect and cruelty one finds and the more
likely children are to have been killed, rejected, beaten, terrorized and sexually
abused by their caretakers. (deMause 1998)

Psychohistorian Lloyd deMause has written extensively on the global history
of child abuse. In *The History of Childhood*, he details the experiences of
children in India and China as particularly abusive. In India, children were
regularly masturbated by their mothers, and adults used children sexually
long before they reached the age of ten. Growing up in China was equally
cruel. Both male and female children were sexually assaulted and forced into
prostitution. Ancient Greek and Roman girls were often raped, and older men
used boys for sex. Until recently, in Western countries children were considered small adults. Labor laws and child abuse protection laws are phenomena
of the twentieth century in the United States.

Child exploitation existed long before the Internet, and networks of offenders communicated before the personal computer was part of our everyday lives.
The North American Man-Boy Love Association is an example. The association
publishes its beliefs and attempts to advance the social acceptability of romantic relationships between men and boys. Prior to the accessibility and instant
communication afforded by the Internet, it took more effort to find and enter
a child exploitation network. The following testimony of Joseph Henry is
illustrative:

During this time, 1975 and 1976, I was actively involved in the San Diego-based
pedophilia organization, the Childhood Sensuality Circle (CSC). I corresponded
with Valida Davila, the head of the CSC, and did some typing for her. As was the
practice with the CSC, Davila also put me in touch with other pedophiles. I can't
stress enough that this group and others, regardless of their publicly stated goals, are
in practice little more than contact services for pedophiles. These groups serve as a
reinforcement for pedophiles and a constant source for new friendships and, thus, a
supply of new victims.

By November 1976, I was back in New York when I received a phone call from
a man named Eric Cross. Cross was a friend of John Duncan, and he said he
understood I was looking for a woman with small children who would agree to marry
me so that I could be a father and feel like an adult, not just to molest children.
At that time, I had no idea who Cross was, but I later learned he was a child
pornographer, publisher of *Lolitots* magazine and a pedophile with connections not
only through the United States, but in several foreign countries as well. I understand
he is now in Florida State Prison and facing a Federal trial on charges of distribution
of child pornography.

I went to Los Angeles in the fall of 1977 to meet with Cross. For several nights, I
met with Cross to look at child porn photos he was sending out of the country. Cross

and I were at the motel examining photos of naked children that he was sending to a source in Canada. As we left the hotel one night, we were arrested. The police had to release me through lack of evidence, and I was able to return to New York, but some weeks later, I was rearrested in New York by U.S. Customs agents.

After my arrest, I learned that numerous other men had come to Los Angeles and San Diego from 1974 to 1976 to molest children John Duncan made available to us. Various motels and homes of two men were used as locations for the molestation. The children were also photographed during sessions with the men.

Although I did not participate in this, one of the men, I can't be sure which, apparently sold photos to the Dutch child porn magazine *Lolita* because in the *Lolita* issues 29, 30, and 31, there were shots of Tammy and Yvonne in various explicit poses. (U.S. Senate 99th Congress)

The growing use of the Internet by adolescents and younger children created the possibility for their victimization by adult sex offenders. As more and more children flocked to the Internet in the 1990s, adults wishing to lure them into sexual relationships welcomed them. What happened before the wide use of the Internet? If an adult had an interest in having sex with a child, the individual would seek contact by gaining employment where there would be exposure to children, or volunteering to work with children, or having one's own children, or befriending the neighborhood children.

Imagine the vast difference in communications technology that has occurred over the past quarter of a century. Anytime prior to 1995, a person seeking sex with a child would become a scout leader, priest, teacher, clown, father, uncle, bus driver. He might join a pedophile network like the CSC described by Joseph Henry. A last resort would be lurking around the neighborhood playground. In the 1980s in some places, citizens band radio was popular among preteens and teenagers, and adults would meet children through that medium. Mostly, though, until the increased use of the Internet, adults met child-victims through the adults' employment or familial ties.

## 1.3) CHILD PORNOGRAPHY

The term "pornography" was first defined in the *Oxford English Dictionary* in 1857 and was referenced earlier in French writing to refer to writing about prostitution, obscenity, and obscene images (Hunt 1993). Each jurisdiction has its own, very specific, definitions of "child" and "pornography." For our purposes in this brief introduction to the matter, "child pornography" can be functionally defined as an image that depicts a clearly prepubescent human being in a sexually explicit manner.[1] There will be no pictures depicting child pornography. Whenever necessary, such as in the discussion about virtual child pornography—that is, child pornography created completely by computer—images will be used for demonstration; however, no images will be used that could be considered child pornography or obscenity in the majority of jurisdictions throughout the world. Undisputedly, there is a great value to seeing the content of the images. After all, it is difficult to really know what something is unless you have actually seen it. We hope that the descriptions given here, taken with your experiences, will be sufficient. Given the nature of the subject and the potential for abuse by those not using the material for legitimate purposes, law enforcement–sponsored training should be the place where images are viewed and analyzed.

Interpol, the international police agency, states that more than 30,000 pedophiles are involved in organized child pornography rings in Europe, which

> **Child pornography** is defined as an image that depicts a clearly prepubescent human being in a sexually explicit manner.

began forming through the Internet. In Europe, countries have been attempting to establish their own individual standards and policies for regulating the Internet. In the United States, law enforcement made an estimated 2,577 arrests for crimes involving the online sexual exploitation of minors between July 1, 2000, and June 30, 2001 (Wolak, Mitchell, and Finkelhor 2003). According to the study's authors, 39 percent of arrests were for crimes against identified victims; 36 percent were for child pornography; and 25 percent of arrests were for solicitations of undercover officers posing as minors. Among all of the offenders, two thirds possessed child pornography. The overwhelming majority of the child pornography that the arrestees possessed depicted children under the age of twelve (83 percent) and explicitly showed the sexual penetration of a minor (80 percent) (Wolak, Mitchell, and Finkelhor 2003). These results demonstrate that Internet-facilitated sexual exploitation of children is prevalent and a very serious social concern.

## 1.4) TECHNOLOGY AND CHILD EXPLOITATION

> If the coming of the Internet has not exactly legalized child pornography of the most worrisome kind, then it has made such material extraordinarily accessible, and almost risk-free to those viewing it. (Jenkins 2002)

---

[1] For ease of discussion, the definition of child pornography is grossly oversimplified here. More detailed treatment of definitions of child pornography will be fully explicated later in this text.

*Figure 1.1*

*Facilitating the sexual exploitation of children: evolution of visual technology*

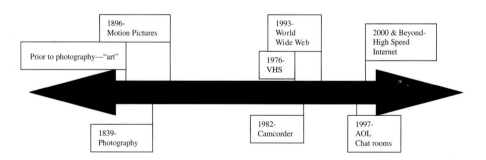

**Facilitating the Sexual Exploitation of Children:**

**Evolution of Visual Technology**

As long as people have been writing, drawing, painting, and sculpting, the human form and sex have been the subject of much of it. It wasn't until the invention of photography in 1839 that depictions of sexual activity could (1) duplicate the act as it happened; (2) clearly depict the individuals involved; and (3) represent a permanent record of the event. Prior to photography, such images could arguably be referred to as "art," because the image was drawn, sculpted, or painted and there was some processing by the artist's creative process. Photographs actually record an event, captured in time forever. When the subject of a photograph is the sexual exploitation or victimization of a child, the recording of the act compounds the damage done in that instant because the victim's suffering is memorialized for all time.

Not long after photography became well known, it was used to exploit children. Each new development in technology translates into a new method of either luring children into illegal sexual activity or portraying child pornography and distributing it. Motion pictures[2] created the ability to view the entire sex act as if the viewer was either involved or watching as a voyeur. VCRs[3] and camcorders[4] substantially enlarged the media market. People who would never dream of venturing out to a peep show or an X-rated movie could rent videos of sexually graphic features with impunity. Similarly, child pornography also increasingly was found on videotape and circulated in that form.

Ann Wolbert Burgess and her colleagues brought the issue to the academic and legal communities for the first time. The following is a brief excerpt from *Child Pornography and Sex Rings* describing the availability of child pornography in Chicago in the late 1970s:

---

[2] Thomas Edison showed the first motion picture in 1896.
[3] VHS, developed by JVC, was introduced circa 1976.
[4] In 1982, both JVC and Sony announced the "CAMera/recorder," or camcorder, combinations.

During 1976 and 1977 there were approximately sixty retail adult bookstores in the city of Chicago. Most, if not all, of these stores received their stock of magazines, films, and videocassettes from three or four major wholesale distributors. The variety and coarseness of pornography available through these retailers was increasing. "Adult materials" appeared to be digressing toward more bizarre and unusual forms featuring bondage, sadomasochism, bestiality, and child pornography. While this material had been available before, it now appeared more readily accessible. The informal consensus among law enforcement agents working in this area was that child pornography had never been as available over the counter as it was in 1976–77. . . .

The typical foreign magazine sold for between $6 and $12, and this for pamphlets with reproduction so poor that in some cases it was hard to distinguish the sex of the model. Domestically produced child pornography sold for approximately $25 per magazine and $50 per film. (Burgess 1984)

Calculated in today's dollars and allowing for inflation, the child pornography magazine that sold for $25 in the 1970s in Chicago would go for about $108, and the $50 film would sell for $215 today.

Law enforcement crackdowns on child pornography were very effective during the 1970s and 1980s. The material was hard to find as it was. Law enforcement efforts made it even harder to find, and even more expensive. Until relatively recently, child pornography was difficult to find anywhere. What was available was of poor quality, and it was expensive.

Many factors converged in the latter part of the 1990s to fuel an explosion in the availability of high-quality child pornography in digital form. The Internet revolutionized the child pornography industry. Illicit materials that in the 1970s and 1980s cost hundreds of dollars to buy and required traveling to an unsavory neighborhood and risking arrest all of a sudden could be accessed easily over the Internet, viewed immediately, and downloaded for later viewing. Older pictures and magazines could be scanned into digital format and posted on the Internet for anyone to access for free.

Scanners—devices that transform documents or pictures into a digital format—went down in price substantially. In 1990 a scanner cost around $1,000. In the mid- to late-1990s a high-quality scanner cost no more than a few hundred dollars. Whereas it would have been cost prohibitive only a few years ago to produce high-quality images in one's home and publish them on the Internet, the cost today is minimal. An Internet-ready personal computer costs less than $700. Used computers cost even less. A digital still image camera costs less than $100. Cameras capable of sending real-time images over the Internet (a.k.a. Webcams) often come as part of the personal computer package.

Storing images in digital format also became easier and more affordable. Whereas storage cost a great deal and required extensive resources when personal computers first became widely available, in the mid- to late-1990s the size of hard drives and removable media increased vastly, while at the same time the cost plummeted. For roughly the same price of one of the first dual-floppy drive personal computers, one can purchase an Internet-ready machine capable of storing as much information as the Library of Congress holds on its bookshelves.

> The advances in technology during the few years between 1985 and 2000 cannot be overstated in terms of their impact on the availability of child pornography. In 1986, a typical personal computer had two $5\frac{1}{4}''$ floppy drives. One booted up the system with a "boot" disk. One disk contained the software and another disk saved the work. Monitors were small and all were monochrome. One could access the Internet using a 1200 or 2400 baud modem, which was very, very slow and the interaction was limited. There were no graphical user interfaces (GUI). The concept of point-and-click did not exist.

Personal computers with small (by today's standards) hard drives of 10 or 20 megabytes (MB) started to be widely used in the late 1980s. It was only as recently as 1993 when the World Wide Web (Web for short) became a significant part of the Internet. Prior to the invention of hypertext markup language (HTML), the Internet was effectively limited to communication among academics, the military, and a few others with the knowledge and resources to access it. The first Web site appeared in 1990. By 1993, there were about 500 Web servers. By 1994, the Web had 10 million users. Between 1994 and today, the number of Internet users has grown exponentially. By 2002, the number of Internet users was estimated at 580,780,000.[5] At the same time, connection speeds have increased, facilitating transmission of larger amounts of data over shorter periods of time.

As stated earlier, the fastest modem connection in the mid-1980s was about 2400 bits per second. Transmitting a small number of commands seemed to take an interminable amount of time. A small document might take one to five minutes to transmit. As shown in Table 1.1, there is a dramatic difference in download times between a 2400 baud modem typically available during the 1980s, a 56 KB, and an ISDN connection. While there is variation in actual download time due to network response and protocol overhead, the findings

[5] http://www.nua.ie/surveys/how_many_online 2003.

*Figure 1.2*

*This is a thumbdrive that holds up to 2 gigabytes of information. Available online for $799 at http://www.usbdrive.com/ website/products/weather proof.html. A gigabyte is equal to 1,024 megabytes. A megabyte is equal to 1,000,000 bytes. A byte is equal to one character.*

| Bits per second | Download time in seconds | Download time in minutes | Download time in hours |
|---|---|---|---|
| 2400 | 100820.2666 | 1680.3378 | 28.01 |
| 14400 | 1803.7298 | 30.0621 | 0.5 |
| 56000 | 590.1963 | 9.8366 | |
| ISDN | 405.7599 | 6.7627 | |
| ADSL | 202.8799 | 3.381 | |

*Table 1.1*

*Estimated Download Times for Different Speed Modems for a 2.5 MB JPEG file*

Source: Samir Termanini, "Modem Speeds: The Evolution of the Modulator/Demodulator Technology with Respect to the Graphics on the World Wide Web." Research conducted for the authors (2002).

are telling. This enormous advance in the transmission speed greatly enhanced the utility of the Internet for trading child pornography.

Of interest for understanding the vast proliferation of child pornography and adult erotica is that no one with access to the Internet need ever pay for any type of access to digital images depicting pornography again. Thousands of newsgroups, Web sites, e-groups, and file servers offer every conceivable sex act with every type of animal and/or object both free and for nominal fees. Amateurs frequently post their own photos—taken either with digital cameras or scanned into digital format. Postings span every interest. Child pornography of every sort is fairly easy to find. Both child erotica—pictures of children in suggestive poses, sometimes partially naked but not depicting any sexual activity, and hard-core child pornography—images of clearly prepubescent children engaged in sexual activity are easily available. The images range in quality from that circulated twenty to thirty years ago, to high-quality video. Home movies of the actual sexual assault of children can easily be made with inexpensive digital video cameras and posted on the Internet within minutes of the event, or may even be posted live.

Consider the vast difference in technology between the 1970s and the early 2000s that can be used to create and distribute child pornography. In the 1970s, it would not have been possible to make even decent quality photocopies of a document, never mind a picture. Developing pictures from camera negatives required specialized equipment, supplies, and knowledge, or the film had to be developed professionally. The risk of taking child pornography to a commercial development lab for processing was high. Many photo processors routinely reported child pornographers to police.

**CASE EXAMPLE**

Nikolai Zarick was convicted of three counts of risk of injury to a child, four counts of being an accessory to risk of injury to a child, two counts of conspiracy to commit risk of injury to a child, one count of sexual assault in the first degree, eight counts of sexual assault in the second degree, twelve counts of being an accessory to sexual assault in the second degree, one count of sexual assault in the fourth degree and one count of employing a minor in an obscene performance. The court sentenced him to twenty-eight years in prison. Shortly after Mr. Zarick's wife dropped off film for developing, the Massachusetts photoprocessor reported seeing sexually explicit photographs of children on the Zarick film. Mr. Zarick's convictions resulted from the investigation started in response to the photoprocessor's complaint.[6]

Even if the manufacturer of child pornography were to get film developed, to distribute the product, it had to be printed professionally, and not many professional printers would risk their business to print contraband. If they did, the cost would be increased. In more recent years, a number of investigations have been prompted by computer shops reporting child pornography found on computers dropped off for repair.

Prior to the Internet, the postal service was the primary means of distributing child pornography. Postal Inspectors were adept at picking up distributors and purchasers. Prohibitions against trafficking in child pornography were enforced through controlled deliveries of child pornography ordered in response to advertisements. A postal worker would deliver the package, and a few moments later the Postal Inspectors would execute a search warrant on the residence and arrest the target on site. Even though the purchaser thought he took fewer risks by ordering the contraband through the mail, he actually provided the Postal Inspectors with more physical evidence because he sent an order and a check and accepted delivery from a Postal Inspector in person. Prior to the Internet, the cost and risk associated with manufacturing and dis-

---

[6] *State v. Zarick*, 227 Conn. 207; 630 A.2d 565 (1993).

tributing child pornography translated into high selling prices for the material and very limited availability.

## 1.5) TECHNOLOGY AND PREFERENTIAL SEX OFFENDERS

Teenagers are drawn to technology. Youth adapt to and learn new technology more easily than adults for many reasons. We tend to stick with things we know and are comfortable doing. Constantly learning new ways to do things is a challenge and fun when we are young, but as we get older, it loses its allure.

Preferential sex offenders study their targets. They know where children of their preferred age group will be and what sorts of things interest them. Before the Internet, preferential sex offenders haunted the citizens band and ham radio. The technology lent itself to use by children. It enabled communication with many people at the same time and did not require a minimum age to use it. Sitting in his or her own living room, a child could talk with other children and adults. Depending on whether citizens band or ham radio frequencies were employed, a child could reach people over considerable distances.

Children's interest in CB radio was eagerly shared by preferential sex offenders who used it as a means to develop relationships with potential victims. Prior to the CB, offenders relied on employment, volunteering, family, and friends to gain access to children in their desired age range. If the preferential sex offender lacked the ability to obtain employment with access to children or possessed a physical characteristic that prevented him from connecting with children, the CB offered the offender access to potential victims and a means of developing a relationship with a potential victim over a period of time. This ability to develop a relationship without face-to-face contact provided the offender with the ability to gradually forge the type of relationship that would enable him to initiate sexual encounters with the victim while dissuading disclosure of the activity.

Preferential sex offenders often use the latest technology to attract victims. For instance, an offender might coax a child to his home with an offer to allow the child to play the latest video game or new gadget.

> A forty-three-year-old Connecticut man who lived with his parents traveled to Keene, New Hampshire, thinking he would meet a young teenager who was interested in a sexual relationship. Instead, police arrested him. A subsequent search of his home revealed hundreds of videotaped assaults of children. The suspect lured children into allowing him to lick their feet and tickle them by letting them play with his video games and giving them rides in his vintage car.

## 1.6) DEVELOPMENT OF CHILD PORNOGRAPHY LAW

Initially, child pornographers were subject to laws in the United States and abroad regulating obscenity. During the 1970s and 1980s, the United States Supreme Court made a number of landmark decisions governing obscenity and child pornography. In 1973, the court decided *Miller v. California* (1972)[7]—the case that set the standard for determining obscenity. The test set forth in *Miller* dictates that for a work to be condemned as "obscene," one must determine that, taken as a whole, it appeals to the prurient interest; portrays sexual conduct in a patently offensive way measured by community standards; and lacks serious social value, whether literary, artistic, political, or scientific.

> "Obscenity" is a legal determination. For material to be **obscene**, it must appeal to the prurient interest; portray sexual conduct in a patently offensive manner as measured by community standards; and lack serious literary, artistic, political, scientific, or other social value.

Shortly thereafter, the court decided *New York v. Ferber* (1984).[8] *Ferber* held the states have a compelling interest in protecting children; that child pornography is inextricably intertwined with child exploitation and abuse because it is both a record of the abuse and it encourages production of similar materials; and that child pornography has very little social, scientific, political, literary, or artistic value. States may therefore regulate child pornography more strictly than obscenity. The court distinguished "child pornography" from "obscenity," and material need not be obscene for it to be illegal child pornography. The court further distinguished child pornography from obscenity in *Osborne v. Ohio* (1990),[9] holding that in contrast to obscenity, states could regulate the "mere" possession of child pornography.

In the United States, little serious public outcry or legal attention was given to obscenity, child pornography, or the sexual exploitation of children prior to the early 1970s. We owe increased sensitivity, new laws, and law enforcement attention in large part to the women's movement. At first blush, it may seem odd that obscenity and child pornography protections—which may appear to be concerns of the more conservative among us—stem from radical feminist theory. An explanation, we hope, will dispel any confusion and make perfect sense of it all.

[7] *Miller v. California*, 314 U.S. 15 (1972).
[8] *New York v. Ferber*, 458 U.S. 747; 102 S. Ct. 3348; 73 L. Ed. 2d 1113; 1982 U.S. LEXIS 12; 50 U.S.L.W. 5077; 8 Media L. Rep. 1809 (1982).
[9] *Osborne v. Ohio*, 495 U.S. 103; 110 S. Ct. 1691; 109 L. Ed. 2d 98; 1990 U.S. LEXIS 2036; 58 U.S.L.W. 4467 (1990).

The term "the women's movement" refers to coalitions of organizations championing feminist issues. At the turn of the twentieth century, the primary concerns of the movement were gaining the right for women to vote and protecting children through child labor laws. The suffragists shifted their focus to prohibition in the 1920s. The women's movement in the 1960s and early 1970s advocated for an Equal Rights Amendment to the United States Constitution, reproductive rights, creation and enforcement of domestic violence laws, and development of sexual assault victim services. Women's advocates were successful in securing greater legal protection and law enforcement response to victims of domestic violence and sexual assault. Only within the past twenty years has mandatory arrest in domestic violence cases been the rule rather than the exception. Services for victims of domestic violence and sexual assault were scarce at best and in many places did not exist until twenty years ago. The advocates for equal rights and sexual assault victim services heavily influenced our current child pornography laws.

Catherine MacKinnon led radical feminist thinking regarding pornography and obscenity. She advocated the idea that pornography is a means of discrimination against women. MacKinnon argued that pornography causes its viewers to objectify, abuse, and sexually assault women (MacKinnon 1993). MacKinnon states in her book, *Toward a Feminist Theory of the State*, that pornography "sells women to men as and for sex. It is a technologically sophisticated traffic in women" (MacKinnon 1989). The reader should note that prior to the 1990s it was exceedingly rare for women to direct or profit from the making of pornography. In the early twenty-first century, it is quite common for women to create pornography and to profit from it. Jenna Jamison, a popular and now wealthy star of adult films, is one example. MacKinnon and Andrea Dworkin were instrumental in persuading the City of Indianapolis to enact an ordinance banning pornography. While the ordinance was subsequently struck down by the Seventh Circuit Court of Appeals, the reasoning behind its original passage became part of obscenity and child pornography analysis.

In 1968 Congress passed the Anti-Pandering Statute (39 U.S.C. §3008) in response to increasing complaints from constituents who received sexually related advertisements in the mail. The law was intended to deter advertisers from sending material to individuals who did not solicit it. Congress enacted the Protection of Children Against Sexual Exploitation Act in 1977, and President Carter signed it into law in 1978. The Act extended the federal government's authority to prosecute producers and distributors of child pornography and prohibited transportation of children across state lines for the purpose of sexual exploitation. Since its initial passage, the Protection of Children Against Sexual Exploitation Act has been modified several times. The development of the law will be dealt with in greater detail in Chapter 10.

## 1.7) INTERNATIONAL: THE UNITED NATIONS CONVENTION ON THE RIGHTS OF THE CHILD

The United Nations General Assembly unanimously adopted the Convention on the Rights of the Child in 1989. The Convention sets forth fundamental rights for individuals under the age of eighteen and establishes them as part of international law. Child pornography is specifically addressed. Each country is required to "take all appropriate national, bilateral and multilateral measures to prevent: . . . . (c) The exploitative use of children in pornographic performances and materials." (Convention Article 34 1989).

Canada added to its obscenity law in 1993, outlawing the possession of child pornography. According to Persky and Dixon, the impetus behind the child pornography possession law was the feminist legal theory of Catherine MacKinnon (Persky and Dixon 2001; *American Booksellers Association, Inc. v. Hudnut* 1985).[10] Applying that thinking to the sexual assault and exploitation of children, the Canadian legislature enacted the child pornography possession prohibition (Persky and Dixon 2001).

## 1.8) CONCLUSION

This text is aimed at both practitioners and students from a wide range of disciplines. Each topic is fully developed to provide a solid treatment of the subject for beginners, and citations to additional resources are liberally provided for more advanced study. Section I deals with The Influence of Technology. In addition to the current chapter, this section covers Internet Applications in Chapter 2, Cyber Victims in Chapter 3, Cyber Offenders in Chapter 4, and Sources of Digital Evidence in Chapter 5.

Section II explores various aspects of Investigating Internet Child Exploitation. Chapter 6 looks at Undercover Operations, Chapter 7 provides guidelines for Collecting and Preserving Evidence on the Internet, Chapter 8 reviews Tracking on the Internet. Chapter 9 begins a discussion of Search & Seizure in Cyberspace addressing Drafting Warrants. Chapter 10 continues the Search & Seizure topic, addressing Executing the Warrant.

Section III provides an overview of Forensic Examination of Digital Evidence. Topics covered in Section III are Overview of the Examination Process in Chapter 11, and Servers and Networks in Chapter 12.

Section IV concludes the text with The Law of Internet Child Sexual Exploitation. Chapter 13 discusses the law governing Child Pornography. Chapter 14 delves into Pre-trial. Trial issues are explored in Chapter 15.

---

[10] *American Booksellers Association, Inc. v. Hudnut*, 771 F.2d 323 (1985) rehearing denied 475 U.S. 1132 (1986).

Chapter 16 concludes the text, summarizing and touching on organizing an Electronic Evidence Examination Unit and the future of Internet child exploitation.

## REFERENCES

Bell, R. Marc Dutroux on www.crimelibrary.com (2003).

deMause, L. "The History of Child Abuse." *The Journal of Psychohistory* 25, no. 3 (Winter 1998).

deMause, L. *The History of Childhood.* London, UK: Souvenir Press, 1976.

Burgess, A. W., ed. *Child Pornography and Sex Rings.* New York: Lexington Books, 1984.

Casey, E., M. M. Ferraro, and M. McGrath. "Sex Offenders on the Internet," in *Digital Evidence and Computer Crimes, 2nd Edition.* E. Casey, ed. Boston, MA: Academic Press, 2004.

Convention on the Rights of the Child, U.N. General Assembly, Doc. A/Res/44/25 (Dec 12, 1989). Available online at www.cirp.org/library/ethics/UN-convention.

"Dutroux Affair Haunts Belgian Police." (January 22, 2002). http://news.bbc.co.uk/1/hi/world/europe/1775576.stm.

Esposito, L. C. "Regulating the Internet: The New Battle Against Child Pornography." 30 Case W. Res. J. Int'l L. 541 (Spring/Summer, 1998).

Hunt, L. ed. *The Invention of Pornography, Obscenity and the Origins of Modernity, 1500–1800.* New York: Zone Books, 1993.

Jenkins, P. "Bringing the Loathsome to Light." *Chronicle of Higher Education* 48, no. 25 (March 1, 2002): B16, 2p.

Meloy, J. R. *Violent Attachments.* Northvale, NJ: Aronson, 1997.

MacKinnon, C. A. *Only Words.* Cambridge, MA: Harvard University Press, 1993.

MacKinnon, C. A. *Toward a Feminist Theory of the State.* Cambridge, MA: Harvard University Press, 1989.

McGrath, M., and E. Casey. Forensic Psychiatry and the Internet. *Journal of American Academy of Psychiatry and Law* 30: 81–94, 2002.

Olson, D. A. "The Swedish Ban of Corporal Punishment." Comment, B.Y.U. L. Rev. 447–456 (1984).

Persky, S., and J. Dixon. *On Kiddie Porn: Sexual Representation, Free Speech and the Robin Sharpe Case.* Vancouver, CA: New Star Books, 2001.

Senate, Testimony of Joseph Henry before the Permanent Subcommittee on Governmental Affairs, Ninety-Ninth Congress.

Sunstein, C. R. "Article: Pornography and the First Amendment." Duke L.J. 589, 1986.

Taylor, M., and E. Quayle. *Child Pornography: An Internet Crime.* Philadelphia, PA. Brunner-Rutledge, 2003.

Wolak, J., K. Mitchell, and D. Finkelhor. "Internet Sex Crimes Against Minors: The Response." Alexandria, VA: Crime Against Children Research Center, University of New Hampshire, National Center for Missing and Exploited Children, 2003.

# CHAPTER 2

# INTERNET APPLICATIONS

*Police have arrested 12 men in a series of raids in a crack-down on people buying "pay-per-view" child porn on the internet. The 12 were arrested at different addresses by North Wales Police who were following up details of Internet users who subscribed to paedophile Web sites. The Web sites charge customers a set rate which gives access to a library of images for a limited time. (Skynews 2002)*

*Deputy Bill Stevenson is one of the men who poses as an underage chat-room visitor who is willing to have sex with someone who will drive to the county for the experience. "I've had as many as 25 or 30 hit on me within a couple of minutes," he said. "You can go to hundreds of different chat rooms. Anytime, day or night, you can go on anytime. There's no good or bad time. They're on all the time," Stevenson said. (Nurenberg 2002)*

In some ways, the Internet is similar to other technologies. It is similar to a cellular phone or VCR in the ways people use it. Some people are familiar with every feature of their cellular phone. They access games, they program the screen saver, and they customize the ringer. They have all of their contacts programmed in and use the calendar. The same people who program their cellular phones are usually the same people who know how to set the time on their VCRs. They know how to program the machines to record their favorite programs. They can program the VCR to tape one show while they watch another. They can program the VCR to tape multiple programs while they are on vacation. Of course, there's a whole other world full of people who use their cellular phone only to make telephone calls. If someone sent them a text message, it would be so foreign to them that they might think it was magic. Should the electricity go out at their home, the VCR time would blink at 12:00 until a technically savvy neighbor or friend dropped by and programmed it properly.

Similarly, there are two worlds of Internet users. Some users simply log onto the Internet to access e-mail, the Web, and Instant Messaging. These folks are unaware that beyond their limited Internet interactions lies an entire universe of online experience that may be used for legitimate or for illegal purposes. More advanced Internet users—the type of people who have their cellular phones programmed and their VCRs display the accurate time—use the less-known services such as peer-to-peer, newsgroups, and Internet relay chat. In this chapter the most prominent Internet features are treated in a way that will provide a fair introduction.

Individuals who are involved with the investigation and prosecution of child exploitation should be familiar with both the basics and more advanced features of the Internet. This chapter begins with the more commonly used Internet services such as e-mail and the Web and progresses to lesser-known services. It is important for those involved with the investigation and prosecution of child exploitation to understand how offenders use these technologies to commit crimes and avoid apprehension. You are encouraged to explore the backstreets of the information highway. It's difficult to patrol if you haven't reviewed a map of your assigned area.

This chapter describes the Internet applications that are most commonly encountered in child exploitation cases. Although the underlying protocols are touched on, an in-depth treatment is beyond the scope of this text.[1] Each section begins with a review of the Internet feature, describes how the feature has been or could be used to exploit children, and incorporates illustrative examples.

## 2.1) IP ADDRESSES AND DOMAIN NAME SYSTEM

To facilitate communication using the Internet, the technology requires that each computer connected to it, and each transaction using the network, be identified. For this function, the Internet primarily uses Internet Protocol (IP) addresses that consist of four sets of numbers that range from 0 to 255.[2] The IP address identifies the Internet connection. A server such as www.missingkids.org has a permanently assigned or "static" IP address. On the other hand, dial-up users generally connect to a randomly assigned IP address through a bank of modems operated by an Internet Service Provider (ISP). This IP address is referred to as "dynamic" because a different address is assigned each time an individual connects to the Internet. Users who connect

---

[1] Many of the protocols are defined in Request For Comment (RFC) documents available on the Internet.

[2] A newer addressing scheme called IPv6 uses a different format.

to the Internet through a cable provider, DSL, or other high-speed connection generally have dynamic IP addresses but, for an added fee, can obtain a static IP address.

To make the Internet more user-friendly, many IP addresses have names associated with them. For example, the Web site for the National Center for Missing and Exploited Children is located at www.missingkids.org, which corresponds to a server accessing the Internet through IP address 165.121.1.2. The Domain Name System (DNS) keeps track of these name-IP address associations. When you enter the name www.missingkids.org, a DNS server translates that name into the corresponding IP address and directs your request accordingly. Individuals can query DNS servers directly using the nslookup command that comes with Windows and UNIX, as shown here:

```
C:\>nslookup www.missingkids.org
Server: dns.home.net
Address: 192.168.0.1

Name: us.missingkids.com
Address: 208.254.21.169
Aliases: www.missingkids.org, www.missingkids.com
```

Note that this server actually has three DNS names that all refer to the same IP address to make it easier for people to locate this online resource.

## 2.2) E-MAIL

E-mail is letter-type correspondence. Using e-mail is a fairly straightforward proposition. Most e-mail software is pretty much the same. It is very much like a memo pad. You type in the addresses you would like to send to, the name of the person you'd like to get a copy, the subject, and then the content. Most e-mail programs allow you to attach a file. The type of file, content, and size may be limited by firewall software[3] and by the transmission speed of the Internet connection. Digital images, music, movie files, spreadsheets, and word processing documents are typical examples of the kinds of files attached to e-mail. Child pornography distributors use e-mail to transmit child pornography sometimes, but do not use it to send the material in any large quantities. Most often, if pictures are attached to e-mail, the sender shares a few images of particular interest with another collector or distributor. More frequently, a preferential sex offender grooming an intended target sends child pornography images attached to e-mail. Sharing pictures in this way allows the offender the oppor-

---

[3] Firewall software is used to secure a computer system from unfriendly Internet or other outside networks.

tunity to give the image a context and to describe not only what might be going on in the attached image(s), but how the images might be relevant to what the offender would like to do with the intended victim.

It is important to discuss how e-mail gets from sender to recipient to appreciate the nature of the communication medium. Many people labor under the misapprehension that their e-mail communication is "private." Well, it could be—if they take precautions, like encrypting it. Of course, most people don't use encryption or other security measures when using e-mail. Using an analogy to post office "snail-mail," e-mail is less like a letter that's sealed, and more like a post card. The content of e-mail is wide open as it travels from one place to another. When an e-mail is sent, the message is broken up into "packets" containing pieces of the e-mail. Each packet is labeled with information, like a set of instructions to all the servers it will pass through telling them where it's going, who sent it, and when. It could be difficult for someone to put together all of the packets to make a whole e-mail message, but then again, it might not. Tools such as Ethereal make this reassembly process trivial, but only an Internet user with advanced knowledge and skills would be aware of the software and take time to use it.

## 2.3) E-GROUPS AND MAILING LISTS

To facilitate communication among groups, various types of e-mail services flourish. Two types of services, e-groups and mailing lists, will be described here because they have been known to facilitate the sexual exploitation of children on the Internet.

There are e-groups for every conceivable interest—and some inconceivable interests. A brief review of some of the nearly unlimited Yahoo! Groups revealed groups catering to bellybutton enthusiasts and dozens of groups dedicated to sharing pictures of people—from children to adults—in diapers. One group closed to new members is described by its creator:

> Hello my friend, I have created this club for me and other dads who truly do it with their pre-teen daughters, to share pics, vids & stories. I don't care about the number of members as long as we all share the same interests.

Another group moderator greets prospective members with this statement:

> This is a group for sharing passes to nn teen and pre-teen sites. Examples, christinamodel.com, Daniela-model.net, etc. . . .) TO JOIN E-MAIL THE PASS TO THE MODERATOR (me) BEFORE YOU SUBMIT THE REQUEST TO JOIN. . . . If you're going to submit pictures/movies whether or not you're approved is solely at my discretion. (teenpassexchange 2003)

Many people subscribe to mailing lists and they are often used to distribute child pornography. Many organizations with a presence online have a mailing list feature to keep members informed and to foster communication. A mailing list requires a subscription. The applicant sends an e-mail to the moderator (either a person or automated program), and the moderator sends the applicant an e-mail that describes the list, sets forth the rules for posting messages or e-mails, and the procedure for unsubscribing. When a message is sent to the moderator, s/he reviews it and, if it meets the list criteria, sends it out to all list subscribers. When the subscriber receives an e-mail, the sender is listed as one individual, whatever the list's name is. Even if the group has a thousand members, only one e-mail address is listed in the sender and recipient address lines. When the moderator sends out the e-mail, it is as if the e-mail is sent to each subscriber individually. The individual subscribers never see all of the list subscriber names and e-mail addresses.

E-groups are quite similar to mailing lists in that people must subscribe, and e-mail to the group of subscribers is one of the features offered. E-groups differ from both traditional e-mail and mailing lists in that other services are offered to subscribers, such as chat, calendars, and bulletin boards. There is also, usually, a home page or central area for members to view e-group statistics, see who is currently online, and access recently posted material. Also, importantly, there are different ways to sign up for e-groups, and each subscriber may choose different access options. A glaring and important example can be taken from the Candyman investigation.

## UNITED STATES V. PEREZ[4]

**CASE EXAMPLE**

**OPINION: CHIN, D.J.**

This case presents difficult questions concerning the Fourth Amendment and the Internet. On the one hand, child pornography and the sexual abuse of children are crimes that have been fueled by the Internet, as those who would exploit children have sought to take advantage of the Internet's vast and largely anonymous distribution and communications network. On the other hand, when law enforcement gathers information about the activity of individuals on the Internet, the potential for unreasonable intrusions into the home—the chief concern of the drafters of the Fourth Amendment—is great. This case demonstrates the tension that can exist: the Government argues, in essence, that it had probable cause to search the homes and seize the computers of thousands of individuals merely because they entered their e-mail addresses into a Website where images of child pornography were available, even without any proof that the individuals uploaded, downloaded or discussed the images, or otherwise participated in the Website.

[4] 247 F. Supp. 2d 459; 2003 U.S. Dist. LEXIS 3162 (2nd Cir. 2003).

Defendant Harvey Perez is charged in a one-count indictment with violating 18 U.S.C. § 2252A(a)(5)(B) by unlawfully and knowingly possessing materials containing images of child pornography transmitted in interstate commerce. The Government also seeks the forfeiture of certain of Perez's computer equipment. This case arises out of Operation Candyman, an undercover FBI investigation into a group that allegedly traded pornographic images of children over the internet.

Perez moves to suppress certain evidence obtained as the result of the execution of a search warrant at his home. For the reasons that follow, the motion is granted and the evidence is suppressed. [ ]

On March 6, 2002, federal law enforcement agents executed a search warrant at Perez's home. They seized a computer, numerous compact discs and floppy discs, computer drives, a scanner, two cameras, and a piece of paper listing various Websites. [ ] The agents also interviewed Perez; he "admitted to visiting child pornography sites" on the internet. [ ]

The search warrant was issued by Magistrate Judge James C. Francis IV on the basis of a 32-page affidavit executed by Special Agent Austin P. Berglas of the FBI on March 1, 2002. [ ] The affidavit requested authorization to search nine residences in Manhattan, the Bronx, Riverdale, West Point, Wappingers Falls, Tarrytown, and the village of Florida, New York. [ ] One of these residences was Perez's home. The agent represented that probable cause existed to believe that the nine residences contained evidence of violations of 18 U.S.C. §§ 2252 and 2252A, which make it a crime to knowingly transport, transmit, or receive child pornography in interstate or foreign commerce by any means, including computer. [ ]

The affidavit provided a lengthy description of how the internet and computers are used—in general terms—to distribute child pornography. [ ] It also described an undercover investigation by the FBI into the "Candyman Egroup." [ ]

The affidavit provided little detail on the Candyman Egroup. It explained that the Candyman Website displayed the following message:

> This group is for People who love kids. You can post any type of messages you like too or any type of pics and vids you like too.

[ ] The affidavit did not represent or assert that the sole or principal purpose of the Candyman Egroup was to engage in unlawful conduct. It represented that the group had 3,397 members. [ ]

The affidavit explained that to become a member of the Website an undercover FBI agent was required to send an e-mail message to the group's moderator requesting permission to join; no fee was required. [ ] The affidavit detailed how, after receiving confirmation of membership via e-mail, the undercover agent was able to download, from the Candyman Website, approximately 100 images and video clips of "prepubescent minors engaged in sexual activities," "the genitalia of nude minors," and "child erotica." [ ] Of these, the majority of the images and video clips fell into the first category. [ ] In addition, the affidavit reported that the undercover FBI agent received some 498 e-mails from the Candyman Egroup, of which approximately 105 had attachments containing child pornography and another 183 had attachments containing "child erotica images." [ ]

The affidavit explained that the Candyman Egroup Website had several features, including a "Files" section that permitted members to post images and videos for other members to download. It also disclosed that the Candyman site offered a "Polls" feature that permitted members to answer survey questions; a "Links" feature that permitted members to post links to other Websites; and a "Chat" section that permitted members to engage in "real time conversations with each other."

The affidavit represented that all new members were immediately added to the Candyman Egroup's mailing list, and it asserted the following:

> Every *Candyman Egroup* member on the *Candyman Egroup* e-mail list automatically received every e-mail message and file transmitted to the *Candyman Egroup* by any *Candyman Egroup* member. Therefore, when individuals transmitted child pornography to the *Candyman Egroup*, those images automatically were transmitted to every *Candyman Egroup* member.

(emphasis added). These representations were critical because they advised the magistrate judge that all Candyman members automatically received all e-mails and that therefore all Candyman members must have received e-mails that contained images of child pornography.

. . .

On August 12, 2002, the Government wrote defense counsel and advised that the above-quoted sentences from paragraph 8(d) of the affidavit were not accurate. [ ]The Government advised that in fact Candyman members had three e-mail delivery options: (1) receipt of all e-mails; (2) receipt of only a daily digest of e-mails; and (3) "no e-mail receipt at all." [ ] A member who selected the no e-mail option would not receive any e-mails from the Candyman Egroup, its moderator, or its members. [ ] Hence, it was not correct that every Candyman member received every e-mail from the group.

. . .

A prospective member of an Egroup run by eGroups (including the Candyman Egroup) could subscribe in one of three ways: (1) via the Website by clicking on the "subscribe" button on the particular group's Website; (2) via e-mail by sending an e-mail to the "subscribe address" listed on the front page of the particular group's Website; or (3) via e-mail by sending an e-mail to the moderator at an address listed on the group's Website. [ ]

A subscriber who joined via the Website was automatically presented with three options for the delivery of e-mail. By clicking on the "subscribe" button, he would be sent to a page that gave him three options: (1) he could have individual e-mail messages sent to his personal e-mail address (selected as the default choice); (2) he could have a daily digest of messages (described on the site's text as "many e-mails in one message") sent to his personal e-mail address; or (3) he could receive no e-mail messages at all (described as "Don't send me e-mail, I'll read the messages at the Web site"). At the bottom of the page was a "join" button.

A subscriber who joined via e-mail to the "subscribe" address would be automatically "signed up" after responding to a confirmation request, if the group was an "open group." [ ] A subscriber who joined via e-mail to the moderator was not automatically signed up; rather, the moderator could choose to subscribe the individual, deny or ignore the request, or send a further invitation. For both e-mail subscription methods, no e-mail delivery options were provided; rather, the default setting was that the new member would start receiving all e-mails. A member could change to a different e-mail option by clicking on the "modify" button on the first page of the Website. [ ]

When he joined the Candyman Egroup on January 2, 2001, Binney had been with the FBI for eight years, all in the Houston division. He had spent two years on the "Innocent Images" project, primarily working undercover on-line to investigate individuals who were seeking to meet children for unlawful purposes. [ ] Binney believed that the FBI was spending "an awful lot of time on-line," and that the effort was not "as productive" as it could have been. [ ] In addition, he wanted to target individuals who were seeking to exploit younger children, i.e., children who were too young to go on-line themselves. [ ] In the fall of 2000, Binney began to look for an opportunity for an on-line, undercover child pornography investigation, and this effort eventually led to Candyman. [ ]

Binney and FBI Special Agent Kristen Sheldon, who took over the case from Binney, knew or should have known, before the search warrant affidavit was executed in this case on March 1, 2002, that Candyman members had e-mail delivery options. At a minimum, they knew that it was an open question.

. . .

On March 18, 2002, Sheldon interviewed Mark Bates, the former moderator of the Candyman Egroup. Bates told her that Candyman members could elect not to receive e-mail. She apparently did not believe him. [ ]

In May 2002, Sheldon learned from an FBI agent in St. Louis that Yahoo had submitted an affidavit in a Candyman case stating that there had been e-mail delivery options. [ ]

At some point in mid-2002, the Government started to acknowledge in the various Candyman cases that the search warrant affidavits had contained an error: it was not correct that all members automatically received all e-mails. As a consequence, defendants in different Candyman cases moved to suppress evidence obtained as a result of the search warrants. [ ]

Not surprisingly, Binney has had to explain his representation that all Candyman members received all e-mails. In an affidavit submitted in opposition to a motion to suppress in another Candyman case in July 2002, Binney gave the following explanation:

> First, I went to the Candyman Website and copied the E-mail address of the moderator, which was listed on the Web page. I then left the Website, went to my Web mail provider, and sent an E-mail to the Candyman moderator asking to join the group. During this entire process, I was never given any opportunity to select any mail delivery options. Nor was there any mention of such options during the joining phase.

[ ] Binney has testified several times in other Candyman cases and provided a similar explanation of subscribing via e-mail and not being presented with e-mail delivery options. [ ] He also included a similar explanation in the search warrant affidavit itself. [ ]

This is also essentially the explanation that the Government gave to defense counsel when it first gave notice of the error. [ ]

The search warrant contained only three paragraphs specifically about Perez. It reported that information obtained from Yahoo and AOL (an internet service provider) as well as from the Department of Motor Vehicles, the Postal Service, and other public records showed: (1) the e-mail address "navajablade@aol.com" belonged to an individual who joined the Candyman Egroup; (2) "navajablade@aol.com" was registered in the name of "Harvey Perez," and (3) "Harvey Perez" resided at one of the premises listed in the search warrant. [ ]

As the Government acknowledged at oral argument, there is nothing in the record to indicate that Perez did anything more with respect to the Candyman site than subscribe. [ ]

Here, as the Government concedes, the search warrant affidavit contained false information: it was not true, as the affidavit alleged, that all Candyman members automatically received all e-mails and therefore it was not true that all Candyman members automatically received the e-mails that contained child pornography. In fact, as the Government now concedes, Candyman members had three delivery options, including a no e-mail option. Hence, two principal issues are presented: (1) whether the false statements or omissions in the affidavit were made deliberately or with reckless disregard for the truth, and (2) if so and the false statements are set aside, whether the "corrected" affidavit would support a finding of probable cause. [ ]

The Fourth Amendment does not require that "every statement in a warrant affidavit . . . be true." [ ] That is, of course, because law enforcement officers often must rely on hearsay information, tips from informants, and information sometimes "garnered hastily." [ ] Rather, as the Supreme Court explained in Franks, the affidavit must be:

> "truthful" in the sense that the information put forth is believed or appropriately accepted by the affiant as true. It is established law, that a warrant affidavit must set forth particular facts and circumstances underlying the existence of probable cause, so as to allow the magistrate to make an independent evaluation of the matter.

. . .

Perez must prove by a preponderance of the evidence that (1) the drafters of the affidavit made the statement that all Candyman members automatically received all e-mails with knowledge that the statement was false, (2) they had a serious doubt as to the truth of the statement when they made it, or (3) they had obvious reason to doubt the veracity of the statement. As to the omitted information that Candyman members had e-mail delivery options, including the choice of receiving no e-mail, Perez must prove by a preponderance of the evidence that any reasonable person would have known that this was the kind of information that the magistrate judge would have wanted to know.

There simply is no support for the Government's initial position, where the source of the information is another government agent. The Government cannot insulate one agent's deliberate or reckless misstatement in an affidavit merely by relaying it through another agent personally ignorant of its falsity.

. . .

I conclude that the law enforcement agents acted recklessly in submitting an affidavit that contained the false information that all Candyman members automatically received all e-mails, including e-mails that forwarded images of child pornography, for the agents had serious doubt as to the truth of the statements or, at a minimum, they had obvious reasons to doubt their veracity. Moreover, I conclude that the agents also acted recklessly in omitting the information that Candyman members in fact had e-mail delivery options, including the option of receiving no e-mail at all.

[A] magistrate judge could not conclude, on the face of the "corrected" affidavit, that a fair probability existed that all subscribers to the site illegally downloaded or uploaded images of child pornography. The extrinsic facts confirm that was the case. As the Yahoo logs show, the vast majority of subscribers, including Perez, elected to receive no e-mails. The vast majority of the e-mails that Binney received did not have images of child pornography attached. Subscribers were not required to post or upload images, and the Yahoo logs show that Perez did not. Subscribers could have engaged in protected, non-criminal activities, such as answering survey questions or chatting. An individual could have joined simply by entering an e-mail address without paying a fee, explored the site without knowingly downloading any images, and left, without ever returning. This would not have been illegal conduct.

. . .

The context here is the Internet, specifically, the use of the Internet to trade child pornography. Law enforcement needs a certain amount of latitude to address those who would violate the child pornography laws and sexually exploit and abuse children. Just as there is no higher standard of probable cause when First Amendment values are implicated, however, there is no lower standard when the crimes are repugnant and the suspects frustratingly difficult to detect.

Here, the intrusion is potentially enormous: thousands of individuals would be subject to search, their homes invaded and their property seized, in one fell swoop, even though their only activity consisted of entering an e-mail address into a Website from a computer located in the confines of their own homes. [ ]

For the reasons set forth above, defendant's motion is granted and the fruits of the search are suppressed.

## 2.4) NEWSGROUPS, DISCUSSION BOARDS, AND BULLETIN BOARDS

Newsgroups are a distinct and "sovereign" feature of the Internet. The word "sovereign" is used here to describe newsgroups because Internet users must generally use a newsgroup reader (a.k.a. newsreader) to be able to use this service.[5] Although newsreaders and newsgroup access are free, many Internet users do not know that newsgroups exist and have never seen or used the feature. Other users "subscribe" to many newsgroups.

Newsgroups allow users to join conversations taking place among a number of subscribers from anywhere in the world who share a common interest. Newsgroups are similar to electronic bulletin board systems (BBS) in that they enable conversation, albeit asynchronous, to take place among a great number of participants. In fact, newsgroups are most like bulletin boards located in public places such as grocery stores where people may post and view written, paper messages. A key difference is the capacity of the newsgroup medium to enable the sharing of text, images, sound, and video files of virtually any size in an international forum. This capability makes newsgroups one of the largest sources of free pornography ever known to the human race.

The majority of newsgroups are collectively called Usenet, with hundreds of thousands of newsgroups covering just about every topic under the sun. By subscribing to a newsgroup, individuals can read postings of interest or can

---

[5] Sites such as Google Groups (http://groups.google.com/) provide a Web interface to newsgroups. Google Groups is also a useful resource for searching past newsgroups' messages.

participate in posting discussions. Newsgroup names usually reflect their focus. Some newsgroups are geared toward pedophiles and the exchange of child pornography—for example, the groups *alt.binaries.pictures.erotica.children* and *alt.binaries.pictures.erotica.pre-teen* (abpep-t). According to one researcher, "by late 2000, *abpep-t* boasted some forty thousand postings, mainly images of young girls ranging from toddlers through young adolescents" (Jenkins 2000). The names of the newsgroups change, but they usually suggest the content in the name for the group.

Usenet is composed of news servers (computers running special software) all over the world that communicate using the very simple Network News Transport Protocol (NNTP). When a user posts a message to one of these servers, it is not immediately seen by everyone; it is gradually disseminated to all of the other Usenet servers until readers around the world are able to read and respond to it. As with e-mail, a newsgroup user can attach computer files, including but not limited to graphic images. Newsgroups allow the message's reader to download the attached computer file or image. Unlike e-mail, each news server stores a separate copy of the message and messages can be retracted, but removing the message from every news server takes time.

Newsgroups are frequently used to post erotica and child pornography in both picture form and video clips. Libraries of images are often off-loaded by collectors onto some form of removable media, such as diskettes or CD-ROMs. Some distributors of child pornography obtain all of their pictures and videos by downloading the files from newsgroups. They create CD-ROMs, DVDs, or videotapes and distribute the material to their customers.

Newsgroup content is rarely regulated, but the Internet Service Provider (ISP) through which an individual accesses the newsgroup may exercise at least some censorship. An explicit child erotica newsgroup that might be readily accessed through one ISP may be blocked by another. Very frequently, newsgroups are plagued by spam (unsolicited commercial e-mail) and other irrelevant material. When the newsgroup topic is something as unsavory as sex with minors, many postings are by people opposed to the group (messages called "flames").

A discussion board is similar to a newsgroup in that the posting of messages is asynchronous and the discussion usually centers around a predetermined topic. The principal difference is where the data resides. Whereas newsgroups reside on servers around the world administered by different people, most discussion boards are maintained on a single server by the owner or operator of the board.

Bulletin board systems are similar to discussion boards and newsgroups. The principal difference is that a BBSs often hosted by the owner or operator, and the Internet is *not* the means of accessing the information. BBSs may be accessed directly via dial-up modem or otherwise. For this reason, because no ISPs or third-party services are utilized, BBSs have become very popular methods of sharing child pornography and other illicit material. Ironically, BBSs were around *before* the Internet was widely available and even before the personal computer. When child pornography first was trafficked using computer-assisted technology, BBSs were used. Now that the Internet has become less open and less accommodating to child pornographers, some of the activity has retreated to BBSs.

## 2.5) WEB SITES

The Web was made possible in 1989 by the invention of hypertext markup language (HTML). The creation of HTML enabled computers accessing the Internet to communicate with each other and to "see" the same information, even though they use different types of operating systems. Since 1989 the Web has proliferated, enabling unprecedented sharing of information worldwide. The Web has also enabled electronic commerce, arguably driving the continued increases in Internet usage.

A Web site is a set of files, called "Web pages," accessible via the Internet; these files contain text, sound, pictures, video, and any combination of the foregoing. Each Web site has an address—a Uniform Resource Locator, or URL. The Web site owner must reserve the address through a service that sells the addresses. Each Web page is composed of HTML "tags" or sets of instructions that tell the browser software how to display the Web page.

Many large-scale, multi-jurisdictional cases have had their beginnings when a law enforcement officer stumbled upon a Web site either by accident or by responding to an invitation in an unwanted e-mail message (spam). The Landslide case, which turned into the multi-national child pornography investigation "Avalanche," began when a police officer came across a Web site containing child pornography. The following is a description of the investigation from the United States Postal Service Inspection Service Web site:

**CASE EXAMPLE**

Operation Avalanche began in 1999, when Postal Inspectors discovered that a Ft. Worth, Texas, company, Landslide Productions, Inc., operated and owned by Thomas and Janice Reedy, was selling child pornography Web sites. Customers from around the world paid monthly subscription fees via a post office box address or the Internet to access the hundreds of Web sites, which contained extremely graphic child pornography material. Ft. Worth Postal Inspector Robert C. Adams and Dallas ICAC Task Force Detective

Steven A. Nelson teamed together to initiate what would become a child exploitation case of unprecedented magnitude.

During the investigation, while Landslide Productions was still in business, the National Center for Missing and Exploited Children's Cyber Tipline received more than 270 complaints from people around the world related to the Landslide case. All credible complaints were forwarded to investigators.

Postal Inspector Bob Adams obtained federal search warrants for the business and personal residence of the Reedy's. The warrants were executed by a task force of 45 officers and agents. They served seizure warrants on Landslide's bank accounts and two unencumbered Mercedes Benz vehicles valued at more than $150,000—and purchased with the Reedy's ill-gotten gains. Landslide was a highly successful financial enterprise, at one point taking in over $1.4 million in a single month.

After reviewing volumes of seized evidence and subpoenaed financial records, the Reedy's were indicted in federal district court on 89 counts of conspiracy to distribute child pornography and possession of child pornography. Following a one-week jury trial, the Reedy's and their company were convicted on all counts as charged. Thomas Reedy was given an unprecedented sentence of life in prison, and his wife Janice received a 14-year prison sentence. [ ]

Working out of the Dallas ICAC Task Force office, Postal Inspectors and other investigators initiated undercover contacts with the most egregious suspects. As cases were developed, the suspects were passed off to other Postal Inspectors and ICAC task forces throughout the United States for further investigation. Investigators obtained and served search warrants, seized huge volumes of child pornography images and materials, identified child molesters, and rescued victimized children from further sexual abuse. To date, over 160 search warrants have been served and more than 120 child sex offenders and pornographers have been arrested.

In one instance, Postal Inspectors and ICAC Task Force investigators searching the home of a 36-year-old computer consultant in North Carolina found videotapes he had produced depicting the sexual abuse of a number of young girls, one of whom was only four years old. The offender recorded the activities with a pinhole camera he had hidden in a bedroom smoke detector and which was connected to a VCR and a computer. On August 7, 2001, the man was sentenced to 17 and 1/2 years in federal prison on various charges of sexual exploitation. (USPS 2003)

Four years after the Landslide Web servers were taken down, leads taken from the customer lists are still being investigated.

## 2.6) CHAT ROOMS AND INSTANT MESSAGING

Chat rooms are often the scene of at least initial meetings and conversations between the victim and offender in enticement cases. Often, in enticement cases, a number of different Internet technologies are used, and it is important for all of the actors—the investigators, prosecutors, defense attorneys, fact finders, and forensic examiners—to be familiar with the features used in the particular case. Chat is real-time conversation between two or more users. The conversation takes place in a "chat room." Usually, all of the participants in the chat are listed so that their screen names, Internet access identification, or online nicknames can be seen by all other participants. Chat rooms often have a theme, or topic that conversation is supposed to center around. Some chat rooms are monitored, but most are not.

Chat appeals to middle school and older children because of the ability to communicate with many people in real time. Chat is most like a party-line, or "total-phone" telephone conversation, with the added value of allowing participants to simultaneously chat with a group, communicate privately via Instant Messaging, and to browse the Web and perform other tasks. Many people use chat to meet others on the Internet. Online victim Katie Tarbox describes her first online experience as a thirteen-year-old:

> It was unbelievable. The list of rooms covered every conceivable interest, and many I would have never imagined, including one called "sexual overdrive," whatever that meant. Many of the rooms were concerned with sex, but there were also teen chat rooms. These weren't divided into interest areas. Instead they were called simply TEEN1, TEEN2, etc. I thought that these would be the tamest areas and that I would stick to them. (Tarbox 2000)

Many different services provide chat facilities. America Online is the largest provider of chat, but other services such as MSN and Yahoo! also provide chat. Web sites also provide chat facilities. Internet Relay Chat (IRC) and ICQ also provide chat facilities. IRC is available free and may be used by anyone with an Internet connection. The limitation of AOL chat is that only AOL users can chat in AOL chat rooms. IRC can be downloaded and used free, making it much more available. Also, IRC does not monitor or censor content.

Anecdotal evidence suggests that AOL and other service provider chat is used to entice minors for sex, whereas IRC is more often used for illicit activity. This may have something to do with the member profile feature in AOL and ICQ. Offenders can look at AOL and ICQ profiles to find likely victims; this is not as feasible on IRC because there is not as much information in profiles.

Instant Messaging (IM) is almost exactly like chat. Communication takes place in real time and consists of individuals typing messages back and forth. The distinguishing feature of Instant Messaging is that it is one-to-one between the conversants and allows file transfer. The Internet is utilized to connect the conversants but in some implementations, the intermediate system drops out after the individuals are connected. Some implementations use an intermediate server to establish the client-to-client connection, and then the server is out of the loop. However, other IM implementations pass all traffic through an intermediate server.

Instant Messaging software maintains a list of people the user "instant messages." This list is often called a "Buddy List." Anyone on the Buddy List may send the user an Instant Message. If the sender is not on the Buddy List, a message will be sent to the receiver stating that the screen name is trying to send an Instant Message and asking whether the user would like to accept. Simply selecting the option not to receive the message may block Instant Messages.

Buddy Lists are important because being on someone's Buddy List allows access to the person. The name itself, "Buddy List," implies an immediate familiarity. If someone is on my Buddy List, that makes him or her my "Buddy," right? Many, many middle school and younger children have literally hundreds of people on their Buddy Lists. The way they acquire so many Buddies is by copying their lists and sending them to their friends. So, kids might have two hundred Buddies on their Buddy List and not know who those people are. It is quite simple for a preferential sex offender to obtain access to a vast number of potential victims by getting their screen names on one Buddy List. Once on a single list, the screen names will be shared with many other people. Being on the Buddy List will then enable communication via Instant Messaging—a private conversation between the preferential sex offender and the potential victim. Since the offender already holds the status of the potential victim's "Buddy," the rest of the way is much smoother.

Instant Messaging is often used in conjunction with chat room conversations to entice minors to engage in sexual activity. Preferential sex offenders use the technology to groom any number of potential victims over a period of time. Offenders have been known to groom as many as fifty or sixty potential victims at a time. Self reports by offenders indicated that they might carry on Instant Message and chat conversations with more than twenty potential victims at any given time.

## 2.7) WEB CAMERAS AND VIDEOPHONES

Many personal computers come with a Web camera bundled with the hardware and software package. A Web camera is a digital camera that takes pictures at set intervals or at the instruction of a user.

> Westchester County New York authorities arrested a middle school teacher who allegedly masturbated in front of a Web camera. He believed he was "performing" the act for a 14-year-old boy, but was in actuality a Westchester County detective. (Venezia 2003)

The preceding example provides just a glimpse of the tip of the iceberg. The ease of use of Web cam and video technology, plus its low cost and portability virtually assure that Web cams, video telephones, and digital cameras will be used during the course of child exploitation. The extent of use of these technologies is just beginning to be seen by law enforcement. It is still very early. Increased access to the technology will, without question, bring a steady and increasing number of cases.

## 2.8) FILE TRANSFER PROTOCOL (FTP)

File Transfer Protocol is used to download large files via the Internet. According to RFC 959, the objectives of FTP are

1) to promote sharing of files (computer programs and/or data)
2) to encourage indirect or implicit (via programs) use of remote computers
3) to shield a user from variations in file storage systems among hosts
4) to transfer data reliably and efficiently

"FTP, though usable directly by a user at a terminal, is designed mainly for use by programs" (Postel and Reynolds 1985). FTP facilitates file transfer between computers. Using FTP, child pornography traffickers have been known to download or trade hundreds of thousands of images at a time. In one case, a college student used FTP on a computer at the university library. By the time law enforcement was alerted, the student had downloaded millions of images. The student's activities would have gone on undetected if he had not devoted hours each day to downloading files.

## 2.9) PEER-TO-PEER (P2P)

Peer-to-peer (P2P) applications were developed only recently. Although most people who use the Internet are at least somewhat familiar with e-mail and the Web, the average Internet user may not have ever heard of or had occasion to use P2P software. P2P is used to share files. While P2P is often used legitimately to share music, video, and other types of files and software, P2P is also increasingly used to traffic in child pornography. Napster was a P2P application. Now that Napster is gone, other programs and services have stepped in to replace it. Whereas the principle is basically the same in that the service allows users to swap files and to search for files among all of the users' materials, the technology and rules governing service use differ from one service to another. Some of the more popular implementations of P2P technology are KaZaA, Morpheus, Gnutella, FreeNet, WinMX, and iMesh.

KaZaA allows users to search for and download audio, video, image, and text files using either the KaZaA Media Desktop P2P client, the Winamp plug-in, or the KaZaA.com Web site. KaZaA can automatically transform more powerful clients into "SuperNodes" able to handle search requests from nearby users. In this way, the KaZaA network organizes itself into clusters of nearby users to make searching and downloading more efficient. If a file cannot be found on a nearby machine, KaZaA extends the search further across the network.

Morpheus is a distributed file-sharing network based on KaZaA. Morpheus uses a centralized user registration and logon system. It does not maintain a central content index or filter content.

Gnutella is a decentralized network that allows users to search for files. Users may opt to share no files, one file, a directory, or their entire hard drives. Searching is decentralized because the files are stored on the users' hard drives, not on a centralized server, and when a search is executed, it searches users' hard drives.

In March 2003 the United States General Accounting Office offered testimony to Congress detailing the prevalence of child pornography trafficking using P2P applications:

---

**What GAO Found**

Child pornography is easily found and downloaded from peer-to-peer networks. In one search using 12 keywords known to be associated with child pornography on the Internet, GAO identified 1,286 titles and file names, determining that 543 (about 42 percent) were associated with child pornography images. Of the remaining, 34 percent were classified as adult pornography and 24 percent as non-pornographic. In another search using three keywords, a Customs analyst downloaded 341 images, of which 149 (about 44 percent) contained child pornography. [ ] These results are consistent with increased reports of child pornography on peer-to-peer networks; since it began tracking these in 2001, the National Center for Missing and Exploited Children has seen a fourfold increase—from 156 in 2001 to 757 in 2002. Although the numbers are as yet small by comparison to those for other sources (26,759 reports of child pornography on Web sites in 2002), the increase is significant. (US GAO 2003)

## 2.10) CONCLUSION

This chapter reviewed Internet features used to exploit children. Each section began with a review of the Internet feature and described how the feature has been or could be used to exploit children. Examples of instances in which offenders used the Internet to exploit or harm children were provided. The technologies addressed were e-mail, e-groups, and mailing lists; newsgroups and bulletin board systems; Web sites; chat rooms, and Instant Messaging; and File Transfer Protocol and peer-to-peer. This overview of Internet technology provides a foundation for understanding other features as they develop. There is no question that as new features emerge, criminals will exploit them to facilitate criminal activities.

## RESOURCES

"Child Porn: Twelve Men Arrested," Skynews U.K. (2002). http://www.sky.com/skynews/article/0,,30100-1062429,00.html.

Jenkins, P. *Beyond Tolerance—Child Pornography on the Internet.* New York: New York University Press, 2000.

Nurenberg, G. "Cracking Down on Online Predators." (August 22, 2002) http://www.techtv.com/news/print/0,23102,3397013,00.html.

Postel, J., and J. Reynolds. "File Transfer Protocol (FTP)." RFC 959, Network Solutions Group, (1985). http://www.w3.org/Protocols/rfc959/.

Tarbox, K., *Katie.com.* New York: Dutton Books, 2000.

United States Postal Service. "Operation Avalanche." (2003) http://www.usps.com/postalinspectors/avalanch.htm.

United States General Accounting Office. "File Sharing Programs: Users of Peer-to-Peer Networks Can Readily Access Child Pornography." Washington, DC: GAO (September 9, 2002).

Venezia, T. "Teacher Did Live Sex Acts on Internet: DA." *New York Post* (May 28, 2003): 027.

Internet FAQs Archive. (2003). www.faqs.org.

# CHAPTER 3

# CYBER VICTIMS

## Michael McGrath, MD

*By their very nature, children make perfect victims. Authorities recognize children's vulnerability and they point to widely recognized factors that make children ideal targets of abusive behavior. (APRI 2003)*

As the Internet becomes easier to access and hardware becomes more afford-able, more children will use it. Increasingly, teachers assign children as early as fourth grade to use the Internet to complete assignments. In the United States, nearly every child has access to the Internet at home, at school, at friends' homes, at the local library, at an Internet café, or at all of those places. Security and supervision of children's Internet use vary widely. For instance, Internet access at an elementary or middle school is usually filtered and closely supervised. On the other hand, many public libraries use no filtering and do not supervise Internet use. Many parents are completely naïve regarding the potential dangers to their children posed by the Internet. Parents often have a completely different Internet experience than their children. Parents use the Internet mostly for e-mail, shopping, and research. Children use the Internet to communicate with people using Instant Messaging, chat, and e-mail; participate in interactive games; download music; do their homework; and perform all sorts of other activities. Today children live a large share of their lives in the virtual world. Unfortunately, the increased exposure to inappropriate content and contact with people often leads to children being victimized.

According to a survey conducted through New Hampshire University (Finkelhor, Mitchell, and Wolack 2000), between August 1999 and February 2000, of 1,501 youths aged 10 to 17 who regularly use the Internet in the year prior to the survey:

- About one in five received some form of sexual solicitation over the Internet:
- One in thirty-three received an aggressive sexual solicitation (request to meet, talk by phone, etc.).

- One in four was exposed to unwanted pictures of nudity or sexual activity.
- One in seventeen felt threatened or harassed (not related to sexual content).
- Girls were targeted at about twice the rate boys were targeted.
- Seventy-seven percent of targeted youth were over fourteen years old.
- Although 22 percent of targeted youth were ages ten to thirteen, this group was disproportionately distressed by the incident.
- Adults (most between the ages of eighteen and twenty-five) accounted for 24 percent of the sexual solicitations.
- Juveniles made 48 percent of the solicitations and 48 percent of the aggressive solicitations.
- Age was unknown for 27 percent of solicitors.
- Slightly more than two thirds of solicitations and online approaches came from males.
- One quarter of aggressive approaches were by females.

While not all the youth who received some sort of sexual solicitation online were bothered by the interaction, some (one in four of those solicited) were "very or extremely upset or afraid" (Finkelhor, Mitchell, and Wolack 2000). The researchers found that few distressing online interactions are reported to parents, let alone police. To make matters more frustrating, even if parents report online harassment of their children, most police departments are ill equipped to follow up on such complaints and may view complaining parents as a nuisance. Issues of jurisdiction and arrest aside, most police departments lack the sophisticated computer skills required to retrieve digital evidence that will pass muster in court. Additionally, parents may balk at turning over their computer to police, either due to the inconvenience involved (including loss of the computer for a period of time) or possibly due to a fear that police may find something illegal on the hard drive and charge a member of the household with a crime. It is common knowledge that online child pornography arrests have stemmed from a computer being brought into a shop for repairs.

Using the same data collected in the New Hampshire study, researchers explored common characteristics of children they considered at risk for online sexual solicitation (Mitchell, Finkelhor, and Wolak 2001). Researchers found that girls, older teens, troubled youth, frequent Internet users, chat room participants, and children who communicate online with strangers were more likely than other children to be solicited online for sex.

A Florida man who owned and operated residential facilities for youths aged eleven to eighteen was arrested after he brought his computer in for repairs and child pornography was found on the hard drive (Burke 2002). A well-known rock performer, Gary Glitter, was convicted in Britain of possessing child pornography after a repair shop discovered it on his hard drive (Sprenger 1999). South Dakota (along with several other states) has passed a law requiring computer-repair shops to report any child pornography to authorities (Kafka 2002). Even without a law in place, many law-abiding individuals are fearful about having contact with anything resembling child pornography and will report such findings quickly to law enforcement. Unfortunately, such community vigilantism can be overdone. There may be developing a societal zero tolerance for pictures of children that in a different era would never have even raised an eyebrow. While there is an expectation that illegal photos of children will be reported to police, there is no guidance to the photo lab as to where to draw the line, if at all. Various fairly innocuous photos have at times resulted in police action (Kincaid 2000).

The online victim of the child molester is not really any different from the real-world victim, other than the fact that the victim is old enough to know how to use a computer and sufficiently literate to interact online. Such children generally tend to have low self-esteem, lack of (online) supervision, dysfunctional families, etc. While all of these traits may be common to the online victim, they are not required. An A-student with excellent self-esteem and a wonderful home life is not exempt from victimization by an online sexual predator. For example, a thirteen-year-old Minnesota eighth grader met a man she believed was eighteen through an AOL chat room before Christmas. They talked by phone prior to New Year's Eve, and she agreed to meet him near her home. She met a forty-year-old man who took her to a motel and gave her video games to play and wine coolers to drink. The man then allegedly raped the girl when she resisted his advances (WCCO 2003), A fifteen-year-old girl was found with a forty-three-year-old psychology professor in a New York State park, allegedly engaged in sexual intercourse in a car. The professor and the victim met online (Associated Press, 2003).

As noted earlier, the victim of an online sexual predator may have cooperated with the offender in one manner or another and may not cooperate with law enforcement. The victim may feel a sense of loyalty to the offender, may have participated in crimes (i.e., downloaded or traded child pornography), or may be simply generally rebellious and not fazed by the fact that s/he has been exploited. It may be difficult for investigators and prosecutors to relate to such a victim. Often, such a victim makes for a less than optimal witness. It is important for law enforcement personnel to refrain from being judgmental and accept the fact that gaining the cooperation of the victim may take a considerable amount of time. Judgmental treatment, disdain, and lack of interest by law enforcement toward such victims only reinforce their poor self-image and further victimize them for acts they engaged in but were poorly prepared for emotionally and were unable to give true informed consent. In an investigation of ten children identified through seized child pornography, for example, none of the ten reported the abuse they had endured to anyone without prompting (Barnen 1996).

The victims of the online sexual predator described above may differ somewhat from the victims of child pornography, whose pictures are distributed over the Internet. The victims described above are likely still living in the home, although that is no guarantee of safety. Child pornography victims are of various types: children and adolescents exploited by their guardians; victims offered alcohol and/or drugs and either videotaped without their knowledge committing sexual acts or performing under various kinds of ruses or threats; runaways seeking shelter or friendship with adolescents. The moral bankruptcy of those willing to exploit others knows no bounds. There are even clubs composed of parents who swap child pornography involving their own children with other like-minded individuals and child pornography distributors (Holmes and Holmes 2002). It has been reported that live child-sex shows have even been sent over the Internet with viewers forwarding instructions to the adult participants as to what they would like to happen (Shannon 1998).

Those who consume child pornography often need to portray it as a victimless crime. But this is clearly not so on several levels. On one level there is simply the issue of being used by those who have a fiduciary relationship toward a child they are raising. Just as a parent should not overtly sell his or her child for sex, the parent should not photograph that child for the sexual benefit of others. By posting even "innocent" photos or making them available to others in any manner, knowing that the ultimate goal is sexual arousal, the parent or guardian has essentially irreparably demonstrated a complete lack of understanding of his or her role. On another level, having children "consensually" engage in sexual relations with other children or with adults places them in a position they are not psychologically (and often physically) prepared for and will cause significant harm to their psychosexual development, as well as their future relationships with others in general. Perhaps worst of all are those situations in which children are forced into sexual activity with others.

A common tactic of pedophiles and child sex traffickers is to show pornography (including child pornography) to children as a way of lowering their inhibitions, getting them sexually aroused, and making it seem that this type of activity is acceptable (Calcetas-Santos 2001). As part of the Blue Orchid pornography ring, videos were produced and distributed involving sadistic behavior with young boys. In March 2001, as an offshoot of the Markean case (Graff 2001), Victor Razumov, a.k.a. "The Punisher," was arrested in connection with abuse of a fifteen-year-old boy during the making of two videos depicting forced sex and sadomasochistic behaviors. The boy is clearly suffering in the video. These videos were part of a series distributed by the Blue Orchid Club. The victims in these tapes were mostly young boys from homeless or dysfunctional families (U.S. Customs 2001).

Orchid Club members gained a perverse infamy when it was discovered that several members, located in several different countries, participated in the real-time sexual abuse of a ten-year-old child by one of the members as he transmitted images over the Internet. Other members communicated suggestions as to further abuse (O'Grady 1998).

There is a culture of pedophiles who prey on Third World children, assuming that either the host government, the family, or both will not care. Asia, Central America, and South America are especially targeted. Victims tend to be poor, uneducated, and easily swayed by money or other gifts. Cases like the one of Marvin Hersh (discussed in greater detail in the next chapter), a Florida professor, happen more often than we would like to believe. Hersh traveled to Asia and Central America to have sex with minors, giving them and their families money, clothes, etc. He targeted his victims by picking out poor children whose parents were uneducated, and convinced them that he was helping the children.[1]

There are no reliable numbers on children involved in commercial sexual exploitation. Official government figures are not reliable because they are too low, and numbers reported by advocacy groups are probably too high (Barnitz 1998).

## 3.1)  VICTIMOLOGY

Victims of online sex offenders do not differ significantly from victims in the physical world. Investigators should be able to apply traditional methods of gaining victim information. **Victimology** in general is the study of the victim from various perspectives, be they statistical, sociological, etc. For the purposes of profiling, victimology refers to the collection of information on a specific victim or series of victims for the specific purpose of furthering an investigation. "Victimology is first and foremost an investigative tool, providing context, connections, and investigative direction" (Turvey 2002). While we are sometimes impressed with the connection that investigators make with victims and victims' families in high-profile cases, it is surprising how, in general, investigators actually know little of value about the victims of the crimes they are attempting to solve.

## 3.2)  HOW TO PROTECT CHILDREN ONLINE

It is not possible to ensure our children are safe from everyone at all times. But it is possible to take reasonable steps to protect our children while online. When

---

[1]  *U.S. v. Hersh*, No. 0014592OPN—07/17/02 (11th Circuit, 2001) http://laws.lp.findlaw.com/11th/0014592opn.html.

we rely solely on educating children about Internet safety, we inadvertently place the responsibility for protecting our children on our children. Protecting children is the responsibility of their parents, the community, and government. Prevention efforts should incorporate components that educate parents, children, police officers, teachers, and health-care professionals.

Organizations such as the National Center for Missing and Exploited Children, PedoWatch, the Child Protection and Advocacy Coalition, getnetwise, and isafe offer information on how to protect children online and where to report trafficking in child pornography. Commercial software can monitor online behaviors, including e-mail, chat room conversations, instant messages, passwords, and Web site visits. Some software can even record keystrokes. Most monitoring software allows the installer to guard access to it with a password, and monitoring takes place unbeknownst to the user. The installer usually has the option of directing the monitoring software to send a report via e-mail that details all computer activity. Some monitoring software allows the installer to monitor the computer user's activity in real time from a remote location. Other software is engineered to allow the installer to conduct a forensic examination of the user's computer system from a remote location.

A frequently invoked misnomer in the online safety field is the concept of a "stranger." It is quite difficult to educate young children about the dangers of strangers when talking about the Internet. A stranger is someone a child does not know. Stranger-hood is easily overcome by child molesters. Even something as simple as using the child's name (perhaps overheard moments before) or asking for help in finding a lost puppy has been enough to overcome intensive "stranger danger" instruction by parents. Adolescents, on the other hand, have already had much experience dealing with adults they do not know. Prevention education efforts are well advised to encourage children and adolescents to feel comfortable in going to their parents or a trusted adult when in need of guidance. Teaching a child to "check with mom, dad, or a trusted adult" before going off with anyone is more helpful than saying, "don't ever talk to strangers." After all, if abducted, a child may be best served by turning to a stranger for help.

**Red flags include**

- Your child receives mail or gifts from people you do not know or have never heard of;
- Your child receives telephone calls from adults or older adolescents you do not know;
- Your child spends significant time online;
- Your child quickly turns off the monitor or switches to other screen content when you enter the room;

- Your child receives unexplained or suspicious gifts, especially digital cameras, cellular phones, phone cards, scanners, computers, or money;
- Your child becomes aggressive, runs away from home, or starts committing criminal acts;
- Your child's grooming habits or hygiene habits change. Changes in dress that hide the child's body or make her appear unattractive should be noted. (APRI 2003)

**Parents should**

- Have rules governing appropriate Internet use and behavior;
- Educate their children about not giving out personal information over the Internet;
- Supervise any picture swapping online;
- Establish a rapport with their children, encouraging them to report any distressing online interaction. If parents cannot or will not talk with their children about online activity, they should designate a trusted adult for the child to talk to;
- Address meeting people met via the Internet with their children. Parents must set forth rules governing how children may meet online friends that take into consideration the level of judgment of each child, his or her age, and how likely the rule will be adhered to.

## 3.3) CONCLUSION

It is good to keep in mind that child abduction in general and Internet child molester abductions are actually rare phenomena. A child molester may be just as likely to meet an FBI agent at the planned rendezvous as a thirteen-year-old girl. While the problem of online predation is real, parents should not be in constant dread that their children will be attacked through the computer. They need to be aware of their children's online habits and who their friends are. It probably makes the most sense to educate children to the fact that some people in the world are willing to exploit them and, that when troubled by an interaction online (or in the real world), they should not be embarrassed to discuss the situation with a parent or other responsible adult.

## REFERENCES

American Prosecutors Research Institute. *Investigation and Prosecution of Child Abuse*. Thousand Oaks, CA: Sage, 2003.

Associated Press. "Prof Accused of Sex with Teen." *Democrat & Chronicle.* January 26, 2003: 7B.

Barnen, R. *Children Who Don't Speak Out.* Sweden: Falun, ScandBook, 1996.

Barnitz, L. A. *Commercial Exploitation of Children: Youth Involved in Prostitution, Pornography & Sex Trafficking.* Washington, DC: Youth Advocate Program International, 1998.

Burke, L. "New Kid Porn Bust in Florida." *Wired News.* (August 17, 2002). http://www.wired.com/news/politics/0,1283,38291,00.html.

Calcetas-Santos, O. "Child Abuse on the Internet: Ending the Silence," in *Child Pornography on the Internet.* C. A. Arnaldo, ed., 57–60. New York: UNESCO Publishing/Berghahn Books, 2001.

Finkelhor, D., K. J. Mitchell, and J. Wolak. "Online Victimization: A Report on the Nation's Youth. National Center for Missing and Exploited Children." (2002). http://www.missingkids.com/download/InternetSurvey.pdf.

Graff, P. "U.S., Russia Unite to Fight Child Sex." *Moscow Times.* (February 12, 2001). http://www.themoscowtimes.com/stories/2001/03/27/003.html.

Holmes, S. T., and R. M. Holmes. *Sex Crimes: Patterns and Behavior,* 2nd ed., Thousand Oaks, CA: Sage Publications, 2002.

Kafka, J. "Crackdown on Child Porn Sees Results." *Associated Press in Midwest News.* (June 15, 2002). http://www.yankton.net/stories/061502/new_20020615020.shtml.

Kavanaugh, J. "Arrest Underlines Perils of Internet: Woman Reportedly Had Sex with Minor She Met Online." *Palo Alto Weekly.* (February 23, 2000). http://www.paweekly.com/PAW/morgue/news/2000_Feb_23.ARREST00.html.

Kincaid, J. R. "Is This Child Pornography? American Photo Labs Are Arresting Parents as Child Pornographers for Taking Pictures of Their Kids in the Bath." Salon.com. (January 31, 2000). http://dir.salon.com/mwt/feature/2000/01/31/kincaid/index.html.

McLaughlin, S. "Indictment in Teen-Sex Case: Woman Was Tutor, School Helper." *The Cincinnati Enquirer.* (November 15, 2000). http://enquirer.com/editions/2000/11/15/loc_indictment_in.html.

McLaughlin, S. "Mother Pleads Guilty to Teen Sex: Faces up to 33 Years in Prison." *The Cincinnati Enquirer.* (April 28, 2001). http://enquirer.com/editions/2001/04/28/loc_mother_pleads_guilty.html.

Mitchell, K. J., D. Finkelhor, and J. Wolak. "Risk Factors For and Impact of Online Sexual Solicitation of Youth." *JAMA* 285, no. 23 (June 20, 2001).

O'Grady, R. Opening address at the Child Pornography on the Internet Experts meeting, Lyon, France, 1998, cited in *Child Abuse on the Internet,* C. A. Arnaldo, ed., 56. New York: UNESCO Publishing/Berghahn Books, 2001.

Shannon, E. "Main Street Monsters: A Worldwide Crackdown Reveals That Child Pornographers Might Just Be the People Next Door." *Time Magazine.* (September 14, 1998).

Sprenger, M. "Glitter Convicted in Online Porn Case." *The Industry Standard.* (November 15, 1999). http://www.thestandard.com/article/0,1902,7689, 00.html.

Turvey, B. "Victimology," in *Criminal Profiling: An Introduction to Behavioral Evidence Analysis,* 2$^{nd}$ Ed. B. Turvey, ed., 137–155. London: Academic Press, 2002.

U.S. Customs Service. "U.S. Customs Service, Russian Police Take Down Global Child Pornography Web Site: 4 Arrests, 15 Search Warrants Thus Far in U.S.; 5 Arrests in Russia." press release. (March 26, 2001). http://usinfo.state.gov/topical/global/ecom/01032602.htm.

WCCO. "13-Year-Old Rape Victim Met Attacker Online." (January 9, 2003). http://www.wcco.com/topstories/local_story_009180608.html.

Wilber, D. Q. "Woman Accused of Having Sex with Boy; Laurel Encounter Began on Internet, Police Say." *Baltimore Sun.* (December 30, 1998): 3B.

## INTERNET RESOURCES

Child Protection Advocacy Coalition (www.thecpac.com).

getnetwise (www.getnetwise.com).

isafe (www.isafe.org).

National Center for Missing and Exploited Children (www.missingkids.org).

Pedo Watch (www.pedowatch.org).

# CHAPTER 4

# CYBER OFFENDERS

## Michael McGrath, MD

*The overriding commonality among child molesters is access to children through career choices, living arrangements, offers to "help" single parents, and volunteer work. (APRI 2003)*

General knowledge of sex offenders and their victims, possessing information specific to an offender, can only further investigative goals of investigators and prosecutors. For example, knowing that the offender lives in a certain geographic area, uses certain idiosyncratic phrases, and probably works in the Information Technology industry can significantly narrow the suspect pool. Similarly, knowing that the offender uses Internet Relay Chat (IRC) to acquire and groom victims, as well as communicate with other offenders, can facilitate evidence gathering on the Internet or on a suspect's computer. Evidence, physical or otherwise, may at times be underutilized due to the investigator's missing its relationship or context to an offender, a series of crimes, or both. Employing a psychological or psychodynamic approach in reviewing various aspects of a crime (evidence, victimology, etc.) can be helpful. Since all behaviors are multi-determined,[1] useful information can sometimes be inferred.

Aside from specific offender information, generalized offender data can be helpful. Knowing that some sex offenders (especially sadists) retain various types of evidence (photos, jewelry, maps, descriptions, etc.) of their crimes can be useful when applying for search warrants. Investigators should be aware that offenders may hide evidence in places easily overlooked. As an example, the notorious Canadian husband and wife team Paul Bernardo and Karla Homolka sexually assaulted and killed several young girls and videotaped the sexual acts they forced the victims to engage in, both when conscious and unconscious. These tapes were missed by the police who searched the couple's home from

---

[1] An act usually has more than one underlying (psychological) cause and, hence, more than one meaning. For example, choosing a career or a spouse is the result of many conscious and unconscious motives for such a decision, as opposed to one. This is true of both simple and complex behaviors.

top to bottom over a three-month period—even though they were specifically looking for the tapes. "The hiding place, Bernardo himself would later say in court, was behind a pot light inside the drop ceiling in the second-floor bathroom. The light had to be pulled down from the ceiling to get at the tapes hidden in the rafters . . . an arm's length up into the rafters, tucking them behind the insulation" (Pron 1995).

Awareness that sex offenders generally target multiple victims may direct investigators to review similar crimes and interview similar victims. Knowing the mindset of an offender may dictate the interviewing approach. It is known that some sex offenders will readily admit to their crimes when treated kindly and offered face-saving explanations of why the sexual exploitation occurred. Other offenders will treat such an approach with contempt. Many sex offenders have an ingrained, strong denial that what they do is not a crime. They feel justified lying to law enforcement.

This chapter presents two approaches to obtaining information about offenders. One approach, often referred to as "inductive profiling," is to review past investigations and offenders to ascertain trends or similarities between offenders. This method suffers from limited reliability and utility. It allows for generation of statistical or "average" profiles that often lack usefulness in a specific investigation. By relying on such profiles, investigators can easily overlook important details and waste resources pursuing false leads. An excellent example of this type of profile derailing an investigation is the 2002 Maryland Sniper investigation, in which police stopped white vans looking for white males. When the offenders were apprehended, they turned out to be black and, in fact, had had contact with police several times during the period of the shootings but were ignored (Boon 2002). Another well-known case in which this type of profile led to the targeting of an innocent man was the Richard Jewel debacle (Edwards 1998). After an explosion in Centennial Park in Atlanta at the 1996 Summer Olympic Games, an inductive profile led authorities to focus investigative efforts on a security guard who actually was later exonerated (LoMonte 1996).

The second approach, known as "deductive profiling," is to infer characteristics of an offender from evidence available in a specific crime or series of connected crimes under investigation. While this approach suffers from offering less information than a statistical profile, the information it does offer may prove to be more reliable. Different offenders do the same things for different reasons and do different things for the same reasons. Additionally, all behavior is multi-determined, making simplistic lists of characteristics drawn from generalized behavior patterns risky. Also, an individual offender can change over time, learning and honing his or her approach to victims and methods of concealing his or her crimes. The astute investigator may learn much from the *modus operandi* and signature behaviors of an offender online. Ultimately, the investigator needs to study the available online and real-world evidence (behavior, language) of an offender to draw relevant inferences about him or her.

This chapter discusses general aspects of offenders and victims and outlines ways to recognize behavioral patterns. It also suggests approaches to profiling a specific offender. Not to be ignored is the option of discussing a case with a forensic psychiatrist or psychologist who has knowledge of the Internet and the behavior of sexual predators online. Such an individual can provide investigative insight (and direction) to narrow the suspect pool, and expert guidance after arrest regarding searches for further evidence and victims and possibly questioning strategies.[2] There is also the consideration of use of the behavioral science expert in the trial phase to provide insight into the motives and behaviors of sex offenders.

## 4.1) THE ONLINE SEXUAL PREDATOR

Child molestation is not a new phenomenon to any society, although awareness of this behavior is higher than in the past. There have always been humans attracted to the opposite sex, the same sex, and to partners younger than themselves and partners significantly younger than themselves. Depending on societal mores, some things that would be considered a crime in Western cultures may not have risen to the same level of concern in the past or in other societies.

In 1996 the Russian parliament voted to lower the age of consent, making it legal for adults to have sexual relations with adolescents from age fourteen and up. Russia may currently be the world's leading exporter of photographs and videos of children engaged in sexual activity. While there was a law against producing pornography for sale or selling it, there was no distinction made between adult and child pornography, and it was considered a victimless offense (Graff 2001). This scenario invited attention from pedophiles who could travel to Russia, have sex with boys as young as fourteen, and not break the law. For example, a forty-four-year-old Indiana man, Glenn Markean, was on a mailing list belonging to Vsevolod Solntsev-Elbe, a notorious Russian child pornographer and operator of the Blue Orchid Web site. The American arrived in Moscow in January 2001 and was tailed by the Moscow police, alerted by e-mails

---

[2] This (assisting interrogations) raises some ethical issues for clinicians because there will be questions as to whether a psychiatrist or psychologist should become involved in a criminal case prior to the accused being provided legal counsel, among other issues.

they found on Solntsev-Elbe's computer. A policeman posed as a pimp and procured Markean a young boy. When Markean asked the boy to undress, he was arrested. Unfortunately, the boy was not young enough. As it turned out, he was fourteen; therefore, the American had not committed a (Russian) crime and was released. The Russian police passed on Markean's name to U.S. Customs, and while he was still in Moscow, U.S. agents searched his Indiana home, finding child pornography. Markean was befriended by an undercover U.S. agent who accompanied him home from Russia and arrested him on the way to his home after admitting to having had sex with about thirty children in the past (Graff 2001). Markean was indicted on charges related to illegal importation of child pornography (from Blue Orchid) and interstate and foreign travel to engage in sexual activity with a minor (U.S. Customs 2001). In June 2002, the Russian Duma voted to raise the age of sexual consent to sixteen, outlaw child pornography, and institute penalties for those who lure children into the sex trade (Graff 2002).

In the year 2005 in the United States, a forty-year-old man having sex with a thirteen-year-old girl would be considered grossly inappropriate, even if the behavior was viewed as "consensual" by the involved parties. Such activity would likely ruin the man's career if he were a professional and result in his arrest. In the year 1066, such a situation might have been the result of an arranged marriage in Europe, and it might not even be an issue in some parts of the world today. The difference is that we, as a society, have decided that people under a certain age (which may vary by state) are unable to give consent to engage in sexual relations with an adult. There is also usually an age differential (generally two to five years when one partner is a minor) that will criminalize sexual activity between a minor and an adult, regardless of the claimed emotional maturity of the younger participant. Heightened awareness in the 1970s and 1980s of sexual assaults against children may have had the unintended effect of leading to false reporting, both intentional and unintentional. Several modern-day witch hunts, related to almost fantastic allegations of sexual abuse against day-care workers and others, have tempered to some degree the belief that child molesters are hiding behind every tree.

Coinciding with the emergence of child molestation concerns has been the explosion of Internet use. Any technology will eventually be utilized by the criminally inclined, and sexual predators' use of the Internet to find and exploit victims was to be expected. This venue offers an (albeit limited) aura of anonymity and a plethora of potential victims. No longer does a predator have to troll for victims in his or her car. The predator can now accomplish this act from his or her home or workplace, or for that matter any site offering access to a computer. Along with the availability of communication with the victims, the Internet allows the predator to literally come into the homes of the victims.

It is quite possible for an offender to be online with a victim while the parents or guardian are at home, even in the same room.

Aside from victim access, the Internet offers the sexual predator something else that had been hard to come by in the past: broad validation of his or her deviant fantasies and/or behaviors by peers. There are Web sites and chat rooms devoted to any and all sexual behaviors. The Internet (and the computer technology accompanying it) offers the pedophile access to child pornography and the ability to trade this commodity with others. Aside from simplifying the trading of child pornography, the current technology might be seen as creating a market for more. Digital cameras and camcorders easily capture images of children that do not have to be sent to a photo lab. These digital images are readily transferred to a computer hard drive and are then available for worldwide distribution. Current technology now even allows for live transmission of sexual abuse. The computer and its associated storage devices (internal and removable) allow for compilation of vast collections of child pornography in small spaces. And, once a victim is located, the Internet can be a treasure trove of information about that individual and/or family. Aside from collecting information, ongoing monitoring can occur through various means, including sending innocuous animations as attachments that attempt to take over the computer (McGrath and Casey 2002).

Child molesters who use the Internet to groom and entice victims are obviously interested in children old enough to operate computers. This does not rule out attraction to even younger children, as an Internet-trolling pedophile could be forced by external restrictions (limitations on movement through an electronic ankle bracelet as a condition of probation or parole, for example) to utilize cyberspace. Grooming victims in chat rooms may force the offenders to interact with children older than a preferred age, but they may still be young enough to be attractive to the offenders. By donning various personas, child molesters troll cyberspace looking for the same things they look for in child victims in general: loneliness, low self-esteem, unhappy family situations, etc. The Internet allows for an almost instant sense of intimacy between people who have never met. The notion may seem surprising to some, but some people will quickly tell a stranger very intimate thoughts. The fact that they are not physically near the person and cannot see him or her lowers inhibitions. Over time children or adolescents can come to believe that the person they have been communicating with actually cares about them. This can occur with or without the knowledge of the demographics of the online pal. The relationship that develops between offender and victim can interfere with an investigation, as the victim may inform the offender of an investigation. Doing so must not be equated with complicity in the context of a criminal act. The victims are no less victims because they have been enticed into a relationship with the offender.

While it is non–Internet-related, the kidnapping of Elizabeth Smart is an excellent example of this phenomenon. After going missing (and presumed by many to be dead) for nine months, the (now) fifteen-year-old was spotted with her abductors in Utah, not far from her home. Police were notified and confronted the group. Elizabeth initially denied who she was to a police officer when it was clear the police were there to help her (Meserve and Rogers 2003). Her early unwillingness to cooperate with the police in her own rescue was a function of the psychological hold the offender had over her, not a sign of cooperation in her own victimization.

## 4.2) THE CHILD MOLESTER

Before honing in on Cyber Child Molesters, we need to look at child molesters in general. It is important to know what a pedophile is because a person can commit a sexual act against a child and yet not be a pedophile. In general, a pedophile can be described as an adult (although adolescents can be diagnosed) who is preferentially sexually attracted to children. More formally, the *Diagnostic and Statistical Manual of Mental Disorders, Fourth Edition* (APA 1994) defines pedophilia as sexual activity with a prepubescent child (a child thirteen or younger). The pedophile must be at least sixteen years old and at least five years older than the victim, although the DSM-IV avoids the use of the term "victim" (or "offender," for that matter). For adolescent pedophiles, no specific age difference (between offender and victim) is given. Technical knowledge of pedophiles may not directly solve cases, but it is important for investigators to have a sense of the terrain in which they are operating.

Per the DSM-IV (APA 1994), diagnostic criteria include (1) recurrent and intense sexually arousing fantasies, urges, or behaviors related to sexual acts with a prepubescent child or children; (2) the fantasies, urges, or behavior lead to clinically significant distress (for example, anxiety or depression), or impairment in social, work, or other important facets of function; (3) the person is sixteen years old or older and at least five years older than the child or children. The DSM-IV provides a disclaimer to avoid labeling as a pedophile someone in late adolescence who has an ongoing sexual relationship with a twelve- or thirteen-year-old child. There are specifiers to identify pedophiles who are preferentially attracted to males, to females, or to both, as well as specifiers indicating when the pedophilia is limited to incest, and also if the pedophilia is exclusive (i.e., sexually attracted to children only) or nonexclusive. Note that if an offender has not suffered any internal or external problems due to his or her sexual interest in children, technically that offender would not be diagnosed as a pedophile by strict DSM-IV standards. This appears to make little sense. This oversight was quietly addressed in the DSM-IV-

TR[3] (APA 2000), where criterion 2 was changed to "The person has acted on these sexual urges, or the sexual urges or fantasies cause marked distress or interpersonal difficulty." This significant change is noted, in spite of a disclaimer (APA 2000, xxix) that "No substantive changes in the criteria sets were considered." It should be kept in mind that the DSM is a diagnostic guide for mental health workers, not a guide for law enforcement officers or prosecutors. As such, the focus is assessing conditions requiring mental health intervention and treatment, not criminal labeling or prosecution.

Most pedophiles are aware of their attraction to children around puberty/late adolescence, although some report onset of pedophilic interests in middle age. Not all people arrested for child molestation meet DSM-IV (APA 1994) criteria for diagnosis as pedophiles. Child molesters can be subdivided by four criteria (Levine 2000): age of the perpetrator (adolescents, young and middle-aged adults, elderly men); sex of the offender (male or female); sexual orientation or preference (to males, females); victim type (male or female or both, infants, toddlers, preschool, grade school, adolescent, or indiscriminant). As noted by Levine (2000) the four categories are not mutually exclusive. The more you learn about sex offenders, including child molesters (and note that it is possible to be diagnosed as a pedophile and yet not be a sex offender), the more it becomes evident that there is no easy way to identify in advance who is likely to commit a sex offense.

Groth (1979) points out that adult sexual interactions generally involve one of three scenarios: negotiation and consent; pressure and exploitation; force and assault. Although negotiation and consent provide the only appropriate course of action, even this option is lacking with underage partners. Clearly, young children lack the ability to give consent, but even sexually mature thirteen-year-old preadolescents lack the psychological maturity to negotiate sexual activity with an adult. "Adults can capitalize in self-serving ways on this immaturity and can exploit the child in a variety of ways . . ." (Groth 1979).

Various typologies of child molesters have been developed with the intent of helping others recognize common traits and behaviors for diagnostic, treatment, and research purposes. They vary in usefulness and target audience. Writing to a clinical audience, Groth (1978) described fixated and regressed offenders. The fixated offender is exclusively or primarily attracted to a particular victim type—for example, ten-year-old boys. The regressed offender had at one point apparently mature or age-appropriate relationships, but for some reason has reverted to a younger partner. A precipitating stressor could be a

---

[3] TR stands for Text Revised, indicating that the accompanying text, not the diagnostic criteria, was updated.

divorce, loss of a job, or any other factor likely to seriously affect self-esteem. The regression may be temporary or prolonged.

Ken Lanning is a former FBI special agent with extensive work in the area of child molestation. Coming from a law enforcement perspective, his opinions and work are directed at investigators and have influenced child pornography laws. In the 1980s he (Lanning 1992) drew on two categories of child molesters, situational or preferential, that had been suggested by Dr. Park Dietz (1983). The situational offender lacks true ongoing preference for children and turns to abusing them during times of stress, although the behavior may continue for significant periods of time. These offenders tend to have lower numbers of victims. Lanning (1992) listed four types of behavioral patterns associated with the situational child molester: regressed, morally indiscriminate, sexually indiscriminate, and inadequate.

Regressed offenders turn to children in times of stress. Such stresses can include divorce, loss of employment, aging, illness, or even a move to a new home. It may be interesting to note that the concept of a regressed offender implies that the individual is not really a pedophile. Yet it is hard to imagine that the initial desire to have sexual contact with an underage victim was not present to some degree before onset of the stressor; otherwise, why did the stressor lead to pedophilic behavior? Morally indiscriminate offenders abuse children as one aspect of a general lifestyle of abusing others in various contexts. For example, morally indiscriminate offenders may verbally and physically abuse a spouse; harass, harangue, and psychologically demoralize their employees; and engage in sexual molestation of their own children and/or their children's friends. Sexually indiscriminate offenders abuse children as one part of a diverse sexual lifestyle. The abuse occurs essentially in the sexual arena, whereas for morally indiscriminate offenders sexual abuse is only one facet of abuse they perpetrate against others. Sexually indiscriminate offenders may be involved in any number of sexual liaisons at any given time. It is not uncommon for such individuals to be bisexual and to have many partners of both sexes and various ages. Inadequate offenders or molesters are limited by social skill deficits, mental illness, retardation, dementia, or some other situation that limits their ability to interact with age-appropriate peers. Inadequate offenders lacking social skills, but having adequate intelligence, may well be drawn to the Internet as a means of contacting victims. Using various online personas, such socially inept individuals can (with the perceived anonymity and rapid sense of intimacy inherent in cyberspace) become emboldened. Interacting from the assumed safety of their home or workplace, inadequate offenders can gain a sense of mastery by grooming those who are as socially inept as they. Adult inadequate offenders may well feel a sense of accomplishment from toying with a pre-adolescent whose level of social maturity is little different from the offenders.

Preferential molesters prefer sexual activity with children and, according to Lanning (1992), exhibit three general patterns: seductive, introverted, and sadistic. These offenders tend to have more victims and are more likely to meet the criteria for a formal diagnosis of pedophilia. Seduction offenders seduce the child, groom the child, and take advantage of him or her emotionally and sexually. Often, the offenders believe they have an actual romantic relationship with the child. "They will court a child in a romantic manner. Attention, affection, and gifts are used to lower the guard of the child" (Flora 2001). Introverted offenders lack social skills for age-appropriate relationships. Introverted offenders are particularly likely to use the Internet as a source of victims due to the lack of face-to-face interaction. The online scenario provides time to think of responses and cushions the anxiety of initial contact. Sadistic offenders enjoy the suffering of the child victim. As you may have noticed, the various categories are not exclusive as to patterns of behavior. More recently, Lanning (2001a) has conceptualized the preferential-situational dichotomy into a continuum with these two categories of molesters at each end. His new typology encompasses sex offenders as a whole, not focusing solely on child molesters.

Richard Romero, a thirty-six-year-old man, is an example of a preferential pedophile. The case (*U.S. v. Romero* 1999)[4] is an interesting read, highlighting the lengths a pedophile can go to in grooming and seducing victims, and worth covering in detail.[4]

---

**CASE EXAMPLE**

In 1995 Romero had met several well-intentioned (so it appears) faith healers in Florida who asked him to come and stay with them in Iowa. Using one of his new friend's AOL account and credit card number, Romero ordered pornography online and by telephone. During his online travels Romero met 12-year-old Erich (a pseudonym) in an Internet chat room devoted to extraterrestrials and UFOs. Romero, presenting himself as 15-year-old "Kyle", and "revealed" to Erich that his father had been murdered by government agents due to knowing "too much" about UFOs. He suggested the boy join him in a "mission" to uncover UFO secrets. One must understand the lure such fantasy-rich ideation may have on a troubled adolescent male. Adrift in a sea of low self-esteem and probable chronic low-grade depression, a young male might find purpose and a sense of worth in being a part of such an undertaking. During the summer of 1995 both e-mails and letters passed between the two as a bond was forged; Erich revealed he was adopted, in treatment for Attention Deficit disorder, viewed his parents as too restrictive and believed they did not understand him. This sce-

---

[4] All information was obtained from the District Court decision. *U.S. v. Romero*, 189 F.3[d], 576 (7th Circuit 1999), http://laws.lp.findlaw.com/7th/982358.html.

nario is the forte of the cyber pedophile. By the end of that summer, 12-year-old Erich believed "Kyle" was his best friend.

During this time, Romero (in the persona of "Ricardo", a Spanish boy hiding in Iowa to avoid an arranged marriage) was also grooming David and Michael (also pseudonyms), two Tampa, Florida, boys he met on the Internet. The two boys had an interest in religion and the occult. Romero ingeniously, or perhaps not, created a religion whose members consisted of Romero, Michael and David, and the boys' friends. Again, one must appreciate the lure of this kind of situation to adolescent boys seeking adventure. Religious rituals were e-mailed to the members of the new religion by Romero. At first these essentially consisted of drops of blood and various seemingly mysterious incantations. As time went on, though, the so-called rites became sexual in nature. The boys refused to conduct the proscribed rituals.

After receiving an enormous ($1200) bill for online telephone usage, and determining that many phone calls were to private homes, not ISPs, the Romero's Iowa friends confronted him and found large amounts of child pornography (magazines and videotapes) in his basement room. The items were destroyed and Romero promised not to buy such things again. Romero's friends closed the AOL account and opened a new one. Prior to being disconnected, Romero (as "Kyle") advised Erich that his mother was restricting his Internet access and that he was depressed and suicidal and would be going away for a while, but that someone would contact Erich on his behalf. Using the new AOL account, Romero contacted Erich as "Rick," "Kyle's older brother. Within months, Erich believed "Rick" and he were best friends. Sometime in October of 1995 Romero's friends discovered he was still using their Internet account to contact underage boys and finally asked him to leave that November. They bought him a bus ticket to Florida. Child pornography continued to arrive in the mail, even after Romero had departed.

Once back in Florida Romero contacted Michael and David. He (as "Ricardo") told them he had run from Iowa because he had refused to return to Spain. The boy suggested he stay at a cheap hotel near where they lived. David ran away from home and stayed with Romero for two weeks. Although Romero made no sexual advances toward the boy, he found child pornography on the man's computer. In January of 1996, posing as "Rick", Romero convinced one of his former Iowa friends to buy him a computer and mail it to him in Florida.

Romero used this computer to move back on the Internet and struck up a correspondence with an Alex Kozlowski, a pornography dealer. Romero told Kozlowski of his attraction to boys in general and specifically to a boy named Erich. He offered to make an erotic video of Erich. Romero had been corresponding with Erich by phone and e-mail and asked Erich to meet him in Florida, requesting a photograph be sent first. Erich complied, sending Romero a photo and a letter. He showed the letter to his adoptive parents as a way of taunting them. They arranged for him to meet with his counselor, who made Erich tear up the letter.

Using a telephone number from a long-distance bill, Erich's mother called Romero, explained that the boy had emotional problems and asked Romero to leave the boy alone. Romero e-mailed Erich and advised him that his mother had said terrible things about him and tried to turn Romero ("Rick") against him. Erich and "Rick" arranged to meet near Erich's home in Illinois. Under a ruse, Romero got a friend to buy him a plane ticket to Chicago, where he went and eventually met up with Erich. The two boarded a bus destined eventually for Florida. Due to past attendance problems, Erich's school notified his mother he had not shown that day. She contacted police and advised them of Romero's online relationship with her son. The two travelers were located on a Greyhound bus in Louisville, Kentucky, and taken into custody. Erich advised police he never would have gone with Romero if he had known his interest in him was sexual.

The following day Romero (or should we say Ricardo) called David in Florida from jail instructing him to destroy evidence on his computer. David set about erasing child pornography files, but being technologically naïve, he failed to do an adequate job and investigators were able to retrieve most of the files. Romero also contacted another friend in Florida with a request to destroy child pornography he had stored in his apartment. The friend found the items, but instead of destroying them, turned the items over to the FBI. Romero was charged with crimes related to traveling across state lines (by himself, from Florida to Illinois) for the purpose of having sexual activity with a minor, kidnapping, transportation of a minor across state lines for purposes of sexual activity, and obstructing justice. Romero admitted to his pedophilic tendencies, but denied ever intending to act out his fantasies with Erich and noted that Erich went with him voluntarily. At trial Romero was convicted of obstruction of justice, acquitted of traveling to Illinois to have sex with a minor, but the jury could not reach a decision on the kidnapping and interstate transport of a minor charges. A second trial on the two unsettled charges led to a conviction on both counts. He was sentenced to 27 years and 3 months in prison and appealed the latter convictions, based on inappropriate admission of expert testimony by Kenneth Lanning on child molesters, among other things. The trial court judgment was upheld.

Knight and Prentky (Knight 1989, 1992; Knight, Carter, and Prentky 1989) have developed a typology for classifying child molesters. This work was originally carried out at the Massachusetts Treatment Center (MTC) for Sexually Dangerous Persons and has been sequentially modified. The most current typology is labeled the MTC:CM3 and is defined by the extent of sexual fixation on children, the level of social competence, and the degree of contact the offender has with children. It is a two-axes typology. The first axis has abandoned the concept of regression and focused on two dimensions: fixation (high or low pedophilic interest) and social competence (high or low). This leads to four types of sexual abusers: (1) high fixation—low social competence; (2) high fixation—high social competence; (3) low fixation—low social competence; (4) low fixation—high social competence. On the second axis the amount of contact with children is dichotomized to high or low. High-contact offenders are divided into those for whom the interaction with the victim substitutes for a more appropriate relationship and those for whom the interaction serves narcissistic (i.e., selfish) needs. Low-contact offenders are divided into four categories related to physical injury (high or low) and sadism (high or low). The variables on axis II allow for differentiation of six types (Knight et al. 1989). The validity data for the typology have been reviewed by Knight (1992), and Prentky, Knight, and Lee (1997) have completed a follow-up study examining some of the typology's dimensions.

While these typologies may offer utility in categorizing child molesters for research, treatment, or descriptive purposes, they tend to offer little prospectively to a law enforcement investigator or the guardian of a potential victim. As was noted in the introduction to this chapter, statistical generalizations or profiles derived from statistical generalizations of past offender data often bear limited or no relation to a specific offender under investigation. While there may tend to be similarities, every case (and every offender) will be different, requiring reliance on solid investigative techniques with occasional innovative approaches. This situation may be compounded by offenders aware of the various typologies proffered. While there is an expectation that the Internet will lure introverted, socially limited molesters, there is also an expectation that socially competent, highly intelligent sadistic offenders will see the advantages of online procurement of victims. Research into the online habits and characteristics of Internet child molesters begs to be done. There is very limited research currently available seeking to determine whether there is any qualitative differences between child molesters who use the Internet and those who do not. One such study (Hernandez 2000a) suggests that Internet sexual offenders tend to share many of the behavioral characteristics of child molesters in general.

## 4.3) MODUS OPERANDI: HOW ONLINE CHILD MOLESTERS OPERATE

To develop an investigatively relevant offender profile, the investigator needs to move beyond general typologies when the offender is unknown. The investigator must examine the offender's behaviors to gain insight into the rationale behind them. Analyzing offender behaviors may reveal information on the offender, such as prior knowledge of victim(s), degree of technical skills, and other evidence-based details that may aid the investigation. This approach is based on the premise that evidence left at a crime scene can reflect offender behavior and traits.

The online child molester, aside from the required computer savvy, relies on the skills that have always been used by such offenders. He or she goes to areas likely to be frequented by victims. In the real world this could be a school, an amusement arcade, or a mall. In the virtual world this would likely be a chat room that caters to children or adolescents. There is no shortage of such groups where a forty-five-year-old man can log on as "Molly" or "Skeet" and start a conversation with other group members. When asked for age or other personal characteristics, the offender can easily offer a profile of a teenage girl or boy. The troll for victims can be as easy as typing a message to the group that: "I just had a fight with my mom. I hate her so much. My parents don't understand me." Within moment's the offender's screen will likely light up with responses from teens mirroring the sentiment: "I know exactly what you mean!" "I hate my parents too," etc. The offender now has tapped into a common adolescent issue and will no doubt have many ears (or eyes). Interestingly, there is a real possibility that some of the responses are from other child molesters inhabiting the chat room. Aside from like-minded offenders bumping into each other pretending to be children, they may interact with law enforcement officers posing as potential victims. This creates a danger for the offenders, but paradoxically, the potential for such danger may increase the excitement of some offenders.

One area child molesters tap is that of young males unsure of their sexuality. The offender may offer to arrange heterosexual activities with alcohol and drugs for the victim, with the ultimate objective to get the intended victim intoxicated and sexually aroused through the use of pornography. Once the victim's guard is lowered, an attempt to engage in sex with the victim occurs through suggestion, coercion, or physical force. Alternatively, if the victim is questioning whether or not he has a homosexual orientation, the offender may act as a mentor with the plan of initiating the victim into homosexual activities. Once the victim is involved in sexual activity with the child molester, even if minimal, the fear of being "outed" by the offender creates powerful leverage in maintaining secrecy. According to the New York Westchester County DA's office, Frank Bauer, a well-liked twenty-nine-year-old male art teacher, was arrested after blackmailing a fifteen-year-old student into making a sexually explicit video of himself (Chen 2000). The teacher reportedly started an online correspondence with one of his students, posing as a woman. The boy and the "woman" sent each other e-mails and photos. Later, communicating under the female persona, Bauer allegedly threatened to alter a photo of the boy to make it appear he was engaged in sex and distribute it to the boy's classmates if he did not videotape himself. The student made the video and then the onscreen "woman" demanded a second video. The boy turned to a trusted adult to discuss the situation. The adult was a teacher, the very person blackmailing the boy for the videos. Eventually, the boy told his parents what was happening and police traced the e-mails to Bauer.

Once victim contact has been initiated, the child molester will groom the victim. Grooming consists of gaining the trust of the victim and also that of those who are in caretaker roles, when necessary. As the offender becomes familiar to the victim, the victim is seduced psychologically and emotionally into lowering his or her guard and telling the offender more and more about himself or herself. This stage can occur quite rapidly online. Although some victims may feel uncomfortable during this stage of the offense, many do not and willingly offer up personal details about themselves and their family. Sometimes the offender does not need to pretend to be a peer of the victim but can openly present himself or herself as a "mature friend" who is willing to relay understanding and advice. If a teenage girl will date a thirty-year-old man in the real world, why should she not interact with such a man online, when in fact this type of communication may even appear safer? According to Lanning (2001b) many online pedophiles are "reasonably honest about their identities, and some even send recognizable photographs of themselves" to potential victims.

Offenders have even been known to start relationships with women only to have access to their children. Once grooming has occurred and sexual abuse has begun, a victim may be torn between wanting the mother to be in a relationship with the offender and not wanting to disappoint the mother. There may be issues of competition between the victim and the mother for the offender's attention, guilt over the abusive relationship, ambivalence over the presence of the offender in the home, a sense of protecting other children by being the abused one, etc. The issues are multi-dimensional and the astute offender is capable of exploiting them. With increased use of the Internet as a means of dating and meeting potential partners, it is expected that offenders prone to seek women with young children will turn progressively to the Internet in search of prey.

Child molesters are quite skilled at grooming victims. In a real-world scenario, an offender might strike up a friendship with a child and slowly get the child to trust him. Although the victim might initially have misgivings about the attention from an adult, eventually this gives way to trust and possibly even affection on the part of the victim. You might be surprised to learn that some child molesters are convinced that not only do they not harm children, but they actually help them by providing companionship, nurturance, and a "loving" introduction to sexual activity. To many child molesters, it is we (the general public) who have a problem, not them. Just as a rapist may attempt to justify a rape by saying the victim asked for it, either through seductive dress or behavior, the pedophile often claims to be the victim of a sexually aware child. These rationalizations are called "cognitive distortions." The North American Man Boy Love Association (NAMBLA) manages to condemn sexual abuse and at the same time espouse it without seeing a problem: "We condemn sexual abuse and all forms of coercion. Freely chosen relationships differ from unwanted sex. Present laws, which focus only on the age of the participants, ignore the quality of their relationships. We know that differences in age do not preclude mutual, loving interaction between persons. NAMBLA is strongly opposed to age-of-consent laws and all other restrictions which deny men and boys the full enjoyment of their bodies and control over their own lives" (NAMBLA 1999).

Online, the sex offender is free to groom the victim at all hours of the day, even in the victim's home. He or she is available to "talk" and interact with the victim, to provide support and advice. The offender can potentially (through instant messaging programs or otherwise) be alerted whenever the victim is online. Once the victim trusts the offender to some extent, the offender may request photos of the victim. These requests may start out as apparently innocent, becoming slowly more erotic in nature. It is amazing where such requests can lead. A victim might acquiesce to a request for "a picture of you in a bathing suit," by sending a fairly modest picture taken that summer, only to be followed up with a request for a topless photo. The victim may then refuse, only to be told by the offender that if such a picture is not offered the first photo will be digitally altered to show the victim nude and will be posted on the Internet as well as be sent to her father. Fearing such a scenario, the victim may then comply. While the average person may find this scenario hard to understand, a young girl (or boy) may see complying with the offender's threat as the only logical thing to do, as telling her parents what is happening may seem unthinkable. Given that Webcams and inexpensive digital cameras are becoming omnipresent, the easy access to photographic equipment and the absence of a need for film processing reduce the offender's risk of being caught and may increase the likelihood of the victim's compliance.

The Internet gives sexual predators the ability to commit an offense without ever physically coming into contact with the victim. One forty-seven-year-old Ohio man posed as a fifteen-year-old and communicated online with a fourteen-year-old girl, eventually convincing her to send him sexually explicit photos and videos of herself performing sexual acts. This cyber relationship went on for a year and a half, from the time the girl was twelve years old. The offender pled guilty to one charge of inducing a minor to produce child pornography (Burney 1997).

Some offenders are content to masturbate to e-mails from the victims or pictures of the victims. Others want to meet the victims in the real world to engage in sexual activity. This step is an important one, as the offender will be leaving the (assumed) anonymity of the computer keyboard and stepping into the light of day. The victim may not be as impressed with the offender as s/he was when corresponding online. Anticipating such a response, many offenders have been arrested carrying articles, such as handcuffs or ropes, to restrain victims when attempting to make a rendezvous. Some victims expect to meet a peer, but some have been groomed so well that they accept that they will be meeting an adult. Regardless of an offender's skill at grooming a victim, sometimes a victim is willing to pursue any offer of love or attention as a way of fleeing an abusive or neglectful home life. Some victims plan to run off with the person they meet online and go missing for various lengths of time. Others are abducted involuntarily. In May 2002, the body of thirteen-year-old Christina Long was found in a ravine in Connecticut. A Brazilian immigrant she met through the Internet strangled her. While attending sixth grade at a Catholic school, Christina developed a reputation as an altar girl, cheerleader, and good student. Unknown to many, she also haunted Internet chat rooms using provocative screen names and had sex with men she met online (CBSnews.com. 2001).

Lanning (2001b) points out that "many of the children lured from their homes after on-line computer conversations are not innocents who were duped while doing their homework. Most are curious, rebellious, or troubled adolescents seeking sexual information or contact." Lanning makes it clear that these adolescents are victims of the child molester they have been interacting with, but the fact that they have participated to some degree in the scenario (possibly by exchanging pornography with the offender, accepting money or gifts) may make them less than honest when cooperating with law enforcement. Depending on the scenario, victim-blaming and media reporting can feed into the public perception of the victim as a co-conspirator in his or her own victimization. While a prepubescent child will always fall under the umbrella of victim-hood, as adolescents get closer to the age of majority, feeling they bear some responsibility for their predicament is easier. But we must emphasize that while their behavior may have contributed to their victimization, this cannot be used as rationalization for lessening the offender's responsibility. Like it or not, the offender bears the weight of the offense. It simply will not wash to play to the alleged consensual nature of sexual relationships between adults and minors. Christina Long is an example of a thirteen-year-old disturbed adolescent who sought clearly dangerous liaisons through the Internet. Not long after her death, critics implied that her behavior contributed to her death. By pointing out how different she was from the usual thirteen-year-old we know, perhaps we somehow feel safer. This does not change the fact that she was thirteen and very much a victim of the men she met and the man who ultimately murdered her.

Once actual sexual contact with the victim has occurred, offenders may take various courses to avoid detection. They might convince the child or adolescent that they love him or her and vice versa. They may tell the victim that if the sexual activity becomes known, they (the offenders) will go to jail. The child or adolescent often cannot imagine being responsible for the incarceration of someone whom he or she believes cares for him or her and may remain silent. If the child or adolescent is unlikely to keep the relationship a secret, threats are key. The victim may be told that he or her enjoyed the sexual activity[5] and that this fact will become known. Or, the offender will tell the child that no one will believe him or her, which is possible when the offender is someone in a significant authority position, such as a policeman, cleric, physician, or parent. If all else fails, physical threats against the victim or family, or even family pets, are often quite potent. Using information known previously to the offender or gleaned subsequently from the victim, an offender can make threats that seem very plausible to a child or adolescent.

The case of a computer scientist and mathematician, Marvin Hersh (*U.S. v. Hersh 2001*), illustrates the lengths (and distances) some predators will go to procure victims.[6]

---

Hersh, a professor at Florida Atlantic University, traveled to third-world countries, ranging from Asia to Central America, to engage in sexual relationships with impoverished young boys, eventually bringing a fifteen-year-old boy from Honduras back to live with him in Florida, posing as his son. Hersh and a friend, Nelson Jay Buhler, of Fort Lauderdale, Florida, were convicted of "traveling for the purpose of sexual contact with a minor, and aggravated sexual abuse of a child in Honduras. According to Title 18,

**CASE EXAMPLE**

---

[5] The victim's enjoyment may be true to some extent, which is why this is often a powerful inducement to silence.

[6] All information, unless otherwise noted, is from the Circuit Court opinion. *U.S. v. Hersh*, No. 0014592OPN-07/17/02 (11th Circuit, 2001) http://laws.lp.findlaw.com/11th/0014592opn.html.

Section 2423, a federal statute in the US, it is a crime for any American citizen to travel abroad with the intent to sexually abuse children. These are the first convictions under the 'Mann Act' extraterritorial laws in the US" (EPCAT 2000).

In the early 1990s Hersh, in his mid-fifties, traveled to Honduras, where he met Moises, an eighteen-year-old boy and offered food and clothing in exchange for sex. Afterward, Hersh asked the boy whether he had any brothers and was brought to Moises' home. Hersh asked the mother for permission to travel with the boys, which she gave, apparently not realizing Hersh wanted the boys for sex. Hersh continued to have sexual relations with Moises, also initiating sex with his three younger brothers in exchange for money and gifts. The youngest brother was ten years old at the time.

Traveling to Thailand in early 1990, Hersh met Nelson Buhler, a pedophile also traveling to a third-world country in search of young men. Hersh tutored Buhler in locating child pornography on the Internet and encrypting the files and saving them to high-capacity (for the time) Zip disks that could easily be destroyed. Hersh invited Buhler to come to Honduras with him. In November 1994 Buhler accompanied Hersh to Central America. At the airport the two men met Moises and two of his younger brothers. The group went to several hotels where the men had sex with the boys. The two Americans visited Honduras together at least five more times over the next twelve months and engaged in sexual activity with the poverty-stricken adolescents, giving their families money and gifts. Hersh made two trips in 1995 alone, during which he convinced the boys' family that the boys would have better educational opportunities in the United States. In August 1995 the fifteen-year-old brother was allowed to travel with Hersh to the states. Hersh had obtained a false U.S. birth certificate for the boy and used it to obtain a passport and a Social Security card. Hersh attempted to pass the Latino boy off as his son.

The boy was brought to Hersh's Boca Raton, Florida, residence and essentially was the middle-aged American's sex partner. In 1996 someone must have made a complaint because the Florida Department of Children and Families placed Hersh under investigation. After searching Hersh's home with his consent, investigators discovered a suitcase with maps indicating where to find boys in impoverished countries and photos of boys unclothed from the waist up. Further search uncovered evidence of digital files of minor males engaging in sexual activity on Hersh's hard drive and encrypted files on Zip disks. The Zip disk files could not be opened, but the file names left little doubt as to the contents. Other evidence was developed indicating Hersh molested boys as young as eight years old. The boys he molested, both

American and foreign, fit a profile: young boys from poor families who turned a blind eye to Hersh's interest in their children in return for food, gifts, and money. It should be noted that Hersh did not pursue one child in Honduras who was a friend of Moises and his brothers because the boy's mother was educated and would likely cause trouble.

Buhler pled guilty to conspiracy in exchange for his testimony against Hersh.

The fifteen-year-old was removed from Hersh's home by authorities. Hersh called his friend, Buhler, and advised him not to call. Hersh was arrested shortly after.

## 4.4) SIGNATURE AND THE ONLINE CHILD MOLESTER

In criminal profiling an aura has developed around the term "signature," implying it is like a fingerprint, allowing for assignment of a crime to a particular person, based on perceived shared characteristics. This concept is generally a fallacy, and the term is more often misused than applied correctly. A so-called signature or "calling card" (Keppel 1995) is best viewed as a class characteristic, capable of placing an item in a class of similar items, rather than an individuating characteristic. By telling someone you saw a blue Ford Taurus drive away from a crime scene, you have supplied class characteristics. The suspect vehicle can be narrowed down from the potential pool of all cars to those that are blue and also a Ford Taurus. If, though, you are able to give the license number, you have now supplied an individuating characteristic. There will be only one blue Ford Taurus with that license plate.

It is hard for criminal profilers to admit that signature evidence is not as good as they would like. One former FBI profiler has even made this claim. An aberrant offender's behavior is as unique as his fingerprint, as his DNA—as a snowflake (Michaud 2000). Aside from the fact that it has never been proven that no two snowflakes are alike, this is simply an unsupportable claim with no scientific basis whatsoever. People do similar things for different reasons and different things for similar reasons. Such proffers of individuating characteristics from items capable only of class characteristics are common in profiling and are rarely seen for what they are (McGrath 2001; Risinger and Loop 2002). In spite of the limitations the concept of signature may have in absolute terms, it may very well be helpful in the investigative phase of a prosecution.

A signature (in the profiling sense) is an offender behavior that is not necessary for commission of a crime and reflects an underlying psychological need (Douglas and Munn 1992; Turvey 1999). Modus operandi is behavior that is necessary to commit the crime, preclude identity, and facilitate escape (Hazelwood and Warren 2001). The distinction between modus operandi behaviors and signature behaviors is not as distinct as it may at first seem. The dichotomy can blur quickly, with some elements of both presenting in a single behavior. For example, wearing a mask to avoid identification would clearly be modus operandi behavior. The kind of mask worn may extend into signature behavior. Using a weapon to keep a victim or victims under control would be modus operandi behavior. The kind of weapon used might be signature behavior. The level of threat to a victim can be modus operandi, signature, or both.

For the investigator, what is important is to have an understanding of the fact that while some behaviors are helpful in facilitating a crime, other behaviors may be more a result of inner needs of the offender. Both types of behaviors may reveal something about the offender that may further an investigation. If an investigator is able to see certain "signature" elements running through a series of crimes (real-world or cybercrime), s/he might be able to connect the crimes from an investigative point of view. For instance, an offender may display modus operandi behavior by choosing specific online chat rooms because they attract the types of children s/he prefers and by using an online nickname (e.g., Zest), designed to gain children's trust. This screen name can also reflect how the offender views himself or herself, thereby imparting a signature aspect to the behavior.

Investigators must be alert for crime-scene staging in cyberspace, just as they must guard against this in the physical world crime scene. Headers on e-mails can be faked. Offenders utilize available technologies to conceal their identities and misdirect investigators. Investigators must also keep in mind that offenders can plant or fabricate digital evidence with the intent of implicating someone else in the commission of a crime. E-mail and Usenet headers can be forged, dial-up accounts can be stolen, and personal computers can be hacked and used as vehicles to commit other crimes. Digital evidence must be treated as any other form of evidence and, therefore, should be closely examined for signs of staging. Once detected, staging can itself reveal significant information about the actual offender, including, but not limited to, skill level; access to various technologies; IP address of actual offender; relationship to, or knowledge of, the individual targeted by the staging; potential motives for staging and/or targeting of the innocent person; potential relationships between the ultimate victim and the staged "offender." Some aspects of staging may uncover signature behaviors, such as language used in planted e-mails, styles of taunting, unnecessary destruction of items (generalized or specific) owned by the targeted individual, etc.

## 4.5) PROFILING THE CHILD MOLESTER

Statistical profiles of child molesters offer little help in an investigation and may even be misleading. Such lists may offer a picture of a "typical" offender, but the information loses its investigative utility when brought out into the real world. The problem is that someone may be identified as having one or several characteristics associated with being a child molester, yet not be a child molester. If we set very broad characteristics, we run the risk of identifying many people, only a few of whom might actually be child molesters. This is called a "false positive": We had a positive finding that subsequently was proven to be false. If we set our criteria too narrowly, we run the risk of letting child molesters slip by. This is called a "false negative": We said there was nothing of concern, when in fact there was. These issues plague all prospective profiling techniques.

An illustration might be the National Basketball Association (NBA). If you watch NBA games on television for any length of time, you might come to the conclusion that almost all professional basketball players are six-feet-four inches in height or taller. Clearly, that height would be one of the outstanding characteristics of a professional basketball player. Using that highly visible criterion, if you set up shop in a mall and stopped every man six-feet-four or taller, it would take a long time before you would accost an NBA player. In fact, after a few days you would likely give up hope of ever finding such a person. Yet you relied on the most obvious characteristic available to you.

So, what might be the most obvious characteristic of child molesters? Clearly, their interest in children, but how does that help us? Do we preventively incarcerate all scout leaders? All day camp operators? All teachers? Obviously not. What we must do is accept that there is no easy answer, no list of things where five or more will allow us to prospectively and positively identify child molesters. On the other hand, one thing stands out: an *intense* age-inappropriate interest in children or adolescents. We are not talking about someone who likes to coach the swim team. But we are talking about someone who likes to coach the swim team, always has an excuse for watching the kids change, likes to rub their backs and necks when talking to them, etc. Ask the kids. They will tell you who they do not feel comfortable around. The reason they will often not volunteer such information is that adults tend to downplay the signs of inappropriate contact. The investigator must put any red flags in perspective but not be naïve when it comes to adults interacting inappropriately with children or adolescents. A thirty-year-old male online communicating with children or young adolescents on a regular basis has a problem, until proven otherwise. He may be immature or have similar interests, but unless there is a good reason for the discourse, this is a matter for concern. Some of those who come to the attention of law enforcement may surprise us, but that only highlights the fact that statistical profiles have limited, if any, utility in predicting who may offend.

One case highlighting the difficulty of identifying potential cyber offenders is that of Patrick Naughton, a thirty-four-year-old executive. Aside from not fitting the expected inductive profiles of those with pedophilic interests, Mr. Naughton displayed incredible naivete for a person with considerable computer savvy. Because he was "[o]ne of the hotshot programmers behind Java and an executive vice president at portal company Infoseek, where he was responsible for content for Walt Disney's Go Network," it is hard to imagine that reportedly, "he gave his home and work numbers to an agent pretending to be a 13-year-old girl in an Internet chat room. Mr. Naughton also pointed the agent to a story (with a photo) about him on Forbes.com, the FBI has alleged" (Aragon 1999). Interestingly, Mr. Naughton's defense lawyers claimed that their client was only fantasy playing with no intention of carrying out any actual physical offense. Unfortunately for Mr. Naughton, he had crossed state lines when he went to meet with a female sheriff's deputy posing as his online thirteen-year-old friend. The lawyers averred that Naughton "was role playing in the fantasy world of chat rooms and never really believed he was going to meet up with a girl who was only 13" (Bowman 1999). At trial Naughton was found guilty of possessing child pornography[7], but the jury could not reach a verdict on charges of crossing state lines to have sex with a minor and arranging to have sex with a minor via Internet messages (ABCNews.com 1999). The week after the conviction, an appeals court judge ruled that virtual child pornography was not illegal, and the child pornography conviction was overturned. Before a second trial, Naughton pleaded guilty to traveling across state lines to have sex with a minor and was sentenced to probation (Bowman 2000).

It could be argued that attempting to profile those interested in child pornography is more likely to lead to befuddlement than insight. Professionals with nothing to gain but everything to lose have engaged in activities related to child pornography online. Some examples: A Minnesota University professor of Greek and New Testament studies was charged with possession and distribution of child pornography; a University of California-Davis computer programmer was charged with distributing child pornography from his computer at work; the head of the English department of a private college in Illinois was arrested after allegedly soliciting images through an Internet child pornography ring using the screen name "Snowy Violet"; a professor at Baylor University in Waco, Texas, was indicted with his wife on child pornography charges (Busse 2001). A Yale professor of geology filmed a boy he was men-

---

[7] Picture files found on his computer.

toring at age eleven and thirteen having sex (allegedly with the professor), and the police investigation uncovered voluminous child pornography on the man's computer. The professor was "respected by hundreds of students as the master of Saybrook College and by thousands of scientists as a pioneer in geochemical kinetics" (Kolber 2000). That he "also has a fondness for child pornography" came as a shock. In February 2003 a fifty-five-year-old rabbi was arrested in Manhattan after traveling from New Jersey to meet an online acquaintance, "Katie," who had advised the rabbi through e-mail that she was thirteen years old. Allegedly, in a bag the rabbi carried were condoms and a lubricant. "Katie" turned out to be an undercover police officer. The rabbi was a well-respected father of six (Italiano 2003).[8]

## 4.6) THE SUBCULTURE OF CHILD PORNOGRAPHY

There is an Internet subculture of child pornography aficionados whose main interest seems to be not only enjoying viewing child pornography, but collecting it. This is a distinct group from the usual online predators, with (allegedly) generally no real intent or need to contact victims in the real world. These individuals post to hard-to-find bulletin boards, do not attempt to meet each other in the real world, are extremely technologically competent, and take pride in staying a step or two ahead of law enforcement. They inhabit a world of proxy servers, anonymous Web connections, and re-mailers. They trade child pornography online through Internet sites that are often only online for a few hours before being taken down, either by design or by an ISP that has been alerted to the nature of the site. They use encrypted Zip files and later in a different online location or bulletin board post passwords for the files. No money passes hands. This is the online equivalent of baseball card trading. There are well-known series of pictures dating back decades, and when someone discovers missing pictures that complete such a series, that person is considered a hero (Jenkins 2001). Research into whether child pornography offenders are a separate group from child molesters is limited. One study suggests the differences may not be as pronounced as some would like to think (Hernandez 2000b).

## 4.7) CONCLUSION

At this point, some might feel we have failed to present a practical scheme to profile the online sexual predator. This is true in one sense, and false in

---

[8] As an aside, these and other cases mentioned might tempt an inductive profiler to assume that the typical Internet sex offender is a university professor. Such an approach, obviously, would lead to poor results in many investigations.

another. The investigator seeking out the "profile" of the cyber predator to target a suspect will be disappointed in this chapter. The reliance on inductive methodology inherent in much of current profiling, including the FBI style (Organized/Disorganized) of profiling, leads to numerous vague and overvalued offender characteristics being offered that ultimately present little if any investigative utility in a specific case. Such criticism may seem unfounded when law enforcement clients may endorse such profiles as "helpful," "accurate," etc. We would argue that such profiles are retrospectively often the equivalent of a cold reading by a "psychic," or no more accurate than a newspaper horoscope written in a vague style to apply to many, but with each individual believing that it has specificity for him or her. So, in a sense, we have failed to present a scheme for producing detailed profiles of offenders that offer little help to the investigator. For that, the investigator should be thankful.

On the other hand, using a deductive approach, relying only on the evidence available in the case or series of cases under investigation, the investigator is more likely to infer useful information about the offender. The available, supportable inferences will be less than in an inductive approach, but we hope more useful in the investigation.

## REFERENCES

ABCNews.com. "Mixed Verdict for Internet Exec: Naughton Convicted Only of Possessing Porn." (December 16, 1999). http://abcnews.go.com/sections/tech/DailyNews/naughton991216.html.

American Prosecutors Research Institute. *Investigation and Prosecution of Child Abuse*, 3rd ed. Thousand Oaks, CA: Sage, 2003.

American Psychiatric Association. *Diagnostic and Statistical Manual of Mental Disorders*, 4th ed., Washington, DC: American Psychiatric Association, 1994.

American Psychiatric Association. *Diagnostic and Statistical Manual of Mental Disorders*, 4th ed., Text Revision. Washington, DC: American Psychiatric Association, 2000.

Aragon, L. "Was Newfound Wealth a Factor in the Naughton Case? *Red Herring*. (September 23, 1999). http://www.redherring.com/insider/1999/0923/news-newmoney.html.

Boon, T. O. "Cops Stopped Sniper Once but Let Him Go." Reuters. (October 27, 2002). http://straitstimes.asia1.com.sg/world/story/0,4386,151338,800.html.

Bowman, L. "Naughton Lawyers Try Role-Playing Defence." *ZDNet UK News*. (December 8, 1999). http://news.zdnet.co.uk/story/0,,t269-s2075702,00.html.

Bowman, L. "Feds Say to Go Easy on Naughton." *ZDNet UK News.* (August 7, 2000). http://crime.about.com/gi/dynamic/offsite.htm?site=http://www.zdnet .com/zdnn/stories/news/0%2C4586%2C2613175%2C00.html.

Burney, M. "Cyber Affair with Teen-Age Girl Leads to Five Years in Prison." The Associated Press. (August 22, 1997). http://www.nandotimes.net/ newsroom/ntn/info/082297/info10_3348_noframes.html.

Busse, N. "Child Porn Scandal Not Unique to US," *Minnesota Daily.* (February 21, 2001). http://www.mndaily.com/daily/2001/02/21/news/new2/.

CBSnews.com. "The Two Faces of a 13-Year-Old Girl." (May 21, 2001). http://www.cbsnews.com/stories/2002/05/31/national/main510739 .shtml.

Chen, D. W. "Teacher Is Accused of Duping Boy to Make a Sexual Video," *New York Times, Late Edition—Final.* (October 5, 2000): B5.

Dietz, P. E. "Sex Offenses: Behavioral Aspects" in *Encyclopedia of Crime and Justice.* S. H. Kadish et al., eds. New York: Free Press, 1983. Cited in Lanning, Kenneth V. *Child Molesters: A Behavioral Analysis for Law Enforcement Officers Investigating Cases of Child Sexual Exploitation,* 3rd ed. Arlington, VA: National Center for Missing and Exploited Children, 1992.

Douglas, J. E., and C. M. Munn. "Violent Crime Scene Analysis: *Modus Operandi,* Signature, and Staging." *Law Enforcement Bulletin* 57 (1992): 1–10.

Edwards, C. N. "Behavior and the Law Reconsidered: Psychological Syndromes and Profiles." *Journal of Forensic Science* 43 (1998): 141–150.

EPCAT. "US Abuser of Honduran Street Kids Jailed for Life." *EPCAT International Newsletters* 31. (June 2000). http://www.ecpat.net/eng/Ecpat_inter/ IRC/articles.asp?articleID=89&NewsID=16.

Flora, R. *How to Work with Sex Offenders: A Handbook for Criminal Justice, Human Service, and Mental Health Professionals.* New York: The Haworth Clinical Practice Press, 2001.

Graff, P. "U.S., Russia Unite to Fight Child Sex," *Moscow Times.* (February 12, 2001). http://www.themoscowtimes.com/stories/2001/03/27/003.html.

Graff, P. "Duma Votes to Raise Age of Consent to 16." Reuters. (June 28, 2002). http://www.ageofconsent.com/russia.htm.

Groth, N. A. "Pattern of Sexual Assault against Children and Adolescents," in *Sexual Assault of Children and Adolescents.* A. W. Burgess, A. N. Groth, L. L. Holmstrom, and S. M. Sgroi, eds., 3–24. Lexington, MA: Lexington Books, 1978.

Groth, N. A. *Men Who Rape: The Psychology of the Offender.* New York: Plenum Press, 1979.

Hazelwood, R. R., and J. I. Warren. "The Relevance of Fantasy in Serial Sexual Crime Investigations," in *Practical Aspects of Rape Investigation: A Multidis-*

*ciplinary Approach*, 3rd ed. R. R. Hazelwood and A. W. Burgess, eds., 83–95. Boca Raton, FL: CRC Press, 2001.

Hernandez, A. E. "Self-Reported Contact Sexual Offenses by Participants in the Federal Bureau of Prisons' Sex Offender Treatment Program: Implications for Internet Sex Offenders." Presented at the 19th Annual Conference Research and Treatment Conference of the Association for the Treatment of Sexual Abusers, San Diego, CA (November 2000a).

Hernandez, A. E. "Self-Reported Contact Sexual Crimes of Federal Inmates Convicted of Child Pornography Offenses." Presented at the 19th Annual Conference Research and Treatment Conference of the Association for the Treatment of Sexual Abusers, San Diego, CA (November 2000b).

Italiano, L. "'Rubber' Rabbi All Set for Sex." *New York Post, Metro Edition* (February 22, 2003): 9.

Jenkins, P. *Beyond Tolerance: Child Pornography on the Internet.* New York: New York University Press, 2001.

Keppel, R. "Signature Murders: A Report of Several Related Cases," *Journal of Forensic Sciences* 40, no. 4 (1995): 670–674.

Knight, R. A. "An Assessment of Concurrent Validity of a Child Molester Typology." *Journal of Interpersonal Violence* 4 (1989): 131–150.

Knight, R. A. "The Generation and Corroboration of a Taxonomic Model for Child Molesters," in *The Sexual Abuse of Children: Theory, Research, and Therapy*, Vol. 2. W. O'Donohue and J. H. Geer, eds., 24–70. Hillsdale, NJ: Lawrence Erlbaum, 1992.

Knight, R. A., D. L. Carter, and R. A. Prentky. "A System for the Classification of Child Molesters: Reliability and Application." *Journal of Interpersonal Violence* 4 (1989): 3–23.

Kolber, M. "Lasaga's Guilty Plea Inevitable: Overwhelming Evidence Supported Child Pornography Charges." *Yale Daily News.* (February 21, 2000). http://www.yaledailynews.com/article.asp?AID=4699.

Lanning, K. V. *Child Molesters: A Behavioral Analysis: For Law Enforcement Officers Investigating Cases of Child Sexual Exploitation*, 3rd ed. Arlington, VA: National Center for Missing and Exploited Children, 1992.

Lanning, K. V. *Child Molesters: A Behavioral Analysis: For Law Enforcement Officers Investigating the Sexual Exploitation of Children by Acquaintance Molesters*, 4th ed. Arlington, VA: National Center for Missing and Exploited Children, 2001a.

Lanning, K. V. "Child Molesters and Cyber Pedophiles—A Behavioral Perspective," in *Practical Aspects of Rape Investigation: A Multidisciplinary Approach*, 3rd ed., R. R. Hazelwood and A. W. Burgess, eds., 199–232. Boca Raton, FL: CRC Press, 2001b.

Levine, S. B. "Paraphilias," in *Kaplan & Sadock's Comprehensive Textbook of Psychiatry*, 7th ed., Vol. 1. B. J. Sadock and V. A. Sadock, eds., 1631–1646. New York: Lippincott Williams & Wilkins, 2000.

LoMonte, F. "A Tearful Richard Jewel Lashes Out," *Headlines@ugusta, Augusta Chronicle Online.* (December 11, 1996). http://www.augustachronicle.com/headlines/102996/jewel.html.

McGrath, M. G. "Signature in the Courtroom: Whose Crime Is It Anyway?" *Journal of Behavioral Profiling* 2, no. 2. (December 2001). http://www.profiling.org/journal/subscribers/vol2_no2/jbp_mm_2-2.html.

McGrath, M. G., and E. Casey. "Forensic Psychiatry and the Internet: Practical Perspectives on Sexual Predators and Obsessional Harassers in Cyberspace." *Journal of the American Academy of Psychiatry and the Law* 30 (2002): 81–94.

Meserve, J., and J. Rogers. "Police: Smart's Cousin Might Have Been Target: Authorities Studying Suspect's Manifesto." CNN.com. (March 15, 2003). http://www.cnn.com/2003/US/West/03/14/smart.kidnapping/index.html.

Michaud, S. G., with R. Hazelwood. *The Evil That Men Do: FBI Profiler Roy Hazelwood's Journey into the Minds of Sexual Predators.* New York: St. Martin's Press Paperbacks, 2000.

NAMBLA. "Nambla: Who We Are." (1999). http://www.nambla1.de/welcome.htm.

Prentky, R. A., R. A. Knight, and A. F. S. Lee. "Risk Factors Associated with Recidivism among Extrafamilial Child Molesters." *Journal of Consulting and Clinical Psychology* 65 (1997): 141–149.

Pron, N. *Lethal Marriage: The Unspeakable Crimes of Paul Bernardo and Karla Homolka.* New York: Ballantine Books, 1995.

Risinger, M. D., and J. L. Loop. "Three Card Monte, Monty Hall, *Modus Operandi* and 'Offender Profiling': Some Lessons of Modern Cognitive Science for the Law of Evidence." *Cardozo Law Review* 24, no. 1 (2002): 193–285.

Turvey, B. *Criminal Profiling: An Introduction to Behavioral Evidence Analysis.* London: Academic Press, 1999.

U.S. Customs Service. "U.S. Customs Service, Russian Police Take Down Global Child Pornography Web Site: 4 Arrests, 15 Search Warrants Thus Far in U.S.; 5 Arrests in Russia." Press Release (March 26, 2001). http://usinfo.state.gov/topical/global/ecom/01032602.htm.

# CHAPTER 5

# SOURCES OF DIGITAL EVIDENCE

*A computer itself is, typically, only one piece of physical evidence, but it can be processed to identify thousands of pieces of digital evidence and each piece of digital evidence can be analyzed to identify ownership, location, and timing. The digital evidence can be analyzed to produce similar characteristics as physical evidence. Therefore, the investigation of billions of bytes of digital data is similar to the investigation of a house where an investigator must look at thousands of objects, fibers, and surface areas and use his/her experience to identify potential evidence that should be sent to a lab for analysis. (Carrier and Spafford 2003)*

By recording offenders' activities in more detail, computers and networks can retain a significant amount of incriminating evidence that can be used to apprehend and prosecute criminals, and that can provide a window into their world, giving us a clearer view of how sex offenders operate. This chapter describes different types of computer systems with examples of digital evidence related to child exploitation that they can contain. The variety of computers that exist is evident in even the small sample shown in Figure 5.1.

The Scientific Working Group on Digital Evidence (SWGDE) defines **digital evidence** as *information of probative value stored or transmitted in digital form.* Although probative generally refers to proof in a legal context, a more general meaning can be adopted to include information that is simply useful for investigative purposes (i.e., a lead) but not for proving a matter in court. However, this definition neglects evidence that simply improves our understanding of an offense, perpetrator, or victim. A broader definition of digital evidence that addresses these limitations is *any data stored or transmitted using a computer that support or refute a theory of how an offense occurred or that address critical elements of the offense, such as intent or alibi* (Casey 2004).

*Figure 5.1*

*An office containing computer systems with a variety of computers and peripherals, including external hard drive, flatbed scanner, wireless access point, and network cables*

When investigators consider the many sources of digital evidence, it is useful to categorize computer systems into three groups: open computer systems, embedded computer systems, and communication systems (Henseler 2000). Open computer systems are what most people think of as computers—systems composed of hard drives, keyboards, and monitors such as laptops, desktops, and servers that obey standards. Embedded computer systems include mobile telephones, personal digital assistants (PDAs), smart cards, and even cars and household appliances that contain computers. Communication systems include traditional telephone systems, wireless telecommunication systems, the Internet, and networks in general.

When dealing with computers as a source of evidence, investigators must make a clear distinction between the physical crime scene that contains a computer and the digital crime scene within that computer. Simply treating a computer as one piece of physical evidence is a dangerous oversimplification that belies the amount of evidence that it contains and the resources required to process them. As stated in the opening quote, each computer is a digital crime scene that can contain thousands of pieces of evidence. One set of procedures is required to collect, document, and examine a computer found in a physical crime scene, and another set of procedures is required to collect, document, examine, and analyze pieces of digital evidence within the digital crime scene created by the computer. "The Good Practices Guide for Computer Based Electronic Evidence" is

*Figure 5.2*

*Laptop with a 128 MB USB thumbdrive, a Firewire cable connected to an 80 GB external hard drive, a 128 MB memory card, and an Ethernet network cable*

an excellent set of guidelines for helping first responders process digital crime scenes properly as a source of evidence, including PDAs and mobile telephones (UKACPO 2004). This guide also provides recommendations for related issues such as welfare in the workplace and control of pedophile images.

## 5.1) OPEN COMPUTER SYSTEMS

Although a full description of how computers function is beyond the scope of this text, a basic understanding is needed to handle them as a source of evidence. The basic components of a computer are the central processing unit (CPU), memory, and input/output (I/O) systems.[1] For example, a laptop might have a 2 GHz Celeron processor, 256 MB of random access memory (RAM), a 40 GB internal hard drive, a keyboard and touchpad for input, a display and speakers for output, and various I/O ports to connect peripheral devices such as an external USB thumb drive, memory card, or hard drive, as shown in Figure 5.2. Laptops and personal computers can also have modems and network cards that enable them to access and store data remotely.

The relevance of these technical details to investigating child exploitation may not be immediately clear. These details provide the foundation for understanding how computers store and manipulate data. Consider the simple act of using a missing victim's mobile telephone to call the last number dialed. This action causes changes in the CPU, memory, and I/O systems, potentially obliterating valuable digital evidence. While performing this action may be necessary in a particular case, understanding the ramifications and carefully weighing the costs against the benefits is also critical.

It is important to know that open computer systems have a battery-powered Complementary Metal Oxide Silicon (CMOS) RAM chip that retains the date, time, hard drive parameters, and other configuration details while the computer's main power is off. In some cases, CMOS data have been lost because investigators did not document them before putting a computer into storage,

---

[1] Information travels between these components via the data bus, address bus, and control lines.

*Figure 5.3*

*A hard drive label listing 903 cylinders, 8 heads, 46 sectors per track, and a capacity of 170 MB*

making it more difficult to determine whether the clock was accurate and to authenticate the associated digital evidence.

More specific knowledge of a given computer system may also be required to extract digital evidence. For instance, when collecting digital evidence from a computer, investigators may need to interrupt the boot process using a specific function key and change the CMOS settings to ensure that the computer will boot from a floppy diskette rather than the evidentiary hard drive. Similarly, when examining some handheld devices, investigators may need to interrupt the system using a special graffiti symbol to obtain a full copy of its memory contents.

It is also important to understand how data are stored on hard drives and removable media. For instance, a familiarity with cylinders, heads, and sectors (CHS) is needed to verify the capacity of hard drives to ensure that all available evidence has been captured. Figure 5.3 shows a hard drive with 170 MB on the label.[2]

However, when a forensic image of this disk is obtained, it copies only 162.3 MB, as shown in this report generated using EnCase:

[2] Drives larger than 8 GB exceed the maximum possible CHS values. Therefore, it is necessary to obtain the total number of sectors by other methods for comparison. For example, drive manufacturers' Web sites and ATA commands for querying drives directly can provide the total number of sectors.

```
File "C:\case153\gamblor\GAMBLOR.E01" was acquired by
Eoghan Casey at 07/22/02 09:48:52AM. The computer
system clock read: 07/22/02 09:48:52AM.

Evidence acquired under DOS 7.10 using version 3.14f.

File Integrity:
Completely Verified, 0 Errors.
Verification Hash: D91CB4F985E5D2473B99EAB5FB14D97E

Drive Geometry:
Total Size 162.3MB (332,304 sectors)
Cylinders: 903
Heads:     8
Sectors:   46

Partitions:
Code  Type   Start Sector   Total Sectors   Size
06    BIGDOS 0              331936          162.1MB
```

Rather than being alarmed by the possibility that some data on the original drive have been hidden or lost, investigators can simply calculate the capacity as follows: Multiplying 903 cylinders × 8 heads × 46 sectors per track gives 332,304 sectors. Each sector contains 512 bytes, giving a total drive capacity of 170,139,648 bytes or 162.3 MB (170,139,648 ÷ 1024 ÷ 1024).

Knowledge of partitions and file systems is also needed to interpret and recover digital evidence, and to understand how data can be hidden on storage devices. For more information about storage devices, file systems, and computer operation, see Casey (2004).

## 5.1.1) DIGITAL EVIDENCE ON OPEN COMPUTER SYSTEMS

Child exploitation investigations often involve images and videos that were created using a computer or downloaded from the Internet. For instance, a suspect's computer might contain child pornography created using a scanner or a Web camera (a.k.a. Webcam) that can be used to prove that s/he committed an offense. The following list, created using the hash utility from Maresware, shows properties of several digital video files:

```
H:\ >hash -p C:\MYDOCU~1\MYPICT~1\QUICKCAM\ALBUM\VIDEOS
Program started Tue Feb 03 17:07:28 2004 Local Time: (timezone not set)

—-- BEGIN PROCESSING MD5 ——-
C:\MYDOCU~1\MYPICT~1\QUICKCAM\ALBUM\VIDEOS\JAKE01~1.AVI
  C87A4452E263C09D462B4BA8823F8535  88320160  11/09/2003  16:31w GMT
C:\MYDOCU~1\MYPICT~1\QUICKCAM\ALBUM\VIDEOS\JAKE03~2.AVI
  2B82CD602E9EFBC7BB8A3B166D46DC29  67271552  11/09/2003  17:41w GMT
```

```
C:\MYDOCU~1\MYPICT~1\QUICKCAM\ALBUM\VIDEOS\JAKE02~3.AVI
  760B22278E052804A82E0B823C297D1B  48025563  11/09/2003  18:26w  GMT
 --- END PROCESSING MD5 ---

Processed 3 files, 203,617,275 bytes: Elapsed: 0 hrs. 0 mins. 2 secs.
```

The location of these files on the disk suggests that they were created using the Logitech Webcam and the Quickcam application on that computer. These videos show the suspect sexually assaulting a child, and witnesses confirm that the suspect was alone with the child at the time these files were created. The MD5 hash values of these files could be used to search a database of videos from other cases to determine whether the suspect distributed them to others. Also, Webcams enable offenders to broadcast incidents of abuse on the Internet in real time.

Evidence relating to child exploitation on open computer systems comes in many other forms. Commercial child exploitation operations may have financial information in spreadsheets on their computers. Information about crimes, victims, or cohorts may exist in an offender's computer diary, buddy list, or address book. Additionally, an offender's communcations via e-mail and online chat can lead investigators to additional evidence.

Also, traces of online activities can help investigators gain a more complete picture of a suspect's behavior and interests. Take the view of a Web browser history file in Figure 5.4 as an example.

These Web browser history entries indicate that the user is interested in CUseeMe, an online videochat network suggesting that this application may have been used to communicate with others on the Internet. Similar history

| Type | Last Visited [GMT] | Secondary Date | Internet History |
|---|---|---|---|
| URL | 24/01/2000 03:35:36 Mon | 24/01/2000 03:35:36 Mon | http://www.cuseemeworld.com/index.asp |
| URL | 24/01/2000 03:35:37 Mon | 24/01/2000 03:35:37 Mon | http://www.cuseemeworld.com/graphics/buttons/login.gif |
| URL | 24/01/2000 03:35:37 Mon | 24/01/2000 03:35:37 Mon | http://www.cuseemeworld.com/graphics/buttons/login.gif |
| URL | 24/01/2000 03:35:38 Mon | 24/01/2000 03:35:38 Mon | http://www.cuseemeworld.com/graphics/logos/world-logo400x208.JPG |
| URL | 24/01/2000 03:35:38 Mon | 24/01/2000 03:35:38 Mon | http://www.cuseemeworld.com/graphics/logos/world-logo400x208.JPG |
| URL | 24/01/2000 03:35:39 Mon | 24/01/2000 03:35:39 Mon | http://www.cuseemeworld.com/graphics/logos/cu-web-logo226x42.JPG |
| URL | 24/01/2000 03:35:40 Mon | 24/01/2000 03:35:40 Mon | http://www.cuseemeworld.com/graphics/logos/WPCo_Logo_k.gif |
| URL | 24/01/2000 03:36:03 Mon | 24/01/2000 03:36:03 Mon | http://www.cuseemeworld.com/graphics/logos/CU-Web_Logo170x31.gif |
| URL | 24/01/2000 03:36:04 Mon | 24/01/2000 03:36:04 Mon | http://www.cuseemeworld.com/graphics/headers/welcome-header.gif |
| URL | 24/01/2000 03:36:04 Mon | 24/01/2000 03:36:04 Mon | http://www.cuseemeworld.com/graphics/headers/welcome-header.gif |
| URL | 24/01/2000 03:36:12 Mon | 24/01/2000 03:36:12 Mon | http://www.cuseemeworld.com/graphics/buttons/logout.gif |
| URL | 24/01/2000 03:36:22 Mon | 24/01/2000 03:36:22 Mon | http://www.cuseemeworld.com/graphics/logos/CU-Web_Logo.jpg |
| URL | 24/01/2000 03:36:25 Mon | 24/01/2000 03:36:03 Mon | http://www.cuseemeworld.com/graphics/banners/cu-pro-text-chat.gif |
| URL | 24/01/2000 03:37:03 Mon | 24/01/2000 03:37:03 Mon | http://www.cuseemeworld.com/cuweb/quick-start.asp |
| URL | 24/01/2000 03:37:05 Mon | 24/01/2000 03:37:05 Mon | http://www.cuseemeworld.com/graphics/screenshots/quick-start-screen.gif |
| URL | 24/01/2000 03:37:25 Mon | 24/01/2000 03:36:06 Mon | http://www.cuseemeworld.com/graphics/2remove/pixel_red.gif |
| URL | 24/01/2000 03:37:25 Mon | 24/01/2000 03:36:06 Mon | http://www.cuseemeworld.com/graphics/2remove/pixel_red.gif |
| URL | 24/01/2000 03:37:25 Mon | 24/01/2000 03:36:24 Mon | http://www.cuseemeworld.com/graphics/buttons/go-to-cuweb-white.gif |
| URL | 24/01/2000 03:37:39 Mon | 24/01/2000 03:36:21 Mon | http://www.cuseemeworld.com/graphics/banners/college.gif |
| URL | 24/01/2000 03:37:47 Mon | 24/01/2000 03:37:03 Mon | http://www.cuseemeworld.com/graphics/buttons/go-to-cuweb-black.gif |

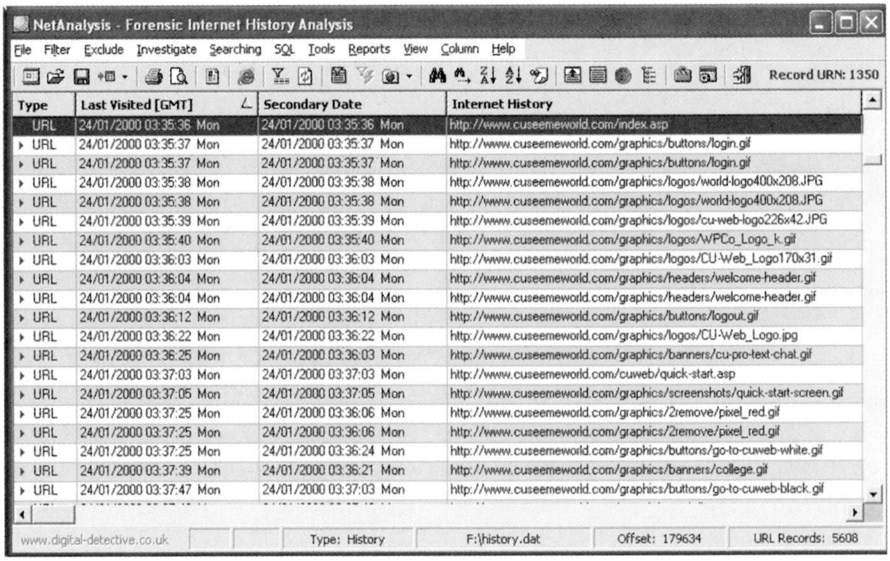

*Figure 5.4*
*Web browser history viewed using NetAnalysis (www.digitaldetective.co.uk)*

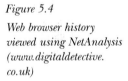

records are created when images or video are downloaded from the Internet. Other applications used to obtain or exchange pornography on the Internet create their own traces on a computer. When forensic examiners encounter new applications, some testing may be required to gain an understanding of what traces are left behind.

Online communications with cohorts and victims can leave traces on personal computers such as the following AOL chat logs showing interactions between a victim and offender:

```
CWhite8147:  we will go shopping and buy u lot of teddys and panties
CWhite8147:  to play in
SwetSara14:    oh i like that
CWhite8147:  then i will video u modeling them for me
SwetSara14:    ok
CWhite8147:  can u take new stuff like that home with u
CWhite8147:  if not i will keep them and bring them back and forth with me
SwetSara14:    yeh i think i can
CWhite8147:  ok cool
CWhite8147:  cant wait to spend some time with u
 .    .   .
CWhite8147:    i almost bought u the neatest neckless today
CWhite8147:    do u like indian jewerlery
SwetSara14:    yeh thats what email said thanks for thinking of me
CWhite8147:    i have never stopped thinking of u
SwetSara14:    i lik that makes me fel specail
CWhite8147:    u are very to me
SwetSara14:    very what
CWhite8147:    SPECIAL !!!!
SwetSara14:    :)
SwetSara14:    ok
CWhite8147:    YOUR MY LITTLE GIRL
SwetSara14:    u are my daddy
CWhite8147:    ummmm i like that
CWhite8147:    cant wait to see u in my corvette
SwetSara14:    cant wait to rid in it
SwetSara14:    ride oops
CWhite8147:    if we can find a place to do it i want to take so pics of u and it
SwetSara14:    k
CWhite8147:    topless and naked
SwetSara14:    k
CWhite8147:    cool
SwetSara14:    oh daddy i gotta go mom is yeling at me to do hw
CWhite8147:    ok baby i love u be good and hope iu talk to u tomorrow
SwetSara14:    k kiss
CWhite8147:    email me
SwetSara14:    k
SwetSara14:    byebye
```

In addition to exhibiting grooming behavior, this chat log indicates that the victim and offender exchanged e-mail that should be sought as another source of evidence. Similar logs can often be found when other chat programs are used.

In essence, every action on a computer, including creating, downloading, viewing, printing, encrypting, and deleting files, can leave traces on a disk and in the Registry. These and other useful artifacts are covered in later chapters and in Casey (2002, 2004).

### 5.1.2) LOG FILES

Some computers also maintain logs such as NT Event Logs and UNIX logon records that can be useful for determining who was using a given computer when it was involved in a crime. The following log entries from a Windows XP computer show that the user account "Jack Smith" was used to log into the computer at the console (Logon Type 2) on October 11 and 13:

```
10/11/2003 10:35:52 528 Jack Smith HOMEPC Successful Logon Logon Type: 2
10/11/2003 16:17:24 551 Jack Smith HOMEPC User initiated logoff
10/13/2003 11:25:19 528 Jack Smith HOMEPC Successful Logon Logon Type: 2
10/13/2003 17:00:44 551 Jack Smith HOMEPC User initiated logoff
```

The following log entries from a Mac OS X computer show that the user account "rsmith" was used to log into the computer remotely on September 29 between 21:13 and 21:28:

```
% last
rsmith  ttyp2  192.168.0.5  Mon Sep 29 21:13 - 21:28 (00:15)
rsmith  console homeunix       Tue Sep 23 16:39 still logged in
reboot  ~                      Tue Sep 23 16:38
```

Although these logs suggest that a particular individual was involved, additional investigative work and corroborating evidence are needed to prove that the owners of these accounts were responsible for the logons and activities during that period.

### 5.1.3) SERVERS

Strictly speaking, a server is any open computer system that provides some service to other computers on a network, called clients.[3] Although any computer can be configured as a server, the focus in this text is on Web, file transfer protocol (FTP), e-mail, and authentication servers. Web and FTP servers can be used to distribute illegal materials, while e-mail can be used for both file sharing and personal communication. Internet Service Providers (ISPs) use authentication servers to verify passwords and record which user account was assigned a given IP address at a specific time period.[4]

In addition to the system logs mentioned in the preceding section, servers generally have their own application logs. These application logs show what was

---

[3] Because computers on a peer-to-peer (P2P) network like KaZaA can function simultaneously as a client and server, they are called *servents*.

[4] As discussed in Chapter 8, ISPs require their subscribers to log onto the Internet with a unique username and password. Most ISPs keep logs of when each subscriber connected to the Internet and what IP addresses he/she was assigned during each period.

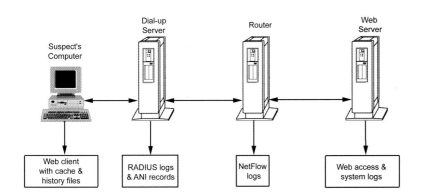

*Figure 5.5*

*Web server (note server logs) being accessed from Web client (note history and cache files)*

accessed, when, and from which IP address. If investigators have seized a Web server containing child pornography, they could use information in the log file to determine who accessed the materials. For instance, the following access log entries show someone accessing illegal images on a Web server:

```
21.218.166.2 - - [15/Sep/2003:17:16:58 -0400] "GET /~rsmith/image1.jpg HTTP/1.0" 404 299
21.218.166.2 - - [15/Sep/2003:17:16:56 -0400] "GET /~rsmith/image01.jpg HTTP/1.0" 200 13946
21.218.166.2 - - [15/Sep/2003:17:19:28 -0400] "GET /~rsmith/image02.jpg HTTP/1.0" 200 35624
```

Investigators could then try to determine who was using the computer with IP address 21.218.166.2 at the time these log entries were created. Each entry in a Web access log has a code that indicates whether the result of the request was successful. The first request in the preceding logs was unsuccessful (code 404) because of a misspelling in the requested file. The second request was successful (code 200), and the last number on the line indicates that the retrieved file was 13,946 bytes in size.

Some individuals who collect child pornography do so at their workplace, storing files on servers that they have access to but that are not directly associated with them. As a result of an international investigation called "Operation Cathedral," a computer technician named Ian Baldock was found to have large amounts of child pornography on his home and work computers. In another case, a professor downloaded child pornography onto a shared UNIX machine in his department.

**CASE EXAMPLE**

Connecticut, 1998: Yale Geology professor Anthony Lasaga admitted to possessing tens of thousands of images of children engaging in sexual acts with adults, animals, and other children. Many of these images were downloaded from the Internet (e.g., Supernews.com) onto a computer in the Geology department and then viewed on Lasaga's desktop computer. A system administrator in the Geology department came across the child pornography on the server in the course of his work. The system administrator observed

> Lasaga accessing the materials on the server from his desktop and reported the incident to law enforcement. Given the severity of the crime and the involvement of several systems, it was necessary to secure and search the entire Geology building and network for related evidence.
>
> Because of his success in attributing the illegal activities to Lasaga, the system administrator was accused by the defense of acting as an agent of law enforcement. Although the system administrator was ultimately exonerated of any wrongdoing, his employers did not provide legal support and he was compelled to hire an attorney to defend himself against the accusations. Notably, Lasaga also admitted to creating a videocassette of a young boy engaging in sexual acts. The tape involved a thirteen-year-old boy whom Lasaga had met through a New Haven child-mentoring program. The tape was shot on the Yale campus, in the professor's Geology classroom and in the Saybrook master's house. (Diskant 2002)

The Internet offers many ways for individuals to store files remotely. Therefore, when examining a suspect's computer, investigators need to look for signs of remote storage, as discussed in Chapters 8 and 11.

## 5.2) EMBEDDED COMPUTER SYSTEMS

Embedded computer systems encompass a wide range of devices that contain the components of a computer. For instance, a mobile telephone might have a 32-bit ARM CPU, 30 MB of RAM, 6 MB of Flash memory, a keypad and digital camera for input, a display and earpiece for output, and various I/O ports (e.g., infrared, Blue Tooth). Permanent storage devices such as memory cards can also be connected to some mobile telephones. Digital evidence relating to child exploitation may be found on embedded computer systems such as digital cameras, personal digital assistants, and mobile telephones. It is important for anyone handling mobile telephones and personal digital assistants as a source of evidence to be aware that data in memory may be lost if a mobile telephone's battery is removed or runs down.

### 5.2.1) DIGITAL CAMERAS

Digital cameras are essentially small computers with a CPU, memory, and I/O systems. Digital cameras make it very easy for offenders to create child pornography and distribute it on the Internet. Some cameras are even sold with equipment to facilitate upload to the Internet.

Although memory cards are the primary source of digital evidence in digital cameras, containing photographs or motion segments, it is important to gather additional details from the camera such as the date and time of the system clock. If the system clock is incorrect, all photographs that the camera stores on memory cards will have incorrect date-time stamps that must be adjusted to correct for the error. Metadata relating to files on memory cards can be useful for reconstructing activities on the system. For instance, the creation and modification times of files can be used to focus a forensic examination of storage media and create a timeline of activities on the system. The following example shows a file listing of a memory card from a digital camera. Each line shows the file name; MD5 hash; size; and created, last written, and last accessed date-time stamps, respectively (using the hash utility from Maresware).

```
C:\>g:\mares\hash -A -p E:\

Program started Tue Sep 30 18:24:11 2003 GMT, 14:24 Eastern Standard Time (-5*)

 —– BEGIN PROCESSING MD5 —–
E:\DCIM\100K3900\DCP_0005.JPG    190D864C9360B85D42B519D4B3A0F0B7    231842
   01/01/1980 00:00:00c 04/05/2003 15:29:18w 01/01/1980 00:00:00a EST . . . . .
E:\DCIM\100K3900\DCP_0007.JPG    8F3E034D4FEF43DB6312E8CFE09F8E70    190300
   01/01/1980 00:00:00c 04/05/2003 17:05:00w 01/01/1980 00:00:00a EST . . . . .
E:\DCIM\100K3900\DCP_0008.JPG    8276B9C099837F1FD74BC4DA1735F8BB    352233
   01/01/1980 00:00:00c 04/05/2003 20:40:02w 01/01/1980 00:00:00a EST . . . . .
E:\DCIM\100K3900\DCP_0009.JPG    75EA61583543E055B6565EB67405AD0E    345653
   01/01/1980 00:00:00c 04/05/2003 20:41:12w 01/01/1980 00:00:00a EST . . . . .
E:\DCIM\100K3900\DCP_0010.JPG    A63E08AD009A17C2A184133202CD867D    281484
   01/01/1980 00:00:00c 04/05/2003 20:42:50w 01/01/1980 00:00:00a EST . . . . .
E:\DCIM\100K3900\DCP_0011.JPG    977814A005B4F47C0A01310465886BD9    220434
   01/01/1980 00:00:00c 04/05/2003 20:45:04w 04/09/2003 00:00:00a EST . . . . .
E:\DCIM\100K3900\DCP_0192.JPG    1EEE7CADC5335B6F0677A0892FD2C739    167111
   01/01/1980 00:00:00c 04/08/2003 22:08:32w 04/09/2003 00:00:00a EST . . . . .
E:\DCIM\100K3900\DCP_0193.JPG    A55E70EA3DC55573EA233CF8923ADAB2    116473
   01/01/1980 00:00:00c 04/08/2003 22:10:44w 04/09/2003 00:00:00a EST . . . . .
 —– END PROCESSING MD5 —–

Processed 8 files, 1,905,530 bytes: Elapsed: 0 hrs. 0 mins. 2 secs.
```

Note that most of the created and last accessed times are 01/01/1980. This date is actually the MS-DOS epoch (start of time) and indicates that these date-time stamps were not updated in the file system on the Flash Card when the photographs were taken. Based on the last written times, one set of photographs was taken on April 5, 2003, and another on April 8, 2003. The last three files in this list were accessed on April 9, 2003, suggesting that they were viewed or copied from the disk on this date.[5] A search of other available storage media for file system and Internet activities on April 9, 2003, might reveal more about what the individual was doing on that day.

---

[5] FAT file systems do not record the last accessed time, only the last accessed date.

### *5.2.2) PERSONAL DIGITAL ASSISTANTS AND MOBILE TELEPHONES*

There are an increasing number and variety of handheld computing devices like the Blackberry and iPAQ Pocket PC. Additionally, the distinction between personal digital assistants and mobile telephones is being blurred as more devices combine aspects of both. These embedded computer systems have calendar, memo, and address applications, and some devices can store data on removable memory cards and can take digital photographs.

In addition to voice conversations, mobile telephones enable person-to-person communication using text, images, and video. Newer mobile telephones can also access the Internet at relatively high speeds, enabling the efficient exchange of larger amounts of data. Offenders use mobile telephones to communicate with victims, create and exchange child pornography, and access Internet services. In 2002, Japan's National Police Agency reported a dramatic increase in the number of crimes, including murder and rape, linked to Internet dating sites and that, in almost all cases, Internet-enabled mobile phones were used to access the dating sites (The Age 2002).

> As part of an international investigation called "Operation Ore," Scottish police found that several suspects had child pornography on their mobile telephones. Some of the images had been downloaded from the Internet and others had apparently been created using the digital cameras embedded in the telephones. (Silvester 2003)

These devices can contain various kinds of digital data that are useful in child exploitation investigations including images, color video clips, and communication remnants. Mobile telephones can store numbers indicating who an offender or victim communicated with, providing investigative leads. Keep in mind that the telecommunication system that the mobile telephone connects to may have related evidence such as numbers called and the place where the device was located at certain times.

Notably, when executing a search warrant, investigators should look for cradles and cables for connecting handheld devices to a computer. However, investigators must keep in mind that these devices can transmit data using infrared or radio (Bluetooth), and the system owner may not use a cable or cradle.

Many other kinds of embedded systems are available such as watches with password-protected 128MB flash memory and a USB connection for connecting the watch to a computer and transferring data between them (www.laks.com). Some watches also have scheduling features that contain information relating to rendezvous with victims. Answering machines with voice messages, caller ID, deleted messages, and last number called may be relevant to the investigation. Although it is not possible to be familiar with every kind of embedded system, it is important to keep them in mind when searching for sources of digital evidence. Also, digital evidence examiners need to understand how data are stored in these devices to enable them to recover deleted and hidden data. An overview of evidence on handheld devices is provided in Casey (2004). A more in-depth treatment of processing evidence on embedded systems and associated tools only available to law enforcement is provided in van der Knijff (2002).

## 5.3) COMMUNICATION SYSTEMS

As was noted in previous sections, open and embedded computer systems are often connected to communication systems like the Internet and wireless telephone networks. Until recently, it was sufficient to look at individual computers as isolated objects containing digital evidence. Computing was disk-centered—collecting a computer and several disks would assure collection of all relevant digital evidence. Today, however, computing has become network-centered as more people rely on e-mail, e-commerce, and other network resources. It is no longer adequate to think about computers in isolation since many of them are connected together using various network technologies. Digital evidence examiners must become skilled at following the cybertrail to find related digital evidence on the public Internet, private networks, and other commercial systems. An understanding of the technology involved will enable digital evidence examiners to recognize, collect, preserve, and analyze evidence related to crimes involving networks.

### 5.3.1) INTERNET

Although there are unquestionably hotbeds of illegal activity on the Internet, any service can be used to facilitate child exploitation. Offenders lure children and exchange child pornography via e-mail, instant messaging programs, peer-to-peer file-sharing networks, Internet Relay Chat (IRC), and many other Internet services. When investigating illegal activities on the Internet, investigators must realize the very real and direct link between people and the online activities that involve them. Doing so is important both because the victims suffer very real and direct harm and because investigators will be most effective if they can combine information from the Internet and physical world.

**CASE EXAMPLE**

In 1996, a six-year-old girl in Greenfield, California, reported that she had been sexually abused at a slumber party by a friend's father, Ronald Riva. At Riva's home, investigators found computer equipment that one ten-year-old girl at the party said had been used to record her as she posed for Riva and a friend of his, Melton Myers (Golden 1996). This led investigators to an international group called the Orchid Club that used Internet Relay Chat to exchange child pornography. This investigation resulted in the discovery of a chat channel called "#w0nderland" that was also devoted to the distribution of child pornography. According to evidence obtained by British authorities during and following the arrest of Ian Baldock, a Briton who belonged to both the Orchid Club and #w0nderland, membership in the latter required the possession of 10,000 images of pre-teen children engaging in explicit sexual activity and the capacity to store these images on a server accessible to other members for electronic transfer via the popular file transfer protocol (FTP). Admission to #w0nderland required acceptance by a "membership committee." Only after admission would an individual be told of the channel's secret Internet address. Authorities also found on Baldock's computer equipment approximately 42,000 computer images of child pornography. A forensic examination of Baldock's computer revealed the existence of other channels similar to #w0nderland, including one titled "#ourplace".[6]

Information relating to suspects in the United States was provided to the Customs Service, and it was determined that one screen name, "sassybabe," had been used to access #w0nderland on April 1, 1998, at 7:14 p.m. Information identifying the account associated with the screen name "sassybabe" showed that the individual using that screen name also had used the screen name "sassywork" and had connected to the Internet using a modem-based service provided by IBM Global Network Services (IBM). According to IBM records, at the time the screen name "sassybabe" was used to access the #w0nderland channel, it was associated with an Internet access account registered to Grant. IBM's records indicated that Grant resided in Skowhegan, Maine, but a search of automobile and telephone records revealed that Grant had moved to South Portland, Maine, in or around August 1998. Grant's IBM Internet account remained active, and was used, through the end of that month.

During August 1998, Grant also maintained a Road Runner Pro (Road Runner) Internet account with Time Warner Cable. Road Runner is a cable-based Internet service through which an individual can maintain an "always-

---

[6] *U.S. v. Grant* (2000) District Court, Maine, Case Number 99-2332.

on," high-speed Internet connection. Road Runner records revealed that Grant's account was used as an FTP server—the type of file-transfer server required for #w0nderland membership.

On August 28, 1998, in relation to another child pornography investigation, the United States District Court of Maine approved a Customs Service application to tap a telephone line not associated with Grant. On August 30, between 9:15 p.m. and 11:30 p.m., Agent Booke observed the targeted individual logging into the secret #ourplace channel. There, Booke was able to observe information identifying other #ourplace users who were, at the same time, also logged into the channel. These users included an individual with the screen name "sassy!sassygal14@slip166-72-215-109.va.us.ibm.net." The "slip166-72-215-109.va.us.ibm.net" portion of the user's identity constitutes a "port address." This particular port address was, at the time, assigned to Grant's IBM account. Contemporaneous Customs Service surveillance revealed that Grant's car and his wife's were both parked at their residence in Portland during the evening of August 30.

To investigate child exploitation on the Internet, investigators need to be familiar with the various services. They cannot simply rely on Google when searching for information on the Internet but must become conversant with Web search engine syntax and should have working knowledge of various online databases (a.k.a. the invisible Web). Investigators must also be able to read e-mail and Usenet headers and to obtain information from online chat networks like IRC. Additionally, as the preceding case example demonstrates, to attribute illegal online activities to an individual, investigators need to understand how the Internet works and where to find evidence that establishes the continuity of offense. Sources of digital evidence on networks include authentication logs like Grant's IBM dial-up logs, network monitoring logs such as those used to determine that Grant's Road Runner account was used as an FTP server, and the contents of network traffic as observed by Agent Booke. An understanding of how to collect and interpret these sources of evidence is necessary to track down unknown offenders via networks and attribute criminal activity to them.

In addition to attributing criminal activity to an individual, evidence on the Internet can be useful for locating a missing victim. In the past, offenders have persuaded victims to destroy evidence by removing and disposing of their hard drives before leaving their home to meet the offenders. In such cases when investigators do not have access to a key computer, it is necessary to reconstruct events using only evidence on networks. Sources of evidence on the Internet that may reveal whom the victim was communicating with include e-mail and log files on the victim's Internet Service Provider's systems and backup tapes.

Additionally, mobile telephone records may help determine whom the victim was communicating with and where s/he went.

### 5.3.2) SMALL OFFICE HOME OFFICE NETWORKS

With the growth of broadband Internet access and inexpensive, user-friendly cable/DSL routers, more people are setting up networks within their homes. These networks are generally called Small Office Home Office (SOHO) networks. Therefore, when searching a suspect's home for potential sources of evidence, investigators need to consider that computers may be located in adjacent rooms or buildings. While investigating a homicide, one investigator found child pornography in the adjacent house on a computer that was connected to the suspect's home network (McLean 2002). Wireless networks make home searches even more challenging because it is not possible to simply follow network cables to locate computers. For instance, in Figure 5.1 notice the wireless router and the laptop with a wireless network card. In this type of environment, computers used to store incriminating evidence can be hidden from view but still be accessible over the wireless network.

In addition to the Internet and home networks, digital evidence may exist on computers in a suspect's workplace. Corporate networks can be a richer source of information than the public Internet because they contain a higher concentration of information about the individuals who use them. Unlike the Internet, all of the potential sources of digital evidence on corporate networks are located in a contained area and are under the control of a single entity. Also, private organizations often configure their networks to monitor individuals' activities more than the public Internet. E-mail and Web browsing activities may be inspected and, in some organizations, all traffic entering and leaving the corporate network may be monitored, resulting in a substantial amount of information.[7]

Capturing network traffic is comparable to making a bitstream copy of a hard drive: A sniffer can capture every byte transmitted on the network. As with any bitstream copy, files and other useful digital evidence can be extracted from network traffic using specialized tools. For example, digital evidence examiners can use a sniffer to monitor a child pornographer on a network and recover images, e-mail attachments, IRC communications with cohorts, and anything else the offenders transmitted on the network.

---

[7] Because e-mail and network traffic contain so much personal data, they are protected by a number of privacy laws that must be taken into consideration when investigating crimes involving networks.

# Chaosreader Image Report
Created at: Wed Feb 18 13:01:27 2004, Type: tcpdump

## Images

*Figure 5.6*

*Images recovered from network traffic*

> **Sniffers** are programs that can capture all data transmitted on a network segment, saving these data to file for later examination.

When investigators are dealing with networks, they will find it useful to have an understanding of two fundamental components: switches and routers. Basically, a switch connects multiple computers together and a router connects multiple networks together. The home network in Figure 5.1 provides a simple example of these devices. The hub connects the Windows and Sun computers together on a private network, and the wireless router connects all of these computers to the Internet via the ADSL modem.

To appreciate how knowledge of network devices can be useful in an investigation, consider a scenario based on a case in which the defendant was distributing child pornography from a Web server in his home. The server in this scenario used a dynamic domain name service (DDNS) to associate the name "family-fun.dyndns.org" with whichever IP address was assigned to the suspect's home network at any given time (Figure 5.7). This configuration created an additional solid link between the suspect and the illegal online activities that led investigators to his home.

Although networks create challenges from an evidence-processing standpoint, they can be very useful in an investigation. While the distributed nature of networks makes it difficult to isolate a crime scene, this distribution also makes it difficult for offenders to destroy all digital evidence relating to their crimes.

*Figure 5.7*

*Netgear router configured to update a dynamic DNS database to enable others to find the suspect's Web server more easily*

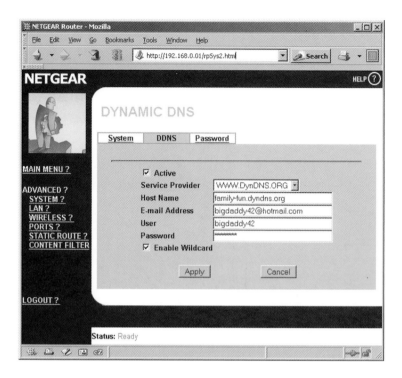

### 5.3.3) WIRELESS NETWORKS

Child exploitation can involve wireless networks in a variety of ways, including exchange of child pornography and communication between offenders and victims.

> Police in Ireland launched an investigation into the circulation of a pornographic image of a schoolgirl by hundreds of students using camera phones in Cork, Limerick, and Kerry. Investigators made an effort to identify the girl and to prevent further distribution of the image, which was illegal under the Child Trafficking and Pornography Act. (RTE 2004)

In addition, wireless networks enable mobile telephones to access the Internet and permit computers to connect to the Internet using a cellular telephone in much the same way as a modem is used to connect using telephone wires. As more offenders use wireless devices to exchange child pornography and communicate with victims or cohorts, it is important for investigators to look for evidence on wireless networks.

Wireless telecommunication systems maintain logs that can be useful in an investigation, such as numbers called from a particular device, the start and end times of each call, and the approximate locations of the telephone when calls were initiated and ended. This location information is based on the radio tower (a.k.a. base station) through which the mobile device was connected. These records can be useful for retracing the movements of offenders or missing victims and determining who they were communicating with. Additionally, investigators may be able to obtain related voice mail, text messages, and photographs or videos from the telecommunication provider.

## 5.4) PERIPHERAL DEVICES

Child pornographers often use devices for digitizing and reproducing photographs. An offender may print photographs downloaded from the Internet to have them in tangible form. Another offender may convert a traditional photograph to digital form using a scanner to make it available to others on the Internet. In either case, a trail of digital evidence will be created. Paper versions of images printed by offenders can be useful, and some printers and photocopiers have internal storage that can contain copies of data printed in the past. Printing a file also creates artifacts such as printer spool files that may be recovered from the computer. Print servers also contain usage logs with times and sometimes file names. Additionally, scanners may create distinctive characteristics when digitizing images that can be used to link the device with the files it created.

## REFERENCES

Carrier, B., and E. H. Spafford. "Getting Digital with the Digital Investigation Process," *International Journal of Digital Evidence* 2 (2003):2.

Casey, E. *Handbook of Computer Crime Investigation.* London: Academic Press 2002.

Casey, E. *Digital Evidence and Computer Crime: Forensic Science, Computers and the Internet*, 2nd ed. London: Academic Press, 2004.

Diskant, T. "After Sentencing, Lasaga, Yale Face Civil Suit." *Yale Herald.* (February 22, 2002). http://www.yaleherald.com/article.php?Article=359.

Golden, T. "16 Indicted on Charges of Internet Pornography." *The New York Times* (July 17, 1996).

Henseler, J. "Computer Crime and Computer Forensics," in *Encyclopedia of Forensic Sciences.* Jay Siegel, ed., London: Academic Press, 2000.

McLean, J. "Homicide and Child Pornography" in *Handbook of Computer Crime Investigation.* Eoghan Casey, ed., London: Academic Press, 2002.

RTE. "Garda Probe into Camera Phone Pornography." (January 22, 2004). http://www.rte.ie/news/2004/0122/pornography.html.

Silvester, N. "Perverts Swap Sick Images of Kids on Mobiles." *Sunday Mail.* (March 27, 2003).

The Age. "Japanese Police to Regulate Internet Dating Services." (December 26, 2002). http://www.theage.com.au/articles/2002/12/26/1040511126218.html.

United Kingdom Association of Chief Police Officers. "The Good Practices Guide for Computer Based Electronic Evidence." National High-Tech Crime Unit. (2003). http://www.nhtcu.org/ACPO Guide v3.0.pdf.

van der Knijff, R. *Embedded System Analysis: Handbook of Computer Crime Investigation* (Chapter 11 Embedded System Analysis). Eoghan Casey, ed., London: Academic Press, 2002.

Wearden, G. "Insecure Networks Exploited by Paedophiles: Could Your Servers Be Hosting Porn?" *ZDNet UK* (October 12, 2002). http://www.silicon.com/news/500009/1/1036746.html.

# SECTION II

## INVESTIGATING INTERNET CHILD EXPLOITATION

# CHAPTER 6

# UNDERCOVER OPERATIONS

*The structure of peer to peer networking presents opportunities to Law Enforcement for proactive investigation. A moment's consideration of the fact that a direct peer to peer connection is established when a download is ordered will be sufficient to allow anyone with a basic knowledge of TCP/IP to work out how this might be done. This results, of course, in prosecutions not for the mere possession of abusive images but rather for distribution; a much more serious offence. (Fellows 2004)*

Online undercover investigations can be used in child exploitation investigations to protect investigators and reduce the risk of alerting criminals when they are under active investigation. Investigators may pose as children or as pedophiles to gather evidence in a case. This chapter provides guidelines for developing undercover identities and conducting undercover investigations, including soliciting personal details to assist in identification and documenting a predisposition of a suspect to avoid entrapment. Considerations for collecting evidence remotely prior to drafting a warrant application are also discussed.

## 6.1) SELF-PROTECTION

It is important for investigators to become familiar with online anonymity to protect themselves and to understand how criminals use anonymity to avoid detection. In addition to concealing obvious personal information such as name, address, and telephone number, some offenders use IP addresses that cannot be linked to them. In their book *Investigating Computer Crime*, Clark and Diliberto demonstrate the dangers of online investigations by outlining the problems they encountered during one online child exploitation investigation:

1. *Telephone death threats*
2. *Computer (BBS) threats*
3. *Harassing phone calls (hundreds)*

4. *Five Internal Affairs complaints*
5. *Complaints to district attorney, state attorney general, and FBI*
6. *Surveillance of officer*
7. *Videotaping of officer off duty (of officer giving presentation in church on subject of "dangers of unsupervised use of computers by juveniles")*
8. *Video copied and sent to militant groups*
9. *Multi-million dollar civil suits filed*
10. *Tremendous media exposure initiated by suspects*
11. *Hate mail posted on Internet resulting in many phone calls*
12. *Investigator's plane tickets canceled by computer*
13. *Extensive files made on investigators and witnesses, including the above computerized information: name, address, spouse, date of birth, physical, civil suits, vehicle description, and license number*
14. *Above information posted on BBS*
15. *Witnesses' houses put up for sale and the bill for advertising sent to witnesses' home addresses by suspects*
16. *Witnesses received deliveries of products not ordered, with threatening notes inside*
17. *Hundreds of people receiving personal invitation to a witness's home for a barbeque (put out by computer)*

*And much more! After eighteen months of such incidents, when all was said and done, the suspect was sentenced to six years, four months in state prison. All the complaints against the investigator were determined to be unfounded, and the investigator was exonerated of any wrongdoing.*

Simply conducting research to gather intelligence online most likely will not open an investigator to these types of attacks. However, the preceding testimonial highlights the imperative that when conducting an investigation involving Internet use and technically savvy targets, investigators must follow proper, predetermined protocol. This chapter discusses undercover best practices in more detail and, in addition to following applicable jurisdictional policies, district attorneys should be consulted prior to conducting online undercover investigations.

To protect yourself during online undercover investigations, defend yourself legally, professionally, and personally. Develop a rough scenario identifying how you intend to proceed, discuss it with your legal counsel, and ask for his or her advice on the entrapment issues. Also, make sure that you have the support of your superiors and/or local law enforcement. To protect yourself personally, never give out personal information. As noted previously, the suspect might target you after the arrest. Develop a full persona but try to make sure that you do not accidentally use an actual person's identity. Also develop a backup identity or two in case the primary identity fails.

Prepare a biography. If the suspect asks you personal questions (e.g., age, birthday, address, phone number), you must be prepared with a consistent answer. You do not want to hesitate, and you do not want to tell the suspect that you are fifteen and then say that your birthday is in 1984. Similarly, make sure that you have notes of all the information that you gave before—you don't want to contradict yourself. Write down these biographical details and/or memorize them. What are you going to do if the suspect asks you for a photo? Are you going to say, "I don't have one"?

Your persona must be realistic. If you are impersonating a thirteen-year-old girl, express age-appropriate concerns (e.g., self-image, parents) and express age-appropriate interests (e.g., music, activities). Does your persona have a beeper or a cellular phone? You might even consider putting information on the Internet to add depth to your persona (Usenet posts, Web pages, etc.). In the United States, the Internet Crimes Against Children Task Forces offer guidelines for conducting undercover operations. The guidelines provide an excellent resource for undercover investigators. Also, the National Center for Missing and Exploited Children sponsors training in online undercover operations. It is strongly recommended that you attend hands-on training prior to embarking on your own undercover online investigation.

## 6.2) USING PERSONAL EQUIPMENT

It is strongly recommended that you do not use your own personal equipment to conduct undercover operations. Everything you do during the course of an investigation is ultimately discoverable, to some extent, later during the prosecution of a suspect. If you use the same computer that you use for undercover operations to also keep track of your personal finances, send personal e-mail, do research, and perhaps view pornography, what will you do when the defense moves for discovery of the contents of *your* computer? What if child pornography is found on your personal home computer, or there are other cases on the computer? The best practice is to avoid any appearance of impropriety.

Not all police departments or law enforcement authorities have the resources to devote to undercover operations. Many organizations purport to take on the "watchdog" function. The practices of volunteers who troll the Internet back alleys collecting evidence of wrongdoing are not held to the same scrutiny that the courts will hold law enforcement officers to, unless the volunteers are acting as the agents of law enforcement.

Besides not having to involve your personal computing behavior in a criminal case against someone else, a major benefit of using a department-owned computer at a secure location is that you ensure limited access and chain of custody of the evidence. Remember, all of your online communications, all of the logs and documentation, are evidence, and everything must be accounted for. If you use your personal equipment and you transport it back and forth to and from work, and your family, friends, coworkers, and others have access to the equipment, your chain of custody is affected. It is one thing to build a case good enough to establish probable cause to arrest a subject for a crime; it's another thing to ensure that you'll be able to give the prosecution enough evidence to convict the suspect.

## 6.3) SETTING UP INTERNET AND TELEPHONE CONNECTIONS

If the suspect wants to call you during the undercover investigation, do not give your home phone number. Use a safe number that the suspect cannot track back to you, your family, or your friends. Also, do not use a phone number that might alert the suspect to the fact that you are with law enforcement. Follow applicable procedures for setting up a "hello" line, like those used to communicate with informants. Ensure that the telephone service is not registered to the law enforcement agency, but to your undercover name and address. For officer safety, it is best to keep the number of people who know about the existence of the accounts to a bare minimum. Although you might be tempted to try to obtain free accounts for law enforcement use or to try to obtain a law enforcement or government discount, it is best practice and most protective of officer safety to keep accounts registered to undercover names and to keep the information confidential.

Remember that the suspect can search the Web for addresses, names, and phone numbers, so you should not use the address of a police station or local prosecutor's office—this could be a dead giveaway. In the case of child exploitation investigations, do not put a child on the line. Instead, for instance, have ready an adult female who sounds young or use a suitable recorded message on an answer machine. Devices capable of altering adult voices to sound younger are readily available for law enforcement to purchase.

The same goes for your Internet connection: Make sure the suspect can't determine who you are through your ISP (you probably have already considered this aspect). If you must use personal accounts, specifically ask your ISP not to disclose any information about you to anyone.

Arrange untraceable payment methods (e.g., undercover credit cards, bank accounts, and money orders), telephone lines (block caller ID), and mailing addresses (e.g., post office box). Keep in mind that, to be realistic, child personas should be paid for by their (fictitious) parents.

Finally, verify that no personal information is disclosed via your online undercover identity by visiting sites that attempt to acquire personal information (e.g., privacy.net).

## 6.4) USING ONLINE UNDERCOVER IDENTITIES

Although undercover investigations can be costly and time consuming, they are useful if all other options are exhausted—for example, when anonymity is a barrier protecting the offender's identity or when it is necessary to confirm a report or link an individual to online activity.

Use a dedicated computer configured with the undercover identity and capable of logging all activities for evidentiary purposes (e.g., clients with logging capabilities, screen capture software). When using a single computer to operate several undercover identities, consider using separate removable hard drives to avoid transfer of evidence and identities.

You can also utilize the methods discussed in Chapter 8 to protect your actual identity such as proxies and other anonymous services. Beware of disclosing information via file exchanges (e.g., Word documents containing registration information for investigating agency) and via active Web/e-mail content (e.g., Java, ActiveX). Java applets and ActiveX components run on the undercover PC and may circumvent an anonymous proxy and disclose your actual IP address and other information that could undermine your undercover identity. Consider configuring your Web browser and e-mail client to deny Java, ActiveX, and other active content. Additionally, register all software on the machine using the undercover identity in case this data leaks out.

## 6.5) CONDUCTING AN ONLINE INVESTIGATION

If you are going to engage the suspect in online chat to gather additional evidence, simulate the sting beforehand to make sure that your chat logging and other evidence collection mechanisms are functioning properly. Make sure that your chat client is naming log files in a useful way (e.g., with the name of the chat session and/or the date). If your client software names the log files in a generic way, consider using a different chat client or making an extra effort to demonstrate that the file was created during your chat session.

Also, try to learn more about the suspects or groups under investigation. This is where your Internet skills come in handy. Search the Web and spend some time on Usenet and IRC learning their slang, interests, associates, hangouts, what they read, etc. If you will be communicating directly with these people, you will have to act like them, or you will stick out like an investigator. If you cannot communicate with them on their level, they will not trust you, and you will learn very little about their criminal activities. In the case of a sexual predator, attempt to figure out what the suspect is looking for in a victim. On the one hand you cannot entrap the suspect, but on the other hand you have to know what characteristics s/he will be attracted by (e.g., low self-esteem vs. confidence, sexual curiosity vs. sexual innocence). If you don't already have a sense of what might be going on in the suspect's head, search the Internet for related fantasy stories.

Additionally, be prepared for (and simulate) as many contingencies as possible and make sure that everyone who is supporting you knows what to do. For instance, if the suspect wants to talk on the phone, your assistant should be prepared with the same biographical information that you have and must be aware of the conversation that you just had with the suspect. If the suspect calls you, have caller identification in place to capture his or her phone number.

An essential consideration for conducting undercover operations online is how your jurisdiction deals with real-time recording of online activity by law enforcement. In some states, such activity may be prohibited by wiretapping/eavesdropping laws. A case of a law enforcement officer who was the target of an investigation by another law enforcement officer has worked its way up to the Pennsylvania Supreme Court.[1]

During the live interactions with a suspect, be sure to keep a log of the session and consider videotaping the computer monitor as well. If one form of documentation is lost or not admitted, perhaps the other one will be accepted. Software that captures the online activity, similar to a videotape, is also available, as discussed in Chapter 7.

Collect as much evidence remotely as possible before seizing a computer/server in case the suspect destroys data. Consider using e-mail to communicate with the suspect to obtain header information and anything else that s/he sends in the e-mail body or attachments (beware of attachments because they may be infected with viruses or Trojan horse programs). Consider using Java, Active X, or other types of "Web bugs" to obtain information about the suspect and examine files obtained from the suspect for identifying information.

> A **Web bug** utilizes a portion of a digital file (that is not visible to the viewer) to contact a remote computer on the Internet and deliver information about the viewer's computer.

Additionally, consider using steganography to embed hidden data in images or files sent to suspects to demonstrate that it was sent by you and received by the suspect. Whatever you do, do not break the law by disseminating child pornography or gaining unauthorized access to a remote system.

After your conversations, document and preserve all of your evidence. In particular, calculate the message digest values of files as soon as feasible for the purpose of demonstrating integrity. A message digest can be used to demonstrate that the file was not changed after it was collected and documented. Additionally, print and sign all log files and save all files to disk (ideally, a write-once CD).

---

[1] *Commonwealth of Pennsylvania v. Robert d. Proetto No. 1076 EDA 2000 Superior Court of Pennsylvania 2001 PA Supper 95; 771 A. 2d 823 (2001).*

Finally, take the time immediately after each conversation to go over the evidence that you collected. As you know, it might take a year or more for this case to go to court, and you will want to have copious notes to jog your memory regarding certain pieces of evidence. Many enticement cases are similar, and after a while one case may run into another. Consider making notes on a copy of the session to highlight significant portions.

## 6.6) DOCUMENTING PREDISPOSITION OF THE SUSPECT TO COMMIT A CRIME

In your interactions with the suspect, you will usually want to demonstrate that the suspect is predisposed to committing a certain crime. For example, in child exploitation investigations, you will need to demonstrate that s/he intends to have sex with you (who s/he thinks is a minor). As discussed elsewhere in this volume, do not initiate conversations about sex with a target. Let the target be the one who brings sex into the picture. If s/he doesn't, there are plenty of targets on the Internet to choose from. Too much time and scarce law enforcement resources go into online undercover cases to be lost at the prosecution phase for entrapment. In child pornography investigations, you may attempt to show that the suspect frequents IRC channels devoted to trading child pornography and to document the suspect asking for images to show his or her disposition. Do not send child pornography via the Internet. This is tricky business. We recommend you talk with the district attorney about this situation to avoid entrapment. The DA will have the best sense of what is acceptable in his or her area.

## 6.7) PREPARING FOR A MEETING OR SEARCH

During an undercover investigation, ask questions that can later be used to verify that the individuals on the other end of the line were indeed the suspects. For example, you might ask where they live, what their birthdays are, what they do for a living, if they have a photo. Also, carefully solicit information from the suspects to help develop a search warrant (system information, etc.) and to link the individuals to online activities (type of car, address/room, photos, etc.). However, do not ask too many personal questions, or the suspects may become suspicious. And ask only questions that you are willing to answer if they ask them back at you.

Compile a dossier on the subjects. Using the information gained from your online interactions, put together identifying information and a profile for your targets. Get the motor vehicle department to give you the cars listed to the subjects' address, their operators' license numbers, and photographs. Search law enforcement databases to determine whether they are registered sex offenders, possess firearms, or have been involved as the accused in other offenses. Search publicly available and law enforcement databases to determine whether the subjects have weapons and/or weapons permits, are licensed weapons dealers, and have a criminal history. Also determine whether the subjects are married; what their Social Security numbers are; whether they are working or receiving public assistance; whether they own a business, possess a professional license, own their residence, have utilities billed in their names; and whether they receive mail at the address. If multiple possible suspects reside at the address, do your intelligence workup on all of them—including the women. You'll have a better sense of whom you may be meeting, and you will be in a better position to gauge potential danger and flight risk.

If you decide to meet, be sure that you will be able to identify the suspects when you arrive. Pick a location that has good surveillance visibility (especially if you decide to video tape the subjects' arrival). If you decide to conduct surveillance, be careful that the suspects will not notice (they might decide to conduct surveillance of the scene before they commit to following through with the meeting).

The following summary of best practices is provided to emphasize these important considerations.

---

**Update—Volume 14, Number 1, 2001**

**Some Golden Rules for Investigating On-Line Child Sexual Exploitation**
By Brad Astrowsky and Susan Kreston, 2001.

**Introduction**

With computer facilitated child sexual exploitation coming to the top of the agenda for both police and prosecutors, new issues are arising concerning what should be regarded as the best practices for investigating these crimes against children. To assist front line law enforcement professionals in responding to these issues, the following suggestions are offered.

**The Golden Rule**

**#1. Never say or do anything you wouldn't want to repeat to a jury.** Keep in mind that whatever is done during the course of an investigation must be presented and justified to a jury. If, for example, a perpetrator sends the undercover detective a sexually provocative piece of clothing and asks the "child" to put it on and send a picture to him, the detective must not do this. Think like a 13-year-old to come up with reasons to decline. "I don't want to send it off to be developed—I might get caught," or "How can I take a picture of myself?" Refusing to pander to the perpetrator's wishes is not the end of the case. Sending a picture of a detective dressed in such an item is.

**#2. Never send child pornography, adult pornography, erotica, pictures of yourself or your child over the Internet.** It goes without saying that the job of law enforcement is not to add to the volume of illegal materials available on the Internet. If the perpetrator wants to swap pictures, the detective may send corrupted images. A lack of digital camera and a scanner might also be raised as a bar. Alternatively, undercover detectives may tell the perpetrator that they don't have pictures, but they do have child pornography videos, so a face-to-face meeting might be better. Finally, if there is no other way, arrange a controlled delivery of the materials with immediate seizure after delivery.

Often, the perpetrator will ask the "child" to send a picture of him or herself. Once an image, no matter how innocent, leaves the possession of the sender, it is forever out of his or her control. There is nothing to prevent the recipient of the image from cutting and pasting the head from the image onto the body of another child being abused in another picture thereby creating new child pornography.

**#3. Log everything. It is important in these cases as in any other to keep complete, well documented records of any transactions that occur in the course of the investigation.** It is of paramount importance to log everything so that a full and absolutely accurate accounting may be made of any correspondence between the victim/undercover detective and the perpetrator. It is incumbent upon the investigator to know what is automatically logged and what is not. For example, Internet Service Providers (ISPs) will not automatically preserve instant messages or chat room conversations on their servers. To do so would be an extreme financial burden. Therefore, if a detective attempts to subpoena an ISP for that information, it will be to no avail. Detectives must know how to save and log all communications between the perpetrator and the "victim" to best facilitate the effective prosecution of the case.

**#4. Never work from your home or your personal account.** Every office should have a protocol delineating the parameters and proper techniques for investigating these cases. When detectives go on-line, they should know what is acceptable and legally defensible in such an undercover operation. Two key pieces of any such protocol should be that no detective ever work from his/her home computer or from a personal account. These two rules simplify the issues attendant to properly backstopping accounts, and also firmly and effectively establish the boundaries within which the detective may pursue these cases. By particularly designating who will be allowed to conduct these investigations and on what computer(s), the protocol additionally preempts and precludes the defense of "I was working on a case/I had no criminal intent" being raised. It also helps to insulate both the detective and his/her office from liability issues.

**#5. Give the defendant an out.** At some point in the correspondence with the perpetrators, give them "an out." In a traveler case this might be "Are you sure you want to have sex with me? Can't you get in trouble?" In a child pornography case it might be "I'm worried about getting together to exchange pictures. Isn't this stuff illegal? Can't we get in trouble?" This will help the prosecutor to show that the perpetrator had the opportunity to abandon the activity but, rather chose to pursue it.

**#6. Don't be the slime ball—that's the defendant's job.** When conducting an undercover investigation, it is crucial that the detective let the perpetrator lead the communication. It should never be the undercover detective who first uses sexually explicit language or suggests a sexual encounter. Issues of both entrapment and jury nullification are always best avoided, particularly in this context. Remember, whatever you say, you will have to repeat in front of the jury. Make certain the jurors know that it was the defendant who escalated the conversation and steered it toward sexual matters, not the detective.

**#7. If you seize it, you must search it.** It is imperative that any computer seized be examined quickly. Jurisdictions in the U.S. are, on average, six months behind in their analysis of computer forensic evidence. With each analysis taking approximately 40 hours to complete, it is extremely easy to fall behind. Backlog, however, is not a legally recognized excuse for failing to conduct a forensic analysis in a timely manner. Charging and pre-trial decisions must be made with all deliberate speed, and with issues of civil liability regarding failing to return the computer to innocent third parties (usually businesses who use the computer(s) in everyday work), it is exceptionally important to conduct the forensic analysis of the materials and then return anything that is not evidence to its owner. It should be remembered that seizure of BOTH the defendant's and the victim's computer is optimal to retrieve all possible electronic evidence relevant to the case.

**#8. Consider the pros and cons of a face-to-face meeting.** One of the best ways to place the perpetrator behind the computer and preempt the Some Other Dude Did It (SODDI) defense is to arrange a face-to-face meeting between the perpetrator and the undercover detective purporting to be a child, or purporting to want to exchange child pornography. Two issues must be addressed when deciding whether or not to arrange such a meeting. The first is officer safety. Simply because the perpetrator is (or seems to be) a preferential sex offender does not mean that there are no issues of officer safety. The offender may be armed and fearful that the meeting is, in fact, a sting. Additionally, there is always the possibility that the person who shows up may be a "cyber vigilante" prepared to attack the presumed pedophile.

The second issue relates to potential defenses that such a meeting might inadvertently support. While the face-to-face meeting will effectively counter the "it wasn't me on the computer" defense, it may pose other problems. By having a very young looking officer impersonate the "child" the perpetrator is supposed to be meeting, the defense of "fantasy" may be given unintentional credibility. With the fantasy defense the defendant claims that he knew the "child" was not really a child and that he was just role-playing. The defendant could allege that he was expecting a young looking adult and, in fact, that is who showed up. Before using this technique, consider whether it is necessary to actually have someone impersonate the child/victim or whether the defendant merely showing up is sufficient. UNDER NO CIRCUMSTANCES WHATSOEVER SHOULD A REAL CHILD EVER BE USED TO EFFECTUATE THE MEETING.

**#9. If you discover that the perpetrator is in another jurisdiction, immediately forward the file to that jurisdiction.** When you find that the Internet account is registered to a John Doe in another state (or even a foreign country), inform that other jurisdiction immediately and decide if it is better for the perpetrator's home county to take over the investigation. The multijurisdictional aspect of these cases cannot be overemphasized. Cooperation is needed to both apprehend the perpetrator and protect the victim.

**#10. Computer forensics is not a substitute for solid, old-fashioned police work.** Two classic areas of police work predominate this area: suspect surveillance and suspect interrogation. Surveillance is one way to put the perpetrator behind the computer. Meeting the untrue SODDI defense may require that the perpetrator's home/business be surveilled to determine who has access to the computer and at what times of the day. It is crucial that information be gained at the investigatory stage to defeat this claim.

Suspect interrogation remains one of the three most critical pieces of the successful prosecution of these cases, the other two being the victim and the forensic/medical/physical evidence in the case. Questions that should be asked of the suspect include: "How many computers do you have access to?" "How many computers did you use to correspond with the child?" "Where are they all located?" "Are there password protected or encrypted files in those computers?" "What are the passwords?"

> **Conclusion**
>
> No one protocol or set of rules can definitively deal with all the issues that might arise in the investigation of a computer-facilitated child sexual exploitation case. However, by adhering to some simple strategies that reflect the best practices to date, many of the problems and pitfalls of investigating these cases can be avoided and the children victimized by these crimes will have a better opportunity to obtain justice in the courts. (http://www.ndaa. org/publications/newsletters/update_volume_14_number_1_2001.html)

As you can see, this process is very involved. If you do not have the necessary resources, consider contacting an agency that already has experience dealing with this type of situation and the necessary resources in place.

A few years ago, a few rural investigators went undercover online and chatted with pedophiles. The investigators often used their own computers and worked from home—sort of a hobby after hours. They donned their online personas as a fourteen-year-old boy or girl and went into chat rooms where they conversed with older men who hit on them and attempted to entice the "minors" into real-world sexual activity. The investigators referred "hot" cases to other jurisdictions in which the suspect lived or in which they planned to meet. When the time came to do further investigation or prosecution, when the other jurisdiction requested a copy of the logs, the undercover investigators did not have any logs to turn over. In at least one case, the investigator was clearly the first person to suggest sexual activity. In a number of other cases we are personally aware of, the investigator sent child pornography to the target.

When the prosecuting jurisdiction brought charges, the investigator had to be subpoenaed, and travel and overtime expenses had to be addressed. At least one investigator was embroiled in so many cases that he could not answer the subpoenas sent for him, and all the cases he referred had to be dropped. Another investigator used his personally owned computer and worked from home. When the otherwise righteous case came to trial, the defense subpoenaed his wife and children as witnesses to attest to the times he stated he was online.

## 6.8) AGENCIES AND RESOURCES

Among the most successful undercover operations are those conducted by the FBI's Crimes Against Children Task Forces, the Innocent Images Initiative, and the Internet Crimes Against Children Task Force Program administered by the Department of Justice Office of Juvenile Justice and Delinquency Prevention, and the National Center for Missing and Exploited Children.

Many of the FBI field offices throughout the country have organized Crimes Against Children (CAC) Task Forces. The program aims to "develop a nation-wide capacity to provide a rapid, effective and measured investigative response to crimes involving the victimization of children; and enhance the capabilities of state and local law enforcement investigators through training programs, investigative assistance and task force operations" (FBI CAC Web site 2003). CAC task forces recruit multi-disciplinary and multi-agency teams, and they promote sharing of intelligence information and specialized skills among all levels of law enforcement and provision of victim and witness services. CAC Task Forces focus on crimes against children but do not exclusively concentrate on computer-assisted or Internet crimes against children.

The Innocent Images National Initiative is a component of the FBI's Cyber Crimes Program. Innocent Images is devoted to investigating computer-assisted and Internet-related crimes against children. The Initiative's primary focus is on "travelers," those individuals who use the Internet to entice minors into sexual activity and travel across state lines to do so, and major manufacturers and distributors of child pornography.

Congress created the Internet Crimes Against Children (ICAC) Task Force program in 1998. Initially funding ten task forces, the program has grown to fund forty-five task forces around the country, and the program expands yearly. The ICAC program encourages the partnering and resource sharing among various levels of government—local, county, state, and federal—and promotes a multi-disciplinary approach to attacking Internet crimes against children. The national ICAC Board provides policy guidance and determines investigative priorities.

Task forces must obtain approval to conduct undercover operations and must abide by ICAC guidelines for conducting undercover investigations. The ICAC guidelines for undercover investigations require that law enforcement officers adhere to high standards of online conduct and mandate that under-cover operations receive prior approval from the ICAC Board. Among the requirements, officers may use only authorized equipment and Internet access methods to conduct undercover investigations. All targets and activity must be reported to a centralized database to ensure duplication of efforts is minimized.

## 6.9) CONCLUSION

This chapter provides guidance and resources for investigators conducting online undercover operations. First and foremost, investigators must be extremely cautious. The offenders you will be encountering have an extremely high motivation to avoid detection. After all, attempting to have sex with a minor or trafficking in gruesome pictures of children engaged in graphic sexual activity is one of the most loathsome criminal activity, and those accused of it will bear the brand of "pervert" forever. Investigators should bear in mind that just as they have the ability to track offenders, many offenders are fairly Internet savvy, and their motivation to avoid detection weighs heavily in inspiring them to learn as much as possible about how to prevent being caught.

## REFERENCES

Astrowsky, B., and J. Kreston. "Some Golden Rules for Investigating On-line Child Sexual Exploitation," *National District Attorneys Association Newsletter* 14 (2001): No. 1. www.ndaa-apri.org/publications/newsletters/update_volume_14_number_1_2001.html.

Fellows, G. "Peer-to-peer networking issues: An overview," *Digital Investigation,* Vol 1, No. 1 (2004): pp 3–6.

## INTERNET RESOURCES

www.fbi.gov/hq/cid/cac/crimesmain.htm
www.ndaa.org/publications/newsletters

# CHAPTER 7

# COLLECTING AND PRESERVING EVIDENCE ON THE INTERNET

The Internet can be involved in child exploitation in a number of ways, resulting in many potential sources of digital evidence. The Internet can be an instrumentality when it plays a major role in the commission of a crime, such as enticement of minors to engage in sexual activity or dissemination of child pornography. In other cases, the Internet may simply indicate that a crime has occurred, and provide investigative leads and useful information about an offender or victim.

When the Internet is used to exploit children, networked systems will obviously have related digital evidence. However, when no related Internet activities are immediately apparent in a case, it is a common mistake to search only a computer and not the Internet. Even if there is no evidence of Internet activity on a defendant's computer, performing an Internet search can uncover useful information. The defendant might have used the Internet from a different computer or might have concealed his or her activities very well. Therefore, child exploitation investigators require strong search skills and need to know how to preserve evidence that they find on the Internet.

Once a major source of evidence has been located on the Internet, investigators may decide to collect data from the system remotely prior to obtaining a search warrant to physically examine the remote computer. This chapter discusses the kinds of information that can be obtained remotely, the reasons remote evidence gathering might be necessary, and some associated risks. In this chapter, some knowledge of Internet search tools is assumed, and the focus is on advanced evidence-gathering and handling techniques. For an introduction to searching the Internet, including the Web, Usenet, and online databases, see Casey (2004).

## 7.1) PRESERVING EVIDENCE ON THE INTERNET

When investigating child exploitation, investigators must keep in mind that one of the main limitations of the Internet as a source of evidence is that it has only the latest version of information. If a Web page is modified or someone retracts a Usenet post, the old information is usually lost. This limitation of Web archives is changing with the emergence of the WaybackMachine and Google's cache feature, but these repositories do not store information from IRC, ICQ, and many other services. Until comprehensive Internet archives are well established, the only reliable way to preserve evidence on the Internet is to collect it immediately. For instance, when examiners are investigating criminal activity on IRC, it is advisable to configure some form of logging to document the search and interactions. E-mail and Usenet messages should be saved to a disk to retain their full headers along with any attachments and associated materials.

When evidence on the Internet is saved in a file, it is necessary to document the key file properties such as the file name, date-time stamps, and MD5 hash value. It is also prudent to document the same evidence in multiple ways in case one form is lost or unclear. Printing evidence, such as e-mail messages and IRC logs, and dating and initialing the pages are effective ways to preserve these sources of evidence, provided all of the information is displayed (e.g., full e-mail headers). In addition to saving and printing copies of data found on the Internet, printing screenshots are useful for documenting what investigators saw at a particular time.

A videotape or similar visual representation of dynamic onscreen activities, such as online chat or file sharing, is often easier for non-technical decision makers (e.g., attorney, jury, judge, manager, military commander) to understand than a static screenshot or text log. Although it may not be feasible to videotape all sessions, important sessions may warrant the effort and expense. Also, software such as Camtasia, Lotus ScreenCam, and QuickTime can capture events as they are displayed on the computer screen, effectively creating a digital video of events. One disadvantage of this form of documentation is that it captures more details that can be criticized. Therefore, digital evidence examiners must be particularly careful to follow procedures strictly when using this approach.

## 7.2) FINDING EVIDENCE ON THE INTERNET

To search the Internet effectively, investigators need to be conversant with various online resources and search strategies. The same is true when searching for information about an individual without the Internet. In the physical world, investigators use phone books, newspapers, and other resources in the geographical area where the individual lives. Investigators also try to determine where the subject works or to uncover personal details such as where the subject socializes. Any distinctive feature or "rough edge" relating to the subject may be used by investigators to search for additional information. Although many

Internet services can be searched via the Web, including Usenet messages, mailing lists, and online databases, many others cannot. Therefore, in some cases investigators may need to learn how to search unfamiliar areas in cyberspace such as online chat or file-sharing networks. Having a solid search strategy and method of documenting all findings can help regardless of what technology is used to perform a search.

### 7.2.1) GEOGRAPHIC SEARCH

One method of searching for digital evidence on the Internet is to look for online resources in a particular geographical area. For instance, if a victim or unknown offender lives in San Francisco, there will probably be a high concentration of related information in that area. Searching online telephone directories, newspaper archives, bulletin boards, chat rooms, and other resources dedicated to San Francisco can uncover unknown aspects of a known victim's online activities and can lead to the identity of a previously unknown offender. Search engines that focus on a particular country (e.g., www.google.it, ie.altavista.com) can also be useful for a geographically focused search.

### 7.2.2) INSTITUTION SEARCH

Another strategy is to search within particular institutions or organizations. For instance, if a victim or offender is affiliated with a particular company or school, associated online resources will probably contain a high concentration of personal information about the subject. As with a geographically focused search, looking through an organization's online telephone directory, internal bulletins or newsletters, discussion boards or mailing lists, and other publicly accessible online resources can lead to useful information. Additionally, it may be possible to query systems on an organization's network for information about users. Although it is permissible to access information on an organization's computer systems in non-invasive ways, care should be taken not to cross the line into unauthorized access.

### 7.2.3) UNIQUE CHARACTERISTICS

Individuals often exhibit distinctive features on the Internet, such as unique nicknames (e.g., sassybabe) and e-mail addresses (e.g., dlbch15@yahoo.com). Also, individuals may reveal unusual interests, use certain phrases, or expose other "rough edges" that can be useful for searching the Internet, leading to additional information about the subject. Besides searching for real names, nicknames, full e-mail addresses, and segments of e-mail addresses, focusing searches around unusual interests can be productive searching areas on the Internet that the victim or suspect frequented. Given the difficulty in making informed guesses of places where an offender or victim might go on the Internet, this type of search usually develops from a lead. For instance, interviews with family and friends or an examination of a victim's computer may reveal that s/he subscribed to a particular newsgroup and frequented a particular IRC chat room to arrange sexual encounters. An offender or victim may have left traces of activities in these online areas. Searching these areas can be particularly productive if the offender and victim communicated with each other in a public area on the Internet, revealing connections between them.

### 7.2.4) DOCUMENTATION

In addition to returning some useful information, thorough Internet searches return significant amounts of irrelevant data. Therefore, to ensure that the source of key items can be recalled, investigators should document their work, indicating when, where, and how specific items were found. Handwritten notes combined with the investigators' Web browser history can help show when, where, and how information was located. Ultimately, investigators can create a report, such as the example shown here, to summarize what they found:

**Date**: January 30, 2004 at 17:00
**Searched**: Google (Web & Groups), Whois, Illinois Department of Corrections, Cook County Sheriffs Department, Chicago Tribune
**Keywords & Search Syntax**: +John +Doe

**Summary of Results**:

*Institution Search*: Usenet messages posted by the subject indicate that he runs a company that sells security systems, mace, pepper sprays, handcuffs, stun guns, and other security gadgets.

*Geographic Search*: Mailing addresses in Usenet posts and Whois databases indicate that subject lives in Arlington Heights, Illinois which leads search sex offender registry, newspapers, and other resources in that area. A search of the Illinois Department of Corrections Web site (http://www.idoc.state.il.us/) reveals that subject is a convicted felon who spent time in 1993 in the Shawnee Correctional Facility in Springfield, Illinois. Searching the Cook County Sheriffs Department's website (http://www.cookcountysheriff.org/) indicates that subject is currently wanted for not re-registering as a sex offender in the state of Illinois.

*Unique characteristics*: Rough edges in Usenet posts, such as his e-mail address and signature line (e.g., Get paid to read email: http://www.sendmoreinfo.com/SubMakeCookie.cfm?Extract-#####) confirmed the subjects identity.

This form of documentation can help investigators recall and explain their findings and can help others repeat the search if needed. Any files that are saved in the course of a search should be documented in Section 7.1.

## 7.3) COLLECTING REMOTE EVIDENCE

When a major source of evidence is found on the Internet, investigators must decide whether it is necessary to collect some information from the system remotely. Remotely collected evidence may be needed to demonstrate probable cause for a search warrant and may help determine how many and what kinds of computers to expect. In addition, data on the remote computer that are visible on the Internet such as personal Web pages or an account name may contain investigatively useful information. For instance, personal Web pages may contain photographs and other information about the suspect, and user accounts or computer names can be useful for attributing online activities to owners of the accounts or computers.

Furthermore, remotely probing a computer may reveal that it is a proxy server or a home computer running a Trojan horse program, alerting investigators to the need for surveillance of traffic to and from that system to determine where the actual offender is located. Without this type of information, investigators risk seizing an innocent person's computer and losing an opportunity to apprehend the actual perpetrator.

Some risks are associated with such remote evidence collection. Incautious exploration of remote systems may be viewed as unauthorized access or may warn suspects of an impending search. Law enforcement officers who decide to investigate online child pornography without proper authorization have been accused of illegal activity themselves after downloading illegal materials from the Internet. Additionally, technically savvy offenders can provide false information such as computer names, MAC addresses, and open ports to mislead investigators. To protect themselves legally and professionally, investigators need to obtain explicit written instructions from a manager or prosecutor before collecting evidence remotely.

### 7.3.1) PREPARING FOR A SEARCH WARRANT

Before obtaining authorization to search and seize computers, investigators may need to gather intelligence about the target systems. For instance, when a Web site is under investigation, investigators need to determine where the Web servers are located and what kinds of computers to expect so that they can bring the necessary tools. They might also want to copy as much of the material from the Web site as possible prior to the search to demonstrate probable cause or to serve as a precautionary measure. The process of gathering information about a network can involve reviewing purchase orders; studying security audit reports; scanning the system remotely; examining e-mail headers; and searching the Web, Usenet, DNS, and other Internet resources for revealing details.

> On a practical level, agents may take various approaches to learning about a targeted computer network. In some cases, agents can interview the system administrator of the targeted network (sometimes in an undercover capacity), and obtain all or most of the information the technical specialist needs to plan and execute the search. When this is impossible or dangerous, more piecemeal strategies may prove effective. For example, agents sometimes conduct on-site visits (often undercover) that at least reveal some elements of the hardware involved. A useful source of information for networks connected to the Internet is the Internet itself. It is often possible for members of the public to use network queries to determine the operating system, machines, and general layout of a targeted network connected to the Internet (although it may set off alarms at the target network) (USDOJ, 2002).

The remaining sections describe some of the information that can be obtained remotely from computers on the Internet during child exploitation investigations.

### 7.3.2) CREATING REMOTE QUERIES

Although access to most networked computers is protected by usernames and passwords, some information may be available without a password. For example, the finger command is used to remotely query UNIX computers that support this service to learn more about a specific user. For instance, in a hypothetical scenario, the following information was obtained from the cyberspace.org server, indicating that the last login to the "BigDaddy" user account occurred on February 22 from IP address 151.196.247.149:

```
C:\>finger bigdaddy@cyberspace.org
[cyberspace.org]
Login: bigdaddy                 Name:   Big Daddy
Directory: /c/t/h/bigdaddy      Shell:  /usr/local/bin/tcsh
Last login Sun Feb 22 12:30 (EST) on ttyud from 151.196.247.149
No unread mail
No Plan.
```

Querying the system at a later date may coincide with the user being logged into the systems, as shown here, giving the IP address of the user's computer (141.157.67.68), which resolves to pool-141-157-67-68.balt.east.verizon.net:

```
C:\>finger @cyberspace.org
[cyberspace.org]
Login      Name           TTY  Idle  Login Time
pronstar  Digital Angel   s4         Feb 25 09:25
thehunte  Maniu adrian    p9    41   Feb 25 10:45
bigdaddy  Big Daddy       uc         Feb 25 11:26
wjgh       john smith     u0     2   Feb 25 11:16

C:\>finger bigdaddy@cyberspace.org
[cyberspace.org]
Login: bigdaddy                 Name: Big Daddy
Directory: /c/t/h/bigdaddy      Shell: /usr/local/bin/tcsh
On since Wed Feb 25 11:26 (EST) on ttyuc, idle 0:01, from 141.157.67.68
No unread mail
No Plan.
```

In addition, people who are not well versed in computer security may inadvertently expose information on their computer to others on the Internet. If the remote computer is a Windows machine that is not protected by a firewall or secured in another way, the nbtstat command can return useful information such as the name of the current user, as shown here:[1]

```
C:\>nbtstat -A 141.157.67.68

Local Area Connection:
Node IpAddress: [192.168.0.6] Scope Id: []

        NetBIOS Remote Machine Name Table

   Name               Type      Status
   ----------------------------------------
   JRSMITH    <00>    UNIQUE    Registered
   HOMENET    <00>    GROUP     Registered
   JRSMITH    <03>    UNIQUE    Registered
   JRSMITH    <20>    UNIQUE    Registered
   HOMENET    <1E>    GROUP     Registered

   MAC Address = 00-08-74-22-80-2D
```

Even when individuals do not use identifying usernames on their computer, this information can still help establish continuity of offense when the computer is seized, providing a link between the seized computer and the online activities that are under investigation. Note that the Ethernet address of this

---

[1] Some computers will disclose this type of information to a remote system only after a NULL session is established using the command net use \\141.157.67.68\IPC$ "" /user:"" (Brown 1999).

machine is generally associated with Dell Computers.[2] Additional information can be obtained remotely from Windows machines using the net command, which lists the resources that are being shared on the network:[3]

```
C:\>net view \\141.157.67.68
Shared resources at \\141.157.67.68

Share name  Type            Used as  Comment
-----------------------------------------------------------------
HPLaser     Print                    HP LaserJet 1200 Series PCL
SharedDocs  Disk
The command completed successfully.
```

However, when querying a computer remotely, investigators must be cautious not to gain unauthorized access to any part of the computer. The fact that something is shared on the network does not mean that the computer owner purposefully made it available for remote access. Care must be taken not to overstep authority by gaining access to systems where the owner has a reasonable expectation of privacy. For instance, the following listing of a shared folder on the remote machine could be viewed as unauthorized access, particularly if the SharedDocs folder was shared on the network without the owner's knowledge:

```
C:\>dir \\141.157.67.68\SharedDocs
Volume in drive \\141.157.67.68\SharedDocs is JohnSmithsHD
Volume Serial Number is D40B-FDA2

Directory of \\141.157.67.68\SharedDocs

02/22/2004  11:45 PM    <DIR>              .
02/22/2004  11:45 PM    <DIR>              . .
05/05/2003  08:15 AM            1,572,864  mygirl.zip
02/22/2004  11:42 PM               31,744  images.doc
02/20/2004  09:47 AM                  653  log.txt
02/04/2004  05:58 PM    <DIR>              My Music
02/04/2004  05:56 PM    <DIR>              My Pictures
02/20/2004  02:55 PM            4,194,304  pornpics.zip
               4 File(s)        5,799,565  bytes
               4 Dir(s)    38,436,818,944  bytes free
```

Even if it is easy to check files on a remote system for illegal content, investigators must be certain that they are authorized to do so before proceeding.

---

[2] A searchable database of these vendor codes can be found on the IEEE Web site at http://standards.ieee.org/regauth/oui/index.shtml. Keep in mind that vendors sometimes use other vendors cards, such as a 3COM card in a Cisco device.

[3] A list of shared file systems on a remote UNIX machine can be viewed using the UNIX showmount command.

Although they may be conducting an investigation and feel that the materials are in plain view, privacy laws relating to data stored on and transmitted using computers are complex and must be carefully considered to avoid spoiling a case.

### 7.3.3) FOLLOWING ONLINE LEADS

Information gathered about a suspect can also be used to search other areas of the Internet. For instance, investigators can use the IP address obtained earlier to search IRC for users connecting from the same ISP (balt.east.verizon.net) using the /who command on IRC (command in bold):

```
/who *balt.east.verizon.net
* BigDaddy H BigD@pool-141-157-67-68.balt.east.verizon.net
*balt.east.verizon.net End of /WHO list.
```

As discussed in the next chapter, additional information about a user, including the chat rooms (a.k.a. channels) s/he joined, can be obtained using the /whois command on IRC (command in bold):

```
/whois BigDaddy
[WHOIS: BigDaddy]
Address: BigD@pool-141-157-67-68.balt.east.verizon.net
Server: mesra.kl.my.dal.net
Idle: 00:06:34
Time Online: 1 Day(s), 02:37:54
Channels: @#childporn #@ #psybnc
[ END WHOIS ]
```

Joining the #childporn channel reveals that this user is advertising a file server on IRC that appears to contain illegal materials, as documented in the investigator's log shown here:

```
Session Start: Wed Feb 25 10:59:24 2004
Session Ident: BigDaddy
[10:59] DCC Chat session
-
[10:59] Client: BigDaddy (141.157.67.68)
[10:59] Time: Wed Feb 25 10:59:24 2004
-
[10:59] Acknowledging chat request...
[10:59] DCC Chat connection established
-
[10:59] <BigDaddy> mIRC v6.12 File Server
[10:59] <BigDaddy> Use: cd dir ls get read help exit
[10:59] <BigDaddy> [\]
[10:59] <BigDaddy>
[10:59] <BigDaddy>        _____
[10:59] <BigDaddy>            Panzer Fileserver v2.4
[10:59] <BigDaddy>            http://arnts.tripod.com/
[10:59] <BigDaddy>
[10:59] <BigDaddy>   Commands:
[10:59] <BigDaddy>     CREDIT  . . . . .Your current credit
```

```
[10:59] <BigDaddy>    QUEUE  . . . . . .Shows your QUEUED files
[10:59] <BigDaddy>    STAT   . . . . .Stat's this File Server
[10:59] <BigDaddy>    AUTO on/off  . . .Auto-shows credit after DIR list
[10:59] <BigDaddy>    XP  . . . . . . .Win XP DCC problem fix
[10:59] <BigDaddy>    MULTIDCC  . . . .Shows how you can download multiple files at once
[10:59] <BigDaddy> Current Credit: FREE Ratio: No Ratio / Leech
[10:59] <BigDaddy> For usage help, type: HELP <topic>
[10:59] <BigDaddy> Topics: Upload - Download - Credit - Ratio - Auto
[10:59] <Investigator> ls
[10:59] <BigDaddy> [\*.*]
[10:59] <BigDaddy> [\*.*]
[10:59] <BigDaddy> 0001.jpg            0009.jpg            003.avi             0038.avi
[10:59] <BigDaddy> 10bang.jpg          10boygir.jpg        10built.jpg         10yopuss.mpg
[10:59] <BigDaddy> 10yr3way.jpg        11-12&13.jpg        11bath.avi          11blonde.jpg
[10:59] <BigDaddy> 11fk10.jpg          11fk11.jpg          11hghscl.jpg        11oooh.jpg
[10:59] <BigDaddy> 11sister.jpg        11suck.jpg          124aastr.htm        12anal.jpg
[10:59] <BigDaddy> 12asia3.jpg         12bj.avi            12jenny.txt         12sprea5.jpg
[10:59] <BigDaddy> 12suckdick.jpg      12toilet.jpg        13cortn.jpg         13yosex!.mpg
[10:59] <BigDaddy> 14&17_yr.jpg        14&uncle.jpg        14.jpg              14cute2.jpg
[10:59] <BigDaddy> 14hand.jpg          14hoop.jpg          14rape.avi          14rug.jpg
[10:59] <BigDaddy> 14sue8.jpg          14yroldgoddess.jpg  15&15fck.jpg        15celebs.jpg
[10:59] <BigDaddy> 15expose.jpg        15-inbed.jpg        15piano.jpg         15school.jpg
[10:59] <BigDaddy> 9thgrad.jpg         PRETEEN             TEEN-A              TEEN-B
[10:59] <BigDaddy> a2e.jpg             a3a.jpg             a4.jpg              a4wyw.china03.jpg
[10:59] <BigDaddy> a4wyw.kuik10.jpg    aa-10273.gif        aacup.jpg           adria1.jpg
[10:59] <BigDaddy> age6-1.avi          agnes03.jpg         akifub45.jpg        album45.jpg
[10:59] <BigDaddy> angela16.jpg        anita01.avi         anita07.avi         ann&dad.jpg
[10:59] <BigDaddy> ba-59.jpg           ba07-110.jpg        ba1yearold.jpg      bab05.jpg
[10:59] <BigDaddy> bab08.jpg           bab09a.jpg          bab10.jpg           bab91.jpg
[10:59] <BigDaddy> babjfm005.jpg       babjfm006.jpg       babjfm007.jpg       babysex1.jpg
[10:59] <BigDaddy> chldr03.jpg         chldr04.jpg         chldr05.jpg         chloe01.jpg
[10:59] <BigDaddy> fc0316c.jpg         fuckje~1.mpg        g1.jpg              geedady.txt
[10:59] <BigDaddy> girl2.jpg           goodgrl2.jpg        gotsomething4u.jpg  grl13.mpg
[10:59] <BigDaddy> jdteen05.jpg        jenny05.jpg         karla15.jpg         kids111.jpg
[10:59] <BigDaddy> legalt1000.jpg      legalt1001.jpg      legalt1002.jpg      legalt1003.jpg
[10:59] <BigDaddy> leslie1.jpg         leslie2.jpg         mygirl.jpg          pornpics.zip
[10:59] <BigDaddy> swt16b05.jpg        swt16b07.jpg        swt16fck.mpg        teen007.mpg
[10:59] <BigDaddy> teensu~2.avi        tiny052.jpg         tripod.sg107.jpg    tripod.sg115.jpg
[10:59] <BigDaddy> wwsupfuk.jpg        x-ltna20.jpg        x-ltna21.jpg        x-ltna22.jpg
[10:59] <BigDaddy> x-ltna24.jpg        xaladdin.jpg        y10uncle.jpg        yngsux12.jpg
[10:59] <BigDaddy> yngsx01.jpg         yngsx02.jpg         yngsx03.jpg         yngsx04.jpg
[10:59] <BigDaddy> yngsx05.jpg         yngsx06.jpg         yngsx07.jpg         yngsx08.jpg
[10:59] <BigDaddy> yngsx09.jpg         yngsx10.jpg         yngsx11.jpg         yngsx12.jpg
[10:59] <BigDaddy> yngsx13.jpg         yngsx15.jpg         yngsx16.jpg         yngsx17.jpg
[10:59] <BigDaddy> yngsx20.jpg         yngsx22.jpg         yngsx24.jpg         yngsx25.jpg
[10:59] <BigDaddy> yoda2.jpg           young.jpg           yungin.avi          zhomrmar.jpg
[10:59] <BigDaddy> End of list
[11:00] <Investigator> get mygirl.zip
[11:00] <BigDaddy> Sending file MYGIRL.ZIP
[11:01] <Investigator> stat
[11:01] <BigDaddy>
[11:01] <BigDaddy>            _____
[11:01] <BigDaddy>                 STAT'S FILE SERVER
[11:01] <BigDaddy>
[11:01] <BigDaddy>
[11:01] <BigDaddy>     Thursday February 26 2004
[11:01] <BigDaddy>     Total files available: unknown Size: Dirs:
[11:01] <BigDaddy>
[11:01] <BigDaddy>              DOWNLOADS           UPLOADS
[11:01] <BigDaddy>     Total:   124    [103.22 MB]   0       [0 KB]
[11:01] <BigDaddy>     Total:   124    [103.22 MB]   0       [0 KB]
[11:01] <BigDaddy>
[11:01] <BigDaddy>     Total:   124    [103.22 MB]   0       [0 KB]
[11:01] <BigDaddy>     Last month: 0     [0 KB]      0       [0 KB]
[11:01] <BigDaddy>
[11:01] <BigDaddy>     Today:   4      [1.22 MB]     0       [0 KB]
[11:01] <BigDaddy> Yesterday:   9      [4.31 KB]     0       [0 KB]
[11:01] <BigDaddy>
[11:01] <BigDaddy>                      VISITS
[11:01] <BigDaddy>     Total:   42     This month: 14    Today:     2
[11:01] <BigDaddy>     This year:  42     Last month: 0    Yesterday:  3
[11:01] <BigDaddy>
[11:01] <BigDaddy>     Server visited by people from 4 different countries
[11:01] <BigDaddy>     Top country by visits: N/A
-
[11:05] DCC session closed
```

In this instance, the investigator downloaded a file named "mygirl.zip" from the file server at 11:00, documented the file properties as discussed in Section 7.1, and determined that it contained child pornography. This action could be taken only by an authorized investigator with the proper controls covered in Chapter 6.

Notably, the IP address of the computer running this file server was confirmed and documented using the `netstat` command on the investigator's Windows XP computer shown here in bold:

```
C:\>netstat -ano -p tcp

Active Connections

 Proto  Local Address        Foreign Address       State         PID
 TCP    0.0.0.0:135          0.0.0.0:0             LISTENING     876
 TCP    0.0.0.0:445          0.0.0.0:0             LISTENING     4
 TCP    0.0.0.0:1025         0.0.0.0:0             LISTENING     976
 TCP    0.0.0.0:1423         0.0.0.0:0             LISTENING     976
 TCP    0.0.0.0:5000         0.0.0.0:0             LISTENING     1892
 TCP    127.0.0.1:4655       0.0.0.0:0             LISTENING     420
 TCP    127.0.0.1:4655       127.0.0.1:4656        ESTABLISHED   420
 TCP    127.0.0.1:4656       127.0.0.1:4655        ESTABLISHED   420
 TCP    192.168.0.4:139      0.0.0.0:0             LISTENING     4
 TCP    192.168.0.4:2597     61.6.39.100:7000      ESTABLISHED   1920
 TCP    192.168.0.4:3425     141.157.67.68:4523    ESTABLISHED   1920
```

However, it is possible for individuals on IRC to conceal their actual IP address by connecting through an intermediate machine running a proxy or IRC "bouncer bot" as detailed in the next section.

## 7.3.4) AUTOMATED PROBING

One useful tool for gathering information about a remote computer is Network Mapper (nmap).[4] In addition to basic port scanning, nmap has features for scanning remote computers through firewalls and has several options to reduce the risk that the scan will be detected by the remote system. A full description of nmap is beyond the scope of this text, but a couple of features that can be useful in investigations are provided in this section. As noted earlier, investigators might want to determine what types of computers to expect when executing a search warrant. The nmap remote operating system identification feature is shown here for a standard Windows XP home desktop system:

[4] http://www.insecure.org

```
C:\>nmap -O -n -v 141.157.67.68

Starting nmap 3.50 ( http://www.insecure.org/nmap/ ) at 2004-02-26 13:31 EST
Host 141.157.67.68 appears to be up . . . good.
Initiating SYN Stealth Scan against 141.157.67.68 at 13:31
Adding open port 135/tcp
Adding open port 1025/tcp
Adding open port 445/tcp
Adding open port 5000/tcp
Adding open port 139/tcp
The SYN Stealth Scan took 1 second to scan 1659 ports.
For OSScan assuming that port 135 is open and port 1 is closed and neither are firewalled
Interesting ports on 141.157.67.68:
(The 1654 ports scanned but not shown below are in state: closed)
PORT      STATE  SERVICE
135/tcp   open   msrpc
139/tcp   open   netbios-ssn
445/tcp   open   microsoft-ds
1025/tcp  open   NFS-or-IIS
5000/tcp  open   UPnP
Device type: general purpose
Running: Microsoft Windows 95/98/ME|NT/2K/XP
OS details: Microsoft Windows Millennium Edition (Me), Windows 2000 Professional or
Advanced Server, or Windows XP
TCP Sequence Prediction: Class=random positive increments
                         Difficulty=5186 (Worthy challenge)
IPID Sequence Generation: Incremental

Nmap run completed - 1 IP address (1 host up) scanned in 7.369 seconds
```

Although nmap could not determine the exact version of Windows, it provides useful information. Notice that the preceding results list which ports are open on the remote computer. Newer versions of nmap have a feature to inspect open ports and discover what version of software is running. For instance, the following scan shows several suspicious programs running on the remote system, including some Trojan horse programs and an unknown service called "Elite" shown in bold:

```
C:\>nmap -sV compromised.host.com
<edited for length>
80/tcp      open http
5801/tcp    open            vnc-http-1
5900/tcp    open            vnc
8080/tcp    open            http-proxy
12345/tcp   open            NetBus?
16959/tcp   open subseven
31337/tcp   open            Elite?
54320/tcp   open            bo2k
Nmap run completed - 1 IP address (1 host up) scanned in 225.752 seconds

C:\>telnet compromised.host.com 31337
Trying compromised.host.com. . .
Connected to compromised.host.com.
Escape character is '^]'.
:Welcome!psyBNC@lam3rz.de NOTICE * :psyBNC2.3.1
```

Connecting to the unknown service reveals that a common IRC "bouncer bot" named psyBNC enabled individuals to connect to IRC through the compromised computer, thus concealing their actual IP address. Unlike many other IRC bots, psyBNC also handles direct (DCC) connections between IRC users, making it more difficult for investigators to determine the actual IP address of an offender.

Although some IRC bots maintain logs, they can be encrypted to prevent investigators from reading them. Therefore, to determine who is connecting through a proxy of this kind, investigators may need to monitor network traffic passing through the compromised system. To perform this type of surveillance, investigators require authorization and the cooperation of the computer owner or ISP that connects the compromised computer to the Internet. Notably, some IRC bots support encrypted network connections (e.g., SSL), thus thwarting attempts to monitor the content of their traffic. However, monitoring network traffic will still reveal the source and destination of connections through the compromised computer. As criminals become more sophisticated, investigators must become more creative.

## REFERENCES

Brown, K. "Security Brief." *Microsoft Systems Journal.* (February 1999). http://www.microsoft.com/msj/0299/security/security0299.aspx.

Casey, E. *Digital Evidence and Computer Crime.* Boston, MA: Elsevier, 2004.

U.S. Department of Justice. "Searching and Seizing Computers and Obtaining Electronic Evidence in Criminal Investigations." (2002). http://www.cybercrime.gov/searchmanual.htm.

# CHAPTER 8

# TRACKING ON THE INTERNET

*Members [of BBS2] were given value on the basis of having technical and/or security expertise. Many of the discussions on BBS2 involved technical or security topics. Members often gave or requested information on the latest hardware or on good encryption devices. Status was gained through sharing information, thus demonstrating expertise on the technical aspects of accessing, downloading, and storing child pornography. Given the nature of their activities, concerns about security were also prevalent in their discussions, and knowing how to evade detection was also a route to gaining status. (Taylor and Quayle 2003)*

When the Internet is used to facilitate child exploitation, the associated online activities leave a cybertrail of digital evidence that can be linked to the associated activities in the physical world. Many offenders do not realize that these cybertrails exist and have a false sense of security when using the Internet, exposing themselves to greater risk than they otherwise would. Additionally, online remnants such as network and server logs are beyond an offender's control, giving investigators highly reliable sources of digital evidence. Investigators of child exploitation need to know how to follow this cybertrail to locate the responsible person and establish the continuity of offense. This chapter provides an overview of this process using common forms of digital evidence relating to the Internet. A basic understanding of the Internet and its operation is assumed; for more detailed coverage of the Internet and the evidence it contains, see Casey (2004).

The key principle in operation here is called Locard's Exchange Principle, which comes from traditional forensic science and is depicted in Figure 8.1. This principle is that anyone, or anything, entering a crime scene takes something of the scene with him or her, and leaves something of himself or herself behind when leaving. Such evidence transfer occurs in both the physical and digital realms and can be useful in Internet investigations

*Figure 8.1*

*Locard's Exchange Principle applied to computer-assisted crime results in a cybertrail connecting illegal online activities to the physical world.*

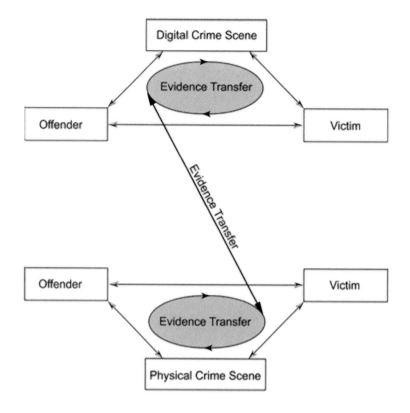

for establishing compelling links between the offender, victim, and crime scene.

## 8.1) ATTRIBUTION AND CONTINUITY OF OFFENSE

To attribute online activities to an individual, investigators must first locate the computer that was used and then determine who was using the computer at that time. Additionally, investigators need to establish a clear connection between the online activities and the suspect's computer, thus establishing the continuity of offense. As demonstrated in the Wonderland case example in Chapter 5, this connection can be established in a "connect the dots" fashion by comparing evidence on the suspect's computer with data from various sources on the Internet.

As an example, consider a case of downloading child pornography from an FTP server on the Internet via a dial-up connection, as depicted in Figure 8.2. Logs on the FTP server show a file named familyfun12.jpg being downloaded to the IP address 172.16.4.24:

```
Nov 12 19:53:23 2003 15 172.16.4.24 780800 /images/famfun/familyfun12.jpg a _ o r user
```

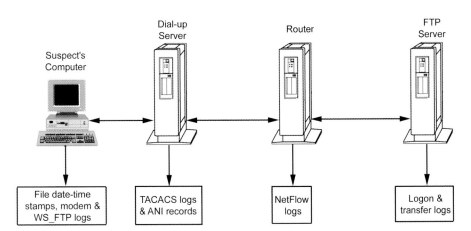

*Figure 8.2*

*Potential sources evidence useful for establishing continuity of offense (from Casey 2004)*

The Internet Service Provider (ISP) responsible for this IP address checks its dial-up authentication (TACACS or RADIUS) logs to determine which user account was assigned the IP address at the time. The ISP's customer records contain the name and billing address of the account owner, providing investigators with a suspect. The ISP also has Automatic Number Identification (ANI) logs—effectively CallerID—connecting the suspect's home telephone number to the dial-up activity. Additionally, the ISP has network (NetFlow) logs from its routers containing summary information for every packet transmitted between the suspect's computer and the Internet. In addition to helping investigators establish continuity of offense, these network logs are useful for refuting the suspect's claims that someone broke into his or her computer via a Trojan horse program and downloaded the offending materials.

An examination of the suspect's computer reveals a file with the same file name and size as the one downloaded from the FTP server (familyfun12.jpg, 780800 bytes). The date-time stamps of the offending files on the suspect's personal computer show when the files were downloaded. Additionally, the following log entry created by WS_FTP shows an image named familyfun12.jpg being downloaded from a remote directory named "/images/famfun" on the FTP server (IP address 192.168.1.45) on November 12, 2003, at 19:53:

```
03.11.12 19:53 A C:\download\image12.jpg <-- 192.168.1.45 /images/famfun familyfun12.jpg
```

Modem logs on the computer confirm that it was connected to the Internet at the time in question.

The more corroborating evidence available to link an individual to online activities, the greater weight the evidence will be given in court and the more certainty investigators can have in their conclusions. In this way, investigators can reconstruct the crime and determine who was involved. It is also important to realize that the best results are attained by combining investigations into online criminal activity with traditional investigative techniques. Recall in *US v. Grant* that the investigators put the suspect's house under surveillance and confirmed that he was at home when they observed illegal online activities involving his IBM dial-up account. In another case, a forty-two-year-old man in San Diego used his AT&T dial-up account to post photographs on Usenet of himself having sex with his daughter. The FBI obtained his name and address from AT&T, compared his driver's license photo with the pictures posted on the Internet, and arrested him at his home (Associated Press 1998).

### 8.1.1) DETERMINING PHYSICAL CONTACTS AND LOCATIONS

Once you have determined the IP address of an offender's computer, how do you determine its physical location? Internet registrars assign blocks of IP addresses to Internet Service Providers, universities, and any other organization that desires them. These Internet registrars maintain online databases, called Whois databases, that anyone can query to obtain the contact information of the organization responsible for specific IP addresses. Importantly, Whois databases rarely contain the name and address of the individual who is using a given IP address. The contact information usually refers to an employee of the offender's ISP who can provide investigators with the information they need.

The many separate Whois databases include those maintained by the main Internet registrars in different countries:

- *United States*: http://whois.arin.net/whois/index.html
- *Europe*: http://www.ripe.net/db/whois.html
- *Asia*: http://whois.apnic.net/

Some Whois databases have information only on high-level domains, whereas others have information on IP addresses. For instance, to find the contact for the State of Connecticut's Web server (www.state.ct.us = 159.247.0.205), investigators can search http://whois.arin.net, as shown here:

```
[Query: 159.247.0.205, Server: whois.arin.net]
OrgName:        State of Connecticut
OrgID:          STATEO-14
Address:        Department of Information Technology
Address:        101 East River Drive
City:           East Hartford
StateProv:      CT
PostalCode:     06108
Country:        US

NetRange:       159.247.0.0 - 159.247.255.255
CIDR:           159.247.0.0/16
NetName:        CTSTATE
NetHandle:      NET-159-247-0-0-1
Parent:         NET-159-0-0-0-0
```

```
NetType:          Direct Assignment
NameServer:       INFO.DAS.STATE.CT.US
NameServer:       DBRU.BR.NS.ELS-GMS.ATT.NET
Comment:
RegDate:          1992-06-18
Updated:          2001-07-02

TechHandle:       GB351-ARIN
TechName:         Blais, Germain
TechPhone:        +1-860-622-2429
TechEmail:        germain.blais@po.state.ct.us

OrgTechHandle:    GB351-ARIN
OrgTechName:      Blais, Germain
OrgTechPhone:     +1-860-622-2429
OrgTechEmail:     germain.blais@po.state.ct.us
# ARIN WHOIS database, last updated 2004-02-06 19:15
```

On the other hand, if illegal activity was originating from within the State of Connecticut domain (state.ct.us), such as e-mail from pop.state.ct.us (159.247.0.202), investigators can search http://www.whois.us/ for the appropriate contact, as shown here:

```
[Query: state.ct.us, Server: whois.nic.us]
<edited for length>
Domain Name:                              STATE.CT.US
Administrative Contact Name:              Michael Varney
Administrative Contact Organization:      State of CT - Department of Information
Technology
Administrative Contact Address1:          101 East River Dr.
Administrative Contact City:              East Hartford
Administrative Contact State/Province:    Connecticut
Administrative Contact Postal Code:       06108
Administrative Contact Country:           United States
Administrative Contact Country Code:      US
Administrative Contact Phone Number:      +1.8606222462
Administrative Contact Email:             michael.varney@po.state.ct.us
Technical Contact ID:                     CT-28-01-2992
Technical Contact Name:                   Andrew  Vincens
Technical Contact Organization:           State of CT - Department of Information
Technology
Technical Contact Address1:               101 East River Drive
Technical Contact City:                   East Hartford
Technical Contact State/Province:         Connecticut
Technical Contact Postal Code:            06108
Technical Contact Country:                United States
Technical Contact Country Code:           US
Technical Contact Phone Number:           +1.8606222463
Technical Contact Facsimile Number:       +1.8602918984
Technical Contact Email:                  hostmaster@po.state.ct.us
Name Server:                              DBRU.BR.NS.ELS-GMS.ATT.NET
Name Server:                              INFO.DAS.STATE.CT.US
Created by Registrar:                     US LOCALITY
Last Updated by Registrar:                US LOCALITY
Domain Registration Date:                 Fri Jan 31 09:29:00 GMT 2003
Domain Expiration Date:                   Sun Jan 30 23:59:59 GMT 2005
Domain Last Updated Date:                 iFri Dec 26 20:52:09 GMT 2003

>>>> Whois database was last updated on: Sat Feb 07 22:16:58 GMT 2004 <<<<
```

*Figure 8.3*

*NetScanTools Pro. This tool can be used to search Whois databases for IP addresses and domain names, and some Whois databases permit searches for other data such as an individual's unique handle (an index field in Whois databases), as shown here*

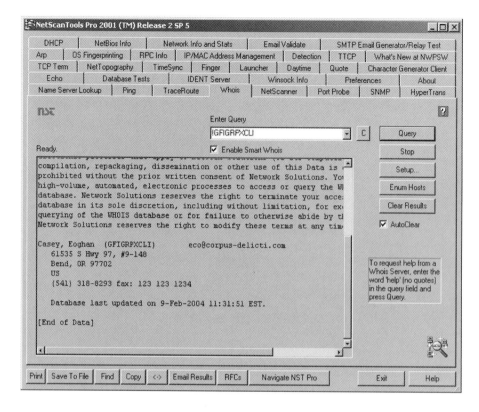

A comprehensive list of registrars is available at InterNIC (http://www.internic.net/whois.html), and a useful online interface for simultaneously searching many Whois databases is the Smart Whois interface (http://www.geektools.com/cgi-bin/proxy.cgi). A convenient Windows GUI tool for performing frequent queries of multiple Whois databases is NetScanTools Pro, shown in Figure 8.3, and UNIX has a `whois` utility that serves the same purpose. Be aware that it is also possible to search some Whois databases for a specific individual, as shown in Figure 8.3, using an e-mail address, full name, or handle—a unique identifier assigned to an individual in the Whois database.

## 8.1.2) INTERNET SERVICE PROVIDER USAGE LOGS

As noted in Chapter 2, ISPs can assign a different IP address each time a customer connects to the Internet (a.k.a. dynamic IP address) or assign a single IP address to each customer indefinitely (a.k.a. static IP address). In either case, most ISPs maintain logs that show which customer account was assigned an IP address for a given period. For instance, when a dial-up account is used to connect to the Internet, the user must provide a password before being given an IP address on the Internet. Similarly, DSL and cable modem subscribers have usernames and passwords that their ISP uses to authenticate them. This authentication process is generally handled by RADIUS or TACACS authentication servers, and the resulting logs can be used for billing purposes or to determine who was responsible for certain online activities. Be aware that these records may be retained only for several days or weeks.

Some ISPs also maintain Automatic Number Identification records on their dial-up modems for security or billing purposes. These records can be very useful in a child exploitation investigation, particularly when an offender is using a stolen dial-up account. In such cases, when the owner of the dial-up account is not involved, ANI information can be used to determine the phone number used to connect to the Internet. Even when the owner of the account is involved, ANI details can be used to confirm that the connections originated from the suspect's residence.

When ANI information is not available, it may be possible to obtain call records from the account owner's telephone company to determine whether the calls to the ISP originated from the account owner's home or office. When dealing with a stolen dial-up account, the ISP may be able to determine which city or geographic area the call was made from, in which case investigators can contact telephone companies in that region to determine who called the ISP at the time in question.

## 8.2) TRACKING INTERNET ACTIVITIES

This section presents techniques and associated tools for tracking down the most common forms of Internet activities encountered in child exploitation investigations: Web, e-mail, and Internet chat and file sharing.

### 8.2.1) WORLD WIDE WEB

Recall from the Landslide case in Chapter 2 that investigations into Web sites that contain child pornography may not require much technical skill to track down offenders. In that case, investigators found a database on Reedy's computer containing details about individuals around the world who were paying to receive child pornography through the Landslide Web site. In other cases, when investigators find a Web server used to disseminate child pornography, they may find log files showing only who accessed the materials. When an individual views a Web page, an entry is made on the server in the following general format:

```
[webserver:/var/log/httpd]% grep 192.168.0.4 access_log
192.168.0.4 - - [08/Feb/2004:14:55:59 -0500] "GET / HTTP/1.1" 200 22000
192.168.0.4 - - [08/Feb/2004:14:56:03 -0500] "GET /IMG000.JPG HTTP/1.1" 404 297
192.168.0.4 - - [08/Feb/2004:14:56:08 -0500] "GET /IMG001.JPG HTTP/1.1" 200 32678
192.168.0.4 - - [08/Feb/2004:14:56:13 -0500] "GET /IMG002.JPG HTTP/1.1" 200 39237
192.168.0.4 - - [08/Feb/2004:14:56:16 -0500] "GET /IMG003.JPG HTTP/1.1" 200 31010
192.168.0.4 - - [08/Feb/2004:14:56:19 -0500] "GET /IMG004.JPG HTTP/1.1" 200 42294
```

The meaning of each item in these log entries is described here using examples from the last line:

- **192.168.0.4** is the IP address of the machine on the Internet that made the request to the server.
- **[08/Feb/2004:14:56:31 -0500]** tells the date and time with the offset from Greenwich mean time or GMT (five hours behind GMT in this instance).
- **"GET /IMG004.JPG HTTP/1.1"** tells which file was accessed on the server.
- The next number is the HTTP result code. The RFC 2068[1] tells that the "200" code means "Success"—the file was successfully accessed. A "404" code means "File Not Found."
- The final number is the file size transferred—so in this case, 42294 bytes.

Investigators still need to demonstrate a link between these server logs and activities on the suspect's computer, establishing the continuity of offense. On the client side, corresponding entries are made in the Web browser's history and cache files. For instance, the following information from Internet Explorer history and cache files on the client computer correspond with the first few entries in the preceding server logs:

```
C:\Documents and Settings\user1\Local Settings\History\History.IE5\index.dat
URL                                 ACCESS TIME
http://192.168.0.5                  Sun Feb  8 19:56:26 2004
http://192.168.0.5/IMG000.JPG       Sun Feb  8 19:56:31 2004
http://192.168.0.5/IMG001.JPG       Sun Feb  8 19:56:36 2004
http://192.168.0.5/IMG002.JPG       Sun Feb  8 19:56:40 2004
http://192.168.0.5/IMG003.JPG       Sun Feb  8 19:56:44 2004
http://192.168.0.5/IMG004.JPG       Sun Feb  8 19:56:46 2004

C:\Documents and Settings\user1\Local Settings\Temporary Internet Files\Content.IE\index.dat
URL                                 ACCESS TIME               SIZE
http://192.168.0.5/                 Sun Feb  8 20:03:47 2004  22000
http://192.168.0.5/IMG001.JPG       Sun Feb  8 19:56:36 2004  32678
http://192.168.0.5/IMG002.JPG       Sun Feb  8 19:56:40 2004  39237
http://192.168.0.5/IMG003.JPG       Sun Feb  8 19:56:44 2004  31010
http://192.168.0.5/IMG004.JPG       Sun Feb  8 19:56:46 2004  42294
```

Because the access date-time stamps in these history and cache files are created by the local system, any clock offset on the computer will become apparent by comparing these date-time stamps with the corresponding entries in Web server access logs.[2] Note, however, that the preceding date-time stamps are presented in GMT, underlining the importance of taking timezone differences into

---

[1] http://www.w3.org/Protocols/rfc2068/rfc2068.

[2] The same concept works with cookie files that are placed on a system by Web servers. Comparing the date-time stamps of these files with the corresponding logs on the server will reveal any differences between the clocks on each system.

account when attempting to establish continuity of offense using data from multiple computers on the Internet.

In some cases investigators will want to ask an ISP to search Web server logs for all information relating to a specific IP address, as in the previous example, or a range of IP addresses.[3] In other cases, investigators will want to know which IP addresses accessed a specific page during a certain time range. As an example, if a Web page contained child pornography, investigators may want to know who accessed the page around a certain time. Alternately, some other piece of evidence may provide a time frame to search Web access logs, as in the following case:

**CASE EXAMPLE**

An unusual lead developed during a serial homicide investigation in St. Louis when a reporter received a letter from the killer. The letter contained a map of a specific area with a handwritten X to indicate where another body could be found. After investigators found a skeleton in that area, they inspected the letter more closely for ways to link it to the killer. The FBI determined that the map in the letter was from Expedia.com and immediately contacted the site to determine if there was any useful digital evidence.

The Web server logs on Expedia.com showed only one IP address (65.227.106.78) had accessed the map around May 21, the date the letter was postmarked. Using their Internet usage logs, the ISP responsible for this IP address was able to provide the account information and telephone number that had been used to make the connection in question similar to the information shown here:

```
Username: MSN/maurytravis
UUNET Resllerer: MSN
IP address assigned: 65.227.106.78
Time of connection: 19:53:34 May 20
Time of disconnect: 22:24:19 May 20
ANI information: (212) 555-1234
```

Both the dial-up account and telephone number belonged to Maury Travis. Investigators arrested Travis and found incriminating evidence in his home, including a torture chamber and a videotape of himself torturing and raping a number of women, and apparently strangling one victim. Travis committed suicide while in custody and the full extent of his crimes may never be known. (Shinkle 2002)

[3] Each time an individual connects to the Internet using a dial-up account, his/her computer is usually assigned a different IP address within a given range. For instance, the Irish ISP called Eircom assigns dial-up customers IP addresses in the range 159.134.0.0–159.134.255.255 (65,534 valid IP addresses) but uses smaller ranges for each region as indicated in the associated names (e.g., 159-134-78-6.as1.crl.dublin.eircom.net).

Web server access logs are also useful when Web-based e-mail is involved. Using these logs, Web-based e-mail providers such as Hotmail, Excite, and Yahoo! maintain a record of IP addresses used to check and send messages, as well as the IP address of the computer that was originally used to create the e-mail account.

### 8.2.2) E-MAIL

Every e-mail message has a header that contains information about its origin and receipt. It is often possible to track e-mail back to its source and identify the sender using the information in e-mail headers. The "Received" headers are the most useful for tracking purposes because they are added to the top of the message by each e-mail server that handles the message and show where the server received the message from. If the message passes through multiple e-mail servers while traveling from its source to the destination, each server adds its own Received header, enabling investigators to trace the exact route the message took.[4] When a Web-based e-mail service is used, a Received header containing the sender's IP address is often included, as shown here in bold;[5]

```
Received: from web14909.mail.yahoo.com (web14909.mail.yahoo.com
         [216.136.225.61]) by lsh110.siteprotect.com (8.11.6/8.11.6) with
         SMTP id i16GIJ303048 for <user32@siteprotect.com>; Fri, 6 Feb
         2004 10:18:20 -0600
Message-ID: <20040206161818.67920.qmail@web14909.mail.yahoo.com>
Received: from [151.196.251.121] by web14909.mail.yahoo.com via HTTP;
Fri, 06 Feb 2004 08:18:18 PST
Date: Fri, 6 Feb 2004 08:18:18 -0800 (PST)
From: Randy Smart <rsmart@yahoo.com>
Subject: Bank transfer information
To: user32@siteprotect.com
```

Because the date-time stamps in legitimate e-mail Received headers are added by an e-mail server, they are generally reliable and can be useful for calculating clock offsets on the sender's computer by comparing them with date-time stamps created by the suspect's system when the message was sent.

When e-mail lists are involved, as in the case of the Candyman Yahoo! e-group discussed in Chapter 2, the mailing list server may add additional Received headers to the top of the message, but the same tracking concepts

---

[4] Because each server adds a Received header to the top of the message like a stack of pancakes, the lowest header was added earliest by the originating server and the uppermost header was added last by the receiving server. Therefore, when tracking e-mail, investigators need to read these headers from bottom to top.

[5] In this instance, the IP address belongs to Verizon Internet Services, and the associated host-name (pool-151-196-251-121.balt.east.verizon.net) suggests that it is assigned to a user in Baltimore, Maryland, on the East Coast of the United States.

apply. Even mailing lists that remove existing Received headers will insert the IP address of the computer that sent the message. The investigation into the Candyman e-group demonstrates the importance of establishing continuity of offense and of becoming familiar with the technology involved. In that case, investigators falsely assumed that all members of the e-group received e-mail messages sent to the group when, in fact, the Yahoo! server logs showed that most members had opted not to receive e-mail.

On the computer that was used to send the e-mail, investigators would expect to find some remnants of the message such as a copy in the Sent folder of the individual's e-mail client. When no such remnants are found on the computer, investigators can use e-mail server logs to establish continuity of offense. Every time an e-mail server sends or receives a message, it records the event in a log file. For instance, the following e-mail log extract shows jake@cyberspace.net sending a message to user13@some-isp.com on February 6 at 15:20 from the IP address 10.10.2.34 in bold:

```
Feb 6 15:20:44 mailserver sendmail[26500]: OAA16500: from=<jake@cyberspace.org>, size=1202,
class=0, pri=31202, nrcpts=1, msgid=<200302061520.HAA00289@mailserver>, proto=ESMTP,
relay=dial-up.cyberspace.org [10.10.2.34]
Feb 6 15:20:52 mailserver sendmail[26513]: OAA16500: to=<user13@some-isp.com>,
ctladdr=<jake@cyberspace.org> (43222/1), delay=00:00:10, xdelay=00:00:08, mailer=esmtp,
relay=mail.some-isp.com. [192.168.1.54], stat=Sent (LAA27108 Message accepted for delivery)
```

These logs can also be useful for calculating clock offsets on the sender's computer by comparing them to the times of e-mail messages from that machine. Incidentally, similar logs are created on the receiving e-mail server when a message is delivered to the recipient. If investigators need to demonstrate that a suspect received and downloaded a particular message, they can use e-mail server logs that show when individuals checked their e-mail. The following log entries show "user13" checking e-mail twice on February 6, once at 11:01 and a second time at 15:30:[6]

```
Feb 6 11:01:26 mailserver ipop3d[26535]: Login user=user13 host=10.10.2.10
Feb 6 11:01:58 mailserver ipop3d[26535]: Logout user=user13 host=10.10.2.10
Feb 6 15:30:48 mailserver ipop3d[27621]: Login user=user13 host=10.10.2.34
Feb 6 15:31:19 mailserver ipop3d[27621]: Logout user=user13 host=10.10.2.34
```

In the event that remnants of the received message cannot be found on the recipient's computer, log entries showing the message being received by the e-mail server and then downloaded using the recipient's account draw a compelling picture. When there is the possibility that someone gained unauthorized

---

[6] In the first log segment, sendmail is the name of a UNIX server that conveys messages using the Simple Mail Transfer Protocol (SMTP). This differs from ipop3d in the second log segment, which is another server that enables "user13" to authenticate and download e-mail from the server (e.g., to a computer at home connected to the Internet via a modem).

access to the recipient's e-mail account, additional corroborating evidence may be needed to attribute these activities to a particular individual.

### 8.2.3) INTERNET CHAT[7]

As noted in Chapter 2, many programs enable individuals to chat with others on the Internet. This section describes tracking in the context of one particular network: Internet Relay Chat (IRC). IRC is frequently encountered in child exploitation investigations, and the associated tracking techniques can be generalized to other chat networks. Before tracking anyone on IRC, investigators need to configure some form of logging to document the search. The reason is that a large amount of data is generated, and it is not possible to document such data manually. For instance, in mIRC logging can be configured as shown in Figure 8.4.

Including the date in the file name is a good practice from an evidence-gathering standpoint, and the "Timestamp logs" feature records the date and time of all lines in a log file, making it easier to keep track of when events recorded in the logs occurred. For instance, when contacting an ISP to identify an individual found on IRC, investigators need to provide the IP address along with the date and time of interest.

*Figure 8.4*

*Logging configuration, accessed via the File, Options menu item*

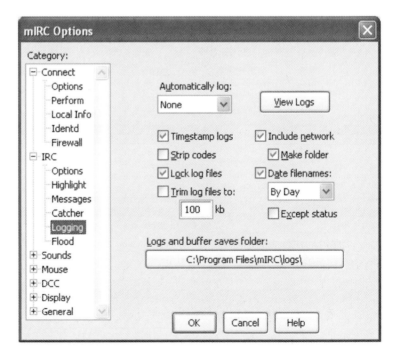

---

[7] This section is adapted from Casey (2004).

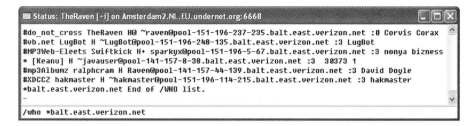

*Figure 8.5*

*Results of the* who *command on IRC*

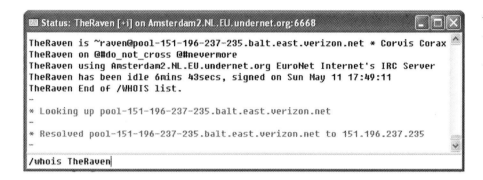

*Figure 8.6*

*Results of the* whois *and* dns *commands on IRC*

When a broad search of a particular IRC subnet is required, the who command is most useful. The who command can search for any word that might occur in a person's hostname or nickname, or can be used to search for people in a particular region. For instance, Figure 8.5 shows the who command being used to find all Verizon users from Baltimore (*balt.east.verizon.net).

Similarly, investigators can search for individuals in a specific country using the commands /who *.se or /who *.ie for all individuals in Sweden and Ireland, respectively. As another example, the command /who *raven* finds all users with the word "raven" in their nickname or hostname. Individuals can make it more difficult to locate them on IRC by using the invisibility feature.[8] However, the invisibility feature does not conceal the individual from others in the same channel, so it offers limited protection.

When a particular individual of interest is found on IRC, the whois command can provide additional details. The whois command on IRC is not the same as the Whois databases mentioned earlier. The whois command uses a person's IRC nickname to get information such as the person's IP address and, if s/he provides it, e-mail address. Figure 8.6 shows information obtained about an IRC user named "TheRaven" using whois, listing channels TheRaven is in (#nevermore, #do_not_cross) and, more importantly, the computer s/he

---

[8] See http://www.mirc.co.uk/faq6.html#section6–26 *and* http://www.irchelp.org/irchelp/misc/ccosmos.html (section 2.7.4).

*Figure 8.7*

*DataGrab used to capture the* whois *and* dns *information about all participants in a channel*

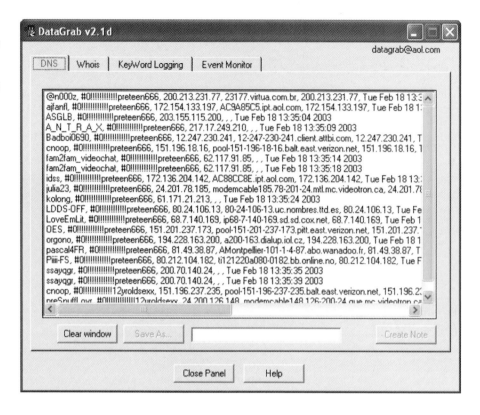

is connecting from (pool-151-196-237-235.balt.east.verizon.net). The IP address associated with this hostname was obtained using the command /dns TheRaven.

Additional information about these and other IRC commands is detailed at The IRC Command Cosmos.[9] Note that it is not advisable to use the finger command on IRC to gather information about an individual because it notifies the other party, whereas the who, Whois, and dns commands do not.

If a particular IRC channel is of interest, using an automated program that continuously monitors activity in that channel can be fruitful. A utility called DataGrab[10] facilitates monitoring activities on IRC and gathering the whois and dns information. Figure 8.7 shows DataGrab being used to gather DNS information about all participants in a channel called "#0!!!!!!!!!!!!!preteen666," saving the date-time stamped results into a text file. The "KeyWord Logging" feature can be configured to record information whenever a particular word occurs in the chat room being monitored.

Chat Monitor[11] is another useful tool for automatically monitoring specific IRC channels and looking for anyone connecting from particular countries.

[9] http://www.irchelp.org/irchelp/misc/ccosmos.html.
[10] http://members.aol.com/datagrab/.
[11] http://www.surfcontrol.com.

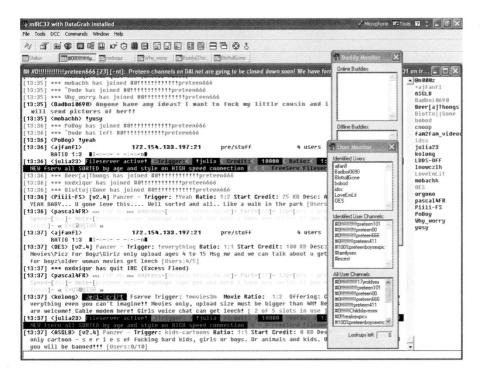

Figure 8.8 shows Chat Monitor logging individuals who are participating in the
IRC channel called "#0!!!!!!!!!!!!!preteen666."

Chat Monitor can also be configured with a list of nicknames that are of interest using its "Buddy Monitor" feature. Additionally, Chat Monitor can be used
to analyze IRC logs for a particular user's activities.

IRC also has a direct client connection (DCC) feature that allows two individuals to have a private conversation and exchange files. As the name suggests,
DCC establishes a direct connection between personal computers much like on
a peer-to-peer network, bypassing the IRC network, leaving little or no digital
evidence on the IRC servers.[12] Another feature of IRC, called "fserve" (short
for fileserver), enables people to make files on their personal computers available to many other IRC users. Many of the people trading files on IRC (e.g.,
pornography and pirated software) use this feature. One of the most sophisticated and popular fserves is Panzer.[13]

When two individuals use DCC or fserve to communicate or exchange information, a direct TCP session is established between the two machines. An investigator can take advantage of this fact, using the `netstat` command to learn
and/or confirm an individual's IP address, as shown here. The first of the two

---

[12]  It can be difficult to obtain logs relating to live chat sessions on the Internet, but it is sometimes
worth the effort. Some chat servers keep logs of which IP addresses connected at which times and
which nicknames were assigned.

[13]  http://www.filetrading.net/irc/fileservers/panzer.htm.

connections to the irc.server.org is the investigator's connection to the IRC server, and the other entry relates to a direct connection with another IRC user's computer. The remote IP address of this direct connection (shown in bold) can be associated with an individual with the help of the associated ISP:

```
C:/> netstat -a -p TCP

Protocol  Local Address   Remote Address          State

TCP       snoop:auth      irc.server.org:1371     TIME_WAIT
TCP       snoop:1150      irc.server.org:7000     ESTABLISHED
TCP       snoop:2341      10.34.156.3:1019        ESTABLISHED
```

To establish continuity of offense, digital evidence examiners may be able to salvage remnants of these DCC sessions from unallocated or swap space. Also, some offenders keep personal logs of the direct, private communications that they have on IRC.

### 8.2.4) FILE SHARING

Many available programs enable individuals to exchange files with others on the Internet, including WinMX, eDonkey, BitTorrent, and the FastTrack network consisting of KaZaA, Grokster, and iMesh. This section focuses on KaZaA, which can be used to share many file types, including images and videos. As with DCC connections on IRC, investigators can use `netstat` to view active connections with remote computers when downloading files.

Once the associated computer is seized, continuity of offense can be established using information stored in the Registry entries and files created by the KaZaA application. The KaZAlyser tool is useful for extracting information such as IP addresses from KaZaA clients, as shown in Figure 8.9.[14]

*Figure 8.9*

*KaZAlyser used to display IP addresses and other details relating to file exchanges*

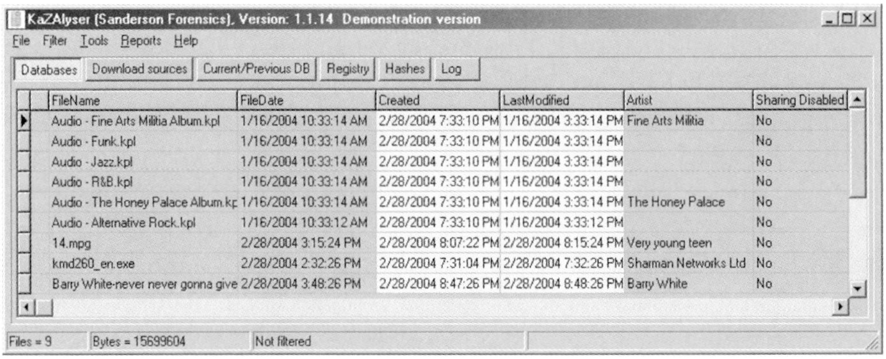

---

[14] http://www.sandersonforensics.co.uk/kazalyser.html.

KaZaA has one feature that can be beneficial from an investigative standpoint: Whenever possible, it obtains files from peers in the same geographic region. Therefore, if investigators find a system with illegal materials, there is a good chance that it is nearby.

## 8.3) OVERCOMING CHALLENGES TO ATTRIBUTION

When attempting to attribute online activities to an individual, investigators need to guard against two fundamental errors. First, they must be careful of transcribing IP addresses and time periods (e.g., 3:14AM versus 3:14PM) when applying for a subpoena or search warrant. Such mistakes have resulted in the wrong person being suspected. Second, offenders may be connecting through an intermediate system such as a proxy or compromised computer. In Toronto, thirty-six-year-old Walter Nowakoski was caught by police driving through a residential neighborhood nude from the waist down, apparently downloading child pornography via insecure wireless access points (CTV News 2003). Notably, defendants in child exploitation cases have used the defense that someone broke into their computer and downloaded child pornography without their knowledge.

To address this risk and solidly establish continuity of offense, investigators should make an effort to verify that the IP address in question is actually the source of the illegal activity. This verification can be achieved using corroborating evidence from multiple independent sources on a network, surveillance, or other methods described in the following section.

### 8.3.1) WEB PROXIES AND MISDIRECTION

Some offenders connect to the Web through a proxy server to conceal their IP address. When a proxy server is used, Web servers generally record only the IP address of the proxy and not that of the offender's computer.[15] Many organizations and ISPs maintain Web proxies for their customers both for security and network management purposes. The use of such professionally managed proxies is generally restricted to customers, and the server may be configured to maintain records similar to Web access logs showing which IP addresses accessed which Web pages. Other proxy servers are simply poorly configured systems that inadvertently allow anyone to use them as a passthrough point when accessing the Internet. Whether these poorly configured systems have logs that can be useful in an investigation depends on the specific situation.

---

[15] Some proxy servers may send the actual IP address of the offender's computer in the "X-Forwarded-For:" HTTP client header when requesting a Web page, in which case the Web server could conceivably record the offender's IP address.

When offenders use anonymous Web proxies that purposefully do not maintain such logs, determining their actual IP address can be very difficult.

**CASE EXAMPLE**

Germany 2003: The AN.ON service (http://anon.inf.tu-dresden.de) at the Technical University of Dresden enables individuals to access the Web through one or more anonymous proxies. In August 2003, the operators of AN.ON were compelled by a Lower District Court in Frankfurt on behalf of the German Federal Bureau of Criminal Investigation (FBCI) to record all connections to a particular IP address via their system. The operators modified the system to record this data and logged one event before the process was suspended a few weeks later while the District Court considered the situation. Before a final decision was reached, the FBCI obtained a warrant from the Lower District Court to search the AN.ON servers for the log of this single event. Rather than having an invasive search of their systems, the AN.ON operators gave the FBCI the data they wanted. However, on appeal the original decision was reversed and the FBCI was required to return the log data. (ICP 2003)

Some Web sites that have an illegal purpose attempt to obfuscate their actual location by using Web redirection services (e.g., www.kickme.to). These types of redirection simply embed the page within a frame or forward the browser to another IP address. As an example, consider the following Usenet message referencing a Web site claiming to contain child pornography. Incidentally, the origin of Usenet messages can often be determined by the optional NNTP-Posting-Host and X-Trace header lines shown here in bold:

```
Path:
typhoon.snet.net!cyclone.swbell.net!cyclone-sf.pbi.net!206.13.28.125!cyclone-
transit.snfc21.pbi.net!205.252.116.205!howland.erols.net!outgoing.news.rcn.net.MISMATCH!
feed1.news.rcn.net!rcn!chnws02.medi
aone.net!chnws05.ne.mediaone.net!24.128.8.70!typhoon.ne.mediaone.net.POSTED!not-for-mail
From: fjnc@gfyrtsxj.com
Subject: The best true Child video server!
Newsgroups: alt.binaries.pictures.erotica.amateur
Organization: =====
Message-ID: <4IQ16T9L.V50TCJ30@gfyrtsxj.com>
Lines: 10
Date: Sun, 25 Jun 2000 17:47:44 GMT
NNTP-Posting-Host: 24.128.110.140
X-Complaints-To: abuse@mediaone.net
X-Trace: typhoon.ne.mediaone.net 961955264 24.128.110.140 (Sun, 25 Jun 2000 13:47:44 EDT)
NNTP-Posting-Date: Sun, 25 Jun 2000 13:47:44 EDT
Xref: typhoon.snet.net alt.binaries.pictures.erotica.amateur:1306872

The best true Child video server!

The best lolitas video site on the Net!
Check this itself!
http://child.lolita.tf/
120 Mb minimum!

Updated bi-monthly!
http://child.lolita.tf/
```

The Web page in this advertisement simply redirected visitors to another Web server (ss8.sexshare.com/~alfers/) that held the pornographic materials. Although the server in Colorado that was directly referenced by http://child.lolita.tf may have some useful logs, the majority of the digital evidence relating to this site was located on a server in Arizona. Therefore, when investigating a Web site that contains child pornography, investigators should be alert for this type of redirection and should open any frames in a new browser window to verify that the page does not bring them to a different Web server.

### 8.3.2) E-MAIL FORGERY

Although the sender can insert forged Received headers into an e-mail message, at least one of the Received headers must be legitimate since the destination server will add one when it receives the message. The following e-mail has two Received headers, but the one added initially (in bold) appears to be fabricated to misdirect attention from the actual source:

```
Received: from 12-217-59-118.client.mchsi.com (12-217-59-118.client.mchsi.com
         [12.217.59.118]) by lsh110.siteprotect.com (8.11.6/8.11.6) with SMTP id
         i155SDv22910 for <user32@siteprotect.com>; Wed, 4 Feb 2004 23:28:15 -0600
Received: from [7.93.244.236] by 12-217-59-118.client.mchsi.com; Sat, 14 Feb 2004 11:26:25
         +0600
Message-ID: <1fr0-8$e-31-5-2-r@6qari3aqno>
From: "Rose Painter" <xfuk00@aol.com>
Reply-To: "Rose Painter" <xfuk00@aol.com>
To: user32@siteprotect.com
Subject: Young teens waiting for you
Date: Sat, 14 Feb 04 11:26:25 GMT
```

One indication that this header is forged is that the date is ten days later than that of the uppermost Received header added by the receiving e-mail server. Another indication is that the IP address (7.93.244.236) belongs to the U.S. Department of Defense, which is not consistent with other information in this case. It is not always safe to assume that an apparently inconsistent originating IP address is an indication of a forgery, but sometimes this will be obvious. When in doubt, investigators should contact the network operators of the apparent source to determine whether the message originated from their network. In the preceding example, the actual source (12-217-59-118.client.mchsi.com) belongs to an ISP named Mediacom Communications Corporation. Therefore, the sender is probably either a customer of this ISP or an intruder who gained unauthorized access to the customer's computer to send the message.

When offenders use pseudonymous e-mail services to conceal their identities, investigators may not be able to determine the sender's IP address from the e-mail header but may be able to obtain this information from log files on the server that provides the pseudonymous service. In the case of truly anonymous e-mail, investigators may not be able to identify the sender without some form of active monitoring on the system that provides the anonymous service.

### 8.3.3) INTERNET CHAT

Increasingly, individuals who want to hide their IP addresses on chat networks are finding poorly configured hosts with open proxy servers (e.g., Wingate or SOCKS proxies) and are using them without authorization. Obtaining log files from these proxies can be difficult, particularly when they are located in another country. To address this growing problem, many IRC networks will not allow connections from hosts that are running a proxy server.

Another way that some offenders conceal their actual IP addresses is using IRC "bots" that are installed on compromised systems. These programs can function like proxies and can be used to perform other tasks such as administering a channel and sharing files. For example, the IRCOffer bot is widely used to share pirated software, movies, and other illegal materials. Another popular type of bot is a "bouncer" (BNC for short) that allows an individual to connect to IRC via the compromised machine. When an individual is connected to IRC via a BNC bot, only the IP address of the computer running the BNC bot is visible; the individual's actual IP address is not visible on IRC.

To determine the actual location of offenders who are connecting through IRC bots, investigators often need to examine the compromised computer to find log files containing IP addresses of individuals who installed or used the bot. However, bots such as "Eggdrop" can encrypt log files on the compromised host to prevent investigators from obtaining the information they contain, in which case it is necessary to monitor network traffic to and from the compromised machine to obtain the IP addresses of those involved.

### 8.3.4) COMPROMISED HOST

When the apparent source of activity is determined, it is advisable to look for signs that the host may be compromised to avoid the wasted effort of seizing the wrong computer. Remotely probing a computer for signs of compromise is a delicate process because if the computer belongs to the actual offender, s/he may notice an inordinate amount of probing. However, skilled investigators can lightly probe a remote computer while remaining indistinguishable from the noise that is created by the large numbers of intruders and worms that are regularly probing computers on the Internet for vulnerabilities.

For example, suppose that illegal activity is tracked back to a computer and the investigator performed the following port scan of the system using nmap:

```
# nmap -sV 192.168.1.5
Starting nmap V. 3.00 (www.insecure.org/nmap/)
Interesting ports on 192.168.1.5:
(The 1579 ports scanned but not shown below are in state: closed)
Port       State      Service
53/tcp     open       domain
135/tcp    open       loc-srv
137/tcp    filtered   netbios-ns
138/tcp    filtered   netbios-dgm
139/tcp    filtered   netbios-ssn
445/tcp    open       microsoft-ds
1080/tcp   open       socks
1434/tcp   filtered   ms-sql-m
3372/tcp   open       msdtc
3389/tcp   open       ms-term-serv
5900/tcp   open       vnc
8080/tcp   open       http-proxy
17300/tcp             filtered kuang2
```

These scan results indicate that the computer is running a Web (HTTP) proxy, SOCKS proxy, Virtual Network Computing (VNC) server, and what might be a Trojan horse program called Kuang. So, an offender might be able to access various Internet services via the Web or SOCKS proxies to conceal his or her IP address. Additionally, the server may be compromised and under the full control of the offender. Like many remote administration tools (a.k.a. Trojan horse programs), VNC has legitimate administrative uses, but it is also used by computer intruders to remotely control a compromised system. Searching Antivirus Web sites for information about the Kuang2 Trojan horse leads to instructions of what to look for on a potentially compromised computer. Instructions for detecting Trojan horse programs commonly include looking for a particular file name in C:\Windows\System32 and for an associated entry in the following Registry key:

HKEY_LOCAL_MACHINE\Software\Microsoft\Windows\CurrentVersion\Run

Using Trojan horse programs, offenders can do almost anything on the remote computer, including downloading files onto the disk and making them available to others on the Internet, thus effectively turning the compromised system into a file server. Investigators may be able to use network level logs from ISPs, such as those described in Chapter 13 to determine whether a computer used to exchange child pornography was compromised. When an ISP's network level logs do not contain signs of intrusion or the ISP does not routinely maintain such network level logs, investigators may be able to perform surveillance of the suspect's network activities using a monitoring system on the ISP's network.

## REFERENCES

Casey, E. *Digital Evidence and Computer Crime.* 2nd Ed. London: Academic Press, 2004.

ICP "District Court in Frankfurt Confirms Legal Claim of AN.ON." (September 18, 2003). http://www.datenschutzzentrum.de/material/themen/presse/anonip3_e.htm.

Shinkle, P. "Serial Killer Caught by His Own Internet Footprint," *St. Louis Post-Dispatch* (June 17, 2002).

Taylor, M., and E. Quayle. *Child Pornography: An Internet Crime.* London: Souvenir Books, 2003.

# CHAPTER 9

# SEARCH AND SEIZURE IN CYBERSPACE I: DRAFTING WARRANTS AND WARRANTLESS SEARCHES

*Although every computer search is unique, search strategies often depend on the role of the hardware in the offense. If the hardware is itself evidence, an instrumentality, contraband, or a fruit of crime, [investigators] will usually plan to seize the hardware and search its contents off-site. If the hardware is merely a storage device for evidence, agents generally will only seize the hardware if less disruptive alternatives are not feasible. (USDOJ 2001)*

Drafting computer-assisted child exploitation search warrants usually requires at least some expertise in both technology and child exploitation. If the officers tasked with drafting the search warrant application do not possess the necessary expertise, it behooves them to seek out someone who can help. This chapter gives officers and prosecutors guidance when preparing search warrants in computer-assisted child exploitation cases. In addition to the advice offered here, officers and prosecutors should consult with local experts. The chapter addresses drafting arrest warrants and offers guidance in approaching complex cases. Thanks to Detective Jim Smith for sharing his search warrant language. The chapter concludes with an overview of situations in which a warrantless search may be considered.

## 9.1) SEARCH WARRANT DRAFTING

The first step is to gather intelligence information to determine whether there is sufficient probable cause to justify a search and seizure. You need to gather as much information as possible about the following before preparing the affidavit and application:

• **An estimated number of computers involved.** The type of criminal activity under investigation should give you some guidance as to whether there is evidence to be found on one computer and possibly removable storage media, such as floppy disks, CD-ROMs and Zip disks, or several computers. For instance, a child pornography possession case might involve one computer and a number of items of evidence such as removable media and videotapes. If the suspect works, evidence might be located on his or her work computer or laptop. On the other hand, if the case involves enticing a minor to engage in sexual activity over the Internet, you will want to examine a number of computers that may be involved: the suspect's computer will have evidence and s/he may have a home PC, a laptop, and a work computer; the victim's computer will contain corroborating evidence that you will want to examine; and the Internet Service Provider may also have information that is important to substantiate the case.

- **Location.** This point may seem obvious, but you need to know where the computers are located. For instance, if your suspect has been communicating with a minor using the Internet, it is safe to assume that s/he is using a computer to do so. The question that should be resolved to support your search warrant application is "Where is the computer that was used to access the Internet?" Internet access can take place from just about anywhere (from home, using a laptop virtually anywhere with a cellular modem, a library, an Internet café, school, work, via a mobile phone, etc.).

- **Type of operating system and software utilized.** Knowing the type of operating system is useful but is not essential at the warrant-drafting stage. However, the Department of Justice advises that, "[u]ntil [an investigator] has learned what kinds of computers and operating systems the target uses, it is impossible to know how the information the system con[tains] can be retrieved, or even where the information may be located. Every computer and computer network is different, and subtle differences in hardware, software, operating systems, and system configuration can alter the search plan dramatically. For example, a particular search strategy may work well if a targeted network runs the Linux operating system, but might not work if the network runs Windows NT instead" (USDOJ 2001). If the plan is to search the system on-site, it is essential to know what type of operating system, hardware, etc., the search team will confront. However, assuming that most of the time the plan will include taking computer systems off-site to conduct the search, knowing the operating system and other details is not critical.

- **The functions the computer is used for.** The functions a computer is used for will have a bearing on how you will want to proceed. For instance, if the computer is used exclusively for personal activity—such as word processing, games, research—you need not proceed as cautiously as you would if the computer were used for an innocent party's business. If the computer is used for conducting business (other than illicit businesses such as narcotics trafficking or child pornography), you need to consult a prosecutor to determine the best way to proceed. Usually, even if the computer is used for the business, if it contains contraband—child pornography—there is no question that law enforcement may seize it, no matter what financial consequences ensue for the business owner. Of course, there are many gray areas, such as when the computer containing the contraband is attached to a larger network and the entire network must be seized to obtain the necessary evidence. In a network case, taking down the entire network may not be justified. The facts of the particular case, the reasonableness of the seizure, and the situation of the computer system's owner will have great bearing on the proper course of action.

Another major consideration is whether a target uses the computer to generate and/or store material intended for publication. Seizing materials intended for publications may implicate provisions of the Privacy Protection Act, a little-used but important protection that is discussed in greater depth in another chapter. Essentially, if child pornography is found on the computer, law enforcement may seize it. In cases in which the computer is used by third parties who are preparing material for publication—such as authors, professors, doctors, journalists, or attorneys—then, upon request, you might need to either provide the owner with a copy of the requested material or return the original and retain a copy.

- **The type of security devices or measures in use.** While it is impossible to anticipate every eventuality, if the affiant can ascertain the level of the target's use of security devices, such as encryption devices and software, data destruction programs and whether counter-surveillance is used, doing so will smooth execution of the warrant when the time comes. Of course, the sophistication of the target plays a major role in the effectiveness of any methods used to conceal illicit behaviors. An anecdote shared with one author by a colleague bears repeating (the truth of the legend is immaterial—the lesson it offers is more important than the facts): Police seized a suspect's laptop and, as they hauled it off, the suspect jeered, "You'll never get anything on me! I installed PGP three times!!!" Indeed, the suspect *installed* PGP three times but never applied the encryption program to any of his files.

- **Whether backup records exist and where they may be located.** While most people don't back up their records, technically savvy people *do* create and maintain backups and so do people who really value their data. It is certainly reasonable to expect that a technologically adept child pornography collector who has spent a great deal of effort and money to acquire the material would be motivated to ensure that it will not be destroyed. When a computer user backs up records, it is accepted and advisable practice to store backups off-site to protect the backups from the same fate visited upon the originals, in case of destruction. It is often not feasible to determine whether backups exist prior to executing the search warrant; however, it is a topic for discussion with the suspect during any interview that may take place.

You might reasonably ask, "Why bother with the backups?" The fact that a defendant backed up data weighs in favor of proving knowledge and intent. If the defendant spent a fair amount of time backing up the data on a hard drive or making duplicates of removable media, s/he *knows* what data is contained therein—after all, s/he is making a special effort to preserve it. (The prosecution is also better able to prove knowledge when the defendant fastidiously arranges files named by content—for example, "my five-year-olds," "angie," "money-shotz," etc.) Backups also tend to prove that the defendant intended to possess the material. If s/he didn't intend to possess the material, then going out of his or her way to make a duplicate of it is nonsensical. Why would anyone who doesn't know the content and character of something make a copy of it? If the defendant did not intend to possess the material, then why didn't s/he delete it or opt *not* to make a copy of it?

## 9.2) SEARCH WARRANTS IN GENERAL

For a search warrant to be valid, it must both particularly describe the property to be seized and establish probable cause for the seizure and search of the property. When drafting an application for a search warrant that includes computer hardware and data, the applicants must particularly describe the property and articulate probable cause that the property: (1) is an instrumentality for the commission of any criminal offense; or (2) is the fruit of a crime; or (3) constitutes evidence of a crime.

### 9.2.1) PARTICULARITY

Whenever complex terms are defined by statute, you should reference the statutory definition and add whatever language is missing. For example, if the term "computer" is defined by statute in the jurisdiction, you can simplify the drafting by substituting the phrase "computer, as defined by . . . (and you cite the statutory reference)." The drafter should be as precise as possible, so if you know that the suspect is using a specific type of PC, the warrant application should state that.

#### 9.2.1.1) Child pornography on a PC hard drive

Electronically stored images of child pornography may be found in a number of places. The suspect's hard drive is one obvious place to look. Suspects may also store images on removable media, such as floppy disks, but more likely larger storage media such as Zip disks, CD-ROMs, magneto optical disks, DVDs, and videocassettes. Investigators should also search for magazines, books, and photographs containing child pornography and child erotica. The following is a sample paragraph from a child pornography warrant application detailing the items sought to be seized:

Evidence of electronic communications from the username "xxxx123" that pertain to the purchase, production, importation, promotion and or dissemination of child pornography;

A "computer system" or systems, as defined by [statute citation] used to contain images of child pornography or evidence of the purchase, production, importation, promotion and or dissemination of child pornography; Notations of any password(s) that may control access to a computer operating system, individual computer files or to access Internet accounts or Websites; Any evidence of "child pornography" as defined in [statute citation], its purchase, production, importation, promotion and or dissemination, by mail or by computer, in the form of envelopes, letters, and other correspondence. Specifically the file named "!!7 girl suck.jpg" but this evidence should not be limited to this specific file; Envelopes, letters, e-mail, and other correspondence (whether stored as "data", as defined by [statute citation], paper or in any other form) "promoting a minor in an obscene performance", as defined by [statute citation], including by mail, by computer or any other means; Correspondence pertaining to the purchase, production, importation, promotion and or dissemination of child pornography, but not limited to: saved electronic communications (e.g., e-mail, instant messages, etc.), paper printouts of same, notes of conversations and any other records of any sort pertaining to the purchase, possession, or receipt of child pornography; Visual depictions, other "material" [statute citation], "data" [statute citation] or "property" [statute citation] that depict "child pornography" [statute citation] in a manner contrary to law, including but not limited to photographs, undeveloped film, videotapes, and electronic media, including but not limited to floppy disks, CD-ROMs, Zip disks and hard drives that may be used to store visual depictions of child pornography; Devices used to create, view or store visual depictions of child pornography including, but not limited to video cassette recorders, cameras or any sort, digital and analog video cassette recorders, photo scanners (used to convert paper photographs to digital form), a "computer system" or systems, as defined by [statute citation] and "data" as defined by [statute citation] that may contain child pornography, software and hardware manuals and passwords necessary to access the computer system, software programs, individual files, Internet Websites or records of visits to Internet Websites, pertaining to possession, importation of child pornography or promoting a minor in an obscene performance; To seize said items and transport them to the Computer Crime Laboratory for investigative examination of digital evidence (the investigative examination will include making true copies of the data and examining the contents of files), to develop and examine undeveloped film taken at the search scene and seized as evidence as potentially containing child pornography.

## 9.3) CHILD PORNOGRAPHY SENT VIA THE INTERNET—SEARCH WARRANT FOR INTERNET ACCOUNT

While you will also want to seize the suspect's computer when the target of an investigation distributes child porn via the Internet, obtaining the Internet account records would be very beneficial. Usually, Internet access providers maintain logs of subscribers' activities. At the very least, they have the contents of e-mail that the account holder has not yet accessed, but often they maintain e-mail sent and recently received. Additionally, some ISPs maintain detailed logs of network activities that can help prove that a defendant downloaded and/or disseminated child pornography on the Internet. Additionally, if an ISP has an intrusion detection system, the associated logs may be useful for establishing whether a defendant's computer was compromised. It is important for investigators to be aware that the company will not store transaction or content information for long—usually not more than a few days for items that have been read or sent and not longer than a few weeks for unread e-mail. This practice is common and necessary because the space that would be required to store e-mail and transaction information for longer periods would be prohibitively expensive.

All information regarding the [Internet company name] account belonging to John Doe of 100 Main Street Anytown, USA to include: screennames and passwords used to access the account; times, dates and Internet Protocol addresses used to access the account for the time period [be specific and be reasonable]; ANI data related to accessing the account; all favorites, buddy lists, newsgroups subscribed to and all data stored by [Internet company name] related to the account, including all e-mail sent, read or unread; all traffic and billing information including payments received and information supplied by the subscriber to establish and maintain the account; all information regarding any other [name of Internet company] account subscribed to by [name and address of target].

When you are requesting information from ISPs, it often helps to speak with them to determine what types of systems and information they have. If such communication is not possible, it is generally acceptable to request a range of information provided limiting language is used to specify the crime, the suspects, and relevant time period. It is also recommended to include explicit examples of the records to be seized and indicate that the records may be seized in any form, including digital and paper. An example of such a request is provided here:

> All records associated with the subscriber and account, including screen name(s) and/or account name(s), phone number(s), address(es), credit card numbers used to establish the account, connection records, to include logon dates and times, IP address assigned for each session, origination information for each call, phone number used for access to the system, newsgroups logs, e-mail logs, quantity of local storage provided and percentage utilized (non content information), credit, and billing information for any and all accounts held in the name of John Doe and the address(s) 192.168.12.14, 192.168.12.16, and john.doe@home.com, for the period of (insert date and time covered as nearly as possible and limited to the period of suspected criminal activity). Furthermore, company policy and activities pertaining to the frequency of backup operations and retention periods of information requested herein. The term "records" includes all of the foregoing items of evidence in whatever form and by whatever means they may have been created or stored.

Note that transcription errors AM versus PM or one wrong digit in an IP address will lead to the wrong individual.

Two nuances in this example deserve emphasis. First, e-mail content is not requested, thus avoiding the privacy issues related to stored personal communications, making it easier to obtain a search warrant. Investigators may be able to obtain a significant amount of information quickly and with relative ease by making this clear distinction between subscriber information and the contents of the individual's account. Some organizations, such as eBay, can even provide law enforcement with certain information about their users (e.g., name, address) without a court order because their user agreement permits such disclosure. Second, log files and "origination information for each call" are included in this sample request to cover Automatic Number Identification (ANI) information to ensure that it is obtained when available.

## 9.4) ENTICEMENT OF A MINOR

When you are investigating an enticement case, you will encounter two main types of scenarios: one in which the "victim" is an undercover officer and the other in which the victim is either a real minor or someone the suspect believes to be a minor. There will be evidence of the offense in at least three places: the suspect's computer, the victim's or undercover's machine, and at the Internet Service Provider. If the enticement took place in a chat room, evidence may exist in other locations, such as on chat room participants' computer systems. However, securing the victim's machine, the suspect's, and the account information will be more than sufficient, if the incident took place and the suspect committed the offense.

The number of separate search warrants required will depend on whether the victim is an undercover officer and, if not, whether the victim is cooperative. Even with a cooperative victim, consent may be withdrawn. And, oftentimes, personal computers are shared with others in the household, so you might consider either getting all users to consent to the search or obtaining a search warrant so that whatever actions you take have the benefit of judicial authorization. The paragraph for the suspect's Internet account in Section 9.3 should be sufficient for his or her online activity. For the suspect's personal computer, the following language provides a starting point:

> A personal computer, any data contained therein and any notes, printouts and material relating to communications over the Internet, by phone and by mail between [THE SUSPECT] and [MINOR(s)] during the time period [DATES, IF APPLICABLE], pictures of the victim, records of Internet accounts subscribed to by [THE SUSPECT], records of gifts purchased by [SUSPECT] for [VICTIM(s)] and trips taken to meet [THE VICTIM/ OTHER VICTIMS].

## 9.5) GROOMING EVIDENCE

Police should search for evidence that the suspect "groomed" the victim or other victims in enticement cases:

> **"Grooming"** refers to the ways that a sexual offender gains control over victims, exploiting their weaknesses to gain trust or instill fear. Grooming usually involves exploiting a victim's needs such as loneliness, self-esteem, sexual curiosity/inexperience, or lack of money and taking advantage of this vulnerability to develop a bond. Offenders use this control or bond to sexually manipulate victims and discourage them from exposing the offender to authorities.

Duncan Brown described "Developing Strategies for Collecting and Presenting Grooming Evidence in a High Tech World." He listed evidence to search for:

- Adult and child pornography: obviously could be used to lower a victim's inhibitions about sex and nudity.
- Adult or child erotica: same use as pornography.
- Photographs of children in underwear or suggestive poses: used as initial grooming device.
- Photography equipment: many molesters first take regular photos of victims to get them used to being in front of the camera.
- Toys, children's clothes, and other items an adult would not, or could not, use: if an adult male has Barbie dolls or the latest Pokemon cards, he may be using them to gain credibility and build rapport with a child victim.

In a computer case, look for these items as well:

- Hard drives or external storage devices that may hold pornographic images.
- Accessories like Web cameras used to record and broadcast acts of sexual exploitation.
- Chat logs and names of Web sites visited by the defendant.
- Passwords for private chat rooms.
- Screen names used by the defendant.
- Notes and profiles about victims met online.
- Items purchased specifically for meeting the victim: online undercover investigators usually ask the defendant to bring an identifying gift for the victim (Brown 2001).

Note that grooming evidence is not evidence of a crime, but it may be used to show the suspect's intent.

## 9.6) THE AFFIDAVIT—PROBABLE CAUSE

No one can provide a simple recipe for developing probable cause. Each case, no matter how much like another, is at least subtly different. Even if the case developed out of the same or similar facts as another, each justification to seize and search property requires that the government establish sufficient probable cause. Piecing together the facts that will fashion an affidavit can be a little easier using some guidance regarding child exploitation warrants. Looking back at the affidavits written by other officers in your own department and in your jurisdiction for similar cases, together with some tips from this text, will help you to include as much pertinent information as possible.

The investigator should consider a number of factors when writing the affidavit. The most important factor in a computer-assisted child exploitation warrant is that a computer and the Internet are involved and how they are involved. Other very important items to address include "freshness" of information.

At some point during the statement of facts, the affidavit should address why the officer believes that a computer is involved and justify its seizure. The way in which the case came to the attention of law enforcement usually makes justification of seizing and searching the suspect's computer a fairly straightforward matter. For example, all of the targets identified in the Avalanche investigation subscribed to an Internet service that allowed them to view and download child pornography. The only way to access the service was with a computer. And the method of identifying the suspects was tied to the use of the individual's credit card, home address, and Internet access account. But such strong facts are not always present, and the computer nexus must be justified nonetheless. Sometimes there simply is not sufficient probable cause to justify searching for a computer, but once the computer is found in plain view during the course of a search for other evidence, there may be sufficient probable cause to support a warrant to seize the computer at that point.

If the crime suspected was importing or distributing child pornography, the affiant may need to address the issue of code words or slang used by collectors. For instance, the terms "lolita," "asparagus," "twink," and "chicken" all refer to minors and have sexual connotations connected to child pornography and child sexual assault. The following is an example of language addressing the term "lolita" used by a suspect when discussing his collection of child pornography in a chat room:

> It is well known within the law enforcement community, and especially among officers who investigate child pornography offenses and sex crimes committed against children that the term "lolita" refers to young, prepubescent females. The origin of the term "lolita" is from the book by that name by Alexander Nabokov, which detailed a romantic and sexual affair between an adult male and a thirteen year-old girl named Lolita. Individuals seeking images depicting prepubescent females frequently use the search term "lolita," and Websites that advertise "lolita" content are explicitly pandering to individuals in search of visual depictions of prepubescent females engaged in sexual activity. This is confirmed by the Federal Court in *US v. Marchant*, 803 F.2d 174 (5th Cir., 1986) and *US v. Porter*, 709 F. Supp. 770 (E.D. Mich S.D., 1989) and as well as others.

## 9.6.1) FRESHNESS

"Freshness" of probable cause in child pornography cases is often an issue used in an attempt to suppress the evidence. Quite often in large, multi-jurisdictional Internet-based investigations, the information used to form the basis of the search warrant application can raise the issue of whether the information is "stale." Staleness of probable cause requires consideration of several factors. Perhaps the most important factor that weighs heavily in influencing whether probable cause is stale is the type of evidence sought. If the evidence sought is narcotics, and the crime under investigation is sale of narcotics, even a few hours may be too long. On the other hand, if the evidence is a buried body, or some durable, tangible item, a longer period is likely warranted. In the case of child pornography stored on computers, the issue should be addressed in the affidavit if there is any delay in the application for the warrant. Investigators and prosecutors are always better off if the judge grants his or her imprimatur, so you need to discuss the issue in the affidavit as shown in this example:

> The affiants know that persons involved in collecting child pornography tend to retain it for long periods of time. Individuals who are interested in child pornography prize the images obtained, traded and/or sold. In addition to their emotional value, the images are economically valuable in return for currency or similar images traded by another pornographer. Therefore, pornographic images are rarely destroyed or deleted by the individual collector. Libraries of images are usually off-loaded by collectors onto some form of removable media, such as diskettes or CD-ROM. Graphic image files can be maintained on the computer system's internal storage device or stored on diskette, CD-ROM, or in similar form. Even when images stored as data are deleted manually, forensic examiners using software developed specifically for that purpose can often restore the image. Forensic examination can also often determine if an image was deleted and when the image was last accessed.

## 9.6.2) QUALIFICATIONS OF THE AFFIANT OR EXPERT CONSULTED

When creating the affidavit, you should detail your qualifications. Discuss the number of similar cases you have investigated and any specialized courses attended. If you don't know what you're talking about, consult an expert and detail his or her experience.

### 9.6.3) INFORM THE JUDGE THAT THE EXAMINATION OF EVIDENCE MAY TAKE TIME

There is nothing fast or simple about forensic examination of digital evidence. Many labs are backed up with casework for more than six months to a year. It is important, therefore, to not only have an idea of how long it will take for any evidence seized to be examined, but to explain this information to the judge in the search warrant affidavit. Most jurisdictions have time limits regarding when the search must be completed following judicial authorization. But there are so many phases of a digital evidence search and seizure that stating precisely when the search began and when the search ended is more speculative than certain.

For instance, in a jurisdiction in which a search must be performed within ten days of issuing the warrant, officers search a suspect's home and seize his computer on day two. The officers transport the computer to the lab for forensic examination on day three, and it is logged into evidence. The computer hard drive and removable media are duplicated ("imaged") about a month later. Two months after that, a forensic examination is conducted on the "image." While it would be preferable to complete the examination within ten days, it is not clear whether doing so is necessary. The search of the home was completed within the ten days. Another issue is whether the forensic examination after the ten-day period is an unauthorized search. But the search is conducted on the "image," not the original. So, if anything, the government may unlawfully retain the computer beyond the ten days, but arguably, examining the image after the ten days is not a search. Another point is that the evidence is duplicated after the ten-day period. One thing is clear: At least some of these issues will be litigated as the backlogs at digital forensics labs mount. In the meantime, the wise affiant will address the amount of time anticipated to conduct a forensic examination of the evidence, as in the following example:

> Computer storage devices can store millions of pages of data. Furthermore, storing incriminating information within innocuous appearing files can hamper identifying data evidence of criminal activity. For instance, a word processing document labeled "vacation.doc" may contain vacation plans as well as evidence of criminal activity such as an image of child pornography or text of an unlawful communication with a minor. This sort of analysis may take weeks or months, depending on the volume of data stored. It would be impractical, if not impossible, to attempt this sort of analysis on site. In order to execute the search properly, the alternative to extricating the items for

analysis in a laboratory setting would be for law enforcement officers to occupy the premises for days or weeks while the search and analysis proceeds. This alternative is far more intrusive and a much less satisfactory proposition for all parties involved.

Based upon the affiants' experience and training (or the experience and training of an expert you consulted and who has informed you of the following), the affiants know that to retrieve "data" [statute citation] stored in electronic format, and to prevent the loss of such data either by accidental or purposeful means, it is usually necessary that the "computer system" [statute citation], related instruction manuals and documentation, be seized, processed and analyzed by a qualified computer specialist in a laboratory setting. Proper examination of the items to be seized requires seizure of the entire computer system(s) and data.

### 9.6.4) PROVIDE BACKGROUND ON INTERNET FEATURES

Many judges are quite Internet savvy. On the other hand, many judges have no idea what the Internet is like—never having turned on a computer or logged onto the Internet. It was not very long ago that a lawyer's fingers never touched a keyboard, never mind typed his or her own correspondence. When drafting the computer-assisted child exploitation search warrant affidavit, you should provide background on the Internet feature so that the judge or magistrate can better understand how the crime in question occurred. Following are samples to explain Internet features. The samples are not meant to cover every possible Internet feature or use. New features premiere almost daily. A search warrant affiant should investigate how the technology works and take pains to describe it accurately. One way to ensure that a description of a feature is accurate is to review the language with a representative of the Internet Service Provider or other expert before attesting to it.

If a description of the Internet feature or computer processing bogs down the affidavit with too much detail, the affiant may consider using a glossary. Because the judge or magistrate may consider only what is within the four corners of the warrant application, a glossary must be incorporated into the affidavit. When the writer first references the glossary, s/he can say something to the effect of "this affidavit contains terms that may be unfamiliar to the reader. These terms are highlighted in bold and defined in the glossary attached to this affidavit and incorporated herein by reference."

### 9.6.4.1) E-mail

People who utilize the Internet can communicate by using electronic mail (e-mail). E-mail is an electronic form of communication that can contain letter-type correspondence as well as graphic images or attached data such as spreadsheets, computer software or graphic images. E-mail is similar to conventional mail in that it is addressed from one individual to another and is usually private. E-mail usually contains a message header that gives information about the individual who originated a particular message or graphic and the return address in order to respond to them. An Internet e-mail address most likely can be traced to a subscription to, membership in or affiliation with an organization or commercial service that provides access to the Internet. While there are e-mail providers that supply e-mail via modem access or a limited access to the Internet, most often, an e-mail address can be traced to an Internet account. A provider of Internet access is referred to as an Internet Service Provider or "ISP."

### 9.6.4.2) Newsgroups

Based upon the affiants' knowledge, training and experience and the experience and training of other law enforcement officers, the affiants know that Newsgroups are an integral feature of communication using the Internet. Newsgroups allow users to join conversations taking place among a community of individuals who share a common interest. Newsgroups are similar to electronic bulletin boards (BBS) and chat rooms. In fact, newsgroups are very similar to the physical bulletin boards located in public places like grocery stores where people may post and view written, paper messages. A key difference is that newsgroups proliferate throughout the Internet. One can find tens of thousands of newsgroup topics and interact with millions of people. A user of a newsgroup can read postings of interest, or can participate in posting discussions. Newsgroup names usually reflect their focus. For example, alt.sex.pedophilia, alt.sex.teen are fictitious examples of the names of newsgroups through which participants may discuss their sexual predilections, share graphic images and other information. The names of the newsgroups change, but they usually suggest the content in the name for the group. When a user posts a newsgroup message, readers around the world are able to read and respond to it. As with e-mail, a user of a newsgroup can attach computer files, including but not limited to graphic images. Newsgroups allow a reader of the message to download the attached computer file or image.

> ### 9.6.4.3) Peer-to-peer applications
>
> Internet users can utilize peer-to-peer (P2P) file sharing networks to share many types of files. Files shared include music, graphics, images, movies and text. In this way, users are able to amass large collections of files. Based on the experience and training of the affiant and information from fellow law enforcement personnel, P2P sharing services increasingly are used to distribute and collect child pornography.

## 9.7) ARREST WARRANTS

Drafting the arrest warrant affidavit in a computer-assisted case requires explaining how the suspect committed the crime. Because the technology can make the explanation seem complicated, it is a good idea to have a framework within which you might work. Particularly when there is a considerable volume of evidence and a long, complicated investigation, having a framework is helpful. The easiest arrest warrant affidavits to follow set forth the elements of the crime and the way the suspect's conduct fits. For example, in a jurisdiction in which there is a statute called "enticing a minor to engage in sexual activity," the elements of the crime are as follows:

> A person is guilty of **enticing a minor** when such person uses an interactive computer service to knowingly persuade, induce, entice or coerce any person under sixteen years of age to engage in prostitution or sexual activity for which the actor may be charged with a criminal offense. For purposes of this section, "interactive computer service" means any information service, system or access software provider that provides or enables computer access by multiple users to a computer server, including specifically a service or system that provides access to the Internet and such systems operated or services offered by libraries or educational institutions.

The easiest way to explain how the suspect committed this crime may be to write a chronological account of what happened and then summarize how the suspect's actions fit with the elements of the crime. Breaking out the elements, the suspect (1) used an interactive computing service (the Internet); (2) to knowingly; (3) persuade or induce or entice; (4) any person under the age of sixteen; (5) to engage in prostitution or sexual activity for which the actor may be charged with a criminal offense. Breaking out the elements of the offense helps to go back through the affidavit to ensure that the writer has addressed each of the component parts of the crime, as in the following example:

> The suspect used the Internet, utilizing screen name "sizzlingcharlie" to communicate with an undercover police officer using the screen name "sweetgirl12" in a chat room operated by [service provider] on November 14, 16 and 21 of 2004. During conversations with "sizzlingcharlie," the undercover officer explicitly stated that she was a twelve-year-old girl, to which "sizzlingcharlie" responded, "ummm, I love them young like you."

## 9.8) WARRANTLESS SEARCHES

There is a strong judicial and prosecutorial preference for a search warrant. Under limited circumstances police can conduct searches without a warrant. When property is seized pursuant to a search warrant, the burden is on the defendant to challenge the legality of the seizure. When property is seized without a search warrant, the burden is on the prosecution (and, therefore, law enforcement) to justify the legality of the seizure by showing that a valid exception to the warrant requirement is present. **When in doubt, apply for a search warrant.** This section briefly addresses some of the types of warrantless searches that may involve computer systems or data.

### 9.8.1) CONSENT SEARCHES

A subject may knowingly and voluntarily consent to search of a computer or electronic evidence. Typical concerns when a subject consents to a computer-related search include that the consent may be revoked at any time, and the subject may lack the authority to give consent to search the entire contents of the computer. Regarding revocation of consent, as soon as a subject revokes consent, police must stop the search. This can present difficulty if police duplicate the subject's hard drive and begin to search and then must stop. At that point, if police have sufficient probable cause to justify a continued search, they should apply for a warrant. If they lack sufficient probable cause, they must return the original evidence and either give the copy to the subject or destroy it.

When police obtain consent to search a computer system or digital evidence, they must determine whether the subject possesses the authority to consent to a search. In many homes, computer ownership and use are shared. Shared use is of particular concern when spouses make complaints against each other and share the same computer system. While it may be expedient to obtain the consent of one of the spouses to search the computer, it is advisable to obtain a search warrant. On the other hand, when the computer belongs to a victim who is unlikely to become a suspect, consent should be sufficient, even when the consent is granted by a co-user or parent. If you obtain consent to search a computer and/or data, ask the subject if there are any passwords or security devices or programs that you should be aware of.

Private employers may consent to a search of a company-owned computer or electronic evidence. Prior to searching an employer-owned device, police should ensure that it is, in fact, owned by the employer and that the employee should have known that he or she had no reason to believe the computer was his or her personal property or that he or she had a reasonable expectation of privacy in the information held by the computer. Usually, the employer has a written equipment or computer use policy that spells out appropriate use of computers, the Internet, and other employer-owned equipment.

A spouse may consent to a search of the entire house, but not of the absent spouse's private or personal effects. It would be reasonable to conclude that the files on an absent spouse's personal computer, particularly those protected by password, are private possessions. Parents may usually consent to a search of their child's room and/or personal possessions. However, if the child is older, pays rent, locks the room when absent from the home, or otherwise exercises exclusive dominion over the room, a search warrant or consent of the child will probably be required. While this is a fact-specific analysis, it is important to bear in mind due to the widespread use of computers and the Internet by minors (Mattei, Blawie, and Russell 2001).

### 9.8.2) SEARCH INCIDENT TO ARREST

Police may search an individual and the area within his or her immediate control pursuant to that person's lawful arrest. Now that computing devices are smaller and more common, an arresting officer may find himself or herself encountering a computer when making a search incident to arrest. Examples of items include PDAs, handheld computing devices, removable media, and mobile phones. An arresting officer would probably not be within his or her authority to view the contents of the subject's PDA, thumb-drive, or other removable media without a warrant. (See *Chimel v. California* 1969; *United States v. Robinson* 1973.)[1]

Federal authorities may search the contents of pagers pursuant to an arrest of the subject.[2] State and local police should consult their supervisors and prosecutors for guidance before conducting any warrantless search. Certainly, if the

---

[1] *Chimel v. California*, 395 U.S. 752 (1969); *United States v. Robinson*, 414 U.S. 218 (1973).
[2] See *United States v. Reyes*, 922 F. Supp. 818, 833 (S.D.N.Y. 1996); *United States v. Chan*, 830 F. Supp. 531, 535 (N.D. Cal. 1993); *United States v. Lynch*, 908 F. Supp. 284, 287 (D.V.I. 1995); *Yu v. United States*, 1997 WL 423070, at *2 (S.D.N.Y. July 29, 1997). See also *United States v. Ortiz*, 84 F.3d 977, 984 (7th Cir. 1996) (relying on an exigency theory).

need to conduct the search is exigent, conduct the search. If the data will be imminently destroyed and they likely contain evidence, it's probably better to err on the side of conducting the search without waiting for a warrant. If the search is unlawful, you will lose the evidence due to suppression. But if the search would have been held lawful, you cannot resurrect evidence once it has been destroyed—even if you have a warrant.

### 9.8.3) INVENTORY SEARCHES

"Inventory searches" are generally permissible without a warrant. The search must serve a legitimate, non-investigatory purpose. Police are allowed to conduct inventory searches to protect an owner's property while in custody; to ensure against claims of lost, stolen, or vandalized property; or to guard the police from danger. These concerns outweigh the intrusion on the individual's Fourth Amendment rights.[3] Conducting an "inventory" search of a subject's PDA, computer disks, or laptop computer while s/he is in custody probably will not be acceptable without a warrant (USDOJ 2001). Such searches tend to be wholly investigatory in nature and more likely to damage the subject's property than to ensure its proper preservation.

### 9.8.4) PLAIN VIEW

As in any other kind of situation in which a law enforcement officer finds himself or herself, a computer and/or data may lawfully be seized without a warrant under the "plain view" exception to the warrant requirement. If a law enforcement officer sees (or hears or feels) the item while lawfully in a position to view (hear, feel, etc.) it *and* has probable cause to believe it is an instrumentality of criminal activity, contraband, or evidence of a crime, s/he may seize it.

**CASE EXAMPLE**

Carey was the subject of an investigation into the sale of cocaine. Police arrested him and pursuant to his consent, searched his residence. Among other evidence, agents seized two computers. Police took the computers to their offices and obtained a search warrant to look for "names, telephone numbers, ledger receipts, addresses, and other documentary evidence pertaining to the sale and distribution of controlled substances." A detective searched for these items but did not discover any files related to narcotics. Despite the negative results, the detective continued to search the contents of the computers, turning from document review to looking for picture files.

[3] See *Illinois v. Lafayette*, 462 U.S. 640, 644 (1983); *South Dakota v. Opperman*, 428 U.S. 364, 369–70 (1976). Second, the search must follow standardized procedures. See *Colorado v. Bertine*, 479 U.S. 367, 374 n.6 (1987); *Florida v. Wells*, 495 U.S. 1, 4–5 (1990).

He found a "jpg" file, which is an image file. When he opened it, he discovered it depicted what appeared to be child pornography. The detective downloaded **19 diskettes** of image files from the computers. He examined them, looking at five to seven files on each disk, confirming that each disk contained images depicting what appeared to be child pornography. Charged with possession of child pornography, the defendant moved to suppress the child pornography evidence. The defendant argued that the detective's search of the image files went beyond the scope of the warrant. The government contended that the image files were within the plain view exception to the warrant requirement and that the detective was within his authority to open and view them. In the detective's own words, he did not suspect that the defendant possessed child pornography until he viewed the first image file. Thereupon, he determined that the defendant did, in fact, possess child pornography. Yet, the detective continued to search despite the warrant allowing the search of the defendant's computer system did not authorize the search for child pornography. The court held that while the detective found the first file viewed in "plain view," the rest of the files viewed were not. The detective should have applied for a search warrant to look for child pornography at the point that he opened the first image file.[4]

## 9.8.5) CONDITIONS OF PAROLE

When an individual enters a parole agreement containing a provision allowing the search of his or her person or residence, that individual relinquishes a portion of his or her reasonable expectation of privacy in his or her residence.[5] If the parole agreement includes a commitment by the parolee to refrain from downloading pornography from the Internet or other provisions prohibiting either the use of the Internet or computer in some way, government agents may be justified in conducting a warrantless search of that individual's computer system.

**CASE EXAMPLE**

A state court in Utah convicted Jeffrey Tucker of sexually abusing a child. As part of his parole agreement, Tucker consented to allow search of himself, his residence and his property without a warrant upon reasonable suspicion that he violated the terms of his agreement. He also agreed that he would not possess child pornography or materials depicting non-consenting sex. Tucker further agreed that he would not have any contact with minors unless someone aware of his deviant sexual history supervised it.

---

[4] *United States v. Carey*, 172 F.3d 1268 (10th Cir. 1999).
[5] See *United States v. Knights*, 122 S. Ct. 587, 591–92 (2001).

In 1998, Utah parole agents received information from unidentified concerned citizens that Tucker was viewing child pornography using his computer and had contact with minors. When agents attempted to seize Tucker's computer, they observed that Tucker had been visiting a newsgroup(3) labeled "alt.sex.preteen." The Utah authorities performed an investigative review of the computer system and determined that Tucker had a large number of deleted files and that Tucker visited newsgroups known to distribute child pornography.

After informing Tucker of his Miranda rights, he waived them. Agents inquired, "what are we going to find?" Tucker responded, "There's some stuff on there that's going to cause me problems." Tucker went on to admit that he possessed over 5,000 images depicting minors engaged in sexually explicit activity. He also admitted to contacting a minor.[6]

## 9.9) CONCLUSION

Drafting warrant affidavits in computer-assisted cases is more complicated than it is for straightforward street crimes. Even when you have a finely crafted boilerplate, technology changes and you must start from scratch. Such changes create a challenge for computer-assisted child exploitation investigators to keep abreast of new technology while doing everything else required. This chapter provides you with tools and guidance for drafting search and arrest warrants in computer-assisted child exploitation cases. The chapter concluded with an overview of situations in which officers may search for digital evidence without a search warrant.

## REFERENCES

Brown, Duncan. "Developing Strategies for Collecting and Presenting Grooming Evidence in a High Tech World." *Update* 14, no. 11 (2001).

U.S. Department of Justice. *Federal Guidelines for Searching and Seizing Computers.* Washington, DC: Computer Crimes and Intellectual Property Section, Criminal Division, United States Department of Justice, 2001.

Mattei (Ferraro), M., J. F. Blawie, and A.G. Russell. *Law Enforcement Guidelines for Computer Systems and Data Search and Seizure.* Middletown, CT: State of Connecticut, Division of Criminal Justice and Department of Public Safety, 2001.

---

[6] *United States v. Tucker,* No. 01-4150 (10th Cir. 09/16/2002). See also *United States v. Fiscus,* No. 02-4172 (10th Cir. 04/29/2003) holding same.

# CHAPTER 10

# SEARCH AND SEIZURE IN CYBERSPACE II: EXECUTING THE SEARCH

*Ways may some day be developed by which the Government, without removing papers from secret drawers, can reproduce them in court, and by which it will be enabled to expose to a jury the most intimate occurrences of the home. Can it be that the Constitution affords no protection against such invasions of individual security?*[1]

This chapter provides guidance on executing search warrants in computer-assisted child exploitation cases. Because technology evolves rapidly, providing definitive guidance is impossible. The suggestions in this chapter are often the subject of current debate in the community. The authors have tried to reconcile multiple sources of record and have consulted a number of practitioners who have executed literally hundreds of high-technology search warrants. Of one thing we are quite certain: Each situation is different and a one-size-fits-all approach will not work. Flexibility and patience are the most valuable tools in the searcher's toolkit. It may be necessary to conduct research from the search scene to determine the best method to seize the evidence. This chapter provides you with direction on determining the best methods for seizing evidence from new technology. Concentrating primarily on searches at the home and businesses, this chapter also discusses searches of the Internet Service Provider. The chapter next reviews interrogating individuals at the scene, including the suspect. Finally, this chapter addresses some special considerations in executing computer-assisted child exploitation warrants.

## 10.1) SEARCH WARRANTS

Now that you are armed with a search warrant drafted with guidance from Chapter 9, planning for execution of the search can begin. Of course, the type of technology involved and the exigency of the search will dictate the degree of planning necessary and possible. For example, in some cases it may be pos-

---

[1] *Olmstead v. United States*, 277 U.S. 438, 474 (1928) (Brandeis, J., dissenting), overruled by *Katz v. United States*, 389 U.S. 347 (1967).

sible to take the time to plan the approach, whereas in other cases there may be a high likelihood that evidence is in danger of being destroyed or, worse, that children are likely to be victimized if action is not immediately taken to avoid it. When there is time, Figure 10 provides an operations plan.

> [T]he next step is to formulate a strategy for conducting the search. For example, will the agents search through the targeted computer(s) on the premises, or will they simply enter the premises and remove all of the hardware? Will the agents make copies of individual files, or will they make exact copies of entire hard drives? What will the agents do if their original plan fails, or if the computer hardware or software turns out to be significantly different from what they expected? These decisions hinge on a series of practical and legal considerations. In most cases, the search team should decide on a preferred search strategy and then plan a series of backup strategies if the preferred strategy proves impractical. (USDOJ 2001a)

Every member of the search team should review the search warrant. It is essential that searchers know exactly what they are looking for. The search team must also know the limits of the search. If the warrant authorized seizure of a specified computer only, and not material depicting child erotica, such as books or magazines, then searchers may not seize the magazines—even if they are in plain sight. Of course, if investigators find *contraband* such as child pornography, stolen property, or narcotics in plain sight, they may seize it.

### 10.1.1) SEARCH TOOLKIT

Investigators cannot execute a search properly without having the proper tools. It's a good idea to put together a search toolkit well in advance of going out into the field. In addition to computer and network-related tools, investigators should also plan to include documentation, sanitation, and sex crime–related tools, Figure 10.2 provides an example of one unit's toolkit.

### 10.1.2) AT THE SEARCH SCENE

Just because a search warrant has been issued for a computer does not mean that officer safety and established protocols should be abandoned. In four out of five of the search warrants executed by one Internet Crimes Against Children Task Force during a two-month period, a handgun was in the same room or right next to the computer system. The entry team should secure the scene, ensure the safety of everyone present, and protect the integrity of all the evidence.

## Sample Search Warrant Operations Plan

Case No: **123ABC**   Date: _____   Supervisor: _____

Case Officer(s): _____

Date and time of operation: _____

Staging / Briefing Location: _____

Diagram/ Pictures   Yes [X]  No [ ]   Attached: [X]
                    Yes [ ]  No [ ]

Type of Operation: **Execution of Search Warrant**   Radio Channel: _____

Background Information: **No weapons or pistol permit registered**

Description of Operation: **Execution of search warrant to find evidence of possession of child pornography**

Violations/ Charges: **Possession of Child Pornography,  Promoting a minor in an obscene performance**

Location of Operation: _____

Other Agencies Involved:   FBI [ ]
                           Postal Inspection Service [ ]
                           Local PD (specify) _____
                           Other (specify) _____
                           _____
                           _____
                           _____

### SUSPECT

Name: _____   DOB: _____

History of Violence:   Yes [ ]   No [X]   Unknown [ ]

Rap Sheet Attached?   No [X]   Yes [X]   Picture?  Yes [X]  No [ ]

### PERSONNEL ASSIGNMENTS

| Name | ID | Phone | Assignment | PD |
|------|----|-------|------------|----|
|  |  |  | **Supervisor** |  |
|  |  |  | **Uniform/Entry** |  |
|  |  |  | **Entry/Evidence** |  |
|  |  |  | **Search/Technician** |  |
|  |  |  | **Search/Technician** |  |
|  |  |  | **Entry/Search/Interview** |  |
|  |  |  | **Entry/Search/Photos** |  |

Local Police Notified: [ ]   Name of PD: _____   Phone: _____
Public Info. Notified: [ ]   Date & Time: _____   Phone: _____

*Figure 10.1*
*Example of a search warrant operations plan for a case involving possessing child pornography and promoting a minor in an obscene performance.*

*Figure 10.2*
*A search toolkit should*
*contain these items.*
*Jurisdictional demands*
*will dictate additional*
*forms and the search*
*team's personal preference*
*will affect the addition of*
*tools.*

**Search Toolkit**

| Documentation Tools | Disassembly and Removal Tools | Package and Transport Supplies | Other Items |
|---|---|---|---|
| Report forms | Flat-blade and Philips-type screwdrivers | Antistatic bags | First aid kit |
| Miranda rights cards | | Antistatic bubble wrap | Antiseptic/antibacterial wipes |
| Digital or 35 mm camera | Hex-nut drivers | Cable ties | |
| Plenty of film | Needle-nose pliers | Evidence bags | Gloves |
| Cable tags | Secure-bit drivers | Evidence tape | Hand truck |
| Indelible markers | Small tweezers | Packing materials | Large rubber bands |
| Stick-on labels | Specialized screwdrivers | Packing tape | List of contact telephone numbers for assistance |
| | Standard pliers | Sturdy boxes of various sizes | Magnifying glass |
| | Star-type nut drivers | | Printer paper |
| | Wire cutters | | Seizure disk |
| | | | Small flashlight |
| | | | Unused floppy diskettes ($3\frac{1}{2}$ & $5\frac{1}{4}$ inch) |
| | | | Black light |

As part of Operation Avalanche, investigators executed a search warrant at the home of Frederick Nichols, an unemployed thirty-four-year old who lived with his parents. As the police drove down his parents' driveway, Nichols spotted them coming. Nichols ran out the back door into the woods and, as police entered the home, they heard a single gunshot. Nichols shot himself in the head and died instantly.

Anyone who is not with the search team should be secured away from potential evidence. If necessary and permissible under local law, individuals should be guarded by uniformed officers and physically restrained if necessary. Do not allow the suspects or anyone else near the computer system, the telephone, or an electronic device. Philip Jenkins reported in his book *Beyond Tolerance—Child Pornography on the Internet* (2001) that collectors of child pornography advise each other to store their CD-ROMs in the microwave so that if the police come to search, they can destroy the evidence by turning on the microwave. The authors confirmed that putting a CD in a microwave and turning it on will obliterate the data contained on it. Search team members should conduct an initial visual scan to identify any perishable evidence, such as on-screen Internet activity or activation of evidence-destruction programs. Check for remote infrared or voice-activated devices in possession of anyone at the scene. Check the roof and area outside. There may be a satellite up-link.

---

**Perform a Visual Scan Upon Entry**

Look for:
- People.
- Anything dangerous within lunge area of occupants.
- Contraband.
- Computer systems.
- Method of accessing the Internet (satellite access, network/wireless connection).
- Electronic devices that potentially contain evidence (PDA, cellular phone, pager).

---

## 10.1.3) DOCUMENT THE SCENE

Document the scene by writing about it and photographing it. Some police departments videotape the search. Some method of visually capturing the scene is advised to facilitate restoring the system later. Reviewing photographs of the scene may also jog a memory or assist in refreshing the investigator's memory. Photograph the screen of the computer, the work area, and the area surrounding the computer. These photographs will assist investigators in restoring the target's computer system should it become necessary when the case comes to trial. Subtle features, such as whether the position of the mouse indicates that the user is right or left handed, may figure prominently in linking the suspect to the criminal activity. People often write passwords, contact numbers, Web site names, and user identifications near their computer workstation. Pertinent information may be taped under the keyboard. Seemingly unimportant scraps of paper scattered around the target's work area may become critical later, so documenting them is important. System documentation, user's manuals, and software reference books should be at least photographed and, if permitted by the search warrant, seized. Perishable data, such as numbers contained on pagers, caller ID records, cellular phones, and other devices should be secured and documented.

Answering machines, pagers, callerID boxes, and similar types of digital devices require that data be retrieved differently than from computer systems that will be seized and examined at a later time. Retrieve data from a pager by reviewing the records and documenting the information manually. The same applies to callerID information. Digital answering systems should be accessed, listened to, and documented. If possible and there is information of evidentiary value, such as a threatening message or communication between a victim and offender, tape record the message.

Document whether the computer system is "on" or "off." If you can hear a fan running and lights are on, the computer is probably "on." Also, if the chassis is warm, it is likely that either the computer was recently "on," or it was recently running. Identify and document components, such as printers, that will not be seized.

---

**Photograph**

- The room in which the computer is located.
- Images on the computer screen.
- The computer, peripheral devices, cabling, etc.
- The area surrounding the computer.

---

### 10.1.4) SECURE EVIDENCE

Do not do anything with evidence that you have not been trained to do. Upon finding a computer or other source of digital evidence, do not turn "on" anything that is "off." Turning on a computer or any other electronic or digital evidence source causes changes to the data contained in storage. The simple act of booting up a personal computer can cause the alteration of hundreds of files. If a computer is "on," pull the power plug from the back of the computer. Seal every component orifice, such as disk, CD-ROM, and Zip drive openings with evidence tape. Many references advise inserting a seizure or wiped disk in open disk drives, but this practice is not necessary to ensure that the evidence is properly seized. The purpose of inserting seizure disks is to ensure that the computer does not boot. Covering the disconnected power supply access on the back of the CPU chassis should be sufficient to ensure that the computer does not boot. Disconnect the computer from its Internet connection. If the computer is connected to a modem line, disconnect the cable from the wall and test the phone line to confirm that it is working. Remove the CPU chassis and photograph the internal components and settings. Disconnect power to any hard drive.

Tag and label all cables and note connections to peripheral devices. Tape and label any empty ports or slots not in use. Make sure to photograph the wiring configurations before disassembling the computer system because you may need to re-create the system prior to trial. Carefully label, log, package, and prepare all seized evidence for transportation. Remember to maintain a tight chain of custody.

More than one computer system may mean there is a computer network. If the scene is a business, searchers can expect to encounter at least one network and possibly several. Networks require the investigators to have specialized experience and training to properly seize the equipment and ensure that the target data is secured. If possible, recruit the assistance of law enforcement personnel who have network seizure experience. Because of the specialized nature of the knowledge, finding a law enforcement officer with the desired training may not be possible. It may be possible to use the expertise of a civilian employee—for example, a system administrator or forensic data examiner. If non–law enforcement personnel will be employed for the search, authorization to allow the civilian personnel to assist, even naming them in the affidavit, is a good idea. Federal law precludes anyone other than the officer being present at the search except for a person "in aid of the officer" (USDOJ 2001a). Searchers can rely on assistance from the system administrator employed by the business being searched or the target himself or herself as a last resort, but there are inherent risks. The target may not be cooperative and may purposely mislead or deceive law enforcement. Similarly, the system administrator may not be completely forthcoming because s/he may be a co-conspirator or have some other interest to protect.

A laptop may be properly seized by eliminating the power source. Since it may be powered by electricity or by battery, disconnect the electrical source and remove the battery. Some laptops have two battery packs, so check to make sure you have removed all power sources.

Wireless telephones may contain a great deal of evidence. Most cellular phones retain numbers dialed, numbers stored for speed dial, callerID, and names and addresses of contacts. If the phone is "on," do not turn it "off." If the phone is "off," leave it off until you are able to contact an expert. The phone may be set to require a password when you attempt to turn it on. Either obtain information by scrolling through the telephone's visual display at the scene or contact an expert to do it off-site. If an expert is unavailable, use a different phone to contact 1-800-LAWBUST. LAWBUST is a service provided by the cellular telephone industry to assist law enforcement with search and seizure of cellular telephones. If possible, locate the user's manual for the phone.

Pagers can be numeric, receiving only numbers, or alphanumeric, capable of receiving numbers and text messages. The stored contents of a pager may be accessed if authorized by the warrant, incident to arrest or with consent. Once the pager is no longer in proximity to the suspect, turn it off because seizing real-time communication without judicial authorization or consent may be an unlawful interception of electronic communication.

Fax machines may contain speed-dial lists and transmission logs. Do not turn off the machine or unplug it before retrieving the information sought. Unplugging the machine or turning it off may wipe out data from memory. Use the manual to ascertain how to retrieve data. If no user's manual can be located, call the manufacturer. Some manufacturers reproduce user's manuals on their Web sites.

CallerID devices contain telephone numbers of incoming telephone calls. Some devices and services also supply the subscriber information of the number calling in. Document stored data instead of seizing the machine. Turning off the callerID device will likely result in loss of any information it contains. Searchers should also be on the lookout for "Smart Cards." A "Smart Card" is a plastic card about the size of a credit card. It contains a small computer chip that can contain time-sensitive passwords or other information (IACP and USSS 2001).

Package the computer by covering all orifices and the power supply connection with evidence tape. Removable media such as CD-ROMs and floppy diskettes should be packaged in anti-static bags, labeled, and inventoried. By all means, follow established procedure for your jurisdiction. If there are no applicable policies in place that control procedures, package removable media according to where you find it. For instance, package together the diskettes found in the workstation. Package together the CD-ROMs found in the bedroom closet. Label the bags with the contents. If a disk or CD has a label, refer to the title on the bag's label. When seizing removable media, ensure that you take the device that created the media (e.g., tape drive, cartridge drives). If the warrant does not specifically authorize seizure of the device, obtain authorization to do so.

Prepare the evidence for transport. Place CPUs and electronic devices on the floor in the back seat of a cruiser or on a flat surface secured so that they will not slide around in a van. Keep the evidence away from extreme heat or cold, and avoid powerful magnetic fields and equipment that might generate electric discharges. Ensure that all components and media are kept away from two-way radios while being transported to or stored in the Evidence Room. You may want to dust the keyboard or certain switches for fingerprints. Fingerprint evidence would be helpful if you need to establish whether the suspect used the computer and/or if s/he had exclusive control. Keyboards, the computer mouse, diskettes, CDs, or other components may have latent fingerprints or other physical evidence that should be preserved. Chemicals used in processing latent prints can damage equipment and data, so collect latent prints after digital evidence recovery is complete.

## 10.2) EVIDENCE HANDLING

Treat the evidence just like you would treat any other kind of evidence. Just as you would not pick up a gun suspected of being the murder weapon in a homicide and pull the trigger a few times to see whether it works, you should not turn on the computer or touch anything when you seize a computer or data unless you know what you are doing. Unfortunately, sometimes overzealous searchers sit at the computer and begin accessing data. More often, supervisory personnel instruct searchers to do so, oftentimes over the searchers' protest. ("Detective, you're good with computers. Find out if there's anything on the computer." "Sir, do you think that's a good idea? It might alter the evidence." "Detective, I told you to do something, didn't I?") If, for any reason, the computer is accessed, make sure to fully document it and inform the forensic examiner. A forensic examination will reveal that the evidence was accessed or altered anyway, so documenting the fact and the reason for doing so will serve to both inform the examiner and head off the defense's attack. ("How do we know that the police officers at the scene didn't plant the evidence on my client's computer?")

Do not examine original evidence such as files on the subject's disks. You wouldn't snort white powder if you found it in a vial during a search, would you? Preserve the original evidence in its original state. Make a true copy of the original evidence. If possible, have the subject sign a stipulation that the copy is an exact duplicate of the original. Make an extra copy to use as your "working copy." Then you can open the files on the "working copy" and look to see what is inside. (Don't forget to run a virus scan before opening any files.)

## 10.3) OBTAINING A SECOND WARRANT

Investigators can include only as much information in an affidavit and application for a search warrant as they possess at the time. As is frequently the case with any other search warrant execution, police may encounter situations in which it will be appropriate to obtain a second search warrant. This may be the case when a computer turns up unexpectedly during a search and is not addressed in the first warrant. However, if you particularly described the computer system and data in a search warrant application and included language requesting analysis of the computer system and/or data, you should not need to obtain a second search warrant to perform a forensic examination. If you will be transporting the evidence to a laboratory for a forensic examination, you really need to obtain judicial authorization to do so. Either include the request for transport and examination by the laboratory in the original search warrant application or apply for a second warrant after seizure.

## 10.4) EXECUTING INTERNET SERVICE PROVIDER SEARCH WARRANTS

Many state and local law enforcement agencies are simply befuddled by the necessity of obtaining information from Internet Service Providers (ISPs). This discussion applies equally to telephone, cellular phone, and credit card companies. The difficulty for an investigator presented by needing information from these service providers is that the companies are usually outside the officer's jurisdiction and the officer is incapable of executing the search on his or her own. Many jurisdictions require that law enforcement officers execute a search warrant. This requirement is intended to ensure that the scope of the search is limited to what the warrant allows. Police officers have been trained in search methods and in the law. Allowing only police officers to execute a search is intended to minimize the intrusion into the privacy of citizens. The judiciary has control over what the police do. The court does not have the oversight of private individuals as it does of the police.

The Electronic Communications Privacy Act (ECPA) authorizes three methods for obtaining information from electronic communications service providers:

> Contents of Electronic Communications in a Remote Computing Service.— (1) A governmental entity may require a provider of remote computing service to disclose the contents of any electronic communication to which this paragraph is made applicable by paragraph (2) of this subsection—(A) without required notice to the subscriber or customer, if the governmental entity obtains a warrant issued under the Federal Rules of Criminal Procedure or equivalent State warrant; or (B) with prior notice from the governmental entity to the subscriber or customer if the governmental entity—(i) uses an administrative subpoena authorized by a Federal or State statute or a Federal or State grand jury or trial subpoena; or (ii) obtains a court order for such disclosure under subsection (d) of this section; except that delayed notice may be given pursuant to section 2705 of this title. 18 U.S.C 2703(b). (2004)

Note that the language of the statute refers to whether a state authorizes the process. An officer in State A may issue an administrative subpoena for subscriber information held by an ISP in his or her state or in another state only if State A authorizes the administrative subpoena. Authorization for such process should come from a statute. The administrative subpoena is not a judicial process; it is an executive branch investigative tool.

State law also must authorize state court orders. A court order, unlike an administrative order, is a judicial process and therefore subject only to the limitations placed on the judiciary of the issuing state. Therefore, a government attorney in State A may apply for a court order compelling an ISP to produce information pursuant to 18 USC 2703(d) if there is a statute authorizing the court to do so or if the court exercises its inherent authority. However, the court in State A does not possess the authority to compel production of records by an ISP located in State B unless (1) the ISP consents to the court's jurisdiction over it; (2) the ISP is subject to State A's jurisdiction based on its corporations statute or long-arm statute, or; (3) State B has a state statute that recognizes the court orders of other state courts.

> United States Code Title 18 Section 2703(d) provides:
>
> A court order for disclosure [ ] may be issued by any court that is a court of competent jurisdiction [ ] and shall issue only if the governmental entity offers specific and articulable facts showing that there are reasonable grounds to believe that the contents of a wire or electronic communication, or the records or other information sought, are relevant and material to an ongoing criminal investigation. In the case of a State governmental authority, such a court order shall not issue if prohibited by the law of such State.

The PATRIOT Act enacted a temporary amendment to the Electronic Communications Privacy Act (ECPA) authorizing a federal court to issue an order under 18 USC 2703(d) that is now valid in another federal court district. This specific and narrow amendment should make it clear that the ECPA has not and does not create any long-arm jurisdictional reach for state governments issuing administrative subpoenas or state courts issuing court orders for ISP data. Likewise, the ECPA, as temporarily amended by the PATRIOT Act, does not mandate State B to honor the search warrants issued by State A for information contained in State B.

Each state has rules governing the issuance and execution of search warrants. Many states restrict execution of state court–issued search warrants to police officers. In *United States v. Bach*,[2] the Eighth Circuit Court of Appeals upheld a search conducted of the suspect's Yahoo! account even though it violated both federal and state law. Police obtained a search warrant for Yahoo! records for Bach, who was party to an incriminating online conversation with a minor. The Minnesota investigator faxed the search warrant to Yahoo! and Yahoo! personnel executed the search and returned the requested data to the Minnesota investigator. Under Minnesota law, a search warrant must be executed by law enforcement officers. In the Bach case, no law enforcement officer was present. Pursuant to the information obtained in the first search, police executed a search warrant at Bach's home, where they found child pornography and additional evidence of Bach's enticement of minors to engage in sexual activity. Bach moved to suppress evidence from both searches. The District Court sup-

---

[2] *United States v. Bach*, 310 F.3d 1063; 2002 U.S. App. LEXIS 23726 (8th Cir. 2002) (reh'r den'd 2003 U.S. App. LEXIS 141).

pressed evidence from the Yahoo! search because it held that the Minnesota officer violated the law governing the execution of a search warrant but upheld the second search. The government appealed the District Court ruling, and the Eighth Circuit Court of Appeals reversed.

The court held that the federal search warrant statute does not codify the Fourth Amendment to the Constitution and that, to force suppression of the evidence, a Fourth Amendment violation must be found. In dicta, the court cited that Congress created a privacy interest in e-mail that under *Smith v. Maryland*[3] would probably otherwise not exist. The court upheld the Yahoo! search's reasonableness, citing a number of state court holdings that approve civilian searches for bank records, software, and other similar matter.[4] This holding worked for this specific case, but it would not work in a jurisdiction that follows a *fruit of the poisonous tree* rule.

A jurisdiction with a fruit of the poisonous tree rule would suppress all evidence obtained illegally. Some jurisdictions do not even allow a good faith exception. Evidence obtained in violation of the law is not admitted. The strict suppression tactic is intended to deter cavalier practices regarding search and seizure by law enforcement. The information governed by the ECPA is often essential to criminal investigations. The states must have settled methods of obtaining the information from out-of-state ISPs that are consistent with state and federal law as well as expedient for law enforcement investigators. After all, facilitating investigation of crimes is a most compelling interest.

One of the issues raised in *Bach* was that a police officer in one state faxed a search warrant to an ISP in another state. That, the court held, violated Minnesota's statute governing execution of search warrants. It should be noted that an argument could be made that the search warrant was executed at the time the police officer faxed the warrant.[5]

The National Institute of Justice (NIJ) has developed a legislative proposal aimed at facilitating state legal processes to obtain information held by Internet Service Providers. The proposed bill is as follows:

---

[3] *Smith v. Maryland,* 442 U.S. 735 (1979).

[4] Civilian searches are sometimes more reasonable than searches by officers. *Harris v. State,* 401 S.E.2d 263, 266 (Ga. 1991) (stating that a dentist may execute a search warrant for dental X-rays and impressions); *Schalk v. State,* 767 S.W.2d 441, 454 (Tex. App. 1988) (providing that a search by a civilian software expert is more reasonable than search by an officer because the officer lacked knowledge to differentiate a trade secret from a legitimate computer software program), cert. denied, 503 U.S. 1006 (1992); *State v. Kern,* 914 P.2d 114, 117–18 (Wash. Ct. App. 1996) (indicating that it is reasonable to delegate search of bank records to bank employees, even when a police officer was not present during the search). Civilian searches outside the presence of police may also increase the amount of privacy retained by the individual during the search. See *Rodriques v. Furtado,* 575 N.E.2d 1124 (Mass. 1991) (body cavity search done outside presence of officers); *Commonwealth v. Sbordone,* 678 N.E.2d 1184, 1190, n.11 (Mass. 1997).

[5] Thanks to Ivan Orton, Sr., Deputy Prosecuting Attorney, Fraud Division, King County Prosecuting Attorney Seattle, WA, for the reference.

> Full Faith and Credit—Any production order issued that is consistent with subsection (b) of this section by the court of another State (the issuing State) shall be accorded full faith and credit by the court of another State (the enforcing State) and enforced as if it were the order of the enforcing state.
>
> Production Order—A production order issued by a State court is consistent with this subsection if—
>
> (1) The order is pursuant to the investigation or prosecution of a crime of the issuing state;
> (2) The order was issued in accordance with the law of the issuing state; and
> (3) Such court had jurisdiction over the criminal investigation or prosecution under the law of the issuing state.
>
> "Production Order" means any order, warrant, or subpoena for the production of records, issued by a court of competent jurisdiction. "Records" includes those items in whatever form created or stored.[6]

The limitation of the NIJ proposal is that it would have very little effect. Although Congress has authority over the Internet by virtue of its Commerce Clause power, it does not have authority over the subpoenas, court orders, and search warrants issued by state courts. There may be an argument that states are obliged to honor these legal processes, but such a duty is moral, not legal or constitutionally imposed. Rather than Congressional action, what is necessary to ameliorate the problem of jurisdiction and enforcement of out-of-state administrative subpoenas, court orders, and warrants is an Interstate compact. In lieu of a state compact, each state may pass its own legislation to honor the subpoenas, court orders, and search warrants issued by other states for ISP and telephone subscriber information and/or long-arm provisions. So far, California, Florida, and Minnesota have statutes to this effect.[7]

According to the United States Supreme Court, police must have judicial authorization to overhear any telephone conversation (unless one of the parties is in another country, which is a topic beyond the scope of this book). But an individual's telephone number is, according to the court, public information beyond the court's protection. In *Smith*, that translated into authorizing police to install pen register and trap-and-trace devices on telephone lines without requiring a warrant. The court reasoned that what an individual willingly offers over to a third party—that is, the phone company—is not protected by the

---

[6] Thanks to Robert M. Morgester, Deputy Attorney General, Special Crimes Unit, California Department of Justice, for the reference.
[7] See, for example, California's Penal Code section 1524.2, which allows service of a search warrant on an out-of-state Electronic Communications Service (ECS) that does business in California.

Fourth Amendment to the United States Constitution (nor the Fourteenth through to the States). Congress clarified the law by codifying wiretap, pen register, and trap-and-trace requirements. (18 U.S.C. 2510 et seq.). That is the foundation for the current law of search and seizure as it relates to stored and real-time electronic communications.

What occurs when a person logs onto the Internet is electronic communication. Just as in the distinction between "content" of a telephone conversation and the telephone numbers dialed or incoming to a telephone account holder, there is a distinction between real-time and stored communications. As the "information superhighway" emerged in its infancy, Congress stepped up to the plate to ensure that the communications would be given similar legal protection to telephone communications. However, and unfortunately, Congress forgot about what its actions could mean to the states and municipal law enforcement agencies. Its actions have impacted individual citizens negatively because the states do not have the jurisdictional reach in criminal matters prior to a final judgment that the federal government has. State and municipal jurisdiction is much more limited and, at the very least, difficult for a patrol officer to figure out when handed his or her first Internet-related call for service.

The ECPA sets forth the requirements and process for obtaining stored electronic communications. The Act directs that real-time electronic communications—like chat and instant messaging, and most cellular phone conversations, for that matter—are covered by the wiretap law (a.k.a. Title III). So, putting the wiretap law and the ECPA together, we now can surmise the following: Content of telephonic and electronic communication is protected by the United States Constitution, and you therefore either need a wiretap authorization to intercept real-time communication or a search warrant to obtain stored communication; subscriber information, such as numbers dialed or the information freely given over to a third-party service provider, is not protected by the Constitution, but it may be protected by Congress. The ECPA requires a search warrant for obtaining the *content* of electronic communications but requires a subpoena for subscriber information—name, address, credit card used to establish the account. A government attorney may obtain a court order to compel production of transactional data—information that is more than simple subscriber and account information but not as detailed or private as content of communications. Attempting to discern the interplay between the federal law and jurisdiction of the states in criminal search and seizure matters is interesting and complex.

Prior to increased competition in the communications industry, telephone service was provided by one local provider. Since deregulation and the breakup of monopolies on telephone service, several different phone service providers are flung throughout the country. As the providers have proliferated, it has become more difficult for law enforcement to obtain simple subscriber information to facilitate investigations. Whereas it was once a simple matter of calling the local telephone company to request information and getting it while still on the line, now it is a significant undertaking to even discover the identity and contact information of the telephone service provider. Once contact information for the service provider has been identified, the process of requesting the necessary information begins. When the service provider is outside the jurisdiction of the law enforcement agency, the process of obtaining and executing the appropriate legal process is a challenge. When the Internet and cellular telephone service began to proliferate and figure prominently in criminal investigations, matters became more complicated for the states and municipal law enforcement.

At the federal level, things were somewhat more straightforward. Most federal agents can issue subpoenas. Federal subpoenas do not require judicial authorization. However, many jurisdictions do not have a process for issuing subpoenas. When a state or local officer contacts a telephone or Internet Service Provider and asks about the proper process for obtaining records, the officer is told to get a subpoena. Often, the response is, "Huh?" Connecticut, for example, does not authorize police to issue subpoenas for investigative information. For a police officer to obtain information about an Internet account serviced by an out-of-state company, s/he must either enlist the assistance of a federal authority to issue a subpoena for the information, persuade an officer in the jurisdiction where the ISP is located to issue a subpoena, or, if that jurisdiction does not possess authority to issue a subpoena for the information, s/he can try to persuade a prosecutor in the jurisdiction to make a motion for a court order. If the jurisdiction prohibits such orders, the officer can request that the law enforcement agency with jurisdiction over the ISP apply for a search warrant [see 18 U.S.C. 2703(d)(2003)]. Of course, to justify a search warrant, the officer must establish probable cause. This is often a circular analysis because s/he often cannot establish probable cause without having the information sought from the Internet or telephone service provider.

What the ECPA does not clarify is that while a state court may issue a court order or authorize a search warrant, a state court's power rests only within its geographic jurisdiction. Whether the receiving state can be mandated to enforce the issuing state's orders is another matter entirely. Extra-jurisdictional reach must be authorized by state statute and be consistent with federal law. Such statutes authorizing state court jurisdiction are called "Long-Arm Statutes."[8] Otherwise, each state possesses authority over the people and property within its borders.

---

[8] See Casad, Long Arm and Convenient Forum, 20 Kan. L. Rv. 1 1971; Currie, The Growth of the Long Arm, U. Ill. L.F. 533 (1963); Cal. Civ. Proc. Code Sec. 410.10; Rest. 2$^{nd}$ Conflicts of Law Sec. 37.

> The several States of the Union are not, it is true, in every respect inde-
> pendent . . . But, except as restrained and limited by [the Constitution], they
> possess and exercise the authority of independent States, and the principles
> of public law . . . are applicable to them. One of these principles is, that every
> State possesses exclusive jurisdiction and sovereignty over persons and prop-
> erty within its territory. (*Pennoyer v. Neff*, 95 U.S. 714 [1878] at 568)

The jurisdiction of a state court may seem obvious, but to many in the field of investigating Internet-related crime, it is a source of great confusion, inconsistent application, and consternation. At least one state court has interpreted the ECPA as having granted to state courts the authority to issue search warrants that have effect in other states. While Congress holds broad authority to regulate interstate commerce, and communication that takes place over the Internet and the subscriber information related to individuals who access the Internet are certainly governed by interstate commerce, the jurisdiction of state courts is governed by state constitutions, statutes, and court rules. The Congress may legislate guidance, but such guidance does not confer power to the courts of the states—the Acts of Congress are thus informative rather than controlling when the subject is state court power.

Without overburdening you with legal minutiae, a brief civics lesson is in order. Federal government authority derives from the United States Constitution. The Constitution delineates the areas of responsibility of the federal government. The listing of responsibilities is called the "enumeration of powers." Whatever is not specifically enumerated by the Constitution as an area of responsibility is reserved to the States or to the People (Engdahl 1987; *McCullough v. Maryland* 1819).[9] With regard to ECPA and the process used to obtain information, Congress does not have the power to mandate one state to recognize or execute the subpoenas, court orders, or search warrants of another state because the federal government was not granted authority to order the states to recognize any acts of state governments other than final judgments of the state courts. Subpoenas, court orders, and search warrants issued in one state can have force in another state only if the receiving state consents.

The Full Faith and Credit Clause of the United States Constitution governs recognition of final judgments issued in one state by another state. Absent a final judgment, the "other" jurisdiction is not obligated to honor the issuing state's order or warrant. The Constitution requires that states honor extradition requests of sister states, but the requirement is limited. In *Kentucky v. Dennison*, the United States Supreme Court held that the Constitutional duty of states to honor the requests by another state for extradition was a *moral* duty

---

[9] *McCullough v. Maryland*, 4 Wheat (17 U.S.) 316 (1819).

rather than mandatory or compulsory [(65 U.S. (How.) 66 (1861) overruled in part by *Puerto Rico v. Branstad*, 483 U.S. 219 (1987)].

## 10.5) CONDUCTING PRELIMINARY INTERVIEWS

Identify all persons at the scene and separate them. Identify the owners of computers and obtain passwords and Internet access identifications from them. Determine what the owner uses the electronic device or computer for. Ask what security measures or devices are in use. Determine whether the owner utilizes offsite data storage.

When you are interviewing the suspect, it is very important to suppress negative emotions. Do not be judgmental, condemning, or cold. Your personal feelings about the suspect have no place in the interview, and unless you can put them aside, you will jeopardize your chances of eliciting helpful information. If all goes as planned, prior to executing the search and interviewing the suspect, investigators have developed an interrogation strategy.

Consider and make a deliberate decision whether you will administer Miranda warnings to the suspect. If you are in the suspect's home and s/he is free to leave, you may consider not administering the warning because it is not a custodial interrogation. This decision is one that must be made taking into account policies and procedures and the advice of local supervisory and prosecutorial personnel. The interviewer needs to establish rapport and create a relaxed atmosphere (USDOJ, 2001b). Start out with questions about the suspect's interests, hobbies, work, and family. Move on to talking about the suspect's relationship with the victim in enticement investigations and his or her interest in erotic images in child pornography investigations.

When talk begins to get close to the offense, the offender will likely attempt to shift blame onto the victim or someone or something else. Let him or her do so. If you give the suspect what s/he believes to be a legitimate reason for committing the offense, s/he will be more likely to provide more information about it. Suspects may rationalize, minimize, or explain the behavior. While it may be loathsome to the interrogator, encourage the suspect to talk about his or her feelings and actions. The more the suspect talks, the more information s/he shares that is potentially incriminating. Any insight that can be gained about the victim, offender, or crime may be useful in an investigation.

---

**Disclosure**

- Assume an understanding and non-judging posture.
- Try to elicit special names or terminology used during the sexual abuse.
- Determine the location of any physical evidence.

## 10.6) NO KNOCK WARRANTS

Some jurisdictions, including federal agencies, recognize exceptions to the "knock and announce" rule. Federal authorities may dispense with the knock-and-announce requirement if

- they have a reasonable suspicion that knocking and announcing their presence, under the particular circumstances, would be dangerous or futile;
- or that it would inhibit the effective investigation of the crime by, for example, allowing the destruction of evidence.[10]

The Federal Guidelines for Search and Seizure advise that federal "agents may need to conduct no-knock searches in computer crime cases because technically adept suspects may 'hot wire' their computers in an effort to destroy evidence. For example, technically adept computer hackers have been known to use 'hot keys,' computer programs that destroy evidence when a special button is pressed. If agents knock at the door to announce their search, the suspect can simply press the button and activate the program to destroy the evidence." (USDOJ 2001a) When a suspect is skilled in technology, and the subject of the search is the sexual exploitation of children, the suspect is both quite capable and highly motivated to destroy data, given the opportunity.

## 10.7) PRIVILEGED DOCUMENTS AND COMMUNICATIONS

Certain professions and relationships have legal privilege attached to resulting communications and documents. Traditionally, privileged relationships include doctor-patient, priest-penitent, lawyer-client, and spouses. Federal privilege protections are much more limited in scope than those in some states, so it is important to know the rules that control. If investigators know ahead of time that there is a potential for privilege to be an issue, they should consult with a local prosecutor right away and enlist his or her assistance in fashioning an appropriate search strategy. In some cases, it may be appropriate to do an in-camera review of files—that is, in the judge's chambers. Some courts have appointed special masters to conduct searches of privileged materials. Another possible alternative is to devise a search method, such as *"officers will perform a forensic examination of the hard drive and removable media seized from the residence and limit the scope of the search by searching only for image files."*

---

[10] *Richards v. Wisconsin,* 520 U.S. 385 (1997).

## 10.8) THE PRIVACY PROTECTION ACT

The Privacy Protection Act (PPA) at the federal level and many individual states provides additional protections. When information is in the hands of a third party, such as a newspaper, lawyer, or priest, the PPA requires a subpoena rather than search warrant. The PPA authorizes a civil cause of action for damages if the government violates its mandates. The law is intended to allow the third party to determine whether the material is relevant rather than allowing a broader search of potentially privileged matter (42 U.S.C. 2000aa). The Act also applies to "work product" and "documentary materials" in an individual's or organization's possession that s/he (objectively) intends to publish. Therefore, if the investigator has a reasonable belief that the target of a search intends to disseminate a newspaper, book, or other form of public communication, the PPA may apply.

There are a number of exceptions to the PPA. The first, and most important, is that contraband is not protected. The Act specifically excludes "fruits of a crime or things otherwise criminally possessed, or property designed or intended for use, or which is or has been used, as the means of committing a criminal offense" (42 U.S.C. 2000aa). Therefore, seizure of a computer system used to store child pornography or that was suspected of being used to contact the victim in an enticement case is beyond the reach of the PPA's protections.

## 10.9) RETURNING SEIZED ITEMS

When the case concludes, and often before then, the law enforcement agency may be ordered by the court to return the items seized. This presents difficulties when there is or may be contraband. Prior to returning anything that might still contain contraband, seek advice from your legal advisor or prosecutor handling the case (Clifford 2001). Many judges issue orders to return computer systems after deleting the contraband (child pornography) or evidence (e-mails, chat logs, etc.). At least one state prohibits distributing evidence alleged to be child pornography to the defendant.[11] But, as you know, deleting some-

---

[11] Cal. Penal Code § 1054.10. Disclosure of copies of child pornography evidence

(a) Except as provided in subdivision (b), no attorney may disclose or permit to be disclosed to a defendant, members of the defendant's family, or anyone else copies of child pornography evidence, unless specifically permitted to do so by the court after a hearing and a showing of good cause.

(b) Notwithstanding subdivision (a), an attorney may disclose or permit to be disclosed copies of child pornography evidence to persons employed by the attorney or to persons appointed by the court to assist in the preparation of a defendant's case if that disclosure is required for that preparation. Persons provided this material by an attorney shall be informed by the attorney that further dissemination of the material, except as provided by this section, is prohibited.

thing on a computer does not eliminate it. The data must be "wiped," or obliterated, and to ensure its destruction, its removal must be confirmed by a qualified technician. Really, the only way to ensure that "all" contraband or evidence is eliminated is to conduct a full-blown forensic examination of the drive or media following the wipe. A quick cost-benefit analysis reveals that this is a completely unproductive and costly procedure. Estimating that the cost of a completely new hard drive ranges between $25 for used to $200 for a new, large drive and that the cost of analysis personnel to wipe and analyze a drive runs about $50 an hour on overtime and the procedure takes at least two hours, simple arithmetic discloses this to be a losing proposition. How many times does the court order that a cocaine-tainted article be cleaned by the seizing agency and returned to the owner? We would guess such incidents do not happen often.

It also frequently happens that a case is nolled or otherwise disposed of without a forensic examination taking place. Returning material that has not been examined is an ethical dilemma for the agency. Consult with the prosecutor handling the case to determine what s/he thinks should happen.

## REFERENCES

Allinich, G., and S. Dreston. "Suspect Interviews in Computer-Facilitated Child Sexual Exploitation Cases." *Update* 14, no. 7 (2001).

*Best Practices for Seizing Electronic Evidence.* International Association of Chiefs of Police and the United States Secret Service, Washington, DC, 2001.

Clifford, R. D., ed. *Cyber Crime—The Investigation, Prosecution, and Defense of a Computer-Related Crime.* Durham, NC: Carolina Academic Press, 2001.

Engdahl, David E. *Constitutional Federalism.* St. Paul, MN: West Group, 1987.

Jenkins, Philip. *Beyond Tolerance: Child Pornography Online.* New York: New York University Press, 2001.

Mattei (Ferraro), M., J. F. Blawie, and A. G. Russell. *Guidelines for Search and Seizure of Computer Systems and Data.* Rocky Hill, CT: State of Connecticut Division of Criminal Justice and Department of Public Safety, 2001.

Shephard, J. et al. *Child Abuse and Exploitation Investigative Techniques,* 2nd ed. Washington, DC: U.S. Department of Justice, OJJDP, 1995.

U.S. Department of Justice. *Electronic Crime Scene Investigation: A Guide for First Responders.* Washington, DC: Technical Working Group for Electronic Crime Scene Investigation, U.S. Department of Justice, 2001a.

U.S. Department of Justice. *Searching and Seizing Computers and Obtaining Electronic Evidence in Criminal Investigations.* Washington, DC: U.S. Department of Justice, Computer Crime and Intellectual Property Section, 2001b.

# SECTION III

## FORENSIC EXAMINATION OF DIGITAL EVIDENCE

# CHAPTER 11

# OVERVIEW OF THE EXAMINATION PROCESS

*Crime scene investigation is more than the processing or documentation of crime scenes, nor is it just the collection or packaging of physical evidence. It is the first step and the most crucial step of any forensic investigation of a possible criminal act. The foundation of all forensic investigations is based on the ability of the crime scene investigator to recognize the potential and importance of physical evidence, large and small, at the crime scene. The subsequent identification of the physical evidence along with determination of the possible source or origin of the evidence, that is, its individualization, are the next steps in the investigation. Finally, proper crime scene investigation is the starting point for the process of establishing what occurred—in other words, it is the initiation of the crime scene reconstruction. (Lee, Palmbach and Miller 2001)*

As noted in the opening quotation, proper evidence collection and documentation form the foundation of any forensic investigation. This is true of both physical and digital crime scenes as covered by many texts (Casey 2004; Mandia 2003). Once evidence has been preserved, investigators need to examine and analyze it to extract important details that combine to create a picture of the crime. This chapter presents the important aspects of examining digital evidence relating to child exploitation investigations. Directions for implementing the structured examination described in this chapter using Maresware, EnCase, or Forensic Toolkit (FTK) are available (Casey and Larson 2004). This chapter also provides an overview of the analysis process to help investigators reconstruct the crime and assess the strength of their conclusions.

Given the pervasiveness of computing devices, it is not feasible for all computer examinations to be conducted in a laboratory environment by highly trained technicians. To ensure that digital evidence is preserved and utilized without further overloading computer crime laboratories, first responders or investigators may need to examine some devices. For such situations, first responders and investigators need clear procedures and associated training. At the same time, it is important to realize that these guidelines and procedures focus on existing technology, and situations not covered by any procedure will arise. Therefore, investigators may need to make judgment calls to deal with new technology and deal with unforeseen circumstances involving digital evidence. It is advisable to have expert resources such as the local crime lab that can talk investigators through unfamiliar situations, if necessary.

Investigators also need to acknowledge from the outset that many laboratories and agencies that investigate child exploitation have limited resources and are suffering from a backlog of cases. This problem is exacerbated by the large amounts of storage media that are common in child exploitation cases involving computers. In addition to large hard drives, these cases often involve many Zip disks, CD-ROMs, memory cards, and other removable storage media. To reduce the examination time for each case, many laboratories and agencies require investigators to specify what they are looking for on the computer and associated media. A request might be for evidence of child pornography and communication with victims or cohorts between 2002 and 2004, for example. Even such a focused examination can result in large amounts of data that must be processed and organized in a methodical fashion. Child pornographers may have tens of thousands of images and may communicate with others through multiple Internet services resulting in thousands of e-mail messages, hundreds of pages of chat logs, and much more.

Additionally, while narrowing the focus of the examination in this way can save time, investigators still need to follow a consistent methodology, and it is important not to become too focused. An examination hastily done, such as simply performing a keyword search or extracting only certain file types, may not only miss important clues but will likely leave the examiners floundering in a sea of superfluous data (Casey and Larson 2004). The increasing use of encryption and data hiding in child exploitation cases renders such cursory searches of media effectively useless. Keyword searches cannot penetrate encrypted files, and child pornography can be embedded in many different file types. Therefore, it is most effective to recover all data from available media and perform some data reduction and organization before performing keyword searches and analysis of certain file types.

The Wonderland child pornography had a "Traders Security Handbook" that instructed members to use Bestcrypt (http://www.bestcrypt.com/) to encrypt incriminating files on their computers. One prosecutor in the UK told the court that the handbook explained how to conceal images and "showed how action could be taken to confuse the hell out of the cops, and what to do if busted." (McAuliffe 2001)

The distinction between examination and analysis is frequently overlooked. "Examination" is the process of extracting and preparing data for analysis. The examination process involves data recovery, translation, reduction, organization, and searching. A thorough examination results in all relevant data being organized and presented in a manner that facilitates detailed analysis. "Analysis" involves gaining an understanding of and reaching conclusions about the incident based on evidence produced during the examination process. Analysis also involves assessing key findings through experimentation, fusion, correlation, and validation.

For instance, in a child pornography investigation, the product of the examination process would include all graphics or video files, as well as Web sites accessed and all Internet communications such as IRC, IM, and e-mail. Furthermore, the examination process would involve a search for specific usernames and keywords to locate additional data that may be relevant. Once most of the data that might be relevant to the investigation have been extracted and made readable, they can be organized in ways that help an individual analyze them to gain an understanding of the crime. As the analysis process proceeds, a more complete picture of the crime emerges, often resulting in leads or questions that require the analyst to return to the original data to locate additional evidence, test hypotheses, and validate specific conclusions.

## 11.1) EXAMINATION

To ensure consistency, thoroughness, and repeatability in their work while keeping examination costs to a reasonable level, digital evidence examiners need an efficient methodology to extract useful evidence from large amounts of digital data. The examination methodology presented in this chapter is part of the investigative process from Casey and Palmer (2004), depicted as a sequence of ascending stairs in Figure 11.1. The terms located on the riser of each step are those more closely associated with the law enforcement perspective. To the right of each term is a more general descriptor that may help to express the essence of each step of the process. Specifically, the examination process involves data recovery, metadata harvesting, data reduction, and organization and search.

Documentation is a critical part of each step; note every action you take and any changes that result from your actions. The aim is not only to give others an understanding of what occurred but also, in the examination and analysis stages, to enable others to reproduce your results. Also, consider making printouts of key evidence and organizing these items in a binder to make it easier to reference them when discussing the case with other investigators or attorneys or testifying in court.

*Figure 11.1*

*Categories of the Investigative Process Model, figure from Casey and Palmer (2004)*

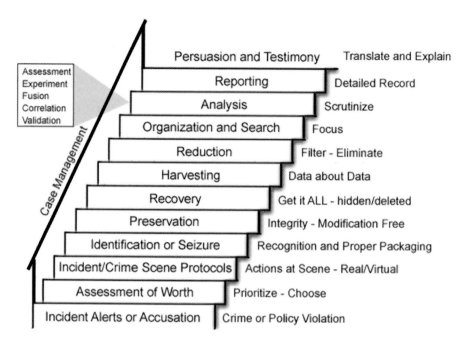

Note that this model takes into account the possibility that certain cases receive priority over others. If a cursory examination of a file system results in sufficient incriminating evidence to build a case, investigators may decide that data recovery is not warranted. In such situations, it is still necessary to harvest the metadata associated with the incriminating digital evidence and process the files as described in the following sections to facilitate analysis.

### 11.1.1) PREPARATION

Before you embark on a forensic examination, some preparation and verification of evidence sources are necessary. It is a good practice to begin a new examination by preparing a sanitized and well-organized working environment. Conducting your examination on a hard drive that has been wiped of all previous data and verified to be empty prevents the possibility of data from past investigations from commingling with the current case. Additionally, assigning unique names to volumes on your work drive can help you keep track of where particular items are located and can help prevent mistakes such as saving recovered files onto the wrong drive.

For each new case, create a set of folders, such as those shown in Figure 11.2, to structure your work. Creating a similar set of folders each time you begin an examination will help you maintain consistency in your work and will make it easier for other examiners to verify your findings if necessary. When the time comes to begin processing storage media, it is advisable to compare them

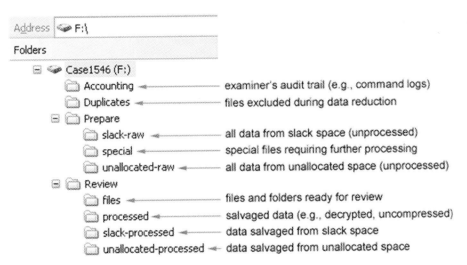

*Figure 11.2*

*Folder structure for beginning examination with brief descriptions of the purpose for each folder based on Casey and Larson (2004)*

against original crime scene documentation, verifying serial numbers of drives, MD5 values data, and any other identifying characteristics. This verification process ensures that items of evidence have not been altered or mixed up with other items since they were collected. Additionally, when it is necessary to examine the original media rather than a copy, be sure to use a method that will not alter the original.

---

**MD5 Algorithm:** The MD5 algorithm is one of the most commonly used methods for calculating message digests. A message digest algorithm, also known as a hash function, takes an item of digital evidence and produces a unique identifying number. Calculating a hash value for a piece of digital evidence enables an examiner to verify that the evidence has not been altered over time. This verification process is accomplished by applying the MD5 algorithm to the item of evidence at any time. If the evidence has changed in any way, the algorithm will produce a different hash value from the original. An MD5 value is the equivalent of digital DNA in that it effectively identifies a particular piece of digital evidence. As such, an MD5 value can also be useful for searching through a large amount of data for a particular item.

---

### 11.1.2) RECOVERY

The first step in the examination process is to salvage all data from storage media and convert unreadable data into a readable form. Although data can be hidden on a drive in many ways and it is not feasible to look for all of them in all cases, examiners should be able to identify the major sources of data or at least be able to recognize large amounts of missing data. For instance, if the combined size of all visible partitions on a drive is much smaller than the capacity of the drive, this may be an indication that a partition is not being detected. Similarly, if a large amount of data cannot be classified or many files of a known type are unusually large, this may be an indication that some form of data hiding or encryption is being used. The following sections cover the main areas on storage media where useful data may be found.

### 11.1.2.1) Deleted files and folders

Criminals often take steps to conceal their crimes, and deleted data often contain the most incriminating digital evidence. Therefore, one of the most fruitful data-salvaging processes is to recover files and folders that have been deleted. When dealing with FAT file systems, most tools can recover deleted files, but not all can recover deleted folders that are no longer referenced by the file system. EnCase has a powerful feature that scours a disk for deleted folders on FAT and NTFS systems. It is useful to have a familiarity with how different tools recover and present information about deleted files. For instance, the SleuthKit is an effective tool for examining UNIX systems because it facilitates the inspection of inodes. Also, the SleuthKit has an added feature of recovering names of deleted files even when the clusters associated with the files have been reallocated, such as the "tempxfer" file shown in Figure 11.3(a). Figure 11.3(b) shows that EnCase does not list the overwritten "tempxfer" file.

Notably, automated file and folder recovery tools make assumptions that are not always correct. For instance, when recovering deleted files, many tools take the starting cluster and file size from a folder entry and assign the next free clusters to the file sequentially. The underlying assumption in this process breaks down when the starting cluster of one deleted file is followed by free clusters that

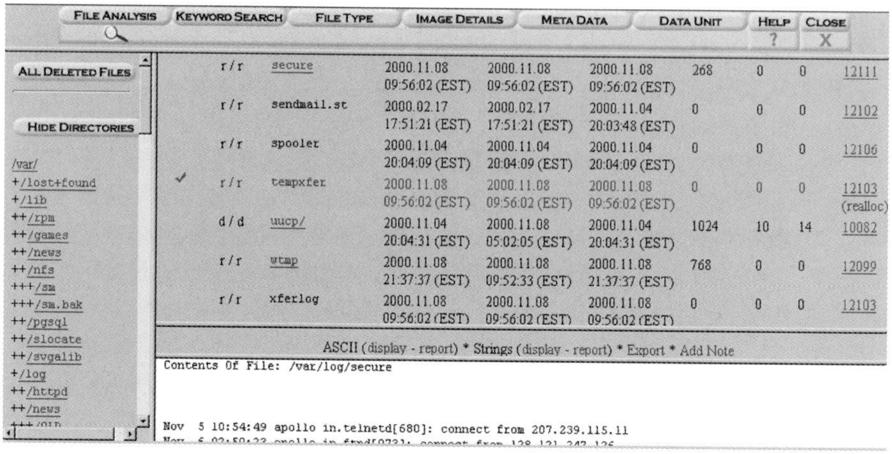

*Figure 11.3(a)*

*Recovering deleted files using The SleuthKit version 1.60*

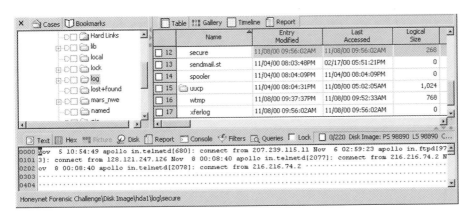

Figure 11.3(b)

Recovering deleted files using EnCase version 4.16a

belonged to a different deleted file. So, automated tools can generate correct or incorrect results depending on the assumptions they make and the particular situation. Furthermore, if two deleted directory entries point to the same cluster, some effort is required to determine which file name and associated date-time stamps referenced that cluster most recently. Some automated file recovery tools distinguish between directory entries that have been deleted versus those that have been deleted and overwritten. However, care must be taken not to assume that files with newer date-time stamps accessed the associated clusters more recently. There are sufficient nuances to file date-time stamps that an apparently newer file could be created before the apparently old one.

The following example clearly illustrates this issue in an Internet child pornography case:

**CASE EXAMPLE**

> [A] JPG file was recovered from cluster 195,018 and two file entries were found pointing to it. The first of these indicated that a file named tn_pbb0915.jpg was written to this cluster at 22:16:06.30 on 10th October 2001 and it was 3,051 bytes in length. The second entry however, indicated that a file named 3e.jpg had been written to the cluster at 00:24:08.75 on 14th January 2002 and it was 6,497 bytes in length. The fact that the drive had been defragmented meant that it was not possible to make the simple assumption that the recovered JPG data was the later file. Even without defragmentation, ascribing the image to the later file entry was still weak because as both file entries were marked as deleted, it was a distinct possibility that the image data had been written after the 14th January 2002 and its attendant file entry had been lost. However, research into the internal structure of JPG files revealed that it is possible to calculate the original length of the file in bytes. The recovered data indicated an original file length of 6,497 bytes, providing a much stronger inferential link to the second file entry. (Bates 2002)

Therefore, if a few recovered files are critical to a case, examiners may want to check these assumptions and seek corroborating evidence from other areas of the computer system or connected networks. Similarly, when recovering deleted subfolders, examiners must be wary of the possibility that, after the subfolder was deleted, another subfolder that was created coincidentally occupies the same cluster as the first subfolder. If the second subfolder is then deleted and its name is overwritten, there is a chance that the original subfolder entry could be associated with the second subfolder's data.

Deleted items in personal digital assistants (PDAs) can be recovered using tools such as PDA Seizure on Windows and pilot-link on UNIX. When examiners encounter a device that their tools are not designed for, the manufacturer may be able to provide them with software to extract data from the device. However, these vendor applications may be able to make only a logical copy that does not include deleted items, or a full memory dump that must be processed like unallocated space, as described in the next section.

Referring back to Figure 11.2, deleted files can be saved in a folder named `Prepare\special\deleted` for later processing. Additionally, documentation relating to this process, such as an inventory of the recovered files and a description of how they were salvaged, should be added to the `Accounting` folder to enable others to see what was recovered. Given the variations between tools and the potential for error, it is advisable to compare the results from one tool using another. Such a comparison can be made by comparing the inventories of undeleted files from both tools for any differences.

### 11.1.2.2) Unallocated, slack, and protected space

Recall that, on storage media, the space that is available to store new data is called "unallocated space." This area on a disk is important from an investigative standpoint because it often contains significant amounts of data from deleted files. Keep in mind that criminals often take steps to conceal their crimes, and deleted data often contain the most incriminating digital evidence. The space between the end of a file and the end of the last cluster assigned to that file is called "file slack." File slack is important because it may contain the remains of previous files or folders that can be retrieved and used as evidence.

Although most tools for examining storage media can extract unallocated space, their approaches are not necessarily consistent. For instance, when EnCase recovers deleted files, it no longer considers the associated data to be in unallocated space, whereas some other tools do, effectively accounting for the data twice. Provided EnCase assigned unallocated clusters to the correct files, there should not be a problem. However, as noted in the preceding section, there is a chance that some unallocated clusters may be assigned to the incorrect file. In some instances, carving the file out of unallocated space may

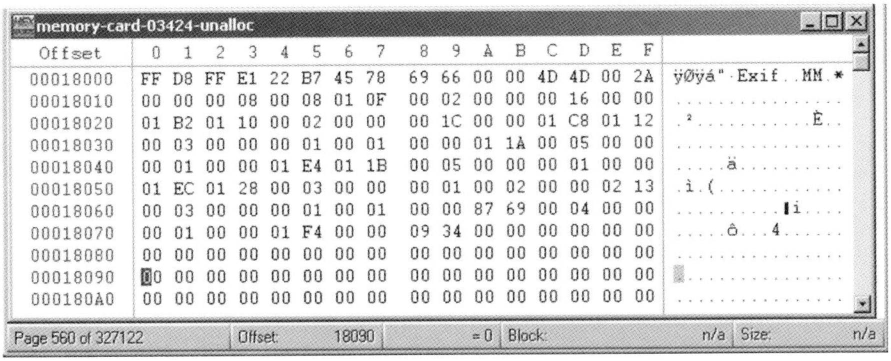

*Figure 11.4*

*Beginning of a JPEG-encoded EXIF file in unallocated space on a memory card*

be more effective, in which case it may be more useful to use a tool that takes a stricter definition of unallocated space. If the undelete and file-carving processes produce the same files, these duplicates can be eliminated in the data reduction step.

File carving uses characteristics of a given class of files to locate those files in a raw data stream such as unallocated clusters on a hard drive. For instance, the beginning and end of a Web (HTML) page are demarked by <html> and </html>, respectively. Figure 11.4 shows another example of digital evidence that is commonly found in child exploitation investigations: digital photographs. The characteristic "FF D8 FF" hexadecimal values indicate that this is the beginning of a JPEG-encoded file and the characteristic "Exif" indicates that it is an Exchangeable Image File Format[1] file common on digital cameras.

Once the beginning and end of the file are located, the intermediate data can be extracted into a file. This carving process can be achieved by simply copying the data and pasting them into a file. Alternatively, the data can be extracted using dd by specifying the beginning and end of the file, as shown here:

```
D:\>dd if=g:\Case1435\Prepare\unallocated-raw\memory-card-03424-unalloc
of=g:\Case1435\Review\unallocated-processed\memory-card-03424-image1.jpg
bs=1 skip=100934 count=652730
```

Some tools automate the file-carving process for various file types, including WinHex,[2] DataLifter,[3] Easy-Recovery Pro,[4] and EnCase[5] for Windows and foremost[6] for UNIX. These tools can be useful for recovering digital video

[1] http://www.exif.org.
[2] http://www.winhex.com.
[3] http://www.datalifter.com.
[4] http://www.ontrack.com.
[5] http://www.encase.com.
[6] http://foremost.sourceforge.net/.

segments created using Webcams that are often in AVI, MPEG, or QuickTime format and may be deleted frequently. This carving technique also works for extracting files from physical memory dumps from handheld computers and from raw network traffic. Additionally, Palm devices and mobile telephones can contain deleted data that may be recoverable using specialized tools (van der Knijff 2002; Casey 2004).

Keep in mind that file carving works on the assumption that a file is stored in contiguous clusters. The advantage of performing file carving on extracted unallocated space rather than on a full forensic image is that the data on disk may not have been arranged in consecutive clusters but may become consecutive when extracted into a single file. Also keep in mind that files salvaged using this technique do not have file names or date-time stamps associated with them, so the examiner needs to assign them names in a systematic way.

Although slack space may not contain complete files, it can contain fragments of deleted files that are useful in an investigation, such as e-mail messages and Internet chat logs. A quick way to examine the contents of slack space is to save it all into a single file and then extract readable text from it using the Gather Text feature in WinHex or `strings` on UNIX. However, slack space can also contain portions of deleted Web browser history files and other artifacts that contain useful binary data such as date-time stamps. Therefore, if a simple string search results in what may be relevant URLs or file names, it is advisable to locate these data on disk and determine whether additional useful information can be extracted from the associated slack space.

Finally, it is important to keep in mind that ATA drives manufactured after 1998, specifically ATA-5 compliant, may have a protected storage area. This protected storage area is implemented using the ATA `setmax` command that instructs the hard drive to report that its maximum storage address is lower than its actual physical capacity.

Most programs cannot access the protected storage area, but companies like Pheonix Technologies are making it easier to utilize this feature, and forensic utilities such as BXDR[7] have been developed to detect and copy this area.

### 11.1.2.3) Special files

Many files on Windows, Macintosh, and UNIX systems require special processing to obtain the useful information they contain. These "special" files include compressed archives, swap files, encoded attachments in e-mail and Usenet messages, and encrypted- and password-protected files. Provided compressed files are not password protected or corrupted, they can be uncompressed with relative ease. For instance, a common method of exchanging large binary files

[7] http://www.sandersonforensics.co.uk/BXDR.htm.

(e.g., images and video clips) on Usenet or in e-mail is to use an encoding algorithm that converts the binary files into a representation that can be sent using mail more easily, often in several parts. The most widely used encoding scheme is called "uuencode," which is most easily recognized by a `begin` at the beginning of the encoded data and an `end` at the end, as shown here:

```
begin 664 baby-jane01.jpg
M_]C_X   02D9)1@ !   $ E@""6   #___@ ?3$5!1"!496H-H-H-H-H-H;F]L;V=I==;@26YC 97-@20@   ?3$5!1"@H-H-H-H-H@26YC@   ?3$5!1"(@@
M+B!6,2XP,0#_VP!_VP!_V_V$@      ("   @("   @("   @("   @("   P,# P,#
M P,#! 4% ! ("   ,! !__ 8  $ 4$0$  @ P, W S  !__ 9__4  @4$4  @44#
M P,%04040040% 5U0440;050% 50504!0504!040504!040504!0504!040504!04%
```

`<cut for brevity>`

```
MI9?]\2?_ !- !_PSYHOI9?]\  ?$G_  ,30 ?\  #/FB^EE_WQ)_\30  ?\,^:+Z6
M7_?$$G_Q- !_PSYHOI9?]\2?_  !- !_PSYHOI9?]\  ?$G_  ,30 ?\  #/FB^EE_
MWQ)_\30!UOA!_X[X;]_?ZA ?V$L^/,XG[/W2R']]R</4 >PE % &!?@ !0 ?0!!0
M % ! !5 ? % ! 4$ ! !$ 4040& $ F( 0 040504?040504? % % % % ! ! !
3 (&1I<<@IF?871B86-K/!!E>&ET"@``
```
`` ` ``

`end`

Notably, this encoded JPG image does not have the JFIF keyword that you would normally look for when scouring a disk for such files. UNIX systems come with both `uuencode` and `uudecode` commands to decode such a message, and similar programs are available for Windows and Macintosh computers such as Aladdin Expander.[8] A MIME-encoded e-mail attachment can be decoded using the `munpack` utility available for Windows and UNIX.[9] However, this utility can decode only one message at a time, and it works only if the message is saved as a plain text file. A different approach is required when processing e-mail stored in a proprietary format such as Microsoft Outlook or AOL. In such cases a tool like the Forensic Toolkit (FTK) can be used to make the examination process more efficient, providing a button to list only e-mail–related data and automatically performing the necessary decoding of attachments and proprietary mailbox formats. FTK can interpret a variety of proprietary formats, including Microsoft Outlook, as shown in Figure 11.5. EnCase can also interpret some of these proprietary formats using the View File Structure feature.

Another approach to viewing proprietary formats, such as America Online (AOL), is to restore them to a disk and view them via the AOL client. In some cases it is possible to recover messages that have been deleted but have not been purged from e-mail files. For additional details about recovering and examin-

---

[8] http://www.aladdinsys.com/.
[9] ftp://ftp.andrew.cmu.edu/pub/mpack/.

*Figure 11.5*

*FTK used to extract e-mail messages and the contents of attachments such as images in a Zip archive shown here*

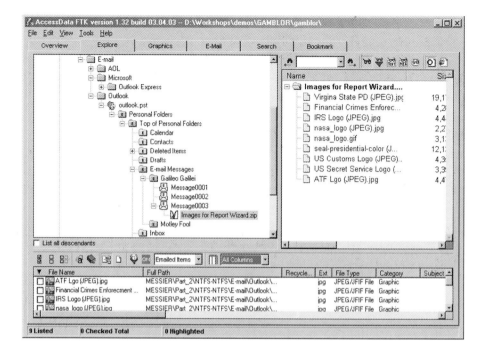

ing e-mail from Microsoft Exchange server, see Chapter 9 of the *Handbook of Computer Crime Investigation* (Casey, Larson, and Long 2002).

When special files are corrupt, it may be possible to repair the damage using specially designed utilities. For example, EasyRecovery Professional from Ontrack can repair a variety of file types from Windows systems, including Outlook files and Zip archives. On UNIX systems, there are tools for repairing a more limited set of files such as `tarfix` and `fixcpio`.

Additional effort is required to salvage data from password-protected or encrypted files (Casey 2001). In some instances, it is possible to use a hexadecimal editor like WinHex to simply remove the password within a file. Some specialized tools can bypass or recover passwords of various files. Currently, the most powerful and versatile tools for salvaging password-protected and encrypted data are the PRTK (Password Recovery Toolkit) and DNA (Distributed Network Attack) from Access Data. The PRTK can recover passwords from many file types and is useful for dealing with encrypted data. Also, it is possible for a DNA network to try every key in less time by combining the power of several computers. DNA can brute-force 40-bit encryption of certain file types including Adobe Acrobat and Microsoft Word/Excel. Using a cluster of approximately 100 off-the-shelf desktop computers and the necessary software, an investigator can try every possible 40-bit key in five days.

When strong encryption is used, such as BestCrypt, PGP, or Windows Encrypted File System, a brute-force approach to guessing the encryption key is generally infeasible. In such cases, it may be possible to locate unencrypted versions of data in unallocated space, swap files, and other areas of the system. For instance, printer spool files on Windows and UNIX systems can contain data from files that have been deleted or encrypted. Alternatively, it may be possible to obtain an alternate decryption key. For instance, some encryption programs advise users to create a recovery disk in case they forget their password. When Encrypted File System (EFS) is used, Windows automatically assigns an encryption recovery agent that can decrypt messages when the original encryption key is unavailable (Microsoft 1999). In Windows 2000, the built-in Administrator account is the default recovery agent (an organization can override the default by assigning a domain-wide recovery agent provided the system is part of the organization's Windows 2000 domain).

Notably, prior to Windows XP, EFS private keys were weakly protected, and it was possible to gain access to encrypted data by replacing the associated NT logon password with a known value using a tool like `ntpasswd` and logging into the system with the new password.

When examiners are investigating child exploitation cases, it is advisable to be on the lookout for other forms of data concealment such as steganography. Examiners can make educated guesses to identify files containing hidden data; the presence of steganography software and uncharacteristically large files should motivate examiners to treat these as special files that require additional processing. In such cases, it may be possible to salvage the hidden data by opening the files using the steganography software and providing a password that was obtained during the investigation. More sophisticated techniques are available for detecting hidden data. Even if encryption or steganography cannot be bypassed, documenting which files are concealing data can help an investigator, attorney, or trier-of-fact determine the intent of the defendant.

### 11.1.3) HARVESTING[10]

The purpose of the harvesting step is to gather metadata relating to the salvaged data from the previous step. These metadata generally come in two forms: class and individual characteristics. Class characteristics are common traits in similar items, whereas individual characteristics are more unique and can be linked to a specific person, place, or object with greater certainty.

---

[10] Portions of this section are adapted from Casey (2004).

For instance, the creation date-time stamp of a file is a class characteristic, whereas an Ethernet address embedded in the document is an individual characteristic.

To begin with, create a list of all active and recovered files, along with associated information, such as long and short file names, extensions, last written or modified dates and times, created dates and times, last accessed dates and times, logical sizes, physical locations on disk, file paths, and file hash values. Many tools have the capability to create this inventory of file properties, including Maresware, EnCase, and FTK (Casey and Larson 2004).

Once the basic file properties are harvested, it is then necessary to look within files for additional metadata. For instance, photographs taken by digital cameras can contain details such as the make and model of the camera, and the date and time the picture was taken (according to the camera's clock) as shown here for the EXIF file from the previous example showing a few seconds' difference between the time the photograph was taken and when it was saved to disk:

```
Pos: 0x1BE, Tag (0x10F) Make = EASTMAN KODAK COMPANY
Pos: 0x1D4, Tag (0x110) Model = KODAK DX4330 DIGITAL CAMERA
Pos: 0x986, Tag (0x201) JPEGInterchangeFormat = 2618
Pos: 0x992, Tag (0x202) JPEGInterchangeFormatLength = 6261
Pos: 0x22E, Tag (0x9000) ExifVersion = 48, 50, 50, 48
Pos: 0x3F6, Tag (0x9003) DateTimeOriginal = 2003:11:13 22:09:26
Pos: 0x40A, Tag (0x9004) DateTimeDigitized = 2003:11:13 22:09:26
```

The data in such photographs found on a computer or on the Internet can be compared with those of a digital camera seized in the defendant's home to determine whether they are consistent, helping to establish the continuity of offense.

Compound files like Microsoft Word documents have date-time stamps, images, and other metadata embedded in them, some of which are shown here:[11]

```
Built-in Document Properties
Property                                    Value
-----------------------                     -----------------------
Title                                       Personal Diary
Template                                    Normal
Last author                                 Harold Smith
Revision number                             53
Application name                            Microsoft Word 10.0
Last print date                             7/7/2003 1:03:00 PM
Creation date                               6/8/2003 10:33:00 PM
Last save time                              9/22/2003 11:11:00 AM
There are 7 inline shapes in the document.
```

[11] These metadata were extracted using a Perl script written by Harlan Carvey (http://patriot.net/~carvdawg/perl.html).

When Word documents or other files are found to contain incriminating images, examiners must return to the previous salvage step, treating them as special files and processing them to obtain all of the images they contain. An efficient way to extract large numbers of images embedded in Word documents is to use the file-carving technique described earlier.

The Windows Registry contains a significant amount of metadata, including the Last Write time of each key. Windows systems use the Registry to store system configuration and usage details in what are called "keys." Registry files (a.k.a. hives) on Windows 95 and 98 systems are located in the Windows installation folder and are named "system.dat" and "user.dat." The Registry on Windows NT/2000/XP is composed of several hive files located in "%system root%\system32\config" and a hive file named "ntuser.dat" for each user account.[12]

Registry files recovered from an evidentiary system can be viewed using the Windows NT `regedt32` command on an examination system using the Load Hive option on the Registry menu. Registry files can also be viewed using third-party applications such as EnCase, FTK Registry Viewer, or Resplendent Registrar.[13] The values in some Registry keys are stored in hexadecimal format but can be converted to ASCII and saved to a text file using the "Save Subtree As" File menu option of `regedt32`. For instance, the following Registry key shows the names of files that were played recently using Windows MediaPlayer (`<sid>` is substituted for the security identifier of the user on the system):

```
Key Name: HKEY_USERS\<sid>\Software\Microsoft\MediaPlayer\Player\RecentURLList
      Class Name:            <NO CLASS>
      Last Write Time:       5/9/2003 - 1:48 PM
      Value 0
         Name:               URL0
         Type:               REG_SZ
         Data:               H:\porn\movie1.avi

      Value 1
         Name:               URL1
         Type:               REG_SZ
         Data:               H:\porn\movie2.avi
```

The Registry values in this example reference files on an external, removable hard drive that was not attached to the system when it was collected. Upon finding these references in the Registry, investigators sought and found the

---

[12] Trojan horse programs such as SubSeven and Back Orifice use Registry keys (and other mechanisms) to persist on a system after it is rebooted. The programs give an individual full remote control of a computer. Although antivirus programs can detect many Trojans in their default state, intruders can modify the programs to avoid detection.

[13] http://www.resplendence.com.

external hard drive. Similar Registry keys exist for other programs and for different file extensions, as shown here:

```
Key Name:
HKEY_USER\<sid>\Software\Microsoft\Windows\CurrentVersion\Explorer\ComDlg32\OpenSaveMR
U\zip
        Class Name:             Shell
        Last Write Time:        5/9/2003 - 1:17 PM
        Value 0
          Name:                 a
          Type:                 REG_SZ
          Data:                 H:\porn\bodyshots1.zip

        <cut for brevity>

        Value 9
          Name:                 j
          Type:                 REG_SZ
          Data:                 H:\porn\bodyshots2.zip
```

As the name suggests, the "Last Write Time" value indicates when the last entry in the Registry was added.

Some keys protect the data they contain, encoding them using a simple cipher, such as the one shown here:

```
Key Name:
HKEY_USER\<sid>\Software\Microsoft\Windows\CurrentVersion\Explorer\UserAssist\{5E6AB78
0-7743-11CF-A12B-00AA004AE837}\Count
        Class Name:             <NO CLASS>
        Last Write Time:        9/11/2002 - 9:28 AM

        Value 1
        Name: HRZR_EHACNGU:T:\sebfg\sebfg.ong

        Value 2
        Name: HRZR_EHACNGU:T:\rapnfr3.rkr
```

The first entry refers to "g:\frost\frost.bat" and the second entry refers to "g:\encase3.exe."

Many other sources of metadata can be useful in child exploitation investigations. As noted earlier, "index.dat" files created by Internet Explorer can be very informative. Windows INFO files show when items in the Recycle Bin were deleted and original file names and locations, shortcut files can contain information relating to files that have been overwritten or stored on removable media, and the $LOGFILE shows file system activities with associated date-time stamps (Sheldon 2002). Data relating to Internet activities such as Usenet access and remote network storage can also be found on Windows and UNIX systems (Casey 2004). The experience and judgment of the examiner must be exercised to determine what data might be available and which might be useful to the investigation.

The data gathered during this step can help generate important leads, pointing to other sources of digital evidence on the system or Internet. For instance, the data extracted from KaZaA, shown in Figure 8.9, contains the IP addresses of computers from which files were obtained. These data can be very helpful to the investigation, demonstrating how the files were obtained and potentially leading investigators to other offenders.

### 11.1.4) REDUCTION

The decision to eliminate or retain certain data for forensic analysis is made based on external data attributes such as MD5 values used to identify known child pornography or to exclude known operating system and application files. It may also be possible to narrow the focus to a particular time period or to certain types of digital evidence relevant to the case. However, keep in mind that offenders might have concealed evidence, and care must be taken when filtering data. Something as simple as video segments having their extensions changed from ".mov" to something like ".exe" could result in an unwary examiner inadvertently filtering out incriminating evidence. Therefore, it is advisable to identify file extension/signature mismatches, move them to the \Prepare\special\sigmismatch folder, and return to the salvage step to determine what data they contain. An even greater risk occurs when steganography is used to hide incriminating evidence within other files.

### 11.1.5) ORGANIZATION AND SEARCH

The primary purpose of a forensic examination is to make it easier for investigators and attorneys to find and identify data during the analysis step and allow them to reference these data in a meaningful way in final reports and testimony. Organization is an implicit part of the examination process described in this chapter, resulting in a reduced set of data grouped into logical categories, as suggested in Figure 11.2. Additionally, investigators often need to search for particular e-mail addresses, IP addresses, or other case-specific details. By making all evidence visible, the examination process enables more complete searches of evidence on a disk.

## 11.2) ANALYSIS AND RECONSTRUCTION

The analysis step involves objectively and critically assessing the available evidence and using this evidence to reconstruct the crime. This process involves developing timelines to identify sequences and patterns in times of events, creating functional reconstructions to ascertain what was possible and impossible, and developing relational reconstructions to determine the relationships and interaction between components of crime. In essence, this step attempts to answer the questions of what happened, where, when, how, who was involved, and why. Although a comprehensive discussion of analysis and investigative reconstruction is beyond the scope of this text, some key issues deserve mention.

Since weak evidence will result in weak conclusions, investigators need to assess the strength of particular pieces of data that are critical to the case. For instance, it is not safe to assume that child pornography found on a defendant's system was created on that system. A careful analysis of class and individual characteristics of the data can lead investigators to additional sources of evidence such as a digital camera or to other offenders depicted in the photograph. This step is particularly important during investigations involving child pornography because it is desirable to locate the original victims and protect them from further abuse.

A **class characteristic** is a general feature shared with similar items such as Kodak digital cameras that embed the make and model names in the photographs they take.

An **individual characteristic** is a unique feature specific to a particular thing, place, person, or action. For example, a scratch on a camera lens that appears in photographs it takes, a distinct monument in the background of a photograph, or the defendant's face appearing in a photograph are all individual characteristics that may help investigators associate the photograph with its source, i.e., a particular camera, location, or person.

As another example, consider the possibility that critical file date-time stamps may have been altered or are inaccurate. Additionally, keep in mind that differences in time zones and daylight savings time can cause date-time stamps to be misrepresented or misinterpreted. In one child abuse case, an expert hired by the defense to examine the defendant's computer concluded that it had been used to access the Internet during the first six hours after it was seized by police. The expert's report indicated that there was substantial evidence of the defendant's computer being altered while it was in police custody, including access to Hotmail login pages and a possible child pornography site. It transpired that the defense expert had not taken the difference in time zones into account when converting the date-time stamps in the Internet Explorer "index.dat" files (Boyd and Forster 2004).

Given the importance of dates and times when investigating computer-related crime, digital evidence examiners need an understanding of how these values are stored and converted. Knowledge of how computers store and

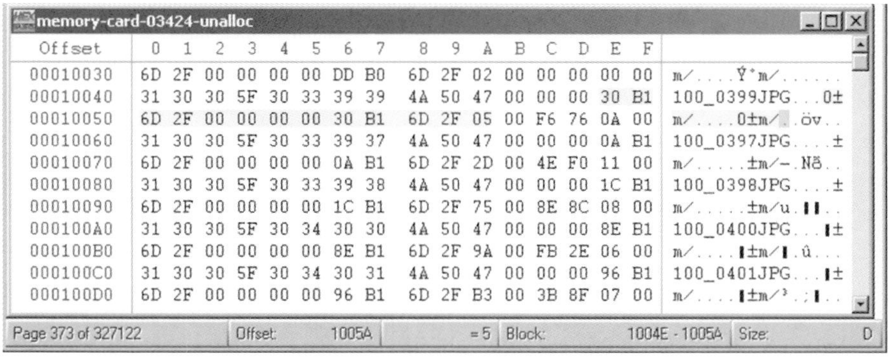

*Figure 11.6*

*Folder entries with 32-bit MS-DOS date-time stamps viewed in WinHex*

calculate date-time stamps will enable examiners to avoid common pitfalls and verify the accuracy of key findings (Forster 2004). For instance, the date-time stamps of files stored on a FAT file system can be verified quite easily from their 32-bit hexadecimal representation, as shown in Figure 11.6.

For example, in Figure 11.6 you can see the date-time stamp associated with the first file (100_0399JPG) is "30 B1 6D 2F" hexadecimal, which is the following in binary:

```
00110000  10110001  01101101  00101111
_____/  _____/  _____/  _____/
 byte 1     byte 2     byte 3     byte 4
```

Converting the binary representation from little-endian to big-endian by reordering the bytes gives

```
00101111  01101101  10110001  00110000
_____/  _____/  _____/  _____/
 byte 4     byte 3     byte 2     byte 1
```

Then, unpacking each portion of the date-time stamp gives
7 bits = 0010111 = 23 years (since 1980)
4 bits = 1011 = 11 months
5 bits = 01101 = 13 days
5 bits = 10110 = 22 hours
6 bits = 001001 = 9 minutes
5 bits = 10000 = 16 = 32 seconds (5 bits cannot store 60 seconds, so time must be incremented in 2-second intervals)

This date-time stamp represents November 13, 2003, at 22:09:32, which can be confirmed with the Data Interpreter in WinHex or using DCode, as shown in Figure 11.7.

*Figure 11.7*

*DCode used to convert
32-bit MS-DOS date-time
stamps from their
hexadecimal
representation*

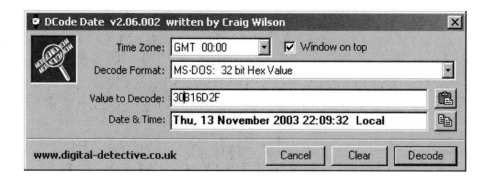

Windows also uses different formats of date-time stamps, including the 64-bit FILETIME that represents the number of 100-nanosecond intervals since January 1, 1600. The FILETIME format is used to represent file dates and times in the NTFS Master File Table (MFT) and for embedded date-time stamps in Microsoft Office documents and Internet Explorer "index.dat" files. For instance, each record in an "index.dat" file contains two date-time stamps, shown here in bold using the history file shown in Chapter 8:

```
Offset        0  1  2  3  4  5  6  7    8  9  A  B  C  D  E  F
00005500     55 52 4C 20 02 00 00 00   90 6B 39 AD 7D EE C3 01    URL . . . .□k9-}îÃ.
00005510     90 6B 39 AD 7D EE C3 01   65 30 17 9F 00 00 00 00    □k9-}îÃ.e0.Ÿ. . . .
00005520     00 00 00 00 00 00 00 00   00 00 00 00 00 00 00 00    . . . . . . . . . . . . . . . .
00005530     60 00 00 00 68 00 00 00   FE 00 10 10 00 00 00 00    `. . .h. . .p. . . . . .
00005540     01 00 20 00 98 00 00 00   14 00 00 00 00 00 00 00    . . .~. . . . . . . . . .
00005550     48 30 17 9F 02 00 00 00   00 00 00 00 00 00 00 00    H0.Ÿ. . . . . . . . . . .
00005560     00 00 00 00 0D F0 AD 0B   56 69 73 69 74 65 64 3A    . . . . . δ_.Visited:
00005570     20 75 73 72 40 68 74 74   70 3A 2F 2F 31 39 32 2E    usr@http://192.
00005580     31 36 38 2E 30 2E 35 2F   49 4D 47 30 30 33 2E 4A    168.0.5/IMG003.J
00005590     50 47 00 10 00 02 00 00   00 00 10 00 00 00 00 00    PG. . . . . . . . . . . .
```

Converting these date-time stamps using DCode, as shown in Figure 11.8, confirms the earlier results (see Section 8.2.1). More in-depth discussions of the format of "index.dat" files and several other files are available in whitepapers from the ODESSA Project (http://odessa.sourceforge.net/).

In addition to checking results with multiple tools, investigators should verify important details by seeking corroborating evidence. For instance, when dealing with date-time stamps of files, look for consistent data gathered during the examination process. As discussed in Chapter 12, investigators may be able to correlate date-time stamps relating to downloaded files with network logs, thus not only validating the findings but also helping to establish continuity of defense.

It is important to keep in mind that the Internet may be a valuable source of evidence even though the offender did not use the Internet to exchange pornography or communicate with victims. An important component of any

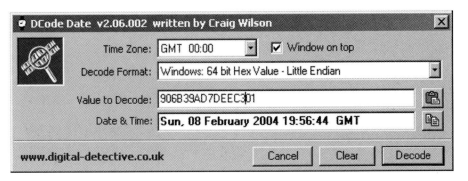

*Figure 11.8*

*DCode used to convert 64-bit FILETIME date-time stamps from their hexadecimal representation*

forensic computer examination is identifying any remote locations where digital evidence may be found. A victim might maintain a Web site, or an offender may transfer incriminating data to a server on the Internet. One of the most common remote storage locations is an individual's Internet Service Provider (ISP). In addition to storing e-mail, some ISPs give their customers storage space for Web pages and other data. So, when examining a computer, search for traces of file transfer applications such as FTP, Secure CRT, and Secure Shell (SSH). Additionally, child pornographers have been known to break into corporate servers and use them to store and trade illegal materials (Wearden 2002). Therefore, when examining a suspect's computer, investigators should look for intrusion tools and signs of compromised systems that the suspects may be using to store incriminating materials.

The value of systematically arranging events and verifying important details in the case cannot be stressed enough. Much insight can be gained from even a simple timeline, relational reconstruction, or functional analysis. Neglecting to perform such analyses can result in missed clues and an incomplete or inaccurate reconstruction of the who, what, where, when, how, and why of the crime. A thorough investigative reconstruction may reveal strong evidence or weaknesses in a case that investigators and attorneys can use to make solid decisions. For a more detailed discussion of analysis and investigative reconstruction, see Chapters 4 and 5 in Casey (2004).

## 11.3) CHALLENGES TO ADMISSIBILITY

One of the most common mistake that prevents digital evidence from being admitted by courts is that it was obtained without authorization. Generally, a warrant is required to search and seize evidence. The main exceptions are plain view, consent, and exigency. If investigators see evidence in plain view, they can seize it provided they obtained access to the area validly. By obtaining consent to search, investigators can perform a search without a warrant, but some care must be employed when obtaining consent to reduce the chance of the search being successfully challenged in court.

> Law enforcement officers obtained permission from the defendant to search his home for evidence relating to a sexual assault of one of his neighbors. During the search, an investigator looked at Turner's computer and identified child pornography. Turner was indicted for possessing child pornography but filed a suppression hearing to exclude the computer files on the ground that he had not consented to the search of his computer and it was not objectively reasonable for the detective to have concluded that evidence of the sexual assault—the stated object of the consent search—would be found in files with such labels as "young" or "young with breasts."[14]

Even when investigators are authorized to search a computer, they must maintain focus on the crime under investigation. For instance, in *United States v. Carey*,[15] the investigator found child pornography on a machine while searching for evidence of drug-related activity, but the images were inadmissible because they were outside the scope of the warrant. The proper action when evidence of another crime is discovered is to obtain another search warrant for that crime.

**CASE EXAMPLE**

> During an investigation into Montgomery Gray's alleged unauthorized access to National Library of Medicine computer systems, the FBI obtained a warrant to seize four computers from Gray's home and look for information downloaded from the library. While examining Gray's computers, a digital evidence examiner found pornographic images in directories named "teen" and "tiny teen," halted the search and obtained a second warrant to search for pornography.[16]
>
> While investigating an online harassment complaint made against Keith Schroeder, a digital evidence examiner found evidence relating to the harassment complaint on Schroeder's computer and noticed some pornographic pictures of children. A second warrant was obtained, giving the digital evidence examiner authority to look for child pornography on Schroeder's computer. Schroeder was charged with nineteen counts of possession of child pornography and convicted on eighteen counts after a jury trial. For the harassment, Schroeder was tried in a separate proceeding for unlawful use of a computer and disorderly conduct.[17]

---

[14] *United States v. Turner* 1999. Appeals Court, 1st Circuit, Case # 98-1258.

[15] *United States v. Carey* 1998. Appeals Court, 10th Circuit, Case # 98-3077.

[16] *United States v. Gray* 1999. District Court, Eastern District of Virginia, Alexandria Division, Case # 99-326-A.

[17] *Wisconsin v. Schroeder* 1999. Appeals Court, Wisconsin, Case # 99-1292-CR.

The other common mistake that prevents digital evidence from being admitted by courts is improper handling. Although courts were somewhat lenient in the past, as more judges and attorneys become familiar with digital evidence, more challenges are being raised relating to evidence-handling procedures.

## REFERENCES

Bates, J. "File Deletion in MS FAT Systems." Technical Paper. (2002). http://www.computer-investigations.com/arts/tech02.html.

Boyd, C., and P. Forster. "Time and Date Issues in Forensic Computing—A Case Study." *Digital Investigations.* 1, no. 1, (2004): 18–23.

Casey, E. "Practical Approaches to Recovering Encrypted Digital Evidence." *International Journal of Digital Evidence*, 1, no. 3 (2002).

Casey, E. "Forensic Examination of Handheld Devices," in *Digital Evidence and Computer Crime: Forensic Science, Computers, and the Internet*, 2nd Edition. London: Academic Press, 2003.

Casey, E., and T. Larson. "Digital Evidence Examination Guidelines," in *Digital Evidence and Computer Crime: Forensic Science, Computers, and the Internet*, 2nd Edition. E. Casey, ed. London: Academic Press, 2003.

Casey, E., and G. Palmer. "The Investigative Process," in *Digital Evidence and Computer Crime: Forensic Science, Computers, and the Internet*, 2nd Edition. E. Casey, ed. London: Academic Press, 2003.

Lee, H. C., T. Palmbach, and M.T. Miller. *Henry Lee's Crime Scene Handbook.* Boston, MA: Academic Press, 2001.

McAuliffe, W. "Wonderland Used Encryption to Swap Child Abuse Pictures." *ZDNet UK* (February 13, 2001). http://news.zdnet.co.uk/business/legal/0,39020651,2084388,00.htm.

Microsoft, "Back Up the Recovery Agent Encrypting File System Private Key in Windows 2000." *Microsoft* KB Q241201.

Sheldon, B. "Forensic Analysis of Windows Systems," in *Handbook of Computer Crime Investigation*, E. Casey, ed., London: Academic Press, 2002.

van der Knijff, R. "Embedded System Analysis," in *Handbook of Computer Crime Investigation*, E. Casey, ed., London: Academic Press, 2002.

Wearden, G. "Insecure networks exploited by paedophiles." *ZDNet UK* (December 10, 2002).

# CHAPTER 12

# SERVERS AND NETWORKS

*Traffic data reveals huge amounts about one's private life. They are your electronic footprints, but unlike the physical fingerprints you leave around you in the real world, they are recorded. For land line phone calls it can reveal the number you dialed, the duration of the call and the time of the call. Traffic data also includes a record of the location of the cell phone in question as it moves about from cell to cell. For this reason, traffic data generated by mobile calls are far more personal and revealing. In relation to the Internet, traffic data would encompass the e-mail addresses on all correspondence to and from the subscriber, a record of date, time, and size of message as well as other transmission details but hopefully excluding message subject and content. It would also encompass a record of every login session, every web page visited and read, every search term entered, every file downloaded, every purchase made, and so forth—in short, virtually the entirety of one's online "session" but hopefully excluding the content of e-mail messages. (Meade 2003)*

The Internet is composed of many networks that child exploitation investigators may need to process for evidence, ranging from large corporate ones to relatively small networks in a suspect's home, as discussed in Chapter 5. Investigators can use log files and traffic from these networks to create a remarkably detailed reconstruction of events surrounding a crime. In addition to examining computers that are directly involved with the commission of an offense, investigators should search for systems used for file storage and for logs generated by other systems on the network. Some examples of these logs were presented in Chapter 8 in the context of Locard's Exchange Principle applied to computers and networks, following the cybertrail, and establishing continuity of offense. In addition to server, application, and authentication logs, useful evidence on networks includes Intrusion Detection System alerts, NetFlow logs from routers, and the contents of network traffic.

This chapter describes how to find and preserve common sources of digital evidence on networks and how to utilize them in child exploitation investigations. This knowledge is applicable whether searching a suspect's home, looking for related evidence on a corporate network, or requesting data from an Internet Service Provider (ISP).

## 12.1) IDENTIFICATION AND SEIZURE

Investigators can locate the most useful sources of digital evidence on a network using the following methodical, three-phased search approach:

1) Determine the endpoints and intermediate systems that the defendant's network connections passed through (e.g., routers, proxies). These systems can contain digital evidence that helps you establish the continuity of offense and gain a more complete understanding of the crime. For example, log files on an e-mail server used to send child pornography can provide a more complete view of the defendant's activities than a single message, such as who else s/he exchanged illegal materials with. Additionally, intermediate systems like routers may generate detailed logs of network activity, which leads to the second search phase.

2) Seek log files that provide an overview of activities on the network, such as NetFlow logs from routers, packet logs from traffic monitoring systems, and alert logs from intrusion-detection systems. These network-level logs are very useful for confirming that a defendant exchanged child pornography via the Internet and determining the IP addresses of the remote systems. Additionally, logs from intrusion-detection systems may reveal that someone gained unauthorized access to the defendant's computer.

3) Look for supporting systems such as authentication servers and callerID systems that can help attribute online activities to an individual. At this point, investigators might decide that live network surveillance is required to attribute the illegal activities to a particular individual, in which case a wiretap or sniffer can be installed provided the necessary authorization is forthcoming.

In practice, these three phases are conducted simultaneously since, in some instances, the second and third phases may lead to other intermediate systems or endpoints. For instance, if an examination of the defendant's computer reveals more illegal Internet activities, requesting additional information from ISPs and telephone companies may be necessary to develop a more complete reconstruction of events.

When dealing with Small Office Home Office (SOHO) networks, investigators can generally find all of the connected systems by following the network cables. However, keep in mind that some systems may be connected wirelessly and that a computer containing the most incriminating evidence may be hidden. Additionally, be aware that some SOHO routers maintain call history records, or logs of when hosts on the network accessed certain Web sites. These types of logs can help establish continuity of offense but may be difficult to obtain because SOHO routers are usually password protected and maintain only a limited number of log entries in memory, expunging old entries to make space for new ones. In any event, such devices connect to ISPs that generally have a log of some form that can help establish continuity of offense.

When investigators are dealing with large networks, an efficient way to locate all relevant systems is to interview the individuals responsible for administering them. Keep in mind that one administrator may not be able to identify all systems in each of the aforementioned search phases. It may be necessary to interview several people to identify all of the systems on their network that may contain useful data. These same individuals probably have access to the systems in question and can often help investigators seize and preserve the associated data. It is advisable for investigators to work closely with these individuals to take advantage of their technical expertise while guiding them through the delicate process of preserving digital evidence, as discussed in the next section.

## 12.2) PRESERVATION

When investigators are dealing with networks, making a forensic image of every system that contains evidence may not be necessary or feasible. When investigators just need logs from a particular system, imaging the entire drive may be a waste of resources, or investigators may not have authority to copy the entire drive. In some instances, investigators need only particular entries from a log file, and it is acceptable to simply request the information from the network owner. For instance, investigators frequently rely on ISPs to preserve evidence from their own systems such as subscriber information and e-mail messages in response to a court order. Furthermore, some data on networks are not stored on hard drives and, therefore, require special measures to preserve them. For instance, in some cases it may be necessary to monitor network traffic to apprehend an offender, in which case a sniffer is used to save a copy of the data into a file.

Even when investigators require only certain entries from a log file, it is advisable to preserve the entire file because they may later find that other portions of the log are relevant to the case. A log file can be preserved by noting the time of the system clock, documenting the file's location and associated metadata (e.g., size, date-time stamps), copying the file to a collection disk, calculating its MD5 value, and labeling the collection disk appropriately. If the log is small enough, it can also be printed in paper form, initialed, and dated to provide another form of documentation. Additionally, it is advisable to save a second copy of the log file to a different medium and verify that both copies are readable on another system.

When logs are stored in a binary format rather than plain text, special utilities may be needed to read them. Therefore, in addition to preserving the binary log file, consider saving a copy of the contents in interpreted form to make it easier to examine later.

As with other forms of evidence, it is imperative to establish chain of custody when collecting evidence on a network by carefully documenting who collected the evidence, from where, how, when, and why.

## 12.3) EXAMINATION AND ANALYSIS

Recall that the first step in the examination process is to make all evidence visible. Although many sources of evidence on networks are stored in plain text format, some logs are stored in binary files and must be extracted using special utilities. For instance, UNIX logon records are stored in binary files and are converted to text using a `last` command. Windows logon records are also stored in binary Security Event Logs that can be converted into text files using `dumpevt`[1] or `dumpel` (Microsoft 2004). Be aware that it is often necessary to extract Event Message Files from a system to obtain complete and accurate information from the Event Logs on that system. A detailed procedure for examining NT Event Logs is provided in the *Handbook of Computer Crime Investigation*, Chapter 9 (Casey, Long, and Larson 2002, 225–228).

As another example, some routers can generate detailed NetFlow logs containing summary information about every packet that passes through the router. Such a detailed record of network activities can be very useful in a child exploitation investigation, showing every connection to and from the defendant's computer. The following NetFlow logs relating to a Hotmail session from a computer with the IP address 192.168.1.105 are displayed using the flow-filter command from the Flow-tools package:[2]

```
examiner1% flow-cat /netflow/2002/2002-08/2002-08-28/ft-v05.2002-08-28.213000-0400 | flow-filter -Sdefendant -f
./defendant.acl | flow-print -f5
  Start              End               Sif  SrcIPaddress    SrcP  DIf  DstIPaddress     DstP  P  Fl  Pkts  Octets

  0828.21:38:19.94   0828.21:38:19.94   2   192.168.1.105   0     19   66.113.201.11    2048  1  0   1     60
  0828.21:38:57.715  0828.21:39:01.339  2   192.168.1.105   1925  13   64.4.53.7        80    6  3   6     609
  0828.21:39:01.539  0828.21:39:02.495  2   192.168.1.105   1927  13   64.4.53.7        80    6  3   18    1172
  0828.21:39:02.299  0828.21:39:05.439  2   192.168.1.105   1928  13   64.4.53.7        80    6  3   15    1081
  0828.21:39:02.323  0828.21:39:05.723  2   192.168.1.105   1929  13   216.33.150.251   80    6  3   8     652

<cut for brevity>
```

[1] http://www.somarsoft.com/.
[2] http://www.splintered.net/sw/flow-tools/.

The preceding logs show only one side of the TCP connection—those made by the Web browser to the Hotmail server. The corresponding flows from the server to the client are listed here, using the -D (destination) option of the flow-filter command instead of -S (source):

```
examiner1% flow-cat /netflow/2002/2002-08/2002-08-28/ft-v05.2002-08-28.213000-0400 | flow-filter -Ddefendant -f
./defendant.acl | flow-print -f5
  Start               End               Sif  SrcIPaddress    SrcP  DIf  DstIPaddress    DstP  P  Fl  Pkts  Octets

  0828.21:38:11.597   0828.21:38:11.597   11   66.113.201.11   0     4    192.168.1.105   0     1  0   1     60
  0828.21:38:50.245   0828.21:38:53.869   11   64.4.53.7       80    4    192.168.1.105   1925  6  3   5     514
  0828.21:38:54.69    0828.21:38:55.25    11   64.4.53.7       80    4    192.168.1.105   1927  6  3   26    12085
  0828.21:38:54.833   0828.21:38:57.969   11   64.4.53.7       80    4    192.168.1.105   1928  6  3   17    6795
  0828.21:38:54.853   0828.21:38:58.257   11   216.33.150.251  80    4    192.168.1.105   1929  6  3   8     3041

<cut for brevity>
```

Each NetFlow entry in the preceding output contains the start and end time of the flow, source and destination IP addresses and port numbers, followed by the number of packets in each flow, a number representing the protocol (e.g., 1 for ICMP, 6 for TCP, 17 for UDP), a number representing the combination of TCP flags in each flow, the number of packets, and the number of bytes (a.k.a. octets) transmitted, respectively. Similar network activity logs can be maintained using other tools such as Argus[3] that store data in binary format but can export them as text.

Unlike traffic data described in the opening quote, captured network traffic includes the full contents of all communications and is analogous to a forensic image of a hard drive. Data can be extracted from captured network traffic using special tools including times, IP addresses, and content (e.g., e-mail messages with attachments) associated with network activities, as shown in Table 12.1. For a more detailed discussion of processing network traffic as a source of evidence, see "Network Traffic as a Source of Evidence: Tool Strengths, Weaknesses, and Future Needs" (Casey 2004).

The next steps in the examination process are to harvest metadata, perform data reduction, and organize the evidence to facilitate searching and analysis.

| Start | Duration | Source (IP:port) | Destination (IP:port) | Bytes | Content |
|---|---|---|---|---|---|
| 2/27/2004 15:02:25 | 64 secs | 172.16.32.214:3387 | 172.16.64.10:80 | 12646 | GIF |
| 2/27/2004 15:04:04 | 77 secs | 172.16.32.214:3394 | 10.13.225.22:1214 | 438984 | MPEG |
| 2/27/2004 15:05:02 | 318 secs | 172.16.32.214:3422 | 172.16.66.248:1214 | 3780694 | MPEG |

*Table 12.1*

*A Summary of Data in a Network Capture File Including Recovered Files such as Images and Video Files*

[3] http://www.qosient.com/argus/.

*Table 12.2*

*Data Extracted from FTP Logs and Organized in a Spreadsheet Showing Files Being Downloaded from an FTP Server Using the "jsmith" User Account*

| Date | Time | IP address | File size | File path | User | Source |
|------|------|------------|-----------|-----------|------|--------|
| 2/23/2004 | 1:14:00 | 172.16.32.13 | 31330 | /pub/jane2/01.jpg | jsmith | xferlog1 |
| 2/23/2004 | 1:14:02 | 172.16.32.13 | 15951 | /pub/jane2/02.jpg | jsmith | xferlog1 |
| 2/23/2004 | 1:14:03 | 172.16.32.13 | 18923 | /pub/jane2/03.jpg | jsmith | xferlog1 |
| 2/23/2004 | 1:14:05 | 172.16.32.13 | 92701 | /pub/jane2/04.jpg | jsmith | xferlog1 |
| 2/23/2004 | 1:14:07 | 172.16.32.13 | 40395 | /pub/jane2/05.jpg | jsmith | xferlog1 |
| 2/23/2004 | 1:14:09 | 172.16.32.13 | 21434 | /pub/jane2/06.jpg | jsmith | xferlog1 |
| 2/23/2004 | 1:14:11 | 172.16.32.13 | 95625 | /pub/jane2/07.jpg | jsmith | xferlog1 |
| 2/27/2004 | 14:56:53 | 172.16.32.214 | 10790 | /pub/amy1/01.jpg | jsmith | xferlog3 |
| 2/27/2004 | 14:57:15 | 172.16.32.214 | 22122 | /pub/amy1/02.jpg | jsmith | xferlog3 |
| 2/27/2004 | 14:57:22 | 172.16.32.214 | 27840 | /pub/amy1/03.jpg | jsmith | xferlog3 |
| 2/27/2004 | 14:57:44 | 172.16.32.214 | 178165 | /pub/amy1/04.jpg | jsmith | xferlog3 |
| 2/27/2004 | 14:57:46 | 172.16.32.214 | 178173 | /pub/amy1/05.jpg | jsmith | xferlog3 |
| 2/27/2004 | 14:57:47 | 172.16.32.214 | 179823 | /pub/amy1/06.jpg | jsmith | xferlog3 |
| 2/27/2004 | 14:57:48 | 172.16.32.214 | 181373 | /pub/amy1/07.jpg | jsmith | xferlog3 |
| 2/27/2004 | 14:57:50 | 172.16.32.214 | 183122 | /pub/amy1/08.jpg | jsmith | xferlog3 |
| 2/27/2004 | 14:57:55 | 172.16.32.214 | 185880 | /pub/amy1/09.jpg | jsmith | xferlog3 |

For some log files, performing these steps simultaneously is most effective. For instance, if FTP server logs contain entries that are unrelated to the investigation, it is most efficient to extract only the items of relevance and organize the associated date-time stamps, IP addresses, usernames, and filenames and sizes in a spreadsheet or database to facilitate searching and analysis, as shown in Table 12.2.

Log files that contain start and end times can be organized in a similar fashion, but it is generally desirable to treat the start and end times as two separate events. Having separate entries for the start and end of events makes it easier to order events chronologically when combining logs from multiple sources. For instance, Table 12.3 contains summarized data from a Windows XP Security Event Log that can be combined with the data in Table 12.2 to demonstrate that the "John Smith" account logged onto the defendant's home computer immediately prior to the FTP downloads and logged off after the downloads were complete.

Although Windows Security Event Logs record logon and logoff events separately, other logs such as UNIX logon databases and NetFlow records have one entry per session containing both the start and end times. For such logs, an examiner must manually separate each log entry into two events in a spreadsheet or database. Some log files, such as RADIUS dial-up authentication logs, are quite difficult to interpret. Fortunately, in child exploitation cases, investigators can usually rely on the ISP to interpret these logs and produce only the relevant entries, such as those shown in Table 12.4.

| Date | Time | Event | Hostname | User | Source |
|------|------|-------|----------|------|--------|
| 2/23/2004 | 1:05:53 | Successful logon | HOMEPC | John Smith | winxp-evtlog1 |
| 2/23/2004 | 1:58:59 | User initiated logoff | HOMEPC | John Smith | winxp-evtlog1 |
| 2/27/2004 | 14:31:48 | Successful logon | HOMEPC | John Smith | winxp-evtlog1 |
| 2/27/2004 | 15:14:46 | User initiated logoff | HOMEPC | John Smith | winxp-evtlog1 |

*Table 12.3*

*Logon and Logoff Events Obtained from a Windows Security Event Log on a Windows XP System Named HOMEPC*

| Date | Start time | End time | RADIUS ID | IP address | Caller ID |
|------|-----------|----------|-----------|------------|-----------|
| 2/23/2004 | 1:07:47 | 1:32:56 | jsmith02 | 172.16.32.13 | 5551467 |
| 2/27/2004 | 14:32:41 | 15:10:19 | jsmith02 | 172.16.32.214 | 5551467 |

*Table 12.4*

*Summarized RADIUS Logs Showing When the "jsmith02" Dial-up Account Was Used to Connect to the Internet and Which IP Addresses Were Assigned to Each Connection*

Once all available data have been filtered and organized, they can be analyzed to gain a greater understanding of the crime. Creating a timeline of events is a fundamental aspect of crime reconstruction that gives investigators an overview of what occurred. Before investigators combine log files to create a chronological reconstruction of events, it is crucial to correct for time zone differences and system clock discrepancies. A failure to do so will create discontinuities in the timeline that will prevent investigators from establishing continuity of offense. Even log files from a single system can contain date-time stamps with different time zones. For instance, Microsoft's Internet Information Server logs are in Greenwich mean time (GMT) by default, whereas the Windows Event Logs generally use the local time. Even large Internet Service Providers like AOL have been known to adjust date-time stamps in their logs into British Summer Time instead of GMT, resulting in a one-hour discrepancy.

Useful patterns can emerge from a timeline, and large gaps may be an indication that an important source of digital evidence has been overlooked. For instance, an offender may have several Internet accounts, but investigators may have discovered only one of them. Analyzing the interactions between entities can also reveal useful patterns. For example, when several individuals share a computer, the remote systems they access and the people they send e-mail to can help investigators differentiate between each person's online activities and thus attribute the illegal activities to a specific person. This type of relational reconstruction can also help investigators find other offenders that the defendant communicated with.

In 1996, while examining the computer of an individual charged with disseminating child pornography on the Internet, Canadian police found an FTP log indicating 19 pictures had been transferred to a computer in the University of Washington. This evidence was given to the U.S. Customs who attributed the activities to Alexander Hay, a student living on the University of Washington campus. Investigators also determined that Hay operated a web site describing his involvement in legitimate activities for young children, including. . . . Although Hay raised numerous objections to the search of his computer, he was convicted for possession and distribution of child pornography.[4]

## REFERENCES

Casey E., H. M. Long, and T. Larson. *Network Analysis, Handbook of Computer Crime Investigation*. E. Casey, ed., Academic Press: London, 2002.

Casey, E. "Network Traffic as a Source of Evidence: Tool Strengths, Weaknesses, and Future Needs, Digital Investigation." 1, no. 1 (2004).

Meade, J. "Retention of Communications Traffic Data." Statement made by the Irish Data Protection Commissioner at the Forum on the Retention of Communications Traffic Data. (February 24, 2003). http://www.dataprivacy.ie/7nr240203.htm.

Microsoft Corporation. *Windows Resource Kits*. (2004). http://www.microsoft.com/windows2000/techinfo/reskit/tools/existing/dumpel-o.asp.

---

[4] *United States v. Hay* (1999). Appeals Court, 9th Circuit, Case #99=30101.

# SECTION IV

# THE LAW OF INTERNET CHILD SEXUAL EXPLOITATION

# CHAPTER 13

# CHILD PORNOGRAPHY

*All ideas having even the slightest redeeming social importance—unorthodox ideas,*
*controversial ideas, even ideas hateful to the prevailing climate of opinion—have the full*
*protection of the [First Amendment] guaranties, unless excludable because they encroach upon*
*the limited area of more important interests. But implicit in the history of the First Amendment*
*is the rejection of obscenity as utterly without redeeming social importance.*[1]

Obscenity and child pornography are crimes that came of age in the twentieth
century. Advances in technology that delivered photography, video, and the
Internet were previously unknown. Although rape and sex abuse undoubtedly
occurred throughout history, the camera first enabled people to capture the
occurrence of such events. A picture of a sexual assault captures the moment,
the horror, and the humiliation of the victim for all time. This chapter explores
the development of child pornography law and its relation to the law of obscenity. The discussion begins by reviewing the landmark United States Supreme
Court decision in *Miller v. California*.[2] This decision defines obscenity and forms
the basis for the discussion of child pornography. Next, the chapter turns to a
discussion of *New York v. Ferber*,[3] the case that explains the difference between
child pornography and obscenity and the reasoning for allowing all child
pornography to be outlawed. The chapter will review the *Ashcroft v. Free Speech
Coalition*[4] decision in which the United States Supreme Court held that
computer-rendered images depicting children in sexually explicit conduct and
images of adults who "appear to be" children engaged in sexually explicit
conduct are not child pornography.

To properly understand the law of child pornography, you must appreciate
its legal foundations. To do that, you must review the complex, subtle, and

---

[1] *Chaplinsky v. State of New Hampshire*, 315 U.S. 568 (1942).
[2] *Miller v. California*, 314 U.S. 15 (1972).
[3] *New York v. Ferber*, 458 U.S. 747 (1982).
[4] *Aschroft v. Free Speech Coalition*, U.S. LEXIS 2789, 122 S. Ct. 1389 (2002). Pub. L. No. 100-690 (1988)
(codified as amended at 18 U.S.C. 2251A-2252).

dynamic relationship between the two legal concepts. Of course, regulation of obscenity and child pornography has to be examined in the context of developments in technology. As technology develops more graphic and instantaneous forms of expression, the law focuses to more precisely define what forms of expression the Constitution protects and what it does not.

United States federal law and the individual states have regulated obscenity since before the Revolutionary War.[5] In the eighteenth century, obscenity took the form of writings, paintings, and drawings. Thinking about such forms today, it seems incomprehensible that United States law allowed regulation of written "obscenity." With the few exceptions of libel, copyright infringement, threatening and inciting to riot, written speech is now fully protected by the First Amendment at the federal level and the states through the Fourteenth Amendment.

In the period between the mid-1800s and the mid-1950s, technology completely revolutionized the nature of obscenity and child pornography. What was regulated when written or drawn was suddenly graphically shown in photographs and movies. The United States Supreme Court struggled through these years, trying to find an acceptable balance between legitimate rights to free speech and the government's need to regulate obscenity and child pornography. Justice Potter Stewart's famous quote sums up the Court's struggle with defining obscenity:

**CASE EXAMPLE**

It is possible to read the Court's opinion in *Roth v. United States* and *Alberts v. California*, [ ], in a variety of ways. In saying this, I imply no criticism of the Court, which in those cases was faced with the task of trying to define what may be indefinable. I have reached the conclusion, which I think is confirmed at least by negative implication in the Court's decisions since Roth and Alberts, [ ] that under the First and Fourteenth Amendments criminal laws in this area are constitutionally limited to hard-core pornography. [ ] I shall not today attempt further to define the kinds of material I understand to be embraced within that shorthand description; and perhaps I could never succeed in intelligibly doing so. **But I know it when I see it**, and the motion picture involved in this case is not that.[6]

[5] "The guaranties of freedom of expression [ ] in effect in 10 of the 14 States which by 1792 had ratified the Constitution, gave no absolute protection for every utterance. Thirteen of the 14 States provided for the prosecution of libel, [ ] and all of those States made either blasphemy or profanity, or both, statutory crimes. As early as 1712, Massachusetts made it criminal to publish "any filthy, obscene, or profane song, pamphlet, libel or mock sermon" in imitation or mimicking of religious services. Acts and Laws of the Province of Mass. Bay, c. CV, 8 (1712), Mass. Bay Colony Charters & Laws 399 (1814). Thus, profanity and obscenity were related offenses." *Roth v. United States*, 354 U.S. 476, 482 (1957).

[6] *Jacobellis v. Ohio*, 378 U.S. 184 (1964) (concurring opinion). (Emphasis added).

Justice Harlan also reflected the Court's frustration when he referred to "the intractable obscenity problem."[7]

During this period, the Court's tortured rulings put them in a position where the docket was laden with obscenity cases. To decide the cases, the Justices had to actually view the films or pictures. The Court created a viewing room where they watched the films. Justice Brennan stated that it created "institutional stress" that was "hardly a source of edification to the members of the Court."[8] In 1972, the Court finally settled on a test for obscenity that rallied the support of a majority of the Justices.

*Miller v. California* (1972) set out the test for obscenity that has remained in force for more than thirty years. For material to be judged "obscene," a court must find that

- The average person, applying "contemporary community standards" would find the work, taken as a whole, appeals to the prurient interest in sex;
- The material portrays in a patently offensive way, sexual conduct specifically defined by applicable state law; and,
- Taken as a whole, the work lacks serious literary, artistic, political; or artistic value (*Miller* at 23–25).

Since *Miller*, the states and the courts have honed the law to more clearly articulate what is prohibited. *Miller* limited the subject matter of obscenity to that which is sexual in nature. That was a big step in narrowing obscenity prohibitions. The *Miller* Court also opted for a "community standards" test rather than a "national standards" test. The Court reasoned that community standards are more appropriate to judge obscenity because it would be too difficult for juries to discern a national standard of acceptable content.

Following the *Miller* decision, child pornography became an increasing problem. Magazines and films littered adult bookstore shelves, and the problem was difficult for law enforcement to address with obscenity statutes. For the most part, obscenity is a misdemeanor offense that was difficult to enforce and yielded minimal sanctions. Some states, such as New York, separated child pornography from obscenity, making it a different offense. In 1982, the United States Supreme Court decided the landmark case *New York v. Ferber*. In *Ferber*,

---

[7] *Instate Circuit, Inc. v. Dallas*, 390 U.S. 676, 704 (1968) (concurring and dissenting opinion of Justice Harlan).
[8] The book *The Brethren* describes this period and the palpable tension on the Court. Woodard, B., and S. Armstrong. *The Brethren*. New York: Simon and Schuster, 1979. *Paris Adult Theatre I v. Slaton*, 413 U.S. 49 (1973).

the Court held that child pornography may be prohibited because it is not protected by the First Amendment to the Constitution. An excerpt of the case follows so that you may appreciate the Court's reasoning and holdings.

**CASE EXAMPLE**

## NEW YORK v. FERBER, 458 U.S. 747 (1982)[9]

**JUSTICE WHITE delivered the opinion of the Court.**

At issue in this case is the constitutionality of a New York criminal statute which prohibits persons from knowingly promoting sexual performances by children under the age of 16 by distributing material which depicts such performances. [ ]

In recent years, the exploitive use of children in the production of pornography has become a serious national problem. [The] Federal Government and 47 States have sought to combat the problem with statutes specifically directed at the production of child pornography. At least half of such statutes do not require that the materials produced be legally obscene. Thirty-five States and the United States Congress have also passed legislation prohibiting the distribution of such materials; 20 States prohibit the distribution of material depicting children engaged in sexual conduct without requiring that the material be legally obscene. [ ]

New York is one of the 20. In 1977, the New York Legislature enacted Article 263 of its Penal Law.[ ] Section 263.05 criminalizes as class C felony the use of a child in a sexual performance:

> "A person is guilty of the use of a child in a sexual performance if knowing the character and content thereof he employs, authorizes or induces a child less than sixteen years of age to engage in a sexual performance or being a parent, legal guardian or custodian of such child, he consents to the participation by such child in a sexual performance."

A "[s]exual performance" is defined as "any performance or part thereof which includes sexual conduct by a child less than sixteen years of age." 263.00(1). "Sexual conduct" is in turn defined in 263.00(3):

> "'Sexual conduct' means actual or simulated sexual intercourse, deviate sexual intercourse, sexual bestiality, masturbation, sado-masochistic abuse, or lewd exhibition of the genitals."

---

[9] WHITE, J., delivered the opinion of the Court, in which BURGER, C. J., and POWELL, REHNQUIST, and O'CONNOR, JJ., joined. O'CONNOR, J., filed a concurring opinion, post, p. 774. BRENNAN, J., filed an opinion concurring in the judgment, in which MARSHALL, J., joined, post, p. 775. BLACKMUN, J., concurred in the result. STEVENS, J., filed an opinion concurring in the judgment, post, p. 777.

A performance is defined as "any play, motion picture, photograph or dance" or "any other visual representation exhibited before an audience." 263.00(4).
At issue in this case is 263.15, defining a class D felony: [ ]

> "A person is guilty of promoting a sexual performance by a child when, knowing the character and content thereof, he produces, directs or promotes any performance which includes sexual conduct by a child less than sixteen years of age."

To "promote" is also defined:

> "'Promote' means to procure, manufacture, issue, sell, give, provide, lend, mail, deliver, transfer, transmute, publish, distribute, circulate, disseminate, present, exhibit or advertise, or to offer or agree to do the same." 263.00(5).

A companion provision bans only the knowing dissemination of obscene material. 263.10. This case arose when Paul Ferber, the proprietor of a Manhattan bookstore specializing in sexually oriented products, sold two films to an undercover police officer. The films are devoted almost exclusively to depicting young boys masturbating. Ferber was indicted on two counts of violating 263.10 and two counts of violating 263.15, the two New York laws controlling dissemination of child pornography. [ ] After a jury trial, Ferber was acquitted of the two counts of promoting an obscene sexual performance, but found guilty of the two counts under 263.15, which did not require proof that the films were obscene. Ferber's convictions were affirmed without opinion [ ]

The New York Court of Appeals reversed, holding that 263.15 violated the First Amendment. [ ] We granted the State's petition for certiorari[ ], presenting the single question: "To prevent the abuse of children who are made to engage in sexual conduct for commercial purposes, could the New York State Legislature, consistent with the First Amendment, prohibit the dissemination of material which shows children engaged in sexual conduct, regardless of whether such material is obscene?" [ ]

The Court of Appeals proceeded on the assumption that the standard of obscenity incorporated in 263.10, which follows the guidelines enunciated in *Miller v. California*, [ ] constitutes the appropriate line dividing protected from unprotected expression by which to measure a regulation directed at child pornography. It was not the premise that "nonobscene adolescent sex" could not be singled out for special treatment that the court found 263.15 "strikingly underinclusive." Moreover, the assumption that the constitutionally permissible regulation of pornography could not be more extensive with respect to the distribution of material depicting children may also have led the court to conclude that a narrowing construction of 263.15 was unavailable.

The Court of Appeals' assumption was not unreasonable in light of our decisions. This case, however, constitutes our first examination of a statute directed at and limited to depictions of sexual activity involving children. We believe our inquiry should begin with the question of whether a State has somewhat more freedom in proscribing works which portray sexual acts or lewd exhibitions of genitalia by children. [ ]

In *Chaplinsky v. New Hampshire* [ ], the Court laid the foundation for the excision of obscenity from the realm of constitutionally protected expression:

> "There are certain well-defined and narrowly limited classes of speech, the prevention and punishment of which have never been thought to raise any Constitutional problem. These include the lewd and obscene. . . . It has been well observed that such utterances are no essential part of any exposition of ideas, and are of such slight social value as a step to truth that any benefit that may be derived from them is clearly outweighed by the social interest in order and morality." [ ]

Embracing this judgment, the Court squarely held in *Roth v. United States*, [ ] that "obscenity is not within the area of constitutionally protected speech or press." [ ] The Court recognized that "rejection of obscenity as utterly without redeeming social importance" was implicit in the history of the First Amendment: The original States provided for the prosecution of libel, blasphemy, and profanity, and the "universal judgment that obscenity should be restrained [is] reflected in the international agreement of over 50 nations, in the obscenity laws of all of the 48 states, and in the 20 obscenity laws enacted by Congress from 1842 to 1956." [ ].

Roth was followed by 15 years during which this Court struggled with "the intractable obscenity problem." [ ] Despite considerable vacillation over the proper definition of obscenity, a majority of the Members of the Court remained firm in the position that "the States have a legitimate interest in prohibiting dissemination or exhibition of obscene material when the mode of dissemination carries with it a significant danger of offending the sensibilities of unwilling recipients or of exposure to juveniles." [ ]

The *Miller* standard, like its predecessors, was an accommodation between the State's interests in protecting the "sensibilities of unwilling recipients" from exposure to pornographic material and the dangers of censorship inherent in unabashedly content-based laws. Like obscenity statutes, laws directed at the dissemination of child pornography run the risk of suppressing protected expression by allowing the hand of the censor to become unduly heavy. For the following reasons, however, we are persuaded that the States are entitled to greater leeway in the regulation of pornographic depictions of children.

First. It is evident beyond the need for elaboration that a State's interest in "safeguarding the physical and psychological well-being of a minor" is "compelling." [ ] "A democratic society rests, for its continuance, upon the healthy, well-rounded growth of young people into full maturity as citizens." [ ]

The prevention of sexual exploitation and abuse of children constitutes a government objective of surpassing importance. The legislative findings accompanying passage of the New York laws reflect this concern:

> "[T]here has been a proliferation of exploitation of children as subjects in sexual performances. The care of children is a sacred trust and should not be abused by those who seek to profit through a commercial network based upon the exploitation of children. The public policy of the state demands the protection of children from exploitation through sexual performances." [ ]

We shall not second-guess this legislative judgment. Respondent has not intimated that we do so. Suffice it to say that virtually all of the States and the United States have passed legislation proscribing the production of or otherwise combating "child pornography." The legislative judgment, as well as the judgment found in the relevant literature, is that the use of children as subjects of pornographic materials is harmful to the physiological, emotional, and mental health of the child. [ ] That judgment, we think, easily passes muster under the First Amendment.

Second. The distribution of photographs and films depicting sexual activity by juveniles is intrinsically related to the sexual abuse of children in at least two ways. First, the materials produced are a permanent record of the children's participation and the harm to the child is exacerbated by their circulation. Second, the distribution network for child pornography must be closed if the production of material which requires the sexual exploitation of children is to be effectively controlled. Indeed, there is no serious contention that the legislature was unjustified in believing that it is difficult, if not impossible, to halt the exploitation of children by pursuing only those who produce the photographs and movies. While the production of pornographic materials is a low-profile, clandestine industry, the need to market the resulting products requires a visible apparatus of distribution. The most expeditious if not the only practical method of law enforcement may be to dry up the market for this material by imposing severe criminal penalties on persons selling, advertising, or otherwise promoting the product. Thirty-five States and Congress have concluded that restraints on the distribution of pornographic materials are required in order to effectively combat the problem, and there is a body of literature and testimony to support these legislative conclusions.[ ]

Respondent does not contend that the State is unjustified in pursuing those who distribute child pornography. Rather, he argues that it is enough for the State to prohibit the distribution of materials that are legally obscene under the Miller test. While some States may find that this approach properly accommodates its interests, it does not follow that the First Amendment prohibits a State from going further. The Miller standard, like all general definitions of what may be banned as obscene, does not reflect the State's particular and more compelling interest in prosecuting those who promote the sexual exploitation of children. Thus, the question under the Miller test of whether a work, taken as a whole, appeals to the prurient interest of the average person bears no connection to the issue of whether a child has been physically or psychologically harmed in the production of the work. Similarly, a sexually explicit depiction need not be "patently offensive" in order to have required the sexual exploitation of a child for its production. In addition, a work which, taken on the whole, contains serious literary, artistic, political, or scientific value may nevertheless embody the hardest core of child pornography. "It is irrelevant to the child [who has been abused] whether or not the material . . . has a literary, artistic, political or social value." [ ]

Third. The advertising and selling of child pornography provide an economic motive for and are thus an integral part of the production of such materials, an activity illegal throughout the Nation. "It rarely has been suggested that the constitutional freedom for speech and press extends its immunity to speech or writing used as an integral part of conduct in violation of a valid criminal statute." [ ] We note that were the statutes outlawing the employment of children in these films and photographs fully effective, and the constitutionality of these laws has not been questioned, the First Amendment implications would be no greater than that presented by laws against distribution: enforceable production laws would leave no child pornography to be marketed.

Fourth. The value of permitting live performances and photographic reproductions of children engaged in lewd sexual conduct is exceedingly modest, if not de minimis. We consider it unlikely that visual depictions of children performing sexual acts or lewdly exhibiting their genitals would often constitute an important and necessary part of a literary performance or scientific or educational work. As a state judge in this case observed, if it were necessary for literary or artistic value, a person over the statutory age who perhaps looked younger could be utilized. Simulation outside of the prohibition of the statute could provide another alternative. Nor is there any question here of censoring a particular literary theme or portrayal of sexual activity. The First Amendment interest is limited to that of rendering the portrayal somewhat more "realistic" by utilizing or photographing children.

Fifth. Recognizing and classifying child pornography as a category of material outside the protection of the First Amendment is not incompatible with our earlier decisions. "The question whether speech is, or is not, protected by the First Amendment often depends on the content of the speech." [I]t is not rare that a content-based classification of speech has been accepted because it may be appropriately generalized that within the confines of the given classification, the evil to be restricted so overwhelmingly outweighs the expressive interests, if any, at stake, that no process of case-by-case adjudication is required. When a definable class of material, such as that covered by 263.15, bears so heavily and pervasively on the welfare of children engaged in its production, we think the balance of competing interests is clearly struck and that it is permissible to consider these materials as without the protection of the First Amendment. [ ]

There are, of course, limits on the category of child pornography which, like obscenity, is unprotected by the First Amendment. As with all legislation in this sensitive area, the conduct to be prohibited must be adequately defined by the applicable state law, as written or authoritatively construed. Here the nature of the harm to be combated requires that the state offense be limited to works that visually depict sexual conduct by children below a specified age. [ ] The category of "sexual conduct" proscribed must also be suitably limited and described.

The test for child pornography is separate from the obscenity standard enunciated in Miller, but may be compared to it for the purpose of clarity. The Miller formulation is adjusted in the following respects: A trier of fact need not find that the material appeals to the prurient interest of the average person; it is not required that sexual conduct portrayed be done so in a patently offensive manner; and the material at issue need not be considered as a whole. We note that the distribution of descriptions or other depictions of sexual conduct, not otherwise obscene, which do not involve live performance or photographic or other visual reproduction of live performances, retains First Amendment protection. As with obscenity laws, criminal responsibility may not be imposed without some element of scienter on the part of the defendant. [ ][10]

*Ferber* made it clear that child pornography is different from obscenity and that the government may regulate it more stringently than obscenity. The government may regulate child pornography without the necessity of proving that it is obscene.

## 13.1) EVOLUTION OF CHILD PORNOGRAPHY LAW POST-*FERBER*

Following the Supreme Court's holding in *New York v. Ferber*, in 1984, Congress eliminated the requirement that material meet the *Miller* test and raised the age of protected children from sixteen to eighteen (Pub. L. No. 98-292 1984).[11]

---

[10] Concurring opinions omitted for ease of reading.
[11] Pub. L. No. Section 98-292 (1984) (codified as amended at 18 U.S.C. Section 2252(b), 2253, 2254).

Four years later, Congress criminalized the use of computers to transport, distribute, or receive child pornography.[12] As early as 1988, Congress foresaw that the Internet and computers would become major facilitators of trafficking in child pornography.

## 13.2) POSSESSING CHILD PORNOGRAPHY CAN BE PROHIBITED

The Court distinguished between trafficking obscene material and possessing it in the privacy of one's own home in *Stanley v. Georgia* (1969).[13] In *Stanley*, the United States Supreme Court struck down a Georgia law that prohibited the mere possession of obscene material. Whether the government could regulate the possession of child pornography was not settled until 1990, when the Court decided *Osborne v. Ohio*.[14]

In *Osborne*, the Court upheld an Ohio law that prohibited possession of child pornography. Citing the holding in *Ferber*, the Court found that the state's interest in protecting children and in destroying the market for materials that exploit children to be compelling. Congress acted quickly to codify the holding in *Osborne*. In 1990, Congress outlawed possessing more than three publications containing child pornography.[15]

## 13.3) THE CHILD PORNOGRAPHY PROTECTION ACT AND THE FREE SPEECH COALITION CHALLENGE

In 1996, Congress expanded the child pornography definition to include "virtual" images and portrayals of sexually explicit conduct that "appear to be" of a minor. "Virtual" child pornography refers to visual images that are completely computer rendered. No actual child is used to create it. Images that depict actors who "appear to be" minors means that the images were produced without using real children, such as through the use of youthful-looking adults.

In *Ashcroft v. Free Speech Coalition* (2002), the United States Supreme Court decided the constitutionality of sections of the child pornography law that criminalized possession of virtual child pornography and images of adults who "appear to be" minors. The focus of the discussion here is on virtual images, as that portion of the *Ashcroft* decision has caused the most confusion. The "appears to be of a minor" language pretty clearly attempted to sweep protected

---

[12] Pub. L. No. 100-690 1(988).
[13] *Stanley v. Georgia*, 394 U.S. 557 (1969).
[14] *Osborne v. Ohio*, 495 U.S. 103 (1990).
[15] Pub. L. No. 101-647, 301, 323 (1990).

speech into the category of child pornography. In the storm of discussions and many media commentaries since the decision, very little if any attention has been paid to the "appears to be of a minor" holding. This may be because the conclusion is so obvious as to generate little comment.

## 13.4) MORPHED IMAGES

The court specifically did not address "morphed" images—those images that are created by cutting and pasting parts of children's bodies onto pictures of adults or vice versa. The distinction is an important one that is often confused. Many non-technical, non-child pornography experts have not had occasion to appreciate the difference. Whereas "virtual" child pornography (the subject matter of the *Ashcroft* decision) is completely rendered by computer, "morphed" images depict an actual child or children. Noting the distinction may seem like splitting hairs, but the difference is quite important. A virtual image victimizes no one. As no actual child is the subject of the rendering, no child's privacy has been invaded, nor has a child been actually sexually assaulted. In the case in which an image is morphed, an actual child is depicted in the image.

Morphed images can be generated using many different components. Images may be cut and pasted using magazines. Products such as Photoshop or some other software can be employed to take part of a digitized picture and paste it together with another, and the software user can blend the images together and add to it. Whether the morphed image will be considered to be child pornography in the post *Ashcroft* age is a tough call. The touchstone of the analysis should be whether a real child is depicted in the morphed image and whether the image depicts sexual conduct that would otherwise be child pornography.

**EXAMPLE 1:** A digital image seized from a defendant's hard drive has been morphed using software. The defendant allegedly took a picture of his nephew licking an ice cream cone and superimposed a picture of his turgid penis in place of the ice cream cone.
**QUESTION:** Is this child pornography?
**DISCUSSION:** The *Ashcroft* case left this question unanswered. There is definitely an actual child depicted. There is sexual conduct. But the child is not engaging in sexual conduct—it is suggested by the defendant's morphing of the image. Until the question is settled, it may be prudent to charge the defendant with child pornography and obscenity. Of course, the limitation in charging a defendant with obscenity is that obscenity can be quite difficult to prove and does not apply to possessing the material.

> **EXAMPLE 2:** Among the items seized during the course of a search of a defendant's home is a photo album. The album contains pictures of naked males posing in provocative ways or engaging in sexual activity with other males, their ages uncertain. Most of the males appear to be in their late teens. The defendant has cut off the heads of some of the images and pasted pictures of boys he is accused of sexually assaulting (ages seven to nine).
> **QUESTION:** Is this child pornography?
> **DISCUSSION:** This example creates a tough call. There are many ways a prosecutor might use the evidence, such as to support a risk of injury to a minor charge, if he showed the pictures to his victims. Whether or not the pictures are child pornography is another matter. You do not know the ages of the people who are engaging in sexual conduct. You do know that they are not the victims of the sexual assault charges, but that the victims' pictures (their heads) are used to suggest that they are the subjects of the pictures.

## 13.5) VIRTUAL CHILD PORNOGRAPHY

The principal holding in *Ashcroft* is that images rendered completely by computer, or virtual images, are not prohibited child pornography. The *Ashcroft* decision caused a panic when it first came out because the media, the defense bar, and a few prosecutors understood it to have held that all child pornography was protected speech. The impact was felt not only at the federal level, but the states suffered from uncertainty. Many prosecutors now hesitate to go forward with a child pornography prosecution, especially when the evidence is in electronic format. Some prosecutors require that the child portrayed in the image be identified and produced for testimony. This interpretation is extreme and unduly onerous in light of the subsequent federal appeals court decisions. The Federal Circuit Courts have decided cases subsequent to *Ashcroft* that provide much needed guidance. The courts in *Wolk*, *Kimler*, and *Deaton* all stand for the principle that a defendant may be convicted of possession or distribution of child pornography without producing the child depicted in the image.

In *United States v. Wolk* (2003),[16] police nabbed the defendant when he attempted to meet a thirteen-year-old girl he chatted with over the Internet. The thirteen-year-old girl was actually a Detective Sergeant conducting an undercover investigation. Wolk sent the police officer "graphic photos of children engaging in sex, incest, and bondage." During the execution of a search warrant at Wolk's

---

[16] *United States v. Wolk*, 337 F.3d 997 2003 U.S. App. LEXIS 15055 (8th Cir., 2003).

house, he admitted to police that he had child pornography on his computer and that he had been collecting it for two years. The defendant was indicted and convicted of transporting child pornography and possessing child pornography. He subsequently appealed his conviction, claiming that *Ashcroft v. Free Speech Coalition* requires dismissal of his indictment. The court disagreed.

While the court admitted that *Ashcroft* held portions of the child pornography law unconstitutional, Wolk did not show that there was plain error in his case. That is, the district court did not deviate from a legal rule, that there was a plain error under current law and that the error affected Wolk's substantial rights. The court held that, "the evidence established that the children depicted in the pictures introduced at trial were actual children [,] no one ever claimed, or even hinted, that the images were of virtual children, [ ] and Wolk stipulated that these were actual children." So, according to the Eighth Circuit, at least, a stipulation to the effect that the subjects depicted in the images are actual children should be sufficient to prove child pornography. And, in addition, the prosecution's case is stronger if the defendant does not claim the images are completely computer rendered, or virtual. The combination of the two factors would likely be sufficient to prove a child pornography case.

*United States v. Kimler* (2003)[17] was also decided subsequent to *Ashcroft*. Kimler was convicted of a number of counts of receiving, distributing, and possessing child pornography. Among many issues raised in his appeal, Kimler argued that "the evidence presented at trial was insufficient to prove that he possessed, received, and distributed depicted real children." The court held that there was sufficient evidence for a reasonable jury to convict Kimler of the child pornography charges, and that there was no need for expert testimony to establish that the images depicted real rather than virtual children. The court reviewed the question of whether *Ashcroft* requires expert testimony using the plain error standard because Kimler failed to properly preserve the issue for appeal. The court held that *Ashcroft* "did not establish a broad, categorical requirement that, in every case on the subject, absent direct evidence of identity, an expert must testify that the unlawful image is of a real child. Juries are still capable of distinguishing between real and virtual images; and admissibility remains within the province of the sound discretion of the trial judge."

Following the *Ashcroft* decision, a few agencies began to collect images depicting identified victims to assist in the prosecution of child pornography cases. One such effort by the National Center for Missing and Exploited Children has helped to identify children in 300 images as of this writing (NCMEC 2003). The way the system works is that a forensic examiner or investigator sends off pic-

---

[17] *United States v. Kimler*, 335 F.3d 1132; 2003 U.S. App. LEXIS 13586 (10th Cir. 2003).

tures to NCMEC for verification. NCMEC personnel check the images supplied against the database of known images. If an image is confirmed as "identified," a person known to the child, or the child himself or herself, provides an affidavit to the effect that he or she was in fact the child depicted in the image, that the sexual activity took place and the age of the parties at the time the image was created. In a case in which hearsay becomes a problem, the witness may actually appear to give testimony.

Known image data has attempted to solve the *Ashcroft* problem. But the difficulties created by relying on known image databases are equally as troublesome as the problem they attempt to solve. The first is that the victim has been identified in only a small fraction of images. A great number of images traded on the Internet prior to *Ashcroft* were old, scanned images from *Lolita* magazines. Now that child pornography traders know that, to prove that an image is child pornography, the victim must be produced, it makes sense that the market for fresh images depicting unidentified images will increase. This issue is of grave concern because the known image databases cannot identify the mass of children depicted in homemade and newly generated images. A second concern is that prosecutors, judges, and defense attorneys may begin to rely on the known image databases as the decision-making factor in child pornography prosecutions. This shifting of responsibility is misplaced, as there are countless images of actual children who will never be identified. As the Tenth Circuit stated in Wolk, "[j]uries are still capable of distinguishing between real and virtual images."

*United States v. Deaton* (2003)[18] provides additional support for allowing the fact finder to decide whether evidence presented is or is not child pornography. Deaton appealed his conviction of possessing child pornography. He argued on appeal that the *Ashcroft* decision required proof that the images depicted actual children. The Eighth Circuit Court of Appeals disagreed. The Court held that there was no plain error because the District Court instructed the jury that it must "find that production of the images involved the use of a minor." When the jury found Deaton guilty, it found that the images in his possession depicted actual children.

*Ashcroft v. Free Speech Coalition* also held that that the "appears to be" and "conveys the impression" provisions of the 1996 Act are overbroad and vague, chilling production of works protected by the First Amendment. Generally, pornography can be banned only if it is obscene under *Miller v. California,* but pornography depicting actual children can be proscribed whether or not the images are obscene because of the state's interest in protecting the children exploited by the production process in prosecuting those who promote such sexual exploitation.

---

[18] *United States v. Deaton,* 328 F.3d 454; 2003 U.S. App. LEXIS 8751 (8th Cir. 2003).

**Significant Developments in United States Child Pornography Law**

| | |
|---|---|
| **1972** | *Miller v. California*<br>Obscenity defined |
| **1982** | *New York v. Ferber*<br>Can prohibit child pornography that is not "obscene" |
| **1984** | **Child Protection Act**<br><br>Raised age of minor from 16 to 18<br><br>Material need not be "obscene" to be child pornography |
| **1990** | *Osborne v. Ohio*<br>CPRPE<br>O.K. to ban possession of child pornography |
| **1996** | **Child Pornography Prevention Act**<br>Prohibits "virtual" child pornography<br>images that "appear to be" of minors |
| **2002** | *Ashcroft v. Free Speech Coalition*<br>"Virtual" images not child pornography<br>"appears to be" minors language unconstitutionally overbroad |

*Figure 13.1*

*From 1972 through the present, child pornography law has begun to develop. This timeline delineates major developments.*

## 13.6) CONCLUSION

The law regulating child pornography has undergone dramatic change during the past thirty years (see Fig. 13.1 for major court rulings). Emerging technology will inevitably bring new ways to exploit children and facilitate their abuse. The future most certainly will bring new challenges to existing child pornography regulations that lawmakers and the judiciary will have to confront.

## REFERENCES

National Center for Missing and Exploited Children. "Secretary Ridge Announces 'Operation Predator' ICE to Begin a New DHS Initiative Targeting Child Predators." Press Release. (July 9, 2003).

National Center for Missing and Exploited Children Web site available online at www.missingkids.org.

# CHAPTER 14

# PRE-TRIAL

*The sexual abuse of a child is a most serious crime and an act repugnant to the moral instincts of a decent people. . . . The prospect of crime, however, by itself does not justify laws suppressing protected speech.*[1]

## 14.1) INTRODUCTION

Prosecutors see it all. From motor vehicle cases to larcenies, narcotics, rape, and murder. Today, she got her first computer-assisted child exploitation case and has no idea where to go. "Oh, come on," the seasoned veteran might say. "What makes a computer-assisted case any different from the cases I've been trying for twenty years?" A lot.

This chapter presents the initial issues a prosecutor will face in preparing a computer-assisted child exploitation case for trial. The next chapter examines issues at trial. This chapter explores some of the many ways in which computer-assisted child exploitation cases and child pornography cases in particular present unique challenges to the prosecutor. The chapter begins with a discussion of charging and determining the number of counts. Important factors to consider when engaging in plea negotiations and frequently used terms of release follow. In preparation for trial, the prosecutor will want to consult the section on selecting and presenting evidence.

## 14.2) CHARGING IN COMPUTER-ASSISTED CHILD EXPLOITATION CASES

A poll of twenty of America's Internet Crimes Against Children Task Forces disclosed that each jurisdiction differed in the number of charges it filed in child pornography possession cases (Danielson 2001). Federal authorities are bound by case law that guides them in the charging decisions. At the state, county, and

---

[1] *Ashcroft v. Free Speech Coalition*, 2002 U.S. LEXIS 2789, 122 S. Ct. 1389 (2002).

municipal level, various approaches are used. The federal cases as well as the variants used by other jurisdictions will be discussed in this section.

A few jurisdictions charge one count of possession, regardless of how many pictures a suspect has. Using this approach, no matter how many pictures a hard drive contains, prosecutors charge only one count of possessing child pornography. The obvious limitation of this approach is that it leaves little room for compromise. Either the one count is proven, or the whole case is thrown away. The benefit of the scheme is that with a number of images, at least one of them should be sufficient to persuade the fact finder that the accused committed the crime.

Few, if any, jurisdictions charge a count for each child pornography image. In many jurisdictions the number of counts is determined by weighing the evidence. If the suspect has a large number of pictures, or the pictures were downloaded on different dates, the prosecutor may file multiple charges. Some prosecutors charge a separate count for each "series" of images. A "series" is a group of pictures taken of the same subject during the course of one session. Some series are well known to law enforcement. The subjects of the pictures in some series have been identified. Some series have circulated in magazines and on the Internet for years.

## 14.3) CASE LAW CONCERNING CHARGING DECISIONS

The courts have upheld charging for each image in the offender's possession when the crime is simple possession of child pornography. However, when the charge is possession with intent to promote, the courts have held that the defendant may be charged with only one count. In *U.S. v. Boos* (2000),[2] the defendant appealed his thirty-month sentence for conspiracy to distribute or receive child pornography. Boos argued on appeal that the district court erred in not "grouping"—that is, merging all counts into one—multiple counts of distribution. He argued that society is the actual victim and not the children in the pictures. Under the federal sentencing guidelines, if society is considered the victim, a lesser sentence is called for than if there is an identifiable human victim.

Government prosecutors conceded that they are able to group the counts under the United States Sentencing Guidelines if the separate crimes are "connected by a common criminal objective or constitute part of a common scheme or plan." However, prosecutors argued that it is in their discretion not to do so. The issue for the court to decide, then, was who the victim was in this case. If

---

[2] *United States v. Boos*, 127 F.3d 1207 (9th Cir. 2000).

society was the victim, then there should have been only one charge of possession, but if the children were the victims, charging multiple counts was correct.
The court held that it was the children who were the victims and, therefore,
multiple charges of possessing child pornography were appropriate. The court
concluded that the children in the pictures were the ones "adversely affected."

*Crosby v. State of Florida* (2000)[3] points up the thorny issues that arise due to
a statute's wording when charging in possession cases. In *Crosby*, the defendant
was convicted of 68 counts of possession of child pornography, some of which
were based on copies of the same image. The defendant appealed, arguing that
it was in error to charge and convict him of multiple counts of possessing several
copies of the same photo. The court held that a defendant found in possession
of copies of the same picture depicting child pornography may be convicted of
a crime for each separate image. The court based its decision on the Florida
statute, which states "possession of each article shall constitute a separate
offense."[4] Each jurisdiction words its statutes differently. Some statutes do not
specifically state that possession of each article shall be a separate offense.

Florida provides another example of the consequences of a statute's wording.
In *Wade v. State of Florida* (2000),[5] the defendant appealed his conviction of three
counts of possession of child pornography with intent to promote. The defendant was arrested when he accepted delivery of three child pornography videos
he had previously ordered over the Internet. A search of his computer resulted
in discovery of reproductions of children involved in sexual conduct.

The court held that the three counts of possession of child pornography with
intent to promote should be reduced to only one count. The court relied on a
previous holding in *State v. Parrella* (1999).[6] In *Parrella*, the court held that the
legislature's use of the word "any" in the statute meant that they intended to
punish only a single crime with regard to the possession of these items. The
statute on which the court relied reads in part as follows:

> *It is unlawful for any person to possess with the intent to promote any photograph,*
> *motion picture, exhibition, show, representation, or other presentation which, in whole*
> *or in part, includes any sexual conduct by a child.*[7]

This court held that the legislature's use of the word "any" barred prosecution
of more than one count of possession with intent to promote child pornogra-

[3] *Crosby v. State of Florida*, 757 So. 2d 584 (Fla. 2d DCA 2000).
[4] Fla. Stat. Ann. § 827.071(5).
[5] *Wade v. State of Florida*, 751 So. 2d 669 (Fla. App. 2000).
[6] *State v. Parrella*, 736 So. 2d 94 (Fla. 4th DCA 1999).
[7] Section 827.071(4), Florida Statutes (1995) (*emphasis added*).

phy. The court also noted that since the photos were found in a single episode, the defendant could be convicted on only one of the three counts. It is unclear whether the court would have upheld Wade's conviction had the photographs been found in three different time periods. The court seems to have decided the case on two different rationales.

## 14.4) WHAT CONSTITUTES POSSESSION?

Aside from the statutory elements of the crime, whether a person "possesses" something is complicated in the virtual world. Whether an individual "possesses" an image that is viewed online is a matter of difference of opinion. On the one hand, some argue that whatever an individual views on the Internet is recorded on the hard drive of a computer (with some exceptions that are beyond the purview of this discussion). Possession is accomplished both by virtue of the individual viewing the image and therefore "possessing" it and by "downloading" it onto the hard drive of the computer. An affirmative action on the part of the viewer to "save" the image is not necessary to establish possession. Reported cases at the federal level are inconsistent from one district to the next, and the states are all over the place on the issue.

*U.S. v. X-Citement Video* (1994),[8] decided before digital media became the preferred method of "possessing" child pornography, contains a detailed treatment of the scienter requirement in the child pornography realm. The *X-Citement Video* case held that a video storeowner was required to have knowledge that an actor in a film s/he distributed was under the age of eighteen when the video was made in order to be charged for distributing child pornography. There have been successful prosecutions of possession cases in which the defendant only viewed the image(s), and there have been unsuccessful cases.

When "viewing" is alleged to be "possession," the only evidence of possession is a record of viewing in the temporary Internet files. Such cases can be difficult for the prosecution because the defendant might claim that s/he did not intend to possess the images. When the prosecution must prove intent to possess, the temporary Internet record, without more evidence, makes this defense difficult to overcome. A prudent prosecutor will ask the forensic examiner to determine whether the defendant sought out the material and whether the defendant did so many times. If the defendant used search terms in Google™ such as "lolita," "preteen," or other similar terms associated with child pornography, such information goes a long way toward proving intent to possess, especially when the only images are located in temporary Internet

---

[8] *United States v. X-Citement Video*, 514 U.S. 64 (1994).

storage. (The authors strongly suggest from experience that asking the forensic examiner about matters such as this be done well before the trial.)

Some child pornography collectors make proving intent easy. The authors have worked on cases in which the defendant has painstakingly organized folders containing pictures and named the folders according to their contents. For example, a folder might be named "my five year olds" or "really young ones," and the folder contains images of what appear to be very young children engaged in sexual conduct. Defendants also have been known to save child pornography images to several different locations or types of media. For instance, a defendant might have images saved to the hard drive of a personal computer and copied to a Zip disk as well. A defendant also might back up selected information to protect it from destruction. Some backup programs will save everything on a hard drive, but most often, the user is required to select what information s/he wishes to preserve. Taking the affirmative step of selecting the files or folders s/he wishes to back up tends to prove that the actor is both aware of the content and character of the files and intends to possess the material contained therein.

## 14.5) MULTIPLE COMPUTER USERS

Multiple computer users pose the problem of proving beyond a reasonable doubt that the defendant charged with possessing the material is the person who both intended to possess the material and actually possesses the material. While child pornography usually bears only a slight resemblance to other types of possession crimes—such as possessing narcotics or stolen property—when multiple users are a factor, there seems to be an exception. "Constructive possession" is a concept unique to possession crimes and, although not often invoked in the child pornography realm, bears discussion here.

Actual possession means that a person knowingly exercises direct physical control over a thing. In the computer world, such control would require that the person is the only user of the computer, and no one else accessed it or had direct physical control over it. This description applies also to removable media on which contraband images are stored. Constructive possession, on the other hand, does not require actual possession but does require that a person either knowingly exercises control over or knowingly has the right to control a thing, either directly or through another person or persons. Constructive possession in the computer or virtual world would apply to all of the parties who access a computer system or removable media containing the contraband.[9]

When multiple users of a computer system lead to a constructive possession theory or argument, the determining factor as to whether the defendant com-

---

[9] See, for example, California Jury Instructions, Criminal, 6th Ed.1.24.

mitted the crime is whether s/he *knowingly* possessed the material. Proving knowledge can be thorny in a time when an Internet user can purposefully enter one Web site and be "mousetrapped" to many others. The term "mousetrap" refers to the Webmaster's trick of sending a user to one Web site after another at the behest of the Web site. The Internet user has no control over where s/he is taken and often must manually shut down the computer system to stop the cycle. The purpose of the mousetrap is usually not malicious, although it can be used that way. Usually, the purpose is to advertise Web sites—most often Web sites that contain pornography of both legal and illegal character. Sometimes mousetrapping is done maliciously by disgruntled employees or an alienated Webmaster seeking to defame or ridicule the previous owner of the site.

For the most part, to establish that a defendant "knowingly" possessed something, the prosecution must prove that the defendant knew the content and character of the item. Mousetrapping is one way in which a person might claim that s/he unwillingly or unwittingly possessed child pornography without the requisite state of mind. A defendant might also argue that either the images were planted on the computer system or that the images belong to a former owner of the computer or someone else who used the computer. The defenses are plausible and should be fully anticipated and investigated.

A full and fairly conducted forensic examination should provide sufficient evidence for the prosecutor to make informed decisions regarding the veracity of any defenses. In the case in which a defendant claims to have purchased a computer owned by someone else, and that the prior owner or another user is responsible for the images, the forensic examination should show when the images were last accessed. In a case in which such a defense is put forth, providing that the computer is second-hand (as opposed to three months old and purchased by the defendant who lives alone), forensic analysis should delineate the illicit files—when they were created and when they were last accessed. If the defendant reformatted the hard drive upon purchase of the computer to start fresh, any files belonging to the prior owner would have been deleted, and a forensic examination would so state. It would be possible to retrieve those files, but they would be marked as "deleted," and the date of deletion would be available to the examiner. In the event that the deleted files were overwritten, the last access date and the deleted status might not be available, and the file(s) would be identified as residing in "unallocated space." Pushing a case in which the only evidence is located in unallocated space is difficult at best. If the computer was previously owned, proving the case beyond a reasonable doubt becomes that much harder.

Forensic examination should also reveal whether another person planted evidence. If a computer system was "hacked"—that is, another computer user entered the computer system either via a network connection or physically and planted evidence—the time and date of the intrusion would likely be evident. As with any other type of crime in which prosecutors must prove knowledge on the part of the defendant, much will depend on the statements of the defendant, his or her conduct, and other evidence.

Statements of the defendant or witnesses can tend to prove knowledge. Often the defendant is quite willing to talk about how s/he accessed illicit images. As with any other type of criminal activity, girlfriends, wives, husbands, boyfriends, and lovers are often quite happy to talk with investigators about the defendant's sexual proclivities (bearing in mind the motivation of the witness, of course). It may be tempting to go forward relying heavily on the digital evidence because it is quite persuasive. But without statements and other supporting evidence, if the digital evidence comes under fire, the whole case may suffer substantially.

Prosecutors also hope that investigators have well documented the defendant's countenance and reaction to questioning about the images on his or her computer system. If there has been an interview or opportunity for observation of the defendant, his or her actions can be evidence of knowledge. For instance, nervousness or sweating when asked about Internet use can be presented to demonstrate knowledge.

Other evidence proving knowledge of the content and character of illicit images include possession of child erotica or child pornography in other media such as magazines and video, and evidence obtained from the forensic examination of any computers, Internet account, or removable media. It is possible in many cases to search for the computer user's "bookmarks" or "favorites,"[10] Web sites visited, chat room conversations, newsgroup subscriptions and postings, and e-mail. Many times child pornography collectors discuss their collections with other people on the Internet in chat rooms, via e-mail, or in postings to newsgroups. The child pornography collector may also have Web sites that cater to collectors of child pornography in his or her list of favorites. While none of these things alone would be proof that the defendant knew the content and character of a particular image, taking each piece of the evidence and putting it together creates a complete picture of what happened.

## 14.6) PLEA BARGAINING CONSIDERATIONS

Computer-assisted child exploitation cases often end in a negotiated plea. The evidence in computer-assisted cases is often so clear that the defendant is guilty

---

[10] An Internet user can "bookmark" Web sites frequently visited. Some services call this feature a "bookmark," and others call it a "favorite."

that s/he will not take the chance of submitting to the mercy of a jury. After all, if the evidence includes child pornography, the jury will see it. Jurors will see each picture and will come to know what the defendant used the pictures for. Desperate to avoid jail and the publicity of a trial, defendants are highly motivated to participate in plea negotiations. Bearing in mind that prosecutors are constrained by the law and policy directives governing plea negotiations and sentencing, this section discusses some of the considerations that prosecutors might weigh in determining terms for a negotiated plea in these cases.

A preliminary matter is to determine whether the jurisdiction considers the crime charged as a sex crime or a crime against a minor. In states that require sex offender registration, whether a crime is a sex crime or not is a very important matter. Allowing an individual who has enticed a minor to engage in sex or a child pornography collector to avoid registering as a sex offender by pleading guilty to a different crime could deprive future victims of the ability to protect themselves. Sex offender registries are frequently referred to by parents and relied upon as a source of self-protection information. While the value and effectiveness of such registries can be argued, whether or not an individual will be placed on the registry as a result of a guilty plea is an important consideration when negotiating with the defendant.

Similarly, the type of crime may have an impact on the sentence. In many jurisdictions there is a difference in the length of time an individual must be registered as a sex offender. For example, a sex offender who has been convicted of raping a child might be required to register for life, whereas an offender convicted of a sex offense against an adult might register for ten years. Also, if the victim is a minor, the court might be able to prevent the offender from having access to children, whereas if the crime is considered to be victimless, or society is the victim, the court may be precluded from limiting contact with children.

Many jurisdictions allow first-time offenders and individuals facing minor charges to take advantage of diversionary programs that come with the benefit of expunging any record of the individual's conviction provided s/he is not re-arrested within a certain period. Some jurisdictions that categorize child pornography as a minor or victimless crime allow those persons charged with the offense to participate in accelerated rehabilitation and other diversionary programs. Even in cases that involve the sexual assault or molestation of a child, some courts have imposed no other sentence than an accelerated rehabilitation program. In one case the court stated that it would not send a sick man to prison. His "sickness," the court believed, was an "addiction" to child pornography. While you may disagree with the judge's thinking in that case, it is important to prepare for such potentialities in advance. It is imperative for the prosecutor to think about the proper sentence in advance because the sentence will have an impact on sex offender registration and the conditions of release.

When considering what conditions suggest that the court impose on supervised release of the defendant, the prosecutor should evaluate the extent of the defendant's sexual interest in children and the likelihood that s/he will re-offend. The prosecutor should consider limiting the defendant's contact with children both online and in the physical world. Conditions of release prohibiting contact with children in the offender's employment, volunteer activities, and on the Internet are an extension of that prohibition. While there is a dearth of successful treatment programs for sex offenders, the prosecutor may determine treatment should be a condition of release.

Treatment often requires the participant to accept responsibility for her or his actions. This is sometimes a thorny issue with offenders who accept a negotiated plea. The individual may want to enter a plea of "nolo contendere," or some similar plea, that allows the party to agree that the government has sufficient evidence to convict him or her of the crime without admitting guilt, and thereby avoiding all of the civil consequences associated with a guilty plea. Prior to allowing treatment to become part of the plea deal, the prosecutor should elicit from the defense the promise to comply with the treatment conditions and fully inform the defendant of what the treatment conditions are.

Any supervised release of an offender convicted of a crime facilitated by computer or the Internet should include regular unannounced home visits during which the client's computer is examined. Those charged with supervising offenders released into the community may wish to install monitoring software on any computer systems the offender will be using. If there are others in the home, the condition of supervised or limited Internet use may preclude others from using the same computer as the client. Many different types of monitoring software can quite effectively be used in conjunction with physical examination and on-site limited forensic examination of the subject's computer system to attempt to ensure compliance with the terms of release.

If the defendant refuses to accept a reasonable plea offer, the prosecution must prepare for trial. The trial preparation process in a computer-assisted child exploitation case will involve wading through sometimes extensive volumes of digital evidence. The prosecutor will have to select the evidence s/he believes will be most salient and persuasive.

> **Considerations for Prosecutors When Negotiating a Computer-Assisted Child Exploitation Plea**
>
> Is the crime the defendant pleads to a **predicate offense for sex offender registration**?
>
> > Is the crime the defendant pleads to a **crime against a child/minor**?
> >
> > If the crime is NOT against a minor, will that affect **sex offender registration**?
> >
> > If the crime is NOT against a minor, will that affect the **ability to limit the defendant's contact with children**?
>
> Will the defendant's record be expunged?
>
> > Will the defendant continue to have contact with children?
> >
> > Is s/he likely to re-offend?
>
> Will the defendant enter a treatment program?
>
> > If so, will the program require him or her to accept responsibility (confess)?
> >
> > How does this affect his or her "nolo contendere" plea?
>
> Will the defendant consent to regular inspection of his or her computer and Internet account?
>
> > If so, no one else may use his or her computer.
> >
> > Explore use of monitoring software and on-site forensic examination.

## 14.7) SELECTION OF EVIDENCE

This section addresses the selection of evidence to be presented at trial. If the charge involves child pornography, which pictures should the prosecutor choose, and how many pictures? If the defendant is charged with enticing a minor to engage in sexual activity, will the prosecution use all of the logs with any attachments, or excise the logs? Are there telephone conversations, and if so, how much of the logs of those conversations will be presented? Of course, the sound discretion of the prosecutor will be final, and in any other type of case, no one would presume to offer advice. The computer-assisted case brings with it some level of complexity that is not present with other cases. Selecting the right evidence to present will help to simplify the case.

Child pornography cases became more complicated when computers got involved. When technology was limited to a camera, it was clearer whether a picture showed an actual child. Technology now allows for morphing images together and creating completely computer-generated images. In 1996, Congress attempted to anticipate that technology would develop to the extent that child pornographers would exploit it for their benefit. The 1996 Amendment added to the definition of child pornography. It included completely computer-generated images of children engaging in sexual conduct ("virtual child pornography") and images created using adults pretending to be minors ("appear to depict a minor"). These two areas, as far as the Supreme Court was concerned, were neither obscene nor were they child pornography. This issue is discussed in depth in Chapter 13. Another important issue in selecting evidence in a child pornography prosecution is how much evidence to present.

## 14.8) HOW MUCH IS ENOUGH?

Judging from published opinions, anecdotes, and experience, we submit that the prudent prosecutor should not go to court with too few images. When selecting the number of images to present as evidence, more is better than fewer. Of course, no one—not the judge, not the jurors, and not the prosecutor—is going to want to go through 100,000 pictures one by one determining whether each and every image meets the statutory criteria. During the pre-trial process, it is quite conceivable that the number of images the court will allow will be pared down substantially. One reason for excluding images has been that the age of the actor could not be estimated because only part of the person's body was displayed. Thus, it could not be determined that the actor was an actual child. Another reason images have been excluded was the court's insistence that only images in which the child had been identified would be admitted.

In preparing for trial, the prosecutor should anticipate evidentiary challenges and have a feeling for what to expect. Selecting images that meet the jurisdiction's statutory criteria for child pornography and also meet the criteria for obscenity (if charged appropriately) is a good step in the right direction. When coordinating with the forensic examiner or investigators in the case, the prosecutor may wish to instruct them to identify the twenty (or whatever number) images that are most repugnant. Or the prosecutor may wish to select only a certain number of images that the examiner can identify were taken with a camera. There is no magic to the selection. The important message here is to put some thought and planning into selecting the evidence in a child pornography trial because a haphazard approach can have negative consequences. Having concluded our discussion of selection of evidence in child pornography cases, we turn to the topic of selecting evidence in sexual enticement cases.

## 14.9) ENTICING A MINOR TO ENGAGE IN SEXUAL ACTIVITY

Enticement cases involving a minor victim present unique issues distinct from cases generated through undercover activity. When a victim is a minor, the prosecutor must deal with two issues right from the start. First, the victim may not make the best witness. If the victim engaged in discussions about sex or, as is often the case, initiated sex talk, the case will be tougher. As with other types of cases involving sexual activity with minors—statutory rape, for example—the victim's appearance and sexual history can become salient factors. Of course, sexual history is touchy stuff that can most often be kept out of evidence. But, when contained in chat conversations and e-mail communications, the victim's sexual life becomes difficult to get around. Often this sort of content is the meat of the communication between the offender and minor victim in an online enticement case.

The prosecutor should review all of the chat logs in the case. Logs should come from both the victim's computer as well as the offender's. The prosecutor should know whether the victim regularly engaged in sex talk with others and how those relationships fared. If the offender engaged in chat or other contact with minors, it may be prudent to contact those individuals to gather information about their relationships with the offender.

The second issue is the age of the victim when the case comes to trial. S/he may have been fifteen at the time the incident occurred but at the time of trial might be seventeen or eighteen. The older the victim, the less likely a jury will be sympathetic to a straightforward "enticing" case. Prosecutors who have tried statutory rape cases have faced the same issue. The jury may be instructed to follow the letter of the law, but the fact that the victim is now an adult and quite possibly does not present as an upstanding and innocent victim has an impact. The prosecutor may wish to present a witness to address how minor victims react, or the prosecutor may choose not to call the victim at all, except to provide foundation to admit chat logs. Many juries have had difficulty convicting someone of trying to persuade a fifteen-year-old to engage in sex via the Internet absent an attempt to meet. It may still be difficult for juries to convict a defendant accused of actually having sex with the minor.

The case resulting from undercover activity in many ways provides fewer challenges but still can present hurdles. It is absolutely essential for the prosecutor to know how the undercover investigation was conducted. Following is a checklist of information the investigators should provide (at minimum):

✓ What guidelines did the undercover officer use to govern the investigation (for example, did s/he follow Internet Crimes Against Children Task Force guidelines)?

✓ What equipment did the undercover officer use—who owns it, is it used for any other purposes?

✓ Did the undercover officer send any pictures to suspects? If so, the prosecutor should see the pictures.

✓ How did the topic of sex come up and at what point in the online relationship?

✓ Who initiated the sex talk and how?

Once evidence selection is complete, the prosecutor can move on to how s/he will present the evidence.

## 14.10) PRESENTING EVIDENCE

On television, every prosecutor has all of the resources and advanced technology s/he would ever need. In reality, thousands of prosecutors in the United States do not even have access to a personal computer of their own at work. Those lucky few who do have computers often lag behind in technology and suffer from a paucity of presentation devices and technology. The computer-assisted child exploitation case will require at least some resource outlay for courtroom presentation, and the prosecutor must become familiar with the means of presentation.

Ideally, the method of presentation will maximize the fact finder's ability to see the evidence without presenting the evidence in an unduly prejudicial manner. In a child pornography case, the images are the cornerstone of the prosecution. How the prosecutor presents the images will say a lot to a jury. Some prosecutors project the images onto a screen using a data projector. Splashing images of children being sexually assaulted over the walls of a courtroom may be perceived as exploitive. Other prosecutors print the images and pass them around. Still others re-create the defendant's computer system and display the images as the defendant would have seen them.

Showing how a defendant imported or distributed child pornography will likely require the use of an expert who can explain how the Internet feature s/he used works and explain how logs from the defendant's computer (or wherever) tend to show that the defendant did what s/he is accused of doing. Evidence presented through expert testimony will be discussed in detail in the next chapter.

## 14.11) CONCLUSION

This chapter examined initial issues the prosecutor might face in preparing a computer-assisted child exploitation case for trial. The chapter began with a discussion of charging in the child exploitation case. Selecting the proper charge and deciding whether to charge multiple counts are major concerns in prosecuting child pornography cases, in particular. Discussion turned to factors a prosecutor should consider when engaging in plea negotiations. Considerations when placing a child exploitation defendant into the community were discussed, and the chapter provided the prosecutor with guidance. The chapter closed with a discussion of courtroom presentation of the evidence.

## REFERENCE

Danielson, Aimee, Memorandum of Law prepared for legal internship with Connecticut Department of Public Safety, Computer Crimes and Electronic Evidence Unit. (November 2000).

# CHAPTER 15

# TRIAL

*The wisdom of our sages and the blood of our heroes has been devoted to the attainment of trial by jury. It should be the creed of our political faith. (Thomas Jefferson, First Inaugural Address 1801)*

The previous chapter discussed pre-trial issues facing the prosecution in a computer-assisted child exploitation case. This chapter drills more deeply down into the issues at trial. The chapter begins with a discussion of jury selection considerations and provides some sample voir dire questions. If children or minors will be testifying, prosecutors should read the section on facilitating their testimony. In addition to selecting the right evidence, prosecutors should be armed with a good expert witness to help them present it. The chapter also explores the use of expert witnesses and describes what to look for in a potential witness. Next, a section offers tips on preparing for court with the expert and areas of inquiry that might be covered. The final section discusses commonly encountered defenses.

## 15.1) SELECTING THE JURY

When selecting a jury in an online exploitation or child pornography case, the prosecutor must consider a few areas. First, the prosecutor should ask potential jurors about their level of computer savvy. Anyone who has tried to explain the Internet to someone who has never used a computer understands that the courtroom may not be the most effective place to introduce jurors to the Internet. Likewise, prosecutors would be wise to steer clear of potential jurors who classify themselves as "experts." A computer expert on the jury could bog down deliberations with his or her own testimony. No one wants to have to re-try a case, and the prosecution needs the jury to stick to deciding the issues the government puts forth. Thomas Temple argues that the best juror for the prosecution is a "user"—someone who uses a computer at work or home but does not participate in chat rooms or newsgroups (Temple 2003).

The prospective prosecution-friendly juror should not be averse to the government's interest in enforcing prohibitions against child pornography and child exploitation that take place over the Internet. And, given that the case will involve at least sex talk and at most hard-core child pornography, jurors must be willing to review the evidence. According to Temple, prosecutors must master the material to be presented and become comfortable in its presentation.

Prosecutors will want to explore the jurors' feelings on the topic of under-age sex and enticement. Although the letter of the law prohibits adults from engaging in sex with minors, the fact is that minors engage in sex sometimes at very young ages. Many potential jurors may have begun sexual activity quite young, and many young people are initiated into sex by adults. These facts, compounded by societal attitudes that tend to blame rape victims, could make it particularly difficult to find a sympathetic jury for a straightforward entice-ment case. The prosecutor will likely have potential jurors in the pool who began having sex at a young age and see nothing wrong with under-age sex. It is also likely there will be potential jurors who will blame the victim for the actions of the accused. Voir dire questioning should address these concerns.

Potential jurors also may have strong feelings about online police undercover operations. Some people believe that it is morally wrong for police officers to lie, and when posing as a minor online to ensnare pedophiles, the undercover officer "lies" about his or her identity. Some people believe that the Internet should be a safe place for all communication and that any monitoring by police is an invasion of privacy. While that position seems extreme, whether we agree or not, some people believe strongly that police officers should not conduct online sting operations. Questions for potential jurors should attempt to "smoke out" any bias against undercover operations, if that was how the defen-dant was caught. When preparing for the voir dire process, the prosecutor may wish to consider using some form of the following questions:

---

**Computer Use**

- On a scale of one to five, how would you rate your ability to use a computer?
- Do you use the Internet?
- If so, what do you use the Internet for?

**Child Pornography**

- Some people think that child pornography should not be illegal. What do you think?

- Part of the evidence in this case will require that you look at pictures that the government alleges are illegal child pornography. By definition, child pornography depicts a child or children engaged in sexually explicit conduct. Will you be able to view pictures that the government alleges are child pornography to discharge your duty as a juror?
- Do you have any experience with child pornography? If so, in what context?

**Enticement**

- Do you have children? If so, do they use the Internet? What for?
- Do you have rules at home about using the Internet?
- Do you monitor your child's Internet use?
- How do you feel about meeting people in person after getting to know them through the Internet?
- In this jurisdiction, it is a crime for an adult to have sex with a person who is a minor (defined as under the age of . . .). Would you have any problem, as a juror, in enforcing that law, even if the evidence shows that the minor was a willing participant in the relationship?

**Bias Regarding Undercover Operations**

- How do you feel about police officers pretending to be minors on the Internet during an undercover investigation?

## 15.2) YOUNG VICTIMS/WITNESSES

Having selected a jury, the prosecutor will need to examine witnesses. As discussed in the preceding chapter, the victim in an online enticement case may be a difficult witness. Facilitating victim/witness testimony may be even more difficult if victims of sex abuse will testify. This section will help you to anticipate issues that may arise with younger victims/witnesses and will discuss strategies for facilitating their testimony.

There is extensive debate in the legal and treatment community about the veracity of children's testimony. Some experts claim that "kids never lie," whereas others take the position that "all children lie" (APRI 2003). The truth, of course, lies (no pun intended) somewhere in between. In child pornography cases, when the participants in the images are identified, investigators will often initiate a sex abuse or assault investigation. In enticement cases, the victim may be older—the average age between twelve and fifteen—but the prosecutor must still be mindful that the victim is not yet an adult. Only recently has the Canadian government begun to question the presumption that children under fourteen are not competent to testify (see www.canada.justice.gc.ca). The keys to ensuring that a child witness provides credible testimony are in proper facilitation by the prosecution and preparation for the case well in advance of trial.

Many jurisdictions organize multi-disciplinary child abuse task forces. Typically, representatives from the police, prosecutor's office, and child protective agencies form a multi-disciplinary team to coordinate interviews of the victim, treatment, preparation of the case against the offender, and prosecution efforts. A principle driving the teams is the belief that using one person to conduct official interviews of the young victim/witness maximizes the legal utility of the sessions. Research has indicated that, when young witnesses are frequently interviewed about an incident, factors such as interviewer bias and suggestive questions can negatively influence the witnesses' responses (Ceci and Hembrooke 1998).

Some states, such as Massachusetts, have Forensic Interviewers. Most states do not, but there are usually experts in interviewing children and teenagers who should be members of the computer-assisted child exploitation investigation and prosecution team. The National District Attorneys Association (NDAA), recognizing the need to develop experts in the field of examining child witnesses, has created a training program called "Finding Words: Half a Nation by 2010." The NDAA requires that teams of investigative and prosecution personnel attend the Finding Words class. This requirement is supported by research and the many experiences of prosecutors and other personnel who have seen the state's case unravel because a child witness was either inappropriately interviewed, interviewed too many times, or interviewed by too many different people. A unified approach to the child interview process will produce the most cogent and usable testimony.

During the Finding Words curriculum, prospective interviewers are taught the RATAC mnemonic method of interviewing developed by Corner House in Minnesota. The mnemonic stands for Rapport, Anatomy identification, Touch inventory, Abuse scenario, and Closure. Students do homework assignments, conduct actual interviews, and receive instruction about child abuse research and child development. (See www.ndaa.org for more information.)

Jennifer Massengale offers several suggestions for facilitating children's testimony. First, prosecutors should have familiarity and understanding of child development. Having a child of one's own helps somewhat, but reading about developmental stages and, if possible, the way the child witnesses' experiences or circumstances may cause him or her to present himself or herself as either more or less advanced in certain areas is important to know. (This issue may be so important to a particular case that the prosecutor may wish to enlist an expert witness to educate the judge and jury about the witnesses' developmental issues.) Besides affording the prosecutor the opportunity to more fully understand the witness, understanding his or her stage of development will make questioning easier. Crafting questions in a language that the witness will best understand will assist him or her to respond more completely.

Second, and along a similar vein, Massengale suggests that questions be kept brief and simple. A glazed-over look should be an indication that the phrasing of the question or its length was too much for the young witness to process. By all means, the interviewer should avoid double-negatives. For that matter, the interviewer should try to avoid all negatives and not ask leading questions. S/he should let the child answer the question himself or herself. (This approach can help to overcome suggestions that the child has been coached.)

Third, Massengale suggests that the prosecutor prepare the child for court. Prosecutors, investigators, and therapists schooled in child abuse are quite familiar with this process, but high-technology professionals may not be. "Preparing" a child for testifying in court does not mean "rehearsing" the child for testimony. ("Preparing" versus "rehearsing" a child for testimony is a notion often brought up by defense attorneys when a child will testify.) The prosecutor can bring the child to the room where s/he will be testifying and let her or him sit in the chairs and walk around to make herself or himself feel more comfortable there. The prosecutor, therapist, or victim advocate—whatever the case may be—should explain the roles of the main players—the judge, prosecutor, defense attorney, sheriff, court recorder—and answer questions. Having settled who all the players are and what they do will reduce anxiety and distractions when it comes time for court.

Fourth, the prosecutor should give the witness notice that s/he is going to transition from one topic to another. Simplicity is the key. For example, the prosecutor might say, "That's the last question I am going to ask you about the defendant's house. Now I am going to start asking you questions about what happened after you entered the house." The prosecutor should clue the child in on where s/he is heading. This approach will help to appease the witnesses' anxiety while testifying and help to make her or him a better witness (Massengale 2001).

## 15.3) EXPERT WITNESSES

As if the computer-assisted child exploitation case weren't difficult enough to pull together, the prosecution will more than likely want to call upon the services of at least one expert witness. The prosecutor may consider using experts in sex abuse cases, young victim/witness testimony, computers, digital imaging, the Internet, or digital evidence forensics. The following sections address why an expert may be employed in a computer-assisted child exploitation case, how to select a good expert, and what to expect. Particular attention is paid to digital forensics experts, and a sample expert report is deciphered.

### 15.3.1) CONSULTING AND TESTIFYING EXPERTS

Consulting experts, who do not testify, can offer expertise in just about any area. A consulting expert can be invaluable in navigating a prosecutor through the voluminous and frequently complicated evidence compiled in a computer-assisted crime. The first contact a prosecutor should make when assigned his or her first computer-assisted child sexual exploitation case is with another prosecutor or attorney who has handled this type of case before. In the United States, there are several excellent resources for prosecutors. Members of the United States Department of Justice Child Exploitation and Obscenity Section are exceptionally helpful (www.usdoj.gov/criminal/ceos/index.html). The National District Attorneys Association–American Prosecutors Research Institute Child Abuse and Cybercrime Divisions have subject matter experts who are available to assist prosecutors in this area also (www.ndaa.org).

Another exceptionally useful consulting expert is one who can point the attorney to good testifying experts and offer advice about questions to ask and presenting the evidence. This person might also review the work of the experts from both sides of the case. A benefit of consulting experts is that there is usually no requirement to identity them to the opposing side or produce the information they provide because these experts will not be testifying (see FRCP Rule 16). Whenever an expert is used, his or her qualifications should be reviewed by someone with knowledge of the appropriate level of education, training, and experience expected of someone offering himself or herself as an "expert" in that field. The consulting expert can be a great asset if s/he does nothing else but keep a prosecutor from putting on the stand an expert who has insufficient or bogus qualifications or provides inconsistent testimony. The following is an excerpt from the examination of a defense expert that points up the value of getting as much information about an expert before employing such a person:

**CASE EXAMPLE**

> **CROSS-EXAMINATION**
>
> *Q: I wish I could say I just had a few questions for you, but, actually, I think I have quite a few. All right. Ms. Lawson, your only formal education is an associates degree; is that correct?*
>
> *A: I have an associates degree, yes, I do.*
>
> *Q: And you took no computer courses during the course of obtaining that associates degree, correct?*
>
> *A: Not obtaining that associates degree, I did not.*
>
> *Q: And you are not a certified forensic examiner, correct?*
>
> *A: You can only be a certified forensics examiner if you are a police officer.*
>
> *Q: But you are not a certified forensic examiner, correct?*
>
> *A: I am not a police officer, nor a certified forensics examiner.*

> *Q: And you have no other certifications, correct?*
>
> *A: No, I do not.*
>
> *Q: Okay. And you have only been working in the area of digital forensics since July of 2000, correct?*
>
> *A: That is correct.*
>
> *Q: Okay. And prior to that, you were a dental assistant—*
>
> *A: Correct.*
>
> *Q:—is that correct? All right. And you indicated that your training came from a course by the name of Key Computer?*
>
> *A: That's correct.*
>
> *Q: All right. And you have not completed that course, correct?*
>
> *A: No, I have not.*
>
> *Q: And you were last active in that course in May of 2002; is that correct?*
>
> *A: I believe that's correct.*
>
> *Q: And you—you talked a little bit about EnCase?*
>
> *A: Yes.*
>
> *Q: Okay. And you've had no formal training in EnCase, correct?*
>
> *A: That is correct. EnCase will only train police officers.*
>
> *Q: All right. So it's your testimony that EnCase will only train law enforcement?*
>
> *A: As far as I know, that is correct.*
>
> *Q: All right. And you have no formal training on Mackintosh [sic] computers, either, right?*
>
> *A: No, I do not.*
>
> *Q: And you indicated that you testified in—you've testified in court once before?*
>
> *A: Yes, I have.*
>
> *Q: Okay. And was that in April of this year?*
>
> *A: I believe it was in April of this year.*
>
> *Q: All right[1]*

In the preceding example, the witness's testimony was admitted, but given her lack of training and experience may not have been given much weight by the trier of fact. Attorneys can hire a witness to offer expert testimony on just about any topic under the sun. The limitations are that the witness may offer opinion testimony only about matters in which s/he possesses sufficient expertise, and the employing side of the controversy must choose a testifying expert carefully because his or her opinions will be subject to discovery. Of course, the witness need possess only sufficient skill and experience as to be more knowledgeable than a lay juror in order to be of assistance to the trier of fact. However, as can be inferred from the preceding example, when the witness is

---

[1] From *State of Washington v. DeGroff*, Super. Court No. 02-1-960-7 (Testimony of Ramona Lawson May 29, 2003).

not adequately trained or experienced, the result may well be that the testimony is admitted, but whether the jury or judge gives it much weight is the overarching concern. Furthermore, by way of association, if one of the defense's experts is successfully impeached, the negative "halo" may spread to other witnesses as well as the defense attorney and the defendant themselves—notwithstanding any cautions by the court to the contrary.

### 15.3.2) EXPERTS IN THE CHILD PORNOGRAPHY CASE

In a child pornography case, there may be several expert witnesses. It may be necessary to employ experts despite the fact that the offense charged is a misdemeanor in many jurisdictions. In the post-*Ashcroft v. Free Speech Coalition* world, the prosecution may call upon experts in imaging technology, child development, and digital forensics, for example. Each expert would testify about different aspects of the same evidence. Each expert would testify only about his or her own field of expertise. A common error in child pornography prosecutions has been for the prosecutor to attempt to elicit testimony from a subject matter expert beyond his or her particular field of study. The following example points up the problem:

---

**EXAMPLE**

The defendant was accused of possessing child pornography. The witness for the prosecution was an examiner in the state's digital forensics laboratory but did not complete the actual examination of the evidence in this case.

**CROSS-EXAMINATION**

*Q: Would you consider yourself a computer expert?*
*A: No. It depends on what you mean.*
*Q: Would you consider yourself an expert in operating systems?*
*A: Again, it depends on what you mean.*
*Q: Well, what would you consider yourself to be an expert in?*
*A: I have experience and training in the forensic examinations of computer systems and digital evidence.*

. . .

*Q: You have the State's exhibits in front of you. Which exhibits would you, in your experience and training, say depict a minor in prohibited sexual activity? (The witness looks to the prosecutor in desperation; the defense attorney is not only asking him a question that is*

> *not within his field of expertise, but he is asking for the witness to testify regarding the*
> *ultimate issue. That is, the defense attorney is asking the expert to render a legal*
> *determination—whether the images are child pornography.)*
>   *A: I cannot testify as to the exact age of the individuals depicted in the images. That is*
>   *beyond my field of expertise.*

To be fair to the prosecutor, the preceding example was his first child pornography case, and the facts were not the best to work with. Unfortunately, the state had no other witnesses prepared to testify as to the age of the children in the images, nor was there a witness to testify as to whether the images were computer rendered. Ultimately, the case was dismissed. The prosecutor hoped to get the images admitted without offering expert testimony as to either the age of the children depicted or whether the images portrayed actual minors (as opposed to computer-rendered images). He hoped that the judge would allow the images into evidence and would be willing to decide whether the images were of children based on his own experience. As with the issue of whether the images depicted children, the forensic examiner could not testify as to whether the images were computer rendered because he felt he did not possess sufficient experience or training to render an opinion.

### 15.3.3) EXPERTS IN THE ENTICEMENT CASE

Besides the issues inherent in offering the testimony of a young witness, as described previously, enticement cases may require the testimony of a witness who can educate the judge and jury about "grooming."

Recall that "grooming" refers to the ways a sexual offender gains control over victims, exploiting their weaknesses to gain trust or instill fear. Grooming usually involves exploiting a victim's needs, such as loneliness, self-esteem, sexual curiosity/inexperience, or lack of money, and taking advantage of this vulnerability to develop a bond. The offender uses this control or bond to sexually manipulate victims and discourage them from exposing the offender to authorities (Casey, Ferraro, and McGrath 2004). The offender develops a relationship with the prospective victim and introduces ideas about sexual content in a way that the child will entertain. The offender uses various approaches to groom the child, depending on the child and the circumstances. If the child is co-operative and interested, the offender enlists the child's trust and loyalty. If the child becomes afraid or wants to end the relationship, the offender may use blackmail to make the child continue the relationship and to ensure his or her silence. An offender may send the child adult or child pornography during the grooming process. The pornography serves many needs: It helps to lower the prospective victim's defenses and introduces him or her to the idea of sexual activity with the offender. The pornography sent by the offender can be used to force the victim to keep the relationship a secret if the offender threatens to tell the victim's parents about his or her interest in pornography and complicity in sexual activity.

Grooming evidence can be used as "other acts evidence." (Currently, only Colorado has a Federal Rule of Evidence 404(b) equivalent that explicitly mentions grooming as other acts evidence.) Other states allow grooming evidence to show motive; preparation, plan, or scheme; intent; opportunity; lack of mistake or accident; identity; and knowledge (Brown 2001). The prosecution may wish to call upon an expert to testify about the grooming process.

### 15.3.4) FINDING A GOOD EXPERT

Prosecutors often ask where and how to find suitable experts. The best approach to finding well-qualified experts is to consult a lawyer or other expert who has experience trying or testifying in similar cases. If a consulting expert is not handy, the prosecutor may find a good expert through an Internet list serve on the subject matter. The High Technology Criminal Investigation Association (HTCIA) has a list serve that may be accessed by members.[2] A prosecutor in search of an expert in digital forensics or digital images could send a request for a referral to the list. If the prosecutor is not a member of the list serve, s/he can ask a member to request the referral. Local colleges and universities are also good sources of expert witnesses. Professors in the discipline in question may be willing to testify or to refer the prosecutor to someone who is willing to testify. Organizations such as the National Center for Missing and Exploited Children and the National District Attorneys Association are also good sources of referral information.

Getting a referral for an expert witness is usually easy. Verifying credentials and ensuring quality testimony are another matter. Those prosecutors who have been burned in the past by shoddy experts approach experts with the necessary trepidation. Although some lessons are most powerfully learned by doing, watching the scene play out in court when a dangerous child sex offender is on trial is unnecessary. The prosecutor should obtain a complete curriculum vita from each prospective expert and employ an investigator to confirm his or her training and experience. The prosecutor should also prepare by sitting down with testifying experts before trial to ensure that s/he asks the right questions.

[2] More information about the HTCIA may be found on its Web site at www.htcia.org.

## 15.4) DISSECTING THE DIGITAL FORENSICS EXPERT'S REPORT

This section will take you through a sample digital forensics expert's report. The entire case report is reproduced first. If you make it through reading the report without scratching your head, congratulations! Move on to the next chapter. If you would like an explanation of the report, explanations follow.

---

### STATE OF CONFUSION[3]

### COMPUTER CRIMES AND ELECTRONIC EVIDENCE UNIT

**Forensic Examination Report**

| | | | | | | |
|---|---|---|---|---|---|---|
| Date | : | 06/05/2004 | Submitting Agency | : | Anytown | |
| Lab Case # | : | 123123 | Agency Case # | : | 12341234 | |

**Executive Summary**

On April 17, 2004 the Forensics Lab received the source media referenced below for forensic evaluation, per the request of Detective X. Based on the search warrant executed on March 27, 2004, Detective X is conducting an investigation regarding possession of child pornography and risk of injury to a minor. She requested a search be done on the storage media for information relating to this investigation, including:

1. Recovery of any child pornography images and/or recovery of any digital images taken by the suspect of the 11 $\frac{1}{2}$ year old female victim.
2. Recovery of any evidence relating to foot fetishes.
3. Recovery of an e-mail address used by the suspect (X@yahoo.com), recovery of e-mails written to or received from the e-mail addresses Y@yahoo.com (Victim) and Y@aol.com, and any recoverable e-mails that may be relevant to this investigation.
4. Other evidence recovered from submitted media.

---

[3] Sample Examination Report provided thanks to Detective Bruce Patterson, State of Connecticut Computer Crimes and Electronic Evidence Unit.

Examination of the evidence generated the following results:

1. Nine images that appear to fit the statutory criteria (penal code §__–__) for child pornography were found.
2. Five images of the victim were found.
3. Forty-five images relating to foot-fetish were found.
4. Chat and e-mails written to and sent from the e-mail addresses Y@yahoo.com (Victim) and Y@aol.com, and other relevant e-mails were discovered detailed in the "Email" section of this report.

### Source Media

The evidence listed below is not necessarily all evidence submitted in the case, but reflects the media where the reported evidence was found / located.

- *Lab Submission # HD-001-001*
  *Seagate hard drive, model ST34342A*
  *SN: X*
  *MD5:* ae3af39664f76d1eb2d652543c536b61

The hard drive was labeled with reference number HD_001-001. The report will refer to this designation when referring to information found on the storage media.

This report may contain terminology unfamiliar to the reader. These items are in *bold italics*. A "Glossary of Terms" containing definitions is located at the end of this report and is incorporated herein by reference.

### Processing

To protect the integrity of the data contained on all fixed and removable media, each item is write-protected, an *MD5 hash* of the data it contains is calculated, and then two separate *sector*-by-sector copies of the data are saved to another storage media. The acquired image is called a "Forensic Image" or "Evidence File" and all examinations were performed on this copy to avoid the risk of altering the original. Throughout the creation of this "Evidence File" the image is continually verified by both a *CRC (Cyclical Redundancy Check)* value for every 32K block, as well as an *MD5 hash* calculated for all data contained in the "Evidence File." Both the CRC and MD5 hash values are immediately assigned to the "Evidence File" upon acquisition. This process not only copies all the standard DOS and Windows compatible files, but it also copies all *file slack*, deleted files and *unallocated space*. This procedure does not affect, change or alter the information on the original storage media in any manner.

The software used to create the evidence file is Encase Version 3.2, distributed by Guidance Software. Encase Version 3.2 has been tested and verified by the National Institute of Standards and Technologies to not alter data on the original media when a sector-by-sector image is created.

**Directory and File Examination**

1. **Recovery of any child pornography images and/or recovery of any digital images taken by the suspect of the $11\frac{1}{2}$ year old female victim.**

Recovered within the ***unallocated space*** of HD_001-001 were five (5) images of the female victim, taken with a digital still camera (DSC) (Refer to Attachment 1). Examination of the ***Exif header***, for each of these images, indicated several pieces of information including the camera make and model and the date and time of image creation. Nine (9) additional images were printed as requested by the investigating officer and are included in Attachment 2. Attachment 3A provides the Exif header information related to all images on Attachments 1 & 2. (Note: The listing is sorted by the column labeled Date & Time Created.)

The investigating officer asked for any child pornography images recovered from the hard drive. Excluding the above mentioned images no additional child pornography was identified.

2. **Recovery of any evidence relating to foot fetishes.**

Forty-five (45) images relating to foot fetishes were recovered from unallocated space on HD_001-001 and were saved to a compact disc (CD) (Attachment 7) and will be included with this report.

In addition to these, four (4) digital camera images, identified as dp193.jpg, dp28.jpg, dp326.jpg and dp730.jpg were located in unallocated space on HD_001-001 (Refer to Attachment 2).

3. **Recovery of an e-mail address used by the suspect (X@yahoo.com), recovery of e-mails written to or received from the e-mail addresses X@yahoo.com (Victim) and X@aol.com (X), and any recoverable e-mails that may be relevant to this investigation.**

Three thousand nine hundred twenty (3,920) *HTML* pages (both whole and in part), that may be relevant to this investigation, were recovered from unallocated space on HD_001-001; a representative sample of these pages were printed and are attached to this report as Attachments 5 and 6. *(Information recovered from unallocated space does not have file names, dates, or time stamps associated with the files; the file names assigned by the forensics examiner to these pages are for the purpose of extracting and saving the information for further review, and are not original file names.)*

The samples printed cover the above mentioned e-mail addresses showing content of various messages exchanged.

The following e-mail accounts have been identified as follows:

| Email Address | Owner |
|---|---|
| X@yahoo.com | X |
| Y@yahoo.com | Y—Victim |
| Y@aol.com | Y |
| X@yahoo.com | X—Suspect |

The recovered information includes:

- **Web Page1058.htm**—Inbox listing for X@yahoo.com
  For Period Covering 01/22 to 03/08
- **Web Page1170.htm**—Sent listing for X@yahoo.com
  For Period Covering 12/24 to 03/05
- **Web Page1943.htm**—Email from X@yahoo.com to X@yahoo.com
  Subject: I will beat you like a bad bad donkey okay
  Mentions about her staying over at his house for a Saturday night

Attachment 7, which is being provided with this report, contains all of the HTML pages recovered.

### 4. Other evidence recovered from submitted media

*Email/Chat*

One hundred forty-eight (148) Web-based e-mails were recovered from the unallocated space of HD_001-001 and are being provided with this report on a compact disc (Attachment 7). For sample e-mails refer to Attachments 5 & 6.

Detective X provided a chat log and several e-mails that had been obtained by him as a result of his investigation. A comparison was conducted between the e-mails obtained and the Web based e-mails printed in Attachment 6. The following is a listing of the Web-based e-mails whose content is consistent with the e-mails obtained by Detective X:

- **Web Page1297.htm**—Email from X@yahoo.com to X@aol.com
  Subject: I wish u were here
  Talks about being lonely and sad
- **Web Page 1331.htm**—Email from X@yahoo.com to X@aol.com
  Subject: Fwd: what is 99% sugar?
  General conversation about Dov

*Images*

Numerous images were also recovered from unallocated space on HD_001-001. Detective X identified one of these recovered images as being that of X (X@yahoo.com). According to Detective X, X sent this picture to the victim, claiming it to be her portrait. The image is being identified as JPG2569.JPG. The image was printed and is provided with this report.

*Documents*

Three (3) word documents were located in the directory \My Documents on HD_001-001.

- **My Documents\WordPad Document.doc**
  The suspect is apologizing to recipient (X) stating that he has ruined the trust of the people who mean the most to him. (Refer to Attachment 4A)
- **My Documents\dear X.doc**
  Same communication as WordPad Document.doc
  (Refer to Attachment 4B)
- **My Documents\dear ?.doc (same file name as above)**
  Believed to be the suspect, apologizing for his actions.
  (Refer to Attachment 4C).

*Text Fragments*

The following text fragments were recovered from unallocated space on HD_001-001.

Path: \Unallocated Clusters\C428368-430927

*Former File Name "One Summer Night.doc"*
Before long they would just lay there in each others arms in the soft glow of the candle she had lit. It was during this quiet as she lay with him on the couch that she would give herself to him. She closed her eyes and let her body be teased and caressed by the gentleness of his finger tips. She became lost in the pleasure as he traced gentle circles over her stomach and her

breasts. He was awakening the woman that lay sleeping deep within her. With every caress of his hand he would bring her closer and closer to the surface. As X's delicate touch began to drift slowly down her belly, X's breath became quicker. She ached for him to touch her there. "Oh", she thought, "please don't stop now !" As he traced his fingers still lower she drew her knees apart almost as if by instinct. Finally, X would trace the very tips of his fingers so gently over her pussy. Instantly a wave of pleasure would come over her. She lay in complete stillness, total anticipation of his every touch. With every stroke of his hand she felt something awakening inside her. A part of her that she never knew existed was emerging. By now she was so hot that she couldn't hold back her feelings. She reached down between her legs and gently opened the delicate lips of her pussy so that X could easily touch her clit. X whispered quietly, " Oh baby, you are so sexy. I'd love to make you cum." With that he put his finger tip to his mouth to wet it slightly. X felt a warm pulse of sexy pleasure as his warm, wet finger tip made delicate circles around her sensitive clit.

Path: Unallocated Clusters\C415568-418127

*Previous path\filename "C:\My Documents\X.doc"*

Y,

I wish someone would create a word that could describe an emotion far deeper than love, a feeling more complete than inseparable, or a devotion that reaches beyond forever.

For those would be the words I would use to express how I feel for you.

They would be words so beautiful that they could only be spoken one time, for this one purpose, and could only be whispered from my heart to yours before they disappeared forever.

If there were such words Y, I would come to you in the quiet of a summer night and look deeply into your endless brown eyes and hold you so tenderly as you felt the completeness of that love . . . . .

Forever, X

**Email Fragments**

Path: Unallocated Clusters\C482128-484687

*Email content matching one obtained by investigating officer, dated 03/14/02*
Subject:</b></td><td width="100%"> when i died</td></tr>
<tr bgcolor=white><td colspan=2><img

src="http://us.i1.yimg.com/us.yimg.com/i/space.gif" border = 0 width=1 height=1></td></tr><tr bgcolor="#eeeeee"><td align=right valign=top nowrap>To:</td><td width="100%">X@aol.com</td></tr>
<tr bgcolor=white><td colspan=2><img
src="http://us.i1.yimg.com/us.yimg.com/i/space.gif" border = 0 width=1 height=1></td></tr></table></td>
<td valign=top bgcolor="#eeeeee"><form name=frmAddAddrs action= "http://address.mail.yahoo.com/yab/us?v=YM&cmode=1&Lang=us" method="post">
<table cellpadding=0 cellspacing=0 border=0 width="100%">
<tr valign=top><td bgcolor="#eeeeee" align=left>
<font face="Arial" size="-1">
<input type="hidden" name="v" value="YM">
<input type="hidden" name="A" value="a">
<input type="hidden" name="fn" value="X,,">
<input type="hidden" name="ln" value="X,,">
<input type="hidden" name="e" value="X@yahoo.com,X@aol.com,">
<input type="hidden" name="m" value="1">
<input type="hidden" name=".done"
value="http://us.f210.mail.yahoo.com/ym/ShowLetter?MsgId=9956_
259006_10829_559_1195_0_143&order=down&inc=&sort=date&view=
&head=&box=Sent&YY=4322">
</font>
</td></tr>
</table>
</form></td>
</tr>
</table>
<br>

<P><FONT color = mediumvioletred>Hi iz me.  Thanks for talkin the other nite. Im soooo sry if I freaked u out with that stuff. I get so angry now for no reason . . .   I feel so bad for what  put my family through my mom iz still REAL upset. I guess if i waz u id be wondering what it waz like too so im not mad that u asked me. I remember the people in the ambu-lance workin over me. Like I could see and hear them from above myself. . I tried to tell them it was okay and to let me go but they couldnt hear me. They used these paddle things on my chest with like an electric shock and i felt like my body was sucking me back into it like a big vaccume (i know that sounds REAL strange) the 2nd time i just started to hear this loud rush of air and felt like i was flying real fast in a tunnel. I remember feeling the

presence of people i should have known but could not recognize quite then. they were telling me no . . . go back . . . it isnt time to come yet but it was my choice. I felt like they loved me like my mom or dad would and that they would always be there when it was time to go. then I felt that sucking back again and I woke up in the hospital the next day. I know that iz prob the most strange thing u have ever heard but that iz what it felt like to me. I do feel like everything was okay when it was happening. like it was as normal as going to school on the bus every day or like i have done it many times before. Any ways thats it . . . hope u arent ashamed of me but i wont blame u if u are. I told Dov that u could tell him bout it if u wanted to. (I was too embarrassed) I hope u have a great time at ur dance !!    Kiss him good Y. . . I will see you soon i hope.</FONT></P>
<P><FONT color = #c71585>Luv X

**Further review and examination of any of this information is available upon request. Please contact me if you have any questions or if you require additional assistance.**

**Signature of Examiner**

**NAME**

**TITLE**

**DATE**

**NOTE:** Curriculum vita available upon request

### 15.4.1) HEADERS AND EXECUTIVE SUMMARY

The first page of the examiner's report should make it clear to the reader where the report came from and what the report is about. A summary of the case, the evidence submitted, and the examiner's findings are essential—especially when the prosecutor is in unfamiliar territory. The summary should be sufficiently clear to allow the reader to explain the examiner's findings to a juror with an eighth-grade education and little or no experience with computers or the Internet. In the sample report provided here, note that the examiner details exactly what the detective asked the laboratory to examine and what he found. He does not overstate what he found. He could have said that he found "child pornography," but he didn't. He stated that he found "images that appear to fit the statutory criteria (penal code §__–__) for child pornography."

## 15.4.2) SOURCE MEDIA

The next section of the sample report contains a delineation of the source media actually analyzed. This section may appear anywhere in the report, but it is essential for the examiner to provide an account of exactly what s/he looked at. Often, police seize and submit for examination more evidence than is necessary. One reason electronic evidence that is submitted is not examined is that the media are too damaged to examine. Another reason is that there is nothing on the media—for instance, a blank diskette. Still another reason might be that the submission is a commercially recorded music CD (this happens more than you may think).

This section of the sample report also refers to a "glossary" contained at the end of the document. The examiner should define and explain within his or her report unfamiliar or technical terms. It is essential for the reader to understand exactly what the examiner means when referring to something, especially when it has bearing on an individual's future liberty or lack thereof.

## 15.4.3) PROCESSING

The "Processing" section describes the steps taken to make the evidence file. It is accepted practice that the examiner should not examine the original evidence, but rather make an exact duplicate of the evidence and examine that duplicate. There are exceptions to this rule, as in the case of CD-ROMs that would not be altered by the examination. To ensure that the evidence file is the exact duplicate of the original, either a cyclical redundancy check, an MD5 hash or, as in the sample examination, both are calculated.

A cyclical redundancy check is a way of checking for errors when transmitting data from one source to another. When original evidence is duplicated, the data are sent from the original media to the evidence file. When the data are sent from the original evidence, the sending "packet" includes a number produced through the application of a mathematical algorithm. The same algorithm, or calculation, is performed when the data packet reaches the destination—the evidence file. If the data were duplicated correctly, the results of the calculations at the source and destination will be the same. If an error occurred during the transmission and the data was changed, the calculations will produce different results.

"MD5 hash" refers to a different algorithm used to check for errors in transmitting data from the original source to its destination. "MD" stands for "message digest." "Hash" refers to what occurs when an algorithm is applied to the data to be checked for errors. The MD5 hash is an algorithm that, when applied to a set of data such as an original evidence file, produces a message digest or numerical "fingerprint." The message digest is one-way, meaning that it can be derived only from the original data—the original data cannot be produced by deconstructing the computation process. The MD5 hash is calculated for the original evidence and then again for the evidence file. The results will be exactly the same for both files if the duplication process was error free. If so much as one character changed—for instance, a "p" was changed to a "z"— the MD5 hash value would differ.

The "Processing" section alerts the reader that all files were copied ("[t]his process not only copies all the standard DOS and Windows compatible files, but it also copies all *file slack*, deleted files and *unallocated space*.") The importance of this distinction in the processing of the evidence cannot be overstated. To understand the importance of the statement, you must first understand how a computer stores and processes data. While these concepts are discussed elsewhere in this book, following is a brief explanation.

When an individual creates a file, such as a document, using a computer, the data is stored in sections called "clusters." Clusters can be imagined as "blocks" that are of the same size. When the individual creates enough data to fill a cluster, it is placed by the computer similar to a building block, one after another, to create the file. (This is an oversimplification of the process, used only for explanatory purposes here.) When the file is completed, even if there is not enough data to fill an entire cluster, the "block" is still placed at the end of the file. The unused space is called "file slack." Once saved, the file will be the same size. If a document is 100 MB and the writer deletes half of it, pasting the deleted half into another document, the original file will remain 100 MB. The half of the file that the writer "deleted" does not appear when the file is opened, printed, or otherwise manipulated, but it is still there and could be resurrected if forensically examined. Figure 15.1 shows how file slack works.

---

### File Slack

Actually, the term "deleted" is a misnomer when dealing with computer files. When you think of "deleting" something, images of using correction fluid and shredding documents come to mind. When you "delete" a file from a computer, it is not "erased." Computers have been engineered to be efficient, and actually "deleting" a file is grossly inefficient. Rather, when you delete a file from computer storage, the reference to the file is deleted. The file remains exactly where it is. The only change made by the computer is to a table that once pointed to the file. So, if you have a memorandum called "memo.doc" and delete it, the computer will remove the reference to "memo.doc" in the filing system (which is different depending on the type of operating system, but the concept remains the same). The computer will replace the pointer with an indication that the section of the storage media where "memo.doc" once resided is available for use by another file. This concept is important because until a file, is overwritten by a new file, it can be resurrected in its entirety.

When you select text from a document, copy it, and paste it into another file, the copied text will not contain evidence that would be contained in the original document. Likewise, simply copying a diskette will not copy all of the evidence on the original diskette to the duplicate. You must use software specifically engineered to copy all of the data on the source media to another location. Without using forensic software, the duplicate may not contain "file slack," deleted files, and "unallocated space."

*Figure 15.1*

*File slack. Data are saved in "clusters," and the size of clusters is predetermined and static. When one cluster is full, the computer will look to the next cluster to write data. File slack refers to the end of a file where the cluster is not completely full of file data.*

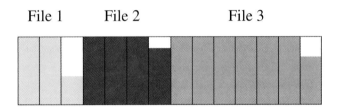

File 1          File 2                    File 3

The "Processing" section next details the forensic software used to conduct the analysis. The examination is only as good as the software used to conduct it. In the sample, EnCase Version 3.2 was used. The version number is important because one version of software may have been verified by the National Institute of Standards and Technologies (NIST), whereas a new version may not. Whether the software has been verified by NIST is not a fatal flaw; knowing this information is important because if the software has not been verified by one source, it should be verified by another before the examination results are submitted as evidence. If the examiner does not state who verified the software and what version was used in his or her report, it is advisable to obtain that information prior to trial because any astute defense attorney will hone in on the forensic software and question its reliability.

### 15.4.4) FINDINGS OF THE EXAMINATION

The examination report should clearly delineate all findings relevant to the request. In the sample report provided here, the examiner takes each request stated in the summary and fully details his findings. When the examination recovers images, the images should be reproduced. When the examination reveals documents that contain relevant text, the text as well as the information necessary to find the file should be provided. All evidence relevant to the investigation should be fully reported—not just evidence tending to prove the prosecution's case. Training in ethics and proper investigative procedures are therefore indispensable for the digital forensics examiner.

### 15.4.5) CERTIFICATION BY EXAMINER

The expert should sign and date the report. The rules change from one jurisdiction to another. The prosecutor should inform the expert about any particular preference regarding certification of the report. For instance, if the prosecutor expects each page of the report to be initialed or signed, or for the report to be witnessed or notarized, s/he should let the examiner know in advance. The examiner should provide his or her curriculum vita for the prosecutor to become familiar with his or her qualifications and to prepare to qualify the examiner as an expert when the time comes. Having the examiner's vita well ahead of trial will allow for the prosecutor's investigator to confirm the expert's training and experience.

## 15.5) DEFENDING THE CHARGE

A good defense attorney can counter any charge. Countering the computer-assisted child exploitation charge is both more difficult and easier than defending other types of charges. A former law student intern once commented on how enormously difficult it must be for the defense in these cases because the digital evidence is so compelling. Certainly, when the evidence is overwhelming, the defendant often pleads guilty to avoid the embarrassment and expense of trial. However, defending this type of case can be easier than other types of cases. A criminal conviction in the United States requires proof beyond a reasonable doubt. Because the evidence in these cases can be complicated and the expert witnesses difficult to understand, creating confusion can spawn reasonable doubt. There are many defenses to computer-assisted crimes, and this chapter will introduce you to some of them. We hope that knowing likely defenses will enlighten the investigator, prosecutor, and forensic examiner in these cases. Because computer-assisted child exploitation cases have only recently begun to be tried, the full exposition of what is required to prove cases beyond a reasonable doubt has not yet occurred.

Defenses to a computer-assisted child exploitation case can be complex, but in their most basic form are no more complicated than those defenses proffered in any other case. The following sections begin with the most obvious. When the evidence is overwhelming, the prosecutor must do anything necessary to prevent it from being introduced. Next, the chapter discusses the defense of false identification. Defendants often claim that computer-facilitated acts were "beyond my control." Sometimes, the law provides for affirmative defenses. The chapter discusses their use (and abuse). Still another claim is that the defendant's online behavior, specifically in the enticement of a minor case, was part of an elaborate fantasy life. Attacking the law itself is another type of defense. Usually, the defendant claims to have a right to engage in the prohibited behavior. The chapter concludes with a discussion of digital evidence as alibi.

Almost all computer-assisted child exploitation cases are circumstantial. Rarely will there be direct evidence such as a picture of the defendant engaging in the criminal activity. This does increasingly happen, however, as the use of digital cameras proliferates. The prosecution often relies on the inference that, if the computer was in the defendant's possession, the defendant consciously saved the data contained within the computer. Of course, where specific intent is not an issue, how the data got on the defendant's computer hard drive is not usually an issue either.

### 15.5.1) SUPPRESSING THE EVIDENCE

Computer evidence can be compelling. In enticement cases the evidence often consists of chat logs between the offender and intended victim, Internet and network records, and pictures. Telephone and cellular phone records also can come into play. In child pornography cases, digital images and network and Internet records often take center stage. Chat logs are difficult to counter. The exact content can be found on the victim's computer, the offender's computer, and sometimes other witnesses' computers. Digital pictures are damning. When they depict the offender himself or herself, there isn't a lot of room to negotiate. When the pictures can be traced to an identified victim, the defense has little to work with. Given that the evidence can be this persuasive, the best way to avoid conviction is to prevent the evidence from being considered.

Motions to suppress evidence focus on how police compiled probable cause, alleging some flaw, or they attack the way the search was executed. In the Candyman investigation discussed previously, some defendants were successful in having evidence suppressed by arguing that the FBI agent misrepresented information about the e-group in the affidavit (U.S. vs. Perez). Operation Avalanche was abandoned by the United States Department of Justice because they interpreted the actions of undercover operatives, in using a similar name to that of the Landslide operation to send e-mail advertising the availability of illicit material, as infringing on the Landslide owner's copyright. If the rights of a party were violated due to government action, it behooves an attorney representing the United States to decline to use such evidence, as it would breach the rules governing professional conduct.

The *U.S. v. Bach* (2002)[4] case started with the defense motion to suppress evidence because the execution of the search warrant was flawed. Of course, in the *Bach* case the evidence was not suppressed notwithstanding the unlawful execution of the search warrant. But the *Bach* case is exceptional due to its facts. In *Bach*, a state investigator faxed a search warrant to an out-of-state service provider. Faxing of the warrant was a violation of the state's requirement that an officer be present to execute the warrant. The *Bach* court admitted the evidence despite the unlawful search warrant execution because the defendant was charged in the federal court, and federal law does not require suppression of evidence unlawfully obtained by a state officer. If the criminal proceeding had taken place in the state court, the outcome likely would have been different.

### 15.5.2) FALSE IDENTIFICATION

Putting the defendant at the computer is the most difficult aspect of proving a computer-facilitated crime. Fingerprinting the keyboard alone is not sufficient to hold a particular defendant responsible for a crime. The prosecution team must prove that the defendant did what they allege s/he did. An increasingly common defense is that the defendant lost control of the computer system. There are several ways this may happen. The first is if a Trojan horse virus takes control of a computer system. Named for the Trojan horse of Greek legend, a Trojan horse virus is sent to the target when s/he visits a Web site or opens an e-mail (usually, though, there are countless other ways). The receiver of the virus thinks one thing is happening, but something quite dangerous to the receiver is infecting his or her hard drive. Most virus-protection software looks for signatures that identify known viruses. Creators of Trojan horse viruses alter the program to suit their needs and thereby make the virus sufficiently different to pass through signature-based detection systems. Once the Trojan horse virus installs on a computer system, it can turn control of the system over to the virus sender.

Defendants sometimes claim that a virus took control of their computer and that they had no knowledge or ability to stop the crime from being committed. In some cases this defense works. Investigators, prosecutors, and forensic examiners should rule out the virus defense before proceeding with a case because it is sometimes plausible. Weighing heavily against the virus defense is forensic

---

[4] *United States v. Bach*, 310 F.3d 1063 (8th Cir. 2002); cert. den'd, 123 S. Ct 1817 (2003); rehr. den'd 2003 U.S. App. LEXIS 141 (2003).

evidence that might show a series of actions in furtherance of the criminal activity over a period of time. Contracting a virus is an acute condition. It is not chronic. Forensic examination often turns up e-mail, pictures, chat logs, and other evidence that, taken together, militate against the virus defense. Of course, the absence of a virus on the system would negate the defense, also.

> Reading, UK, resident Karl Schofield was found not guilty of possessing child pornography in April 2003. Experts testifying on Schofield's behalf persuaded the court that a Trojan virus was responsible for downloading fourteen images of child pornography (Leyden 2003).

A variant of this type of defense is that the defendant was "mousetrapped." "Mousetrapping" refers to when the computer system is involuntarily taken to a series of Web sites or displays a cascade of pop-up advertisements that the user cannot extricate himself or herself from. Usually, mousetrapping requires shutting down the system to end the experience. The mousetrap defense is often employed in child pornography possession cases. It is most persuasive when the evidence is located only in temporary Internet storage, the number of images is small, and the images themselves are thumbnail-sized rather than full size. Thumbnail-size images are more often associated with Web sites and advertisements due to the ability to transmit them more quickly than the larger, higher quality full-sized images. The mousetrap defense is more difficult to accept when the defendant has a high volume of full-size images, when the images have been saved to folders and off-loaded onto disks, when the images have been backed up, when the defendant performed searches on the Internet looking for illicit material, or when the defendant used his or her credit card to purchase the child pornography.

### 15.5.3) THE GOOD SAMARITAN

Although such stories are far-fetched, some defendants have claimed they were merely aiming to assist law enforcement (Casey, Ferraro, and McGrath 2004). Some people believe, in earnest, that they are doing the right thing and have the best intentions. Some do not. But whatever one's intentions, the law does not make exceptions for good intentions. Take, for example, cases in which mothers kill their children because they believe they are possessed by demons. If the law excused people from criminal conduct because they had good intentions, vigilantes could cleanse communities of wrongdoers with impunity. Fortunately, the law regulates voluntary actions, no matter what misguided intentions an individual may have.

Steven Frederick Dodd admitted to downloading child pornography. "There was no dispute at trial that appellant downloaded and possessed six images that came within the statutory definition of pornographic work involving a child and that he did so with knowledge of the work's content. Instead, appellant continued to present his "good-faith" defense, arguing that after receiving unsolicited pornographic images of children as online "pop-up" advertisements, he began collecting the images and attempting to physically locate their disseminators, intending to ultimately share this information with the authorities." The Court of Appeals upheld Dodd's conviction.[5]

### 15.5.4) AFFIRMATIVE DEFENSES PURSUANT TO STATUTE

Some child pornography statutes provide for an affirmative defense for the lawful possession of images of nude minors or child pornography. Defendants sometimes claim that they had every right to possess the material. The claims take different forms. Larry Matthews, a news reporter for National Public Radio, claimed to be conducting research for a story by collecting and distributing child pornography. The court upheld his conviction stating that "admission that he knew he was receiving and transmitting child pornography is all that was required".[6] Likewise, the New York court held that there is no basis for allowing a "research" defense to a child pornography charge.[7]

"It shall be an affirmative defense [] that the defendant—(1) possessed less than three images of child pornography; and (2) promptly and in good faith, and without retaining or allowing any person, other than a law enforcement agency, to access any image or copy thereof—(A) took reasonable steps to destroy each such image; or (B) reported the matter to a law enforcement agency and afforded that agency access to each such image." 18 U.S.C. 2252A(c).

In child pornography cases, since the *Ashcroft v. Free Speech Coalition* decision, prosecutors must prove that alleged child pornography depicts a minor. Many defendants claim that the images in question are either of older people posing as minors or are computer rendered, or "virtual." For example, in *U.S. v. Laufer* (2003)[8] the defendant unsuccessfully claimed that the material seized from his

---

[5] *State v. Dodd*, 2003 Minn. App. LEXIS 1447 (unpublished, December 9, 2003).
[6] *United States v. Matthews*, 209 F.3d 338 (2000).
[7] *People v. Fraser*, 96 N.Y.2d 318; 752 N.E.2d 244; 728 N.Y.S.2d 115 (2001).
[8] *United States v. Laufer*, 245 F. Supp. 2d 503 (W.D.N.Y. 2003).

residence could be either of individuals who were not minors or "virtual." This defense is headed off using many different tools. First, the National Center for Missing and Exploited Children in the United States and COPINE in the Republic of Ireland have established databases that track images depicting identified minors. These images are known to be of human victims who were minors when the images were created. Second, when the defendant makes a request for child pornography, either through an Internet search or by responding to an advertisement, such requests usually make his intent to acquire child pornography fairly clear. Third, in cases in which the defendant admits to knowing the content of the image, it would be hard to persuade a fact finder that the image depicts virtual or adult actors. Admission to knowing the content of an image can be accomplished through interviewing the defendant, showing him or her the pictures, and asking what they depict. Another method of proving knowledge would be for an undercover officer who receives the child pornography to ask the defendant what the image depicts. Often, when the defendant sends an image to an undercover officer, s/he describes the content. For example, "this is a picture of me with my last girlfriend."

### 15.5.5) THE FANTASY DEFENSE

You can pretend to be anyone you'd like to be on the Internet. Many people enjoy pretending to be someone else and trying on different personas. Defendants accused of attempting to entice minors into engaging in sexual activity often claim that they never intended to complete the crime. Rather, the defendants argue that they merely engaged in fantasy and believed they were really communicating with an adult the whole time.

**CASE EXAMPLE**

Vincent Filipkowski went on the Internet and entered a chat room entitled "JAXFL M4M." The abbreviation "M4M" means "men for men," indicating a chat room catering to homosexuals. He began communicating through instant messages with a person using the screen name "OUTDRBOYFL," who said he was 15 years old. Using instant messages, they had a sexually charged conversation and arranged to meet that day at a local mall.

OUTDRBOYFL was actually an undercover police officer. Although police intended to arrest Filipkowski at the mall that day, technical difficulties prevented it. Police later contacted Filipkowski to tell him that OUTDRBOYFL was unable to go to the mall. After another sexually explicit instant message discussion, they arranged to meet again. Police arrested Filipkowski when he arrived at the meeting spot.

> On appeal, as he did at trial, he argued that he did not have the specific intent to commit the charged offense when he engaged in the conversations over the computer. "The thrust of the appellant's argument is that the electronic conversation on the Internet was simply a fantasy—an "Internet play game"—and that he had no intention of ever meeting the other person or engaging in sexual relations." He argued that he never believed that the person communicating with him was fifteen.
>
> The court found no merit in the fantasy defense, citing the fact that the defendant drove to meet the child not once, but twice.[9]

### 15.5.6) ATTACKING THE LAW—"I DIDN'T DO ANYTHING WRONG"

Attacking the law that criminalizes the defendant's behavior is a defense that alleges "I didn't do anything wrong." An example of this approach was taken by Thomas Foley of New York, who was convicted of promoting a sexual performance by a child and attempting to disseminate indecent material to minors.

**CASE EXAMPLE**

> Defendant contends that the following terms are vague: "sexual contact", "importunes, invites or induces", "sexual conduct", and "harmful to minors". We disagree. "Sexual contact", while not defined in Penal Law § 235.22, is defined elsewhere in the Penal Law as "any touching of the sexual or other intimate parts of a person not married to the actor for the purpose of gratifying sexual desire of either party. It includes the touching of the actor by the victim, as well as the touching of the victim by the actor, whether directly or through clothing"[] In addition, the meaning of "sexual contact" can be inferred from the other prohibited conduct, i.e., sexual intercourse and deviate sexual intercourse. The terms "importunes, invites or induces" are common terms with common ordinary meanings [] "Sexual conduct" is defined as "acts of masturbation, homosexuality, sexual intercourse, or physical contact with a person's clothed or unclothed genitals, pubic area, buttocks or, if such person be a female, breast."[]. All the terms within that definition are commonly used terms and are not vague. Finally, "harmful to minors" is defined in Penal Law § 235.20 (6) and has been held sufficient to give adequate notice to individuals.[10]

---

[9] *United States v. Filipkowski*, 2002 CCA LEXIS 70 (unpublished opinion, 2002).
[10] *People v. Foley*, 257 A.D.2d 243; 692 N.Y.S.2d 248 (1999).

Foley also unsuccessfully claimed that the enticement statute was an impermissible restriction on his right to free speech and violated the Commerce Clause of the United States Constitution.

### 15.5.7) DIGITAL EVIDENCE AS ALIBI

A defendant may quite convincingly claim that s/he could not have done what s/he is alleged to have done. The defendant claims to have been elsewhere at the time and has witnesses to prove it. Changing the time and date stamp on a digital device can be a simple proposition. Often a proper forensic examination will pick up on changes to logs. Some personal computers maintain a log of time and date changes. When the time and date are changed on a computer connected to a network, inconsistencies will be pronounced.

## 15.6) CONCLUSION

This chapter discussed trial issues in computer-assisted child exploitation cases. It began with a discussion of jury selection and provided insight into choosing a prosecution-friendly panel. The chapter offered advice to facilitate children's testimony. Types of experts that may be used in trying computer-assisted child exploitation cases and guidance regarding how to select a good expert were discussed. A sample digital forensics examination report was dissected and explained in detail. Finally, potential defenses were explored.

## REFERENCES

American Prosecutors Research Institute. *Investigation and Prosecution of Child Abuse.* 3rd ed. Thousand Oaks, CA: Sage, 2003.

Babitsky, S., and J. J. Mangraviti. *Writing and Defending Your Expert Report: The Step-by-Step Guide with Models.* Falmouth, MA: Seak, 2001.

Brown, D., S. J. Ceci, and M. Bruck. *Jeopardy in the Courtroom.* Washington, DC: American Psychological Association, 2000.

Casey, E. *Digital Evidence and Computer Crime,* 1st Edition, Boston, MA: Academic Press, 2000.

Casey, E., M. M. Ferraro, and M. McGrath. "Sex Offenders on the Internet," in *Digital Evidence and Computer Crime, 2nd ed.* Boston, MA: Academic Press, 2004.

Ceci, S. J., and H. Hembrooke. *Expert Witnesses in Child Abuse Cases: What Can and Should Be Said in Court.* Washington, DC: American Psychological Association, 1998.

Leyden, J. "Trojan Defence Clears Man on Child Porn Charges." (April 24, 2003). www.theregister.co.uk.

Massengale, J. "Facilitating Children's Testimony." *Update* 14, no. 6 (2001).

Smith, F. C., and R. G. Bace. *A Guide to Forensic Testimony: The Art and Practice of Presenting Testimony as an Expert Technical Witness.* Boston, MA: Addison-Wesley, 2003.

Temple, T. W. "Voir Dire in the Computer-Based Sexual Exploitation Case." *Update* 13, no. 3 (2000).

# CHAPTER 16

# FINAL THOUGHTS

This chapter wraps up the book. Why else would we call it "Final Thoughts"? We take this last opportunity to share our thoughts on setting up an Internet child exploitation unit, resources for investigators, and future challenges for investigating and prosecuting online child exploitation.

## 16.1) SETTING UP AN ONLINE CHILD EXPLOITATION UNIT

Several ingredients go into making a successful online child exploitation unit. The first step is to gather a dedicated, qualified, and motivated group of multi-disciplinary professionals. Resources to fund ongoing training and purchase computer hardware, software, Internet services, and undercover operations are essential. Sufficient staff and the support of upper management are absolutely required. The unit must communicate with the community, network with other agencies, and share its knowledge and intelligence as broadly as it can. The following sections focus on each of these factors in greater detail.

### 16.1.1) SELECTING PERSONNEL

Investigating and prosecuting online child exploitation are not for the faint of heart. Online child exploitation units must be staffed only by people who really want to be there and fully understand what they are getting into. Investigators, evidence examiners, and prosecutors will definitely see exceptionally explicit child pornography and obscenity of the most gruesome sort. Few human beings can escape being moved or emotionally affected by viewing such images. Only those who really know what they will be seeing and doing and will not allow the work to encroach on other aspects of their lives will be able to effectively work with child exploitation. Seeing an idealistic individual break down under the pressures of investigating child exploitation is almost as tragic as the crimes s/he sought to resolve and prevent. For the sake of the individual and the unit, such situations should be avoided if at all possible.

Among volunteers who seek to work in the unit will undoubtedly be pedophiles and those who are interested in the work for the sake of its titillating aspect. While there is no foolproof method of screening out all but the pure of heart, there are a few methods that help. A thorough background investigation should be conducted on each prospective member of the unit, no exceptions. The background investigation should include interviews with family members and past employers. Contracting with a psychologist to evaluate applicants can assist in selecting only the best prospects.

Once selected, unit administrators need to focus on maintaining a high level of morale. Ensuring that there are sufficient resources for personnel to do their jobs effectively is a good start. Providing ample opportunities for training and networking with other practitioners can also be rewarding. Taking time to meet as a team on a regular basis and, if the administrator feels comfortable with it, practicing team-building exercises can increase satisfaction among coworkers and bolster morale. Something as simple as having a regularly scheduled pizza lunch together or an annual picnic can provide the glue that keeps a team together.

Some child exploitation units contract with a therapist to provide ongoing support and evaluation of unit personnel. Confidential sessions with the therapist on a regular basis, such as monthly or quarterly, serve several purposes. First, providing such services sends a message to personnel that the administration is concerned about their welfare and mental health. If the opposite sentiment is perceived, resentment will build, and the effectiveness of the unit will diminish. Second, it conveys to team members that their work is recognized as important and that it is expected to be stressful. Such reassurances encourage the team to pull together during difficult periods rather than to neglect members who are having difficulty. Third, ongoing sessions provide a benchmark to compare an individual's functioning and mental health so that if the work environment takes a toll, such changes can be readily identified and intervention may be swift. A prompt response to such problems can minimize the resulting damage to the individual and the cases s/he is working on. Finally, unit personnel reap the benefits of an ongoing supportive relationship with someone who understands their work and can talk about it with them.

Many people who deal with child exploitation and sexual assault are reluctant to talk openly about their work, especially with their loved ones. Of course, each individual is different, and some people talk about work at home and with friends more than others. But the nature of the subject matter child exploitation workers deal with is so objectionable that they may not want to burden a significant other with details. Some individuals may not want to return home and tell their spouse, "I was reviewing some evidence today, and the suspect has hundreds of pictures of himself having intercourse with his eighteen-month-old baby and then ejaculating on her face." It is natural to want to protect loved ones from such disturbing feelings. Having an ongoing therapeutic relationship offers personnel the opportunity to share their experiences and feelings with someone who will not be shocked by what they hear and can be supportive and accepting.

## 16.1.2) DETERMINING THE SCOPE OF THE UNIT'S RESPONSIBILITY

The scope of a new unit's responsibility will no doubt be influenced by the level of staffing and funding available. Considerable thought should be given to the specific functions the unit will perform. Will the unit perform forensic examinations in addition to conducting investigations? Will the unit conduct undercover online investigations? These questions need to be answered at the planning stage so that the appropriate resources can be put in place.

If the unit will conduct forensic examinations, consideration should be given to whether examiners will be police officers or civilian staff. At some point, administrators will need to decide whether to seek accreditation for the forensic function from the American Society of Crime Laboratory Directors/Laboratory (ASCLD/LAB) Accreditation Board. If accreditation will be pursued, administrators will take standards into consideration when crafting policies and procedures, and ensure that they have sufficient resources to accommodate accreditation requirements. Generally, lab accreditation schemes require a system of technical and administrative review of examination reports. Examiners must follow established procedures and document their findings. The lab must conduct proficiency testing of examiners. Testing can be internal as well as external and can use blind and/or open samples with results that are unknown to the examiner but known to the test administrator. Additionally, examiners must pass competency examinations in each area in which they will perform examinations. With regard to computer forensic examiners, that means they must be competent in each software and hardware tool they use. Finally, examiners must possess certain minimum academic credentials and training. The standards applicable to computer laboratory personnel require that examiners have at least a bachelor's degree with science courses (Ferraro and Russell 2004).

If the unit will conduct undercover investigations, administrators must assemble sufficient resources to have an online presence that is effective yet protects officers' safety. An undercover persona should be created, complete with a corresponding mail box, checking account, and credit card account, to facilitate online purchases if permissible. Personnel should use the credit card or a debit card attached to a checking account to set up an Internet access account. Bear in mind that, to open a bank account post-PATRIOT Act, an individual must supply a Social Security number and present identification. This requirement complicates the process but does not make it impossible. Administrators should consult with leaders of other units that conduct undercover investigations for assistance in setting up the necessary accounts and documentation.

Administrators should also determine whether the unit will have a training function. Many Internet Crimes Against Children Task Forces have components that provide Internet safety training to the public and technical training to law enforcement and prosecutors. Many presentations occur in the evening, so administrators should be prepared to authorize overtime or accommodate either a flexible schedule or shifts for personnel assigned to this function.

### 16.1.3) *OBTAINING FUNDING*

Online child exploitation units require funding. Some efforts require less funding than others, but whatever the size of the unit, it will require funding. If the unit can be set up and funded within existing allocations, that is the best possible scenario. However, most jurisdictions find that they must search for funding outside their allocated funding. There are a few sources of grant funding, and there are also ways to obtain necessary resources without requiring funding.

The United States Department of Justice funds Internet Crimes Against Children (ICAC) Task Forces through the Department of Justice Office of Juvenile Justice and Delinquency Prevention. Task Forces are regional and generally serve more than one jurisdiction. Currently, there are forty-five Task Forces, but the program expands by several Task Forces each funding cycle. The average award through the program is around $300,000 for an eighteen-month period. Historically, this funding has been renewed.

The ICAC program has enormous benefits. In addition to providing funding, the program offers ongoing exposure and collaboration with other Task Forces. The benefits of the nationwide network of ICAC Task Forces cannot be calculated. The collaboration is unparalleled in United States law enforcement. The ICAC program offers opportunities for training through the National Center for Missing and Exploited Children and the Fox Valley Community College. The training curriculum for Task Force personnel is state of the art and consistent.

There are drawbacks to receiving ICAC funding, however. Any grant program will require an application, budget, and administrative commitment to a plan. Regular progress and spending reports are also required. Not every agency will have the human resources necessary to complete this paperwork. Participation in the program also requires adherence to program guidelines for conducting undercover investigations, and prior to embarking on an undercover effort, Task Forces must obtain approval from the national ICAC Board.

Some jurisdictions utilize block grant funding to set up new units. The Edward Byrne Memorial Grant Program is one resource. As with other grant programs, the agency must submit a written proposal and provide progress reports. The Byrne Grant funding is limited to four years, so if the agency plans to continue the effort, it must incorporate the unit into budgetary funding. If the agency budget will fund the unit, at a point in the future, it must be prepared to assume the replacement cost of hardware, the expense of upgrading software, and ongoing training for personnel.

## 16.2) LOCATING RESOURCES FOR INVESTIGATORS AND PROSECUTORS

Few resources are directed solely at online child exploitation investigators and prosecutors. That being said, several excellent resources can be pooled. The High Technology Crime Investigation Association (HTCIA) is a worldwide organization with regional chapters made up of law enforcement, private investigators, legal professionals, and educators. The organization has an active list serve that members can query when stuck. HTCIA also offers affordable training—usually less than $100 a session or free—in Internet and computer-related investigations. Several other very valuable list serves and online resources are available, including

- Computer Forensic Investigators Digest (CFID)—for discussions in the field of high-technology investigations.
- Computer Forensics Tool Testing (CFTT)—forum for discussing and coordinating computer forensics tool testing.
- Digital Detective Forum—forum for discussions in the field of digital investigations.
- Digital Forensics Digest (DFD)—forum for discussions in the field of digital forensics.
- Digital Forensic Science List Server (DFSci)—hosted by the Digital Forensic Research WorkShop (DFRWS) but provides a service beyond the scope of the DFRWS alone.
- Forensics@securityfocus—a broad discussion covering digital forensics and its application to information security.
- InternetCrime-L—forum for individuals who have an active role in the investigation and prosecution of crimes involving the Internet.
- Linux-forensics—forum devoted to digital forensics using the Linux operating system.

The National Center for Missing and Exploited Children is another excellent resource. The organization's Web site, located at www.missingkids.org, lists contact numbers and services it provides for law enforcement. Prosecutors have a wealth of expertise and ready assistance in the National District Attorney's Association and the American Prosecutors' Research Institute. They employ subject matter experts who provide assistance on individual cases. They publish a newsletter, called *Update*, that addresses current practice issues. They also conduct training for prosecutors on technology and child abuse and child exploitation.

The National White Collar Crime Center (NW3C) offers training in basic and advanced digital data recovery, some of which addresses handling Internet evidence and conducting online investigations. The SEARCH Group also offers training to law enforcement on technology issues and online investigations.

Two journals dealing with advances in digital forensics are *Digital Investigation*[1] and the *International Journal of Digital Evidence*.[2] Additional information about training, conferences, and related resources is listed at http://www.disclosedigital.com/resources.html.

## 16.3) LOOKING FORWARD

A central theme of this book is that preferential sex offenders exploit each new development in technology to carry out their criminal activity. There is absolutely no question that, as the Internet gets faster and computing devices get smaller and perform more functions, children will be victimized through the new devices and media. Our task is to be constantly vigilant. We know that advances in technology will bring new methods of victimizing our children. When they come, we need to examine the development and try to stay a step ahead. As you find technology making your life easier, ask yourself how each feature could facilitate criminal activity. How does it make it easier to establish contact with children? How does the new technology make it easier to contact criminal associates anonymously or traffic in illicit material while avoiding detection or apprehension?

Wireless access to the Internet will undoubtedly create new challenges for law enforcement. Wireless computing devices are by nature highly mobile, and wireless Internet access is more difficult to track than hard-wired systems. Security weaknesses also can wreak havoc because attributing criminal activity to an individual can become difficult.

---

[1] http://www.digital-investigation.net.
[2] http://www.ijde.org.

Smart phones will also be a challenge. Mobile phones with cameras, Internet access, and increasing ability to transfer data may soon replace the old ball-and-chain personal computer. The increased ability to access potential victims and exchange child pornography will be limited only by the criminal imagination and our response.

As criminals take advantage of new technologies to commit crimes and avoid apprehension, digital investigators and attorneys find new ways to protect and serve the public. This effort requires creative application of the investigative process, digital forensics, and the law. It is our hope that we have provided sufficient historical, legal, and technical background to further this noble endeavor.

## REFERENCE

Ferraro, M. M., A. G. Russell. "Current Issues Confronting Well-Established Computer-Assisted Child Exploitation and Computer Crime Task Forces." *Digital Investigations*, 1, no. 1 (March 2004).

# INDEX

**A**

Admissibility of evidence challenges, 213–215

Affidavit and probable cause, 159–165

Age of consent, 54

Agencies and resources for undercover operations, 112–113

Analysis of digital evidence examination versus, 195
reconstruction and, 209–213
for servers and networks, 220–224

Analyzing offender behavior. *See* Modus operandi

Anonymity, 4, 54, 58; *see also* Undercover operations

Arrest warrants, 165–166

Attribution
compromised host, 148–150
continuity of offense and, 130–135
e-mail forgery, 147–148
Internet chat, 148
overcoming challenges to, 145–150
web proxies and misdirection, 145–147

**B**

Bouncer (BNC) bot, 125, 127, 148

**C**

Caller ID devices, seizing and securing, 178

Calling card. *See* Signature and online child molester

Camcorders, 55

Case examples, 5–6, 14, 33–34, 59–61, 67–69, 87–88, 92–93, 137, 146, 168, 169–170, 199, 214, 228, 230–235, 262–263, 282, 283–284

Charging in computer-assisted child exploitation cases, 243–244

Chat log example, 85

Chat rooms and Internet relay chat
attribution determination, 148
grooming victims in, 55
instant messaging and, 35–36
providers, 35
tracking activities and, 140–144

Child exploitation
investigating Internet, 99–190
photography and, start of, 10
sexual, history of, 6–7
technology influence overview and, 9–15

Child exploitation unit, setting up online, 287–291
funding, obtaining, 290–291
personnel selection, 287–289
responsibility determination, scope of, 289–290
therapist for personnel, 288–289

Child molester, 56–62; *see also* Pedophiles
behavioral patterns, 58

case example, 59–61
categories of, 57, 58, 59, 62
criteria for, 57
fixations, 62
inadequate offenders, 58
introverted offenders, 59
modus operandi, 63–69
profiling of. *See* Profiling child
    molester
sadistic offenders, 59
scenarios, 57
seduction offenders, 59
sexually indiscriminate offenders,
    58
signature and online molester,
    69–70
stressors, 57, 58
typologies, 57–58, 62
Child pornography
availability (1970s) example, 10–11
case examples, 228, 230–235
definitions, 5, 8, 9
experts in cases of, 264–265
law and, 27–241
law development, 16–17, 241
law evolution post-*Ferber*, 235–236
morphed images, 237–238
obscenity versus, 16
overview, 8–9
possession of, 236
subculture of, 73
virtual, 236, 237, 238–240, 253
Child sexual exploitation history,
    6–7
Children versus parental use of
    Internet, 41
Class characteristic, 210
Cognitive distortions, 65
Compromised host, 148–150
Computer hacking, 70, 248–249
Computer repair shops finding
    pornography, 42–43
Computer storage capacity, 4, 12, 83
Computer systems

capacity, calculating, 83
communication, 80, 91–97
components, basic, 81
download times, 13
embedded, 80, 88–91
hard drive label photograph, 82
open, 80, 81–88
photography of, 80
servers, 86–88
Computers, seizing and securing,
    176–177, 178, 179
Conducting online investigation,
    105–107
Consulting experts for trial.
    *See* Expert witnesses
Cookies, 136
Crimes Against Children (CAC) Task
    Force(s), 103, 112, 113
Cyber offenders, 51–77
categories, 57, 58, 59, 62
child molester, 56–62
criteria, 57
deductive profiling, 52–53
inductive profiling, 52
justification by, 52
modus operandi, 53, 63–69, 70
multiple victims of, 52
online sexual predator, 53–56
physical contact necessity, 66
profiling child molester. *See*
    Profiling child molester
relationship with victim, 55–56
scenarios, 57
signature and online child
    molester, 53, 69–70
subculture of child pornography,
    73
Cyber victims, 41–49
protecting children online, how to,
    45–47
statistics about, 41–42
traits of, 43
victimology, 45
Cyber vigilante, 111

**D**

Deductive profiling, 52–53

Defending the charge, 278–285
  affirmative defenses pursuant to statute, 282–283
  attacking the law, 284–285
  digital evidence as alibi, 285
  false identification, 280–281
  fantasy defense, 283–284
  good samaritan, 281–282
  suppressing evidence, 279–280

Digital cameras, 55, 65, 88–89, 206

Digital evidence
  botting systems, 82
  chat logs, 85
  communication systems, 80, 91–97
  computer components, basic, 81
  definitions, 79
  digital cameras. *See* Digital cameras
  embedded computer systems, 80, 88–91
  Internet, 91–94
  log files, 86
  mobile phones. *See* Mobile telephones
  open computer systems, 80, 81–88
  peripheral devices, 97
  personal digital assistants. *See* Personal digital assistants (PDAs)
  physical crime scene versus digital crime scene, 80, 81
  servers, 86–88
  small office home office networks, 94–96
  sniffers, 95
  sources, 79–98
  staging, 70
  video files, 83–84
  web browser history, 84–85
  wireless networks, 96–97

Digital forensics. *See* Forensics, digital

Documentation
  evidence on Internet, 118
  predisposition of suspect to commit a crime, 107

Domain name system (DNS) and IP addresses, 22–23

Download times, 13

**E**

E-groups and mailing lists, 24–31

E-mail, 23–24
  attachments, 23–24
  description for affidavit example, 164
  encryption, 24
  evidence gathering and, 84
  file sharing using, 86
  forged headers, 70
  forgery, 147–148
  printing, 116
  saving, 116
  tracking activities and, 138–140
  undercover operations and use of, 106

Electronic Communications Privacy Act (ECPA), 180, 181, 182, 184, 185, 186

Encryption, 24, 194, 204–205

Enticement of a minor
  definition, 165
  drafting warrants and, 158
  to engage in sexual activity and pretrial, 253–255
  expert witnesses for case of, 265–266
  jury selection and case of, 258

Entrapment, 107

Evidence
  as alibi, digital, 285
  amount determination for trial, 253
  grooming, 158–159
  handling, 178–179

presentation of, courtroom, 255
securing, 176–178
selection for trial, 252–253
suppression, 279–280
Evidence on Internet, 115–127
  characteristics, unique, 117–118
  collecting remote evidence,
    119–127
  creating remote queries, 120–123
  documentation, 118
  e-mail, 116
  finding, 116–118
  geographic search, 117
  institution search, 117
  leads, following online, 123–125
  locating, 116–118
  preserving, 115–116
  probing, automated, 125–127
  search types, 117–118
  search warrant, preparing for,
    119–120
  underutilization of, 51
  videotaping onscreen activities, 116
Expert witnesses, 261–266
  case example, 262–263
  in child pornography cases,
    264–265
  consulting and testifying experts,
    262–264
  in enticement cases, 265–266
  locating, 266

**F**

Fantasy
  defense, 111, 283–284
  development, 4
  stories, researching, 106
Fax machines, seizing and securing,
    177–178
File sharing and tracking Internet
    activities, 144–145
File slack, 276–277
File transfer protocol (FTP), 37, 86
Firewall software, 23, 81, 121, 125

Fixated offender, 57
Forensic examination of digital
    evidence, 110, 162, 191–224
  admissibility challenges, 213–215
  analysis and reconstruction,
    209–213
  backlog, 194
  case examples, 199, 214
  certification of personnel, 289
  date-time stamps importance,
    210–212, 213, 223
  deleted files and folders, 198–200
  documentation, 195
  examination and analysis of servers
    and networks, 220–224
  examination versus analysis, 195
  foundation, 193
  harvesting, 205–209
  hash function, 197
  identification and seizure and
    networks, 218–219
  MD (message digest) 5 algorithm,
    197, 209, 219
  methodology, 195, 196
  narrowing focus, 194
  organization and search, 209
  overview of process, 193–215
  preparation, 196–197
  presentation of evidence, 219–220
  recovery, 197–205
  reduction, 209
  servers and networks, 217–224
  special files, 202–205
  unallocated, slack, and protected
    space, 200–202
Forensic Toolkit (FTK), 203, 204
Forensics, digital, 4
  definition, 4
  expert's report dissection,
    267–278
  report sample, 267–274
Fruit of the poisonous tree rule,
    182
Future outlook, 292–293

**G**

Grooming
definitions, 158, 265–266
evidence, 158–159, 265–266
victim, 64–65, 66

**I**

Individual characteristic, 210
Inductive profiling, 52
Innocent Images National Initiative,
112, 113
Instant messaging (IM)
chat rooms and, 35–36
Internet.
account, search warrant for,
156–157
applications, 21–40
chat rooms and Internet relay
chat, 35–36
digital evidence sources and,
91–94
e-groups and mailing lists, 24–31
e-mail, 23–24
evidence on. *See* Evidence on
Internet
features description for affidavit,
163–165
file transfer protocol, 37
instant messaging, 35–36
IP addresses and domain name
system, 22–23
newsgroups, discussion boards,
and bulletin boards, 31–33
peer-to-peer, 38
setup for undercover operations,
104
tracking. *See* Tracking on Internet
web cameras and videophones, 37
web sites, 33–35
Internet Crimes Against Children
(ICAC) Task Force Program,
103, 112, 113, 243, 254, 290–291
Internet Relay Chat (IRC) and
tracking activities, 140–144

Internet service providers (ISPs), 86,
131
executing search warrant for,
179–187
providing evidence, 219
requesting information from, 157
search warrant execution for,
180–184
usage logs, 134–135
IP addresses and domain name
system, 22–23

**J**

Jury selection, 257–259

**L**

Law(s), 225–286
Anti-Pandering Statute (1968), 17
*Ashcroft v. Free Speech Coalition*, 227,
236, 237, 238, 239, 240, 241,
264, 282
case law concerning charging
decisions, 244–246
child pornography, 227–241
court struggle to define obscenity,
228–229
development of child pornography
law, 16–17, 241
Internet service providers and
executing search warrants for,
180–184
Long Arm Statues, 185
*Miller v. California* (1972), 16, 227,
229, 240, 241
*New York v. Ferber* (1982), 16, 227,
229–235, 241
*Osborne v. Ohio* (1990), 16, 236, 241
plea bargaining considerations,
249–252
pretrial. *See* Pre-trial
privacy, 94
Protection of Children Against
Sexual Exploitation Act (1977),
17

real-time recording, 106
timeline of major developments, 241
trial. *See* Trial
*U.S. v. Hersh* (2001), 67–69
*U.S. v. Romero* (1999), 59–61
*United States v. Perez* (2003), 25–31
virtual child pornography and, 236, 237, 238–240, 282, 283
Live child-sex shows on Internet, 44
Locard's Exchange Principle, 129–130, 217
Log files, 86

**M**

Mailing lists, online. *See* E-groups and mailing lists
Mann Act, 68
Miranda warnings, 187
Mobile telephone(s), 88, 90–91, 94, 96, 177, 293
Modus operandi, 53, 63–69, 70
Molestation definition, 5
Morphed images, 237–238
Mousetrapping, 248, 281
Multiple computer users, 247–249

**N**

National Center for Missing and Exploited Children (NCMEC), 103, 239–240, 266, 283, 290, 292
Networks. *See* Servers
Newsgroups, discussion boards, and bulletin boards, 31–33
Newsgroups description for affidavit example, 164
No knock warrants, 188

**O**

Obscenity, legal determination of, 16
Overview, 3–20
background, 5–6
child pornography, 8–9

development of child pornography law, 16–17
history of child sexual exploitation, 6–7
technology and child exploitation, 9–15
technology and preferential sex offenders, 15
United Nations Convention on the Rights of the Child, 18

**P**

Pagers, seizing and securing, 177
Parole conditions and warrantless searches, 169–170
Pedophiles
definition, 56
diagnostic criteria for, 56–57
Internet and, 55
Interpol on, 9
onset of, 57
rationalizations, 65
Russia and, 53–54
truthfulness of many online, 64
volunteering for online child exploitation unit, 288
Peer-to-peer (P2P), 38–39
description language for affidavit example, 165
proactive investigation and, 101
servents versus servers, 86
U.S. General Accounting Office on, 38–39
Peripheral devices, 97
Personal digital assistants (PDAs), 88, 90–91, 200
Personal equipment usage and undercover operations, 103–104
Plea bargaining considerations, 249–252
Possession, what constitutes, 246–248
Predator, sexual. *See* Sexual predator

Preferential sex offenders
  Buddy List and, 36
  patterns, general, 59
  technology and, 15
Pre-trial, 243–256
  case law concerning charging
    decisions, 244–246
  charging in computer-assisted
    child exploitation cases, 243–244
  enticing a minor to engage in
    sexual activity, 253–255
  evidence amount determination,
    253
  evidence presentation, 255
  evidence selection, 252–253
  introduction, 243
  multiple computer users, 247–249
  plea bargaining considerations,
    249–252
  possession, what constitutes,
    246–247
Privacy Protection Act (PPA), 153,
  189
Privileged documents and
  communications, 188
Probably cause, 159–165
  consent searches and, 166
  freshness of, 161
Procuring victims case example,
  67–69
Profiling child molester, 52–53, 69,
  70–73
  difficulty of profiling examples,
    72–73
  false negative, 71
  false positive, 71
  red flags, 71
  statistical, 71, 72
  undercover operations and, 107
  vagueness of, 74
Protecting children online
  how to, 45–47
  parental controls, 47
  red flags, 46–47

Protection of Children Against
  Sexual Exploitation Act
  (1977/1978), 17

R
Recovery of computer files, 197–205
  case example, 199
  deleted files and folders, 198–200
  special files, 202–205
  unallocated, slack, and protected
    space, 200–202
Red flags, 46–47, 71
Regressed offender(s), 57, 58
Relationship between offender and
  victim, 55–56
Resources and agencies for
  undercover operations, 112–113
Resources location for investigators
  and prosecutors, 291–292
Returning seized items, 189–190
Routers, 95, 96

S
Search and seizure in cyberspace,
  151–190; see also Search
  warrants; Warrantless searches
  arrest warrants, 165–166
  drafting warrants and warrantless
    searches, 151–170
  enticement of minor case, 158
  executing the search, 171–190
  grooming evidence, 158–159
  language example, 155–156
  no knock warrants, 188
  preliminary interviews,
    conducting, 187
  preparing for, 119
  privileged documents and
    communications, 188
  probable cause, 159–165
  requesting information from ISPs
    language sample, 157
  returning seized items, 189–190
  search warrant drafting, 151–154

search warrant in general,
154–156
warrantless searches, 166–170
Search warrant(s)
affidavits, 159–165
document the scene, 175–176
drafting, 151–154
examples of language for items to
be seized, 155–156
executing, 171–178
factors for, 160
general information, 154–156
handheld devices and, 90
for Internet account, 156–157
Internet features background for,
163–165
for Internet service providers,
executing, 179–187
offender information and applying
for, specific, 51
operations plan form sample, 173
preliminary information needed,
151–153
preliminary interviews,
conducting, 187
preparing for, 119–120
search scene, at the, 172, 174–175
second search warrant, obtaining,
179, 214
securing evidence, 176–178
soliciting information for, 107
toolkit for serving, 172, 174
visual scan upon entry checklist,
175
Searches on the Internet, 117–118
Self-protection and undercover
operations, 101–103
Servers, 86–88
access log, 87
accessed from web client diagram,
87
case example, 87–88
identification and seizure,
218–219

networks and, forensic
examination of, 217–224
preservation of evidence,
219–220
small office home office networks,
94–96, 218–219
Sexual abusers types, 62
Sexual assault definition, 5
Sexual predator
definition, 6
online, 53–56
weaknesses of, 6
Signature and online child molester,
53, 69–70
Situational offenders, 58
Small office home office (SOHO)
networks, 94–96, 218–219
Smart phones, 293
Sniffers definition, 95
Statutory rape definition, 5
Storage on computers
capacity, 4, 12
images, 12
remote, 88
Subculture of child pornography, 73
Switches, 95

T
Technology influence, 1–98
1970s versus 2000s, 14
child exploitation and, 9–15
cyber offenders, 51–77
cyber victims, 41–49
evidence sources, digital, 79–98
evolution of visual technology
diagram, 10
Internet applications, 21–40
overview, 3–20
preferential sex offenders and, 15
Telephone connection setup for
undercover operations, 104
Testifying experts. See Expert
witnesses
Threatening victim, 67

Toolkit for serving search warrants, 172, 174
Tracking on Internet, 129–150
    activities, 135–145
    attribution, overcoming challenges to, 145–150
    attribution and continuity of offense, 130–135
    case examples, 137, 146
    chat, 140–144
    compromised host, 148–150
    determining physical contacts and locations, 132–134
    e-mail forgery, 147–148
    file sharing, 144–145
    Internet service provider usage logs, 134–135
    Locard's Exchange Principle, 129–130, 217
    potential sources diagram, 131
    web proxies and misdirection, 145–147
    Whois databases, 132–134
    World Wide Web, 135–138
Travelers, 3
Trial, 257–286
    affirmative defenses pursuant to statute, 282–283
    attacking the law, 284–285
    case examples, 262–263, 282, 283–284
    consulting and testifying experts, 262–264
    defending the charge, 278–285
    digital evidence as alibi, 285
    dissecting digital forensics experts report, 267–278
    evidence suppression, 279–280
    expert witnesses, 261–266
    experts in child pornography case, 264–265
    experts in enticement case, 265–266
    false identification, 280–281
    fantasy defense, 283–284
    good samaritan defense, 281–282
    jury selection, 257–259
    locating experts, 266
    young victims/witnesses, 259–261
Trojan horse programs, 19, 149, 207, 280

**U**
*U.S. v. Hersh* (2001), 67–69
Undercover operations, 101–114
    agencies and resources, 112–113
    conducting online investigation, 105–107
    documenting predisposition of suspect to commit a crime, 107
    dossier on subjects, 107–108
    entrapment, 107
    give defendants an out, 110
    identities, using online undercover, 105
    Internet and telephone connections setup, 104
    Internet Crimes Against Children Task Force, 103, 112
    jurisdiction, 111
    log everything, 109
    message digest, 106
    National Center for Missing and Exploited Children training, 103
    personal equipment, using, 103–104, 109–110
    prepare biography, 103
    preparing for meeting on search, 107–112
    problems, examples of, 101–102
    protesting yourself, 102
    real-time recording laws, 106
    rules for, golden, 108–112
    seize and search, 110
    self-protection, 101–103
    videotaping monitor, 106
    watchdogs, 103

United Nations Convention on the
Rights of the Child (1989), 18
*United States v. Carey* (1998), 214
*United States v. Perez* (2003), 25–31
Usenet, 31–32
determining message origin, 146
forged headers, 70
saving messages, 116

**V**

Victim blaming, 66–67
Victimology, 45
Victims/witnesses, young, 259–261
Videophones, 37
Virtual child pornography, 236, 237,
238–240, 253, 282, 283

**W**

Warrantless searches, 166–170,
213–214
conditions of parole, 169–170
consent searches, 166–167, 213
inventory searches, 168
plain view, 168–169, 213
search incident to arrest, 167–168
Warrants. *See* Arrest warrants; No
knock warrants; Search warrants
Web bugs, 106
Web cameras (webcams), 37, 65,
83–84
Web proxies and misdirection,
145–147
Web server access logs, 138
Web server accessed from web client
diagram, 87
Web sites, 33–35, 119
Whois databases, 132–134
Wireless networks, 96–97, 292
Witnesses/victims, young, 259–261
Women's movement and
pornography and obscenity,
16–17
World Wide Web and tracking
activities, 135–138